PETRARCH TO PIRANDELLO

Edited by Julius A. Molinaro

PETRARCH
•TO•
PIRANDELLO

Studies in Italian Literature
in honour of Beatrice Corrigan

University of Toronto Press

© University of Toronto Press 1973
Toronto and Buffalo
Printed in Canada
ISBN 0-8020-5271-1
Microfiche ISBN 0-8020-0171-8
LC 72-185725

Contents

Contributors

DANILO AGUZZI-BARBAGLI
Department of Hispanic and Italian Studies,
University of British Columbia, Vancouver

ALDO S. BERNARDO
Center for Medieval and Early Renaissance Studies,
State University of New York, Binghamton, New York

THOMAS G. BERGIN
Department of Romance Languages, Yale University, New Haven, Connecticut

C.P. BRAND
Department of Italian, University of Edinburgh, Edinburgh, Scotland

GIOVANNI CECCHETTI
Department of Italian, University of California, Los Angeles, California

S.B. CHANDLER
Department of Italian and Hispanic Studies, University of Toronto, Toronto

LOUISE GEORGE CLUBB
Department of Comparative Literature, University of California,
Berkeley, California

DANTE DELLA TERZA
Department of Romance Languages, Harvard University,
Cambridge, Massachusetts

MADDALENA KUITUNEN

Department of Italian and Hispanic Studies, University of Toronto, Toronto

KURT L. LEVY

(translator of article by Ulrich Leo [deceased])

Department of Italian and Hispanic Studies, University of Toronto, Toronto

HANNIBAL S. NOCE

Department of Italian and Hispanic Studies, University of Toronto, Toronto

J.H. PARKER

Department of Italian and Hispanic Studies, University of Toronto, Toronto

OLGA RAGUSA

Department of Italian, Columbia University, New York

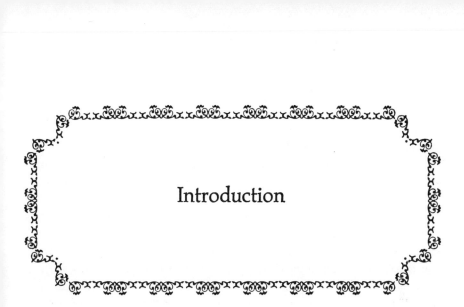

Introduction

THE PRESENT COLLECTION of studies ranging from Petrarch and the Renaissance to Pirandello and twentieth-century Italian literature represents some of the varied interests of Professor Beatrice Corrigan who retired recently from active teaching at the University of Toronto. The book was envisaged as encompassing some, if not all, of those many areas, and each contributor was accordingly invited to present a paper of his own choice within the established framework. This work is composed of one translation, in itself a valuable interpretation, eleven essays covering a period from the fourteenth to the twentieth century, and a bibliography of the publications of Beatrice Corrigan. In his introduction to this bibliography, Parker reviews Professor Corrigan's most fruitful academic career which combined achievements in scholarship with a lively interest in teaching.

The first contribution is by Thomas G. Bergin, distinguished for his translations of Dante, Petrarch and numerous other Italian poets. Bergin presents for the first time in English his version of the first eclogue of Petrarch's *Bucolicum carmen*. It will be recalled that this work, which contains twelve Latin poems, was composed during a crucial period in Petrarch's life and touches upon themes which re-appear in many of his other works. Petrarch consciously follows the tradition of the pastoral handed down by Virgil, who had adopted it from Theocritus, transforming it in the process. The dialogues, in which Petrarch's dramatic intent is evident, were composed between 1346 and 1348, and revised in 1357. In allegorical style the *Carmen* treats the problem of the religious versus the worldly life, contemplation of God as opposed to the pursuit of glory. Petrarch discussed the eclogue which here appears in English in one of his letters to his brother, Gherardo, a Carthusian monk. The poem possesses 'its own virtues,' in Bergin's opinion, and may almost be considered a defence of poetry and a humanist's tribute to his cherished classical authors, his two 'great masters,' Homer and Virgil.

In the second essay on 'Petrarch and the Art of Literature,' Aldo Bernardo explains the apparent paradox in Petrarch's attitude towards his vernacular works after examining the poet's general view of letters. Petrarch's conception of the function of poetry, which differed from Dante's in the contrasting approach to Virgil, can be seen in many places. In one of his letters to his brother, Petrarch, for whom the distinction between the theologian and the poet was slight, argued that poetry was not improper reading for a monastic. Petrarch's theory of literature was also developed in the *Africa* and in the *Trionfi* where the poet's 'religiosity' is viewed no longer as a 'religion' but rather as a product of artistic taste. There was no transformation of love into religious ecstasy as in Dante. Petrarch's coronation oration, whose theme was taken from Virgil's *Georgics*, Bernardo points out, was primarily a short statement on poetics. Poetry must be based on reality which it transforms through symbols and present the truth behind a veil. The *Canzoniere* is the clearest indication of the fusion between Petrarch's theoretical and applied poetics. In that work are to be found innumerable examples of the poet's complete awareness of the complexity of poetic composition. The collection was the best evidence of the poet's belief that he must not only have a divine mission but must also possess a thorough humanistic background.

In the article, 'The Making of the Pastoral Play: Italian Experiments Between 1573 and 1590,' Professor Louise George Clubb contends that our view of the Italian pastoral play has been obstructed by certain generally accepted ideas. Tasso's *Aminta* and Guarini's *Pastor Fido* were considered to represent all there was to know about the genre. It was long held that experimentation in pastoral drama ended with the *Aminta*. To correct the false conclusions which it is maintained have been given credence for too long a time, Professor Clubb examines a large number of pastoral plays, published between 1573, the date of composition and performance of *Aminta*, and the printing of the *Pastor Fido* in 1590. Her classification and analysis of some twenty plays traces the evolution of the genre through a variety of experiments revealing a mixture of elements from the courtly and popular tradition in Italian drama, and enables a reader to appreciate the distance between *Aminta* and *Pastor Fido*. The classification, Professor Clubb argues, throws into relief some elements significant to Elizabethan drama. Elizabethan plays including elements such as the effect of multiplicity achieved through the juxtaposition of contrasting features and levels of style should no longer be considered exceptional because they could not be related to either Tasso's *Aminta* or Guarini's *Pastor Fido*, the models or prototypes of Italian pastoral drama.

Tasso's name is synonymous with the age of the Counter Reformation and its innovations in poetic language, which is one of the principal concerns of Aguzzi-Barbagli's essay. In his book on Italian seventeenth-century literature, Carmine Jannaco stated in 1966 that the idea of the marvellous in the critical literature of the Counter Reformation and that of Marino and his followers were distinctively different. Aguzzi-Barbagli begins his article with Jannaco's suggestion that the concept of the marvellous underwent a process of evolution, and concentrates on analysing the validity of this assertion. The essay studies the gradual elaboration during the sixteenth century of the concepts of *acutezza*, and closely related to it, those of *ingegno* and *meraviglia* from 'their somewhat surreptitious beginnings in the Counter Reformation to their baroque triumphs.' Late sixteenth-century commentators of Aristotle's *Poetics* devoted much attention to a discussion of metaphor and naturally included the pertinent thoughts of Quintilian and Cicero, who were vividly present in most Renaissance treatments of the matter. This was readily acknowledged by Robortello who claimed that together with Demetrius Phalereus, Quintilian and Cicero were responsible for suggesting the terms *ingegno* and *acutezza*. Aguzzi-Barbagli examines closely the critical writings of the sixteenth-century theorists by probing the complexity of that vast subject and concludes that the concepts of metaphor elaborated during the *Cinquecento* by the great commentators of Aristotle's *Poetics* were reexamined and amplified and provide valuable literary connections between the sixteenth and seventeenth centuries.

Centring his essay on the Renaissance, Counter Reformation, and English literature, C.P. Brand examines the reaction of Tasso and Spenser to the *Orlando Furioso* and the extent to which Ariosto anticipated their attitudes. Tasso shared many of the misgivings about the *Orlando Furioso* felt by sixteenth-century critics who, primarily concerned with structure, tone and standard of ethics, wanted to avoid the kind of criticism directed against it. Spenser was similarly inspired and moved not merely to rival Ariosto but to surpass him, with none of his deficiencies. And so both Tasso and Spenser simplified the structure of the romance created by Ariosto. Tasso rejected the realistic elements he found distasteful in Ariosto, an aversion Spenser did not share. Tasso, a product of the Counter Reformation, and Spenser of Elizabethan England, each used Ariosto as a starting point, but in doing so they refashioned the romance to suit their own artistic purposes and thus each created a world distinctly his own.

It has sometimes been said, perhaps unfairly, that heroic drama came to an end in England with Addison's *Cato*, which was acclaimed as a masterpiece when it was performed at the Royal Theatre in Drury Lane 14 April, 1713. In his essay, 'Early Italian Translations of Addison's *Cato*,' Hannibal S. Noce examines a significant aspect of the broad field of Italian and English literary relations. As Noce shows, the play was given new life in Italy where six Italian versions appeared within the short space of five years, that is, between 1713 and 1718. In October 1713 Anton Maria Salvini, a learned academician, completed a version which was performed in the spring of 1714 and published the next year, in 1715. Addison's warm appreciation of the quality of Salvini's translation was not shared by Luigi Riccoboni, versatile in every aspect of the theatre, who censured it because it was too stiff, hence unfit for either actor or audience. Riccoboni went on to produce a more lively and supple version of his own, and one he considered more acceptable to a Venetian audience in 1715. Pier Jacopo Martello's version is not only a translation but in some respects an adaptation of Addison's *Cato*, adding a human dimension to the character of the hero not present in the original, exalting Caesar as liberator of Rome, and in general contributing genuine Senecan touches to the play. Noce concludes that these translations enhanced Addison's reputation in Italy and that 'no other English play had previously received so much attention; none can be said to have been more effective in preparing the way for the eventual re-appraisal of English dramatic literature by the Italians.' Noce makes clear that the Italian translations of *Cato* represent an early stage in the development of closer Anglo–Italian literary relations.

Within the same broad framework it was recently demonstrated that Leopardi, the subject of the next essay, was well known in England. Ulrich Leo's study, however, revolves around the motif of the *passero solitario*, the 'lonely sparrow.' The title of Leopardi's poem is a good example of the rigorous stylistic and philological approach so successfully employed for over three decades by the former student of Karl Vossler. The motif, the late Ulrich Leo points out, is as old as the Old Testament at least, as Psalm cii:8 makes clear. It re-appeared in the early centuries of the Christian era. Paulinus Nolanus, a fourth-century Church Father, used the allusion to refer to the soul reaching its zenith of meditation in an allegorical interpretation of the Biblical passage in the Psalms. In the late Middle Ages, Albertus Magnus became the forerunner of the literal description of the 'passer solitarius,' while Petrarch later used the motif in a literary form anticipating Leopardi, thus broadening the meaning of the term so as to resemble its Hebrew model. Medieval and Renaissance authors including Old French and Provençal Psalters, and finally, Leopardi in the nineteenth century, gave a different treatment to an old motif, as varied in literary form as its authors. In tracing an old motif through a series of literary documents from the Bible through Romance cultures, Ulrich Leo has contributed to a better appreciation of the Western literary heritage in the fine tradition of Ernst Robert Curtius.

If Leopardi never ceases to fascinate the scholar, the same may be said of Alessandro Manzoni who continues to inspire new studies. If Leo went back to the Bible, the author of 'The Moment in Manzoni,' S.B. Chandler selects a passage in St Augustine's *Confessions* as his point of departure, pointing out that Manzoni in his *Osservazioni sulla morale cattolica* in 1819 first conceived the profound significance of the moment for the interpretation of the individual human personality. Manzoni's sources were the seventeenth-century authors Massillon, Bossuet, the Jansenist Pierre Nicole, and Paolo Segneri, whom he had read in the preparation for this work. In his study Chandler defines the function of the moment in this interpretation, discusses its realization in the *Promessi Sposi*, and its effect on Manzoni's treatment of characters, their attitude towards life, religion, the finite and the universal order, and finally, the responsibility of the individual.

The ninth essay of the volume is devoted to Giovanni Verga, another major novelist of the nineteenth century. In his essay, Giovanni Cecchetti holds that while engaged in the writing of the *Vita dei campi*, a collection of short stories, Verga was impressed by the need of creating a style that would match the way of life of his new characters and truly reflect their day-to-day existence. It was during this period that Verga reached artistic maturity. As work proceeded on the drafts of his major novel, Verga experimented with a series of short narratives which, Cecchetti contends, compare favourably with the best of European fiction of the second half of the nineteenth century. Verga's short pieces in the *Vita dei campi* must be considered not merely as a work of transition but as an introduction to *I Malavoglia*. Verga was in quest of a language and style which would be distinctively his own, and free of worn-out expressions. His efforts were thus concentrated, not on reproducing the simple language of popular narration, but rather on rejecting all linguistic patterns not genuinely fresh and unadorned. Verga believed that an author must find in his own inner consciousness the language of his characters and feeling for their environment. Verga could not, Cecchetti contends, simply record the every day speech of his humble characters without first thoroughly assimilating it himself, subjecting it later to a severely disciplined process of re-creation. Verga was not satisfied until he had created a suitable medium of expression for his poor and illiterate characters. Cecchetti concludes that Verga had succeeded in acquiring an original style so individual as to be identified with no one, and this he mastered in *L'Amante di Gramigna*.

Reappraisal of an author's style and of the influences which leave their mark on him is the object of periodic, if not always, continual investigation, as is the theatre of Roberto Bracco in the next essay. Ibsen's plays became known in Italy at the end of the nineteenth century, with the result that it was fashionable for critics to see the influence of the Norwegian dramatist in all of the plays written at that time. Giacosa, Praga, D'Annunzio, and Pirandello were included among those similarly charged, but it was the Neapolitan dramatist, Roberto Bracco, who suffered most by comparison. In her essay 'Ibsen and the Theatre of Roberto Bracco,' Maddalena Kuitunen argues that Bracco was considered a poor imitator of the Norwegian dramatist, or else was praised excessively for personal or sentimental reasons. After pointing out the features the two dramatists possessed in common, she analyses their differences. Under this heading, their dramatic techniques, their use of ideas derived from naturalism, their treatment of character, and above all, their views on the problem of the emancipation of women receive close scrutiny. From this study Bracco emerges as a dramatist in his own right who must be appreciated for his own unique accomplishments.

Unique also would be a suitable attribute to apply to Luigi Pirandello whose accomplishments are manifold. In her article, 'Pirandello's *La Patente*: Play and Story,' Olga Ragusa analyses the playwright's peculiar technique of transforming a short story into a play. *La patente* (The Licence), a one-act play published for the first time in January 1918, was performed in February 1919, then forgotten by critics who were more attracted to the numerous and more successful three-act plays preceding and following it. Olga Ragusa contends that *La patente* belongs to that group of plays 'embodying the progressive unfolding of a character without an author' and was written at a time when Pirandello was making significant discoveries about dramatic conventions. In her examination of the play's structure, Professor Ragusa notes that Pirandello added two functional characters who have no counterparts in the story, and goes on to make other important observations about the play. It is noteworthy that in the short story Pirandello conceived of the meeting of the two principal characters as a scene in the form of a dialogue. There remained little for Pirandello to do later but to incorporate the dialogue into the play using stage directions to connect the narrative material. It is by a process of considering story and play, each in the light of the other, that Pirandello, according to Professor Ragusa, can be appreciated at his creative best.

The historical premise of the last essay in the collection lies in the second decade before the end of the nineteenth century, in the age of naturalism and of scientific ideas. It embraces Pirandello and the ensuing natural developments in the novel. Della Terza initiates his discussion on 'The Italian Novel and the Avant-Garde,' when the term existed in substance if not in name. In the early 1880s two important elements of the avant-garde were present: a reaction against traditional cultural values and a lively concern for new ideas and the future. In Della Terza's opinion, Capuana's review of Verga's newly published *I Malavoglia* which became a manifesto of new literary taste and Verga's mild criticism of a novel by Capuana represent two antagonistic narrative structures anticipating twentieth-century likes and views. Pirandello attracts a critic's attention, Della Terza's article point out, because of his questioning attitude towards the problem of the novel rejecting traditional modes of narration to concentrate rather on an understanding of existence. His novels which are the product of these views are 'parables, the events impatient fictions and metaphors of the immutable drama of existence and the human condition.' Della Terza pursues his discussion of the novel from Pirandello to its logical development in the narrative art of the last decade in Italy.

These studies in our *Festschrift* examine some of the most significant moments in Italian literature: Petrarch and the Renaissance, Italy's cultural contacts with England, a subject which is always open to new discoveries, and her productive association with Ibsen. Leopardi and Manzoni similarly continue to pose problems relevant today, while Verga and Pirandello initiate trends in the novel and drama with enduring effect. It is hoped that this volume which grew out of an occasion will succeed in its dual function of honouring a great scholar and of stimulating further inquiry into a great literature.

I am grateful to Vittorio Klostermann for giving me permission to publish an English translation of the late Ulrich Leo's article, *Il passero solitario: Eine Motivstudie*, which first appeared in *Wort und Texte: Festschrift für Fritz Schalk*, edited by Harri Meier and Hans Sckommodau, Frankfurt-am-Main, 1963. I am indebted also to my colleague Michael Ukas for reading the translation and checking references.

This work has been published with the aid of grants from the Humanities Research Council of Canada, using funds provided by the Canada Council, and from the Publications Fund of the University of Toronto Press.

J.A.M.

PETRARCH TO PIRANDELLO

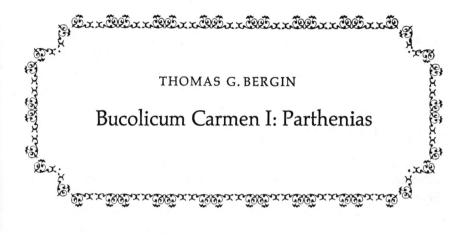

THOMAS G. BERGIN

Bucolicum Carmen I: Parthenias

THE INTENTION HERE is not to offer an edition or even a commentary but simply a translation of Petrarch's first eclogue. A few words of presentation may, however, be useful.

The *Bucolicum carmen* contains twelve Latin poems, sometimes called 'eclogues.' They are cast in the form of conversations between shepherds, whose words have allegorical significance. The *Carmen* was begun in 1346 and essentially finished by 1353, although there are subsequent revisions, some even after the poet's own 'final' draft of 1357.[1] The years of composition mark a crucial period in Petrarch's life: they are the years of his breach with the Colonna and his involvement with Cola di Rienzo; 1348 brought the plague and the loss of 'l'alta colonna e 'l verde lauro.' All of the concerns of these years: personal, public, literary, spiritual, and political, find an echo in the *Carmen*; this mélange of motifs is, to be sure, characteristic of many of Petrarch's works, not excluding the *Canzoniere*.

The *Carmen* has long been overshadowed by other works of the poet and it is true, perhaps, that whatever he says in the eclogues he says better elsewhere. Yet the little work has its own virtues. The pastoral posture, imitated from Virgil (with perhaps some emulation of Dante) is ingenuous and not without charm. Boccaccio found the eclogues much to his taste.[1] They have one special feature, noted by Tatham;[2] composed

Translation and notes by Thomas G. Bergin

1 For chronological details see Enrico Carrara, 'I commenti antichi e la cronologia delle ecloghe petrarchesche,' *Giornale storico della letteratura italiana*, vol. xxviii (1896), 138–53.

2 His opinion is quoted, with pertinent comment, by E.H.R. Tatham in his *Francesco Petrarca: His Life and Correspondence* (London, 1926), ii, 390.

in the form of dialogues, they have a latent dramatic intention and, given a little good will, we may see in them touches of authentic characterization and some hint of theatrical purpose. At any event, for their novel form, for their rich substance and perhaps most of all for their economy in composition they seem to me to invite translation. So far as I know only one of the eclogues has as yet been given English dress.[3]

The first Eclogue, of which I submit a version here, depicts the lifelong conflict of the poet, both as a man and as an artist torn between his conviction of the values of Christian other-worldliness and his enthusiasm for the classical tradition, between David and Virgil, as he puts it here. It is not hard to believe that actual discussions on this subject had taken place between the poet and his brother. But whether the poem reflects real conversations or an ideal one it gives a true picture of the enduring predicament of the restless 'Silvius.'

With some trepidation I have decided to translate the verses into English hexameters, following the metre of the original. The strong beat of the hexameter in English, a language characterized by heavy accentuation, is likely to become, in the long run, either soporific or obsessive. But for a short poem I think the risk is not so great, and the metre, it seems to me, has a part in the intention of the poet to associate himself with the Virgilian tradition. It would be a pity not to reproduce this effort in English.

I follow Antonio Avena's edition of the autograph manuscript.[4]

I am grateful to John L. Ryan of the University of New Mexico for his careful reading of my translation and his useful suggestions for its improvement.

3 The fifth eclogue, 'Dedalus,' was translated, under the title of 'The Shepherds' Affection,' by M.E. Cosenza in his *Francesco Petrarca and the Revolution of Cola di Rienzo* (Chicago, 1913), 109–25.
4 *Padova in onore di Francesco Petrarca* MCMIV/I/ *Il Bucolicum Carmen e i suoi commenti inediti / Edizione curata di Antonio Avena* (Padova, 1906). The text of the first eclogue covers pp. 95–9.

Opening page of *Bucolicum carmen*, 1473.
Courtesy of the Cornell University Library

Bucolicum carmen meum incepit

EGLOGE PRIME TITULUS: PARTHENIAS

COLLOCUTORES SILVIUS ET MONICUS

SIL. Monice, tranquillo solus tibi conditus antro,
Et gregis et ruris potuisti spernere curas;
Ast ego dumosis colles silvasque pererro.
Infelix! Quis fata neget diversa gemellis?
Una fuit genitrix; at spes non una sepulcri!   5
MO. Silvi, quid quereris? Cunctorum vera laborum
Ipse tibi causa es. Quis te per devia cogit?
Quis vel inaccessum tanto sudore cacumen
Montis adire iubet, vel per deserta vagari
Muscososque situ scopulos fontesque sonantes?   10
SIL. Hei michi! Solus Amor. Sic me venerata benigne
Aspiciat, spes nostra, Pales. Dulcissimus olim
Parthenias michi, iam puero, cantare solebat
Hic, ubi Benacus, vitrea pulcherrimus alvo,
Persimilem natum fundit sibi. Venerat etas   15
Fortior; audebam, nullo duce, iam per opacum
Ire nemus, nec lustra feris habitata timebam;
Mutatamque novo frangebam carmine vocem,
Emulus, et fame dulcedine tactus inani:
Ecce peregrinis generosus pastor ab oris,   20
Nescio qua de valle, canens nec murmure nostro,
Percussit flexitque animum; mox omnia cepi
Temnere, mox solis numeris et carmine pasci.
Paulatim crescebat amor; quid multa? canendo
Quod prius audieram, didici, musisque coactis,   25

Bucolicum carmen

ECLOGUE I: PARTHENIAS

SPEAKERS: SILVIUS AND MONICUS

SIL. Monicus, hidden away alone in your quiet cavern,
You have been free to ignore the cares of the flock and the pastures;
I must continue to range over thorny hills and through thickets.
Destiny – who could deny it? – has shaped different lots for twin
                                                                        brothers,
Born of one mother but having no hope of last rest together.   5
MO. Silvius, why do you grumble? The true cause of all of your
                                                                        troubles
Lies in yourself and no other. Who leads you into such pathways?
Who, pray, bids you ascend with so much painful exertion
Lofty, unscaled mountain peaks, or to wander through desert
                                                                        wastelands,
Over moss-covered crags or where lonely cataracts thunder?   10
SIL. Love 'tis, alas, only love. May Pales, our hope, whom I worship
Graciously look upon me. Time was, the gentle Parthenias,
(True, 't was a long time ago, in my boyhood) was wont to sing
                                                                        with me
There, where Benacus, made fair by crystalline waters transparent,
Sends forth an offspring like to itself. But an age followed after   15
Bolder; I dared with no guide make my own way into the forest,
Dense as it was, unafraid of the savage beasts that roamed in it.
There, in a voice now changed, I broke into new song and new
                                                                        measures,
Lured by the charm of false glory, driven by keen emulation.
Lo, then there came a generous shepherd from far away
                                                                        meadows,   20
Native of what vale I know not, but with song not couched in
                                                                        our language,
Stirring and moving my soul so that only in notes and in numbers,
Only with song was I happy, all other matters despising;
Little by little love grew; what more to tell you? Why, briefly,
Later, comparing their muses I learned, and in practice of verses,   25

Quo michi Parthenias biberet de fonte notavi.
Nec minus est ideo cultus michi; magnus uterque,
Dignus uterque coli, pulcra quoque dignus amica.
Hos ego cantantes sequor et divellere memet
Nec scio, nec valeo; mirorque quod horrida nondum   30
Silva, nec aerij ceperunt currere montes.
Verum ubi iam videor, collectis viribus, olim
Posse aliquid, soleo de vertice montis ad imas
Ferre gradum valles; ibi fons michi sepe canenti
Plaudit, et arentes respondent undique cautes.   35
Vox mea non ideo grata est michi, carmina quanquam
Laudibus interdum tollant ad sidera Nimphe.
Dum memini quid noster agat, quidve advena pastor,
Uror et in montes flammata mente revertor.
Sic eo, sic redeo. Nitar, si forte Camene   40
Dulce aliquid dictare velint, quod collibus altis
Et michi complaceat, quod lucidus approbet ether;
Non rauce leve murmur aque, nec cura, nec ardor
Defuerint. Si fata viam et mens tarda negarit,
Stat, germane, mori. Nostrorum hec summa laborum.   45
MO. *O! si forte queas durum hoc transcendere limen.*
Quid refugis? turpesque casas et tuta pavescis
Otia? quid frontem obducis? Nemo antra coactus
Nostra petit; plures redeunt a limine frustra.
SIL. *Non pavor hic animi fuerat; si forsitan aures,*   50
Dulcibus assuetas, inamena silentia tangunt,
Miraris? Natura quidem fit longior usus.
MO. *O! iterum breve si mecum traducere tempus*
Contingat, sileatque fragor rerumque tumultus,
Dulcius hic quanto media sub nocte videbis   55
Psallere pastorem! Reliquorum oblivia sensim
Ingeret ille tibi; non carmen inane negabis,
Quod modo sollicitat, quod te suspendit hiantem.

What I had heard by report: the source my Parthenias drank of.
Not that I honour him less, for truly both are great masters,
Both most worthy of awe and of the fair mistress they cherish.
Let them but utter a note and I follow, for truly to leave them
Neither my strength nor my wit avails. I cannot but wonder   30
How it can be that their songs have not moved wild forests and
                                                          mountains.
Some days, when I have summoned my strength and feel I am
                                                          ready,
Down from the loftiest summit I make my way to the valley's
Depths, where a gushing spring sometimes applauds my singing,
Where from all sides the arid rocks seem to echo in answer.   35
Yet, for all that, the sound of my own voice doesn't please me,
Even though sometimes the nymphs will praise to the skies my
                                                          verses;
Nay, when I think what our shepherd has wrought and his alien
                                                          comrade
I am inflamed and return with spirit afire to the hilltops.
Thus do I go back and forth, in the hope that perchance the
                                                          Muses,   40
Smiling may deign to dictate some sweet notes, likewise appealing
Both to the crags and myself and which the bright air may shine on.
Nor do I want for deep murmuring waters nor study nor ardour,
And if my way is impeded by fate or my own sluggish spirit
I am resolved to die, brother. Such is the end of my labours.   45
MO. Oh, if but only you might step over this stony threshold!
Why do you turn aside? Can it be that you fear these squalid
Huts or your well guarded leisure? Don't frown; none under
                                                          compulsion
Enters our caves, nay, many are turned away disappointed.
SIL. Such is not really my fear. Say, rather, does it surprise you   50
That ears accustomed to song are wounded by unpleasant silence?
Habit, you know, when confirmed, becomes a part of our nature.
MO. Oh, can you not once more with me spend yet a short season,
Letting the noise of the world be stilled and the sound and the
                                                          tumult?
Here, in the depths of night, you will see a shepherd tuning   55
Notes of unrivalled sweetness, such as to make you forgetful,
Heedless of all other matters. And surely you cannot call idle
Music which now can arouse you, now hold you fixed and
                                                          enraptured.

f. 5b SIL. *Quis, queso, aut quonam genitus sub sidere pastor*
      Hoc queat? Audivi pastorum carmina mille,   60
      Mille modos; quenquam nostris equare caveto.

  MO. *Audisti quo monte duo fons unicus edit*
      Flumina? sive ubinam geminis ex fontibus unum
      Flumen aquas, sacrumque caput cum nomine sumit?

  SIL. *Audivi, ut quondam puer hispidus ille nitentis*   65
      Lavit Apollineos ad ripam gurgitis artus.
      Felices limphe que corpus tangere tanti
      Promeruere dei! Fluvius, si vera loquuntur,
      Per cinerum campos ultricibus incidit undis.

  MO. *Hunc igitur, dulci mulcentem sidera cantu,*   70
      Illa tulit tellus; licet experiare, iuvabit.

  SIL. *O! ego novi hominem. Cives et menia parve*
      Sepe Jerosolime memorat, nec vertitur inde;
      Semper habet lacrimas et pectore raucus anelat.
      Hi Roman Troiamque canunt et prelia regum,   75
      Quid dolor et quid amor possit, quidve impetus ire,
      Qui fluctus ventosque regat, qui spiritus astra;
      Necnon et triplicis sortitos numina regni
      Expingunt totidem, varia sed imagine, fratres;
      Sceptriferum summumque Iovem facieque serena,   80
      Inde tridentiferum moderatoremque profundi
      Ceruleumque comas medium, fuscumque minorem;
      Torva latus servat coniunx, aterque paludis
      Navita tartaree piceas redit itque per undas,
      Tergeminusque canis latrat; tum dura severis   85
      Pensa trahunt manibus, fixa sub lege, sorores;

SIL. Tell me, pray, who is this shepherd you speak of, so gifted in
                                      singing?
Under what skies was he born? Shepherds' songs I have heard
                           by the thousands,   60
Thousands of modes. So take care: my champions are surely
                                 peerless.
MO. Happily you may have heard of the mountain where two mighty
                                   rivers
Spring from one source alone, or where there pours forth from
                           two fountains
One sacred stream which from them draws its source and its name
                           and its waters?
SIL. This I have heard: it is said that once on the shores of that
                           sparkling   65
River a hirsute youth laved the golden limbs of Apollo.
Blest were the wavelets that were, if the tale I heard is a true one,
Privileged to touch that immortal body. The stream, so they tell us,
Rolls with avenging current on through fields turned to ashes.
MO. That in truth is the land that bore him whose welcome notes
                           flatter   70
Heaven on high; you too will find it a joy if you listen.
SIL. Him I know well; of little Jerusalem's walls and its townsmen
Never he wearies of telling nor ever is willing to leave them.
Tearful he is, pouring forth from his breast unmusical groanings.
My champions sing of great Rome and of Troy and of kings
                         locked in combat,   75
Telling of love and its power, the effects of grief and of anger,
Who governs the flood and the winds, what spirit rules the high
                           heavens.
Under designs ever varied they paint for us the great brothers,
Given by lot to share dominion of the three kingdoms.
Sceptre in his hand, mighty Jove, with visage serene stands
                         before us,   80
Grasping his trident we see the Ruler of the vast Ocean,
Blue as the sea is his hair; with them stands their swarthy brother
And by his side his grim consort, while back and forth over the
                           pitchy
Ooze of the stream of the marshes of Tartarus wends the dark
                         boatman.
Hark to the three headed hound a-baying, mark there the sisters   85
Spinning as the law bids them, the harsh threads with fingers
                         relentless.

Quinetiam stigias eterna nocte tenebras
Anguicomasque simul furias templumque forumque,
Tum silvas et rura canunt atque arma virosque
Et totum altisonis illustrant versibus orbem.   90
MO. Hic unum canit ore deum, quem turba deorum
Victa tremit, celum nutu qui temperat almum,
Ethera qui librat liquidum, qui roris acervos,
Quique nives spargit gelidas et nube salubri
Elicit optatos herbis sitientibus imbres;   95
Qui tonat et trepidus rapidis quatit aera flammis,
Tempora sideribus, qui dat sua semina terris;
Qui pelagus fluitare iubet, consistere montes;
Qui corpus mentemque dedit, quibus addidit artes
Innumeras, geminum cumulans ab origine munus;   100
Qui vite mortisque vices, queque optima fessos
Fert super astra, viam docuit repetitque monendo.
Hunc meus ille canit; neu raucum dixeris, oro:
Vox solida est penetransque animos dulcore latenti.
Jure igitur, patriis primum celebratus in arvis,   105
Attigit et vetros saltus, lateque sonorum
Nomen habet: que rura Padus, que Tybris et Arnus,
Que Rhenus Rodanusque secant, queque abluit equor
Omnia iam resonant pastoris carmina nostri.
SIL. Experiar, si fata volent; nunc ire necesse est.   110
MO. Quo precor? aut quis te stimulus, que cura perurget?
SIL. Urget amor Muse; quoniam modo litore in Afro
Sidereum iuvenem genitumque a stirpe deorum
Fama refert magnis implentem pascua factis;
Te, Polipheme, tuis iam vi stravisse sub antris   115

Aye, and they sing of the shades of the Styx and of eternal darkness;
Snake-headed furies they tell of and likewise of temple and forum;
Meadows and groves they describe and celebrate arms and great
                             heroes.
So they light up the whole world with their lofty verses'
                            effulgence.   90

MO. Oh, but my master sings of the One, whom the gods He defeated
Reverence, Who, with His nod can temper the fostering heavens,
Moderating the air, distilling dew in abundance,
Scattering the icy snow and out of the clouds, life-giving,
Bringing the thirsty grasses the gentle showers they long for,   95
Thundering down and shaking the atmosphere with sharp flashes,
When He is moved giving seeds to the earth, to the stars each its
                            season,
Bidding the tides of the ocean to flow and the hills to be stable.
He has endowed us with body and soul and to each He has added
Arts beyond number, ever increasing His first-granted bounty.   100
He it is who first taught us – and daily repeats His good counsel –
Life and death and their meaning and the heavenly way to the
                            weary.
He it is my master sings of, and do not, I pray you say 'hoarsely';
Rather say 'firmly,' deep reaching into souls with mysterious
                            sweetness.
First – and with reason – acclaimed in the distant land that he
                          springs from,   105
Now he has come to your hills and your pastures. His glory,
                          far-sounding,
Spreads wide abroad over lands bathed by Po and Tiber and Arno,
Even the vales of the Rhine and the Rhone and the shores that the
                            ocean
Borders resound to the fame and the sacred songs of our shepherd.

SIL. Well then, if chance permit I will listen. But now I must leave
                            you.   110

MO. Whither, I ask you? What spur drives you hence? What care now
                            assails you?

SIL. Love of the Muse compels me. Fame tells of a youthful hero,
Favoured by heaven and born of the race of the gods and now
                            filling
Meadows and fields of the African shore with report of his exploits.
Say, has he not, Polyphemus, by force thrust into your cavern?   115

Dicitur et lybicos silvis pepulisse leones,
Lustraque submissis audax incedere flammis.
Hunc simul Italidesque nurus, puerique, senesque
Attoniti adverso certatim a litore laudant.
Carmine fama sacro caret hactenus, et sua virtus   120
Premia deposcit; pavitans ego carmina cepi
Texere: tentabo ingenium, vox forte sequetur
Orphea, promeritum modulabor harundine parva.
MO. *I sospes, variosque vie circumspice casus.*

Aye, and 'tis said that, much daring, he has also driven the lions
Out of the Libyan wastelands, firing their lairs with his torches.
He it is that all Italy hails; young and old and women and children
Vie in applause and cheer him from the great sea's opposite
                                                    shoreline.
Hitherto, great though his fame, he has wanted a singer. His
                                              virtue   120
Merits a proper reward. So timidly I have been shaping
Verses to laud him. I'll try my skill and my voice, it may be,
Orpheus will second; I'll choose a modest pipe for my music.
MO. Go then, if you must, in safety. Have a care for the road and its
                                              hazards.

COMMENTARY

One of Petrarch's letters, *Fam.* x 4, deals with this poem in some detail. The Letter is addressed to Gherardo; it tells how the notion of writing the *Carmen* occurred to the poet during a summer sojourn at Vaucluse,[5] then proceeds to a summary of the contents of the first eclogue and concludes with an explanation of the allegory. The Letter provides all that is necessary for an understanding of the meaning the poet wanted his verses to convey; there are, however, other commentaries. One is by Benvenuto da Imola,[6] another is of greater interest because its *argomenti* have been attributed to Petrarch himself.[7] Avena, however, who prints the *commento* with the text of the *Carmen*, assigns the *argomenti* to Donato degli Albanzani, the poet's friend (to whom he addressed *De sui ipsius et multorum ignorantia*) and the *commenti* to an unknown hand.[8] The commentaries contain substantially the same material as is found in the Letter, although they tend to be more discursive. Much of the allegory, in fact, will be quite clear to the reader without any exegesis; we shall cite here only such items as seem useful, relying on the Letter[9] as our source, unless otherwise indicated.

Petrarch begins by explaining the significance of the names assigned to his speakers. He has called himself Silvius, he says, both because the poem was composed in the woods and because he has had all his life such great affection for the country and such a horror of cities that he might as well be called Silvanus as Franciscus. Gherardo is here 'Monicus,' after the designation of the Cyclops, signifying 'monoculus' or 'one-eyed,' for of the two eyes which nature gave us for seeing the things of earth and the things of heaven Gherardo keeps open only that one that is fixed on the heavens. The solitary cave is Montrieux, whither Gherardo has withdrawn to profess the monastic life.

5 The wording of the letter is ambiguous but Tatham (*Francesco Petrarca*, II, 387, n.1) fixes the date of composition of the eclogue as the summer of 1346. Wilkins (*Life of Petrarch*, Chicago, 1961, 67) seems to concur: 'The first four eclogues,' he writes, '[were] written certainly or probably in 1346.'
6 Published in Venice, 1503, as an appendix to the third edition of the poet's Latin works. See *Catalogue of the Petrarch Collection bequeathed by Willard Fisk*, compiled by Mary Fowler (London-New York, 1916), 3–4.
7 Such was the view of Attilio Hortis, *Scritti inediti di Francesco Petrarca* (Trieste, 1874), 221–75.
8 Antonio Avena, x *Il Bucolicum Carmen*, etc. 69–74, 84–5. For the text of the commentary on the first eclogue, see 169–75.
9 I follow the text of the edition of Vittorio Rossi, *Francesco Petrarca: Le familiari* (Firenze, 1934), II, 301–10.

For further exegesis it will be convenient to follow the poem line by line. Reference is to the Latin text; in most cases the line of the translation will correspond.

5 *spes ... sepulcri*: This may be taken either as a reference to their eternal abode, says Petrarch, for Gherardo is sure of heaven and the poet is not, or to their gravesites, for Gherardo will be buried in his monastery but the poet cannot say where his wandering life will end.

8 *inaccessum cacumen*: fame

9 *deserta*: 'sunt studia; hec vere deserta hodie et vel lucri cupidine derelicta vel ingeniorum desperata segnitie.'[10]

10 *muscosos ... scopulos*: the rich and powerful *fontes sonantes*: men of intellect and learning

11 *Amor*: that is, *Muse non alium*

12 *Pales*: 'Pales est enim pastorum dea; posset apud nos intelligi Maria, non dea sed Dei mater.'[11] The anonymous commentary adds a refinement: as Pales was the goddess of ancient shepherds, so Mary is the protector of mankind and especially its 'shepherds,' that is, its leaders and governors.

13 *Parthenias*: '... ipse est Virgilius, non a me modo fictum nomen; in vita enim eius legimus quod Parthenias, quasi *omni vita probatus*, dici meruit ...'[12]

15 *persimilem natum*: the Mincio

20 *generosus pastor*: Homer

28 *amica*: fame

30–1 *horrida/silva*: 'populus et vulgus'

31 *aerij montes*: 'principes eminentes'

33–4: The summits would signify theoretical reflections on poetry, the valleys the practice of verse.

34 *fons* 'homines litterati et studiosi,' the community of scholars and men of letters

35 *arentes ... cautes*: 'ydiote,' who respond without understanding

37 *Nimphe*: 'divina studiosorum hominum ingenia'

46 *limen*: the Carthusian order

56 *pastorem*: David

10 'studies, which to-day are truly deserts, either ignored because of the greed for lucre or abandoned because of the hopeless sluggishness of intellects.'

11 'Pales is the goddess of shepherds; by her we may understand Mary, not a goddess but the mother of God.'

12 'Nor did I make up the name for we learn in reading of his life that he earned the name of Parthenias for the probity of his whole manner of living.'

62–4: The two rivers with one source are the Tigris and the Euphrates (cf. *Purgatorio* xxxiii, 112–3); the one river with two sources is the Jordan, rising as it does, from the two springs Jor and Dan. The irrelevant first reference is intended as a bit of humorous characterization; Petrarch writes: 'Monicus quasi pastoria ruditate non nomen reddit, sed describit patriam et more ruralium sepe in verbis errantium, duorum fluminum mentionem facit uno fonte nascentium, ac statim velut errore recognito, verba prevertit et quod de duobus inceperat, de uno flumine duobus ex fontibus descendente prosequitur; utrumque sane in Asia est.'[13]

65 *puer hispidus*: John the Baptist

66 Apollo, the son of Jove and the god of human wit aptly symbolizes Christ, the second person of the trinity: 'ipse sapientia Patris est.'

69 *cinerum campos*: because of Sodom and Gomorrah, which also explains the 'ultricibus undis'

106 *vetros*: clearly a misprint for *vestros*

113 *iuvenem*: Scipio

120 *Polipheme*: Hannibal, one-eyed like the Cyclops; he had lost the other during his campaigns in Italy

121 *leones*: 'Carthaginensium duces' whose ships (*lustra*) Scipio burned

117 *incedere*: read *incendere*

121–2 *carmina cepi/texere*: the reference is to the *Africa*, begun in 1338 or 1339, according to Wilkins[14]

124: with moral meaning which, as Petrarch says, needs no gloss

---

13 'Monicus, with a kind of rural simplicity, does not give the name but describes the fatherland of his subject and as is the habit of country folk who often make mistakes in their words, he first mentions two rivers springing from one source and then at once as if realizing his mistake changes his discourse and goes on to speak of one river flowing from two springs; to be sure both are references to things of Asia.'

14 *Life*, 19. G. Martellotti, in his edition of this eclogue (*Francesco Petrarca: Rime, Trionfi e Poesie latine*, Milano, 1951, p. 816) reminds us that Petrarch could not have known of the *Punica* of Silius Italicus, re-discovered in 1416, and, on the authority of Valerius Maximus, thought the verses of Ennius on Scipio must have been too crude to do his subject justice.

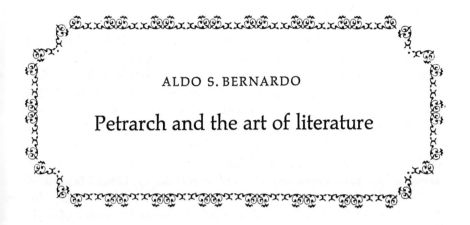

ALDO S. BERNARDO

Petrarch and the art of literature

PETRARCH'S APPROACH TO LITERATURE was as complex as his personality and
life. To begin with, he was deeply sensitive to the classical schools of
criticism, with Plato on one end of the spectrum and Aristotle on the
other. Then, too, he had read widely on the position of the church fathers
on the subject, and had a special predilection for St Augustine. Thirdly,
he was well versed in contemporary theories and felt strongly the distinction between classical and vernacular literatures.

Insights into Petrarch's approach to literature are scattered throughout
his works. As I have shown elsewhere,[1] however, the most sustained
discussion of this subject is in his correspondence with Boccaccio regarding his attitude towards Dante. There several things become apparent
with respect to Petrarch's literary sensitivity. There is, for example, his
admiration for Dante's 'noble theme,' but it is accompanied by a reservation about his style which is 'very popular.' There are the many allusions
to the 'windy plaudits of the multitude' enjoyed by Dante, as well as the
ironical reference to his own 'enemies' who accuse him of envy towards
Dante simply because Dante is so 'extremely popular' with them. There
is also the reference to Dante's undisputed 'genius.' The note of irony
continues in his strange explanation to Boccaccio of why he did not possess a copy of the *Comedy*. He had not purchased a copy in his early
years when the *Comedy* 'would naturally have attracted me most,' and
at a time when 'I too was devoting my powers to compositions in the
vernacular,' simply because he feared the temptation to imitate Dante.
Besides, at that time he 'had not yet learned to look higher.' In his late
fifties, therefore, he is willing to yield to Dante 'the palm for skill in the

1 A.S. Bernardo, 'Petrarch's Attitude Toward Dante,' *PMLA*, LXX (1955), 488–517.

use of the vulgar tongue.' He is particularly irked at the way 'the common herd' befouls the 'noble beauty of his lines.' He himself has abandoned this vernacular style of composition because of the fear of having his works fall into similar hands. In fact, when he did dabble in the vernacular, it was as 'mere sport, a pastime, the first essay of my powers.' This was far different from Dante who made such writing his primary occupation. He is convinced that Dante could 'easily have written in another style had he wanted to,' but he chose not to. Therefore how could he be envious of 'the hoarse applause which our poet enjoys from the tavern keepers, fullers, butchers, and others of their class.' He himself is grateful for having avoided such a fate, as had Virgil and Homer. Basically, for Petrarch, Dante's principal weakness was a certain inequality of style between his vernacular and his Latin poetry (*carminibus*), an inequality present even in his prose.

As late as 1365 we find Petrarch returning to the subject in another letter to Boccaccio (*Epistolae seniles*, v.2). Once again we find a spirit of condescension as Petrarch first proceeds to cede first place to Dante as the 'prince of our vernacular' and then inveighs against an age that had caused Boccaccio to destroy his vernacular poems to keep them from falling into the hands of the common and stupid populace and critics. The vogue for the new and the contemporary was actually getting out of hand and had made him cease writing in the vernacular altogether. Thus Dante remained for Petrarch until the very last years of his life primarily a vernacular stylist whose appeal was chiefly among the 'volgo' ('rabble').

On the surface it would appear, therefore, that among those qualities that Petrarch felt were essential for poetry and literature, one of the most important was its intellectual and aristocratic nature. It was not intended for mere aesthetic enjoyment or pleasure but for those mental activities in which only lofty minds truly indulged. Furthermore, the best vehicle for such communication was the classical Latin language, which presumably still remained partially inaccessible to the man in the street.

II

Considering this position of Petrarch towards Dante and towards literature, there is in his attitude towards his own vernacular works a paradox that must be explained if there is to be any cohesiveness in his general approach to literature. As is well known, notwithstanding his anti-vernacular stand, not only did Petrarch work and rework his vernacular poems and then take great pains to place them in a particular sequence before he was satisfied with the *Canzoniere*, but he worked steadily and almost feverishly on his *Triumphs* until the very last days of his life. If, indeed, the vernacular was to be used for a kind of poetry that could be considered similar to a hobby or to the writing of 'trifles,' why did Petrarch expend so much time and energy perfecting his vernacular pieces? Before venturing an answer, we must first examine at greater length his general view of literature.

As I have shown briefly (494–85) in the study already cited, there is little question that Petrarch subscribed to the allegorical and exclusive approach to literature derived from the tradition of scriptural exegesis which had started with St Augustine and had enjoyed widespread popularity down to Petrarch's own time. Like Dante, however, Petrarch also had great esteem for Virgil as a kind of apex of poetic perfection. Interestingly, it is in their attitude towards Virgil that Petrarch and Dante begin to part company in their respective views on the function of poetry.

III

Perhaps the clearest explanation of Petrarch's poetics may be found in *Epistolae Familiares* x. 4, which he wrote to his brother in 1348. The letter accompanies one of his eclogues, a genre cultivated by Petrarch not only in imitation of Virgil but as a form truly appropriate for poetry at its best. In the letter Petrarch reassures his brother who was a Carthusian monk that the poem is not improper reading for a monastic because 'the difference between poetry and theology is very slight indeed.' He then proceeds to elaborate on the Augustinian concept of theology which is but poetry with God as its subject: 'for is that not poetry that refers to Christ at one time as a lion or at another as a lamb and still another time as a dragon?' The very parables of Christ are nothing more than continuous allegorical discourse which is at the heart of poetry. It may be true that the subject is different inasmuch as theology deals with God and divine beings while poetry deals with gods and men. Nevertheless, they both deal with 'first causes which rule and govern mortal things' in words 'completely different from everyday speech.'

The distinction between the theologian and the poet, Petrarch continues, is slight indeed when one considers the etymology of the word 'poet,' according to Aristotle, and then examines what such authorities as Varro, Tranquillus, and Isidore had to say on the subject. The objection that poetry is too sweet for the rigours of monastic life is not necessarily so. The Psalter was written in Hebrew metrics and the first fathers of the Old Testament, including Moses, Job, David, Solomon, and Jeremiah, did not hesitate to use heroic song and poetic metre. Even St Jerome could not help retaining the metrical form of the psalms in his Vulgate, while Ambrose, Augustine, and Prudentius, for the most part, wrote in the fashion of poets. It is the *sentence* (*sensum*) that matters for, if it is true and salutary, style may matter little. Poetry is indeed like a golden platter on which ordinary but basic food prepared in an earthen vessel may be served. This does not necessarily make the food any better, but it improves its looks much as the use of a ruler in drawing a line assures its being straighter than if drawn free hand. By providing a dimension of beauty as a result of its 'variety and glitter,' poetry appeals to the learned and sophisticated minds of lofty intellects.

Thus for Petrarch the Christian distrust of style or form is irrational. Such style or form is as important for theology as it is for poetry. Both try to achieve a 'discourse different from the sense meanings, which we usually call allegory.' If there is a distinction between poetry and theology it lies exclusively in the subject matter.

Petrarch's letter to his brother also proceeds to explain the allegorical significance of the accompanying eclogue. As part of the explanation we find the distinction between David, the preferred poet of the monastic, and Virgil and Homer, the preferred poets of the man of letters. The latter poets 'sing of Rome, Troy, the battle of kings, the power of grief and love and wrath, the spirit that rules the waves and the winds and the stars; ... they also sing the eternal night of the Stygian shades, the snaky-haired Furies, the temple and the forum; they sing of the woods and fields, arms and heroes, and they depict the entire world with lofty verses.'

A poet such as David, on the other hand, 'sings instead of one God who caused the vanquished throng of the gods to tremble; who governs the bountiful heavens with his nod; who holds the liquid ether in equilibrium and spreads heaps of dew and cold snow ... who assigns age to the movement of the stars and seeds to the earth ... who gave us our body and soul to which he added innumerable other skills ... who, by showing us the alternating of life and death, taught us the best road that leads tired men above the stars, and brings us back to it by warnings.' In the eclogue itself, to Petrarch's charge that poets like David are 'hoarse,' his brother counters that David's voice is instead powerful and penetrates souls with a mysterious sweetness.

The distracted reader may forget that Petrarch's main point in the letter is that the eclogue forwarded to his brother is itself an example of what he considers true poetry. Analysing it on the basis of what he says in his letter, we find that it seems to conform to the requirements that Petrarch's interpretation ascribes to true poetry. On a literal level, it deals with 'gods and men ... the first causes which rule and govern mortal things,' and does so with words that are 'completely different from every-day speech.' It is enclosed in an allegorical covering *resembling* that of theology. And finally it reflects a kind of moral lesson consistent with theological teachings. This is true notwithstanding the ambiguous ending of the eclogue which shows the earthly Silvius (representing Petrarch) responding to Monicus (representing Petrarch's brother) in terms that leave the reader uncertain as to the precise meaning intended. Silvius takes the position that perhaps some day he ought to consider the writings of David more seriously, but for the time being he must hurry away, pulled by 'love of the Muses.' His haste is prompted by the need to sing of the exploits of Scipio Africanus whose fame 'is still bereft of sacred song, and virtue demands its reward.' Just as the prophets and the testament writers had been moved to record the exploits of the servants of the Hebraic–Christian God, so it is that the true poet is moved to sing of the exploits of outstanding human activity. To concentrate on the 'citizens and walls of the Little Jerusalem and never wander from there,' may be appropriate for sacred writing, but much may also be learned from writings that deal with 'gods and men.' It is necessary to wander from the walls of Jerusalem to get away from the tears and the hoarse voices of expiation and atonement. In the variety, glitter, and inspiration present in literature dealing with human values, lessons may be learned as important as those taught by theology. The byways of great literature may well lead to the same straight and narrow path of theology.

One might conclude therefore that in the eclogue both Monicus and Silvius represent extremes. The great poet deals with subject matter that lies somewhere between their two positions. He understands the importance of both and therefore is concerned with something that transcends either one. This is why for Petrarch literature and poetry must possess an aristocratic and exclusive character. Presumably a poem such as Dante's *Comedy* resembles the work of David, while the one that Silvius has undertaken resembles those of Homer and Virgil. Both types have nourishing food to serve, but true poetry provides a 'golden platter' for the food, thus appealing to the learned mind.

IV

Another interesting dimension given by Petrarch to his theory of literature is developed rather thoroughly throughout his *Africa*. We shall return to it later, but for the present shall simply point out the manner in which it is indirectly implied in *Fam.* III. 12, in which he discourages a local ruler from abandoning his political activities simply because he had wished to enter the religious life to assure the salvation of his soul. He points out that service to mankind is as important as the contemplative life. This view, he adds, was widely held by the church fathers when they wrote that the cares of the active Martha are just as important to salvation as the contemplation of Mary. The province of true poetry is the active life and its relationship to the problem and mystery of salvation. It too seeks to promote Charity but in a manner intended for lofty intellects. This may be seen in a work such as the first eclogue, but it really permeates most of Petrarch's other works whether finished or unfinished. It is certainly present in the *Africa*. But perhaps the clearest example, since it consciously counterpoints Dante's *Comedy*, is to be found in the *Triumphs*.

In this strange unfinished poem whose potential and intent reflect the nature of Petrarch's literary stance better than any of his other works, we find a number of qualities that stand clearly in contrast to Dante's *Comedy*. The surface similarities have been pointed out many times in the past. There are certain ambivalent characteristics, however, that bear mentioning. First there is what appears to be a strong sense of objectivity which is missing in the *Comedy*. And yet a close examination of the poem's movements shows it to be far more subjective than is supposed. Then there is the *persona* of the poem who also seems to mirror a certain objectivity unlike Dante's protagonist. As the *persona* of his poem, Petrarch appears to remain an onlooker over the spectacle of humanity. And yet the vision presented is once again totally personal. The same may be said of the subject matter. In a sense Petrarch's poem also deals with a guided pilgrimage. Instead, the different triumphs represent what the poet himself calls 'an extended picture in a brief moment.' (IV. 164)

Then there are, of course, the real distinctions and differences between the two poems. For example, in Petrarch's poem there is no vision of the *perduta gente*. We see almost exclusively *anime gentili*. The concluding visions also contrast strikingly. Whereas Dante's celestial happiness is anchored in the Beatific vision, eliminating completely any possible comparison with earthly counterparts, Petrarch's realm of Eternity represents but sublimated human experiences and remains throughout a place and a state in the future. His God thus becomes only a projection of his own humanity, and the angle of perspective is from the vantage point of earth rather than of eternity. Laura, as a sublimation of earthly beauty, does become one with the divine, but as a transfiguration of the divine rather than of the human. As Goffis has shown,[2] Petrarch seemed to

---

2 C.F. Goffis, *Originalita dei "Trionfi"* (Firenze, 1951). All page references immediately following in the text are to this work.

emulate the *Comedy* by substituting for the song of a soul reaching for the transcendental an extremely modern sigh for 'immortal beauty,' which is the basic theme of all his art. By composing a work 'responding to an exigency that he was the first to feel,' and by using Christian doctrine to achieve new artistic ends, Petrarch could be said to have actually tried to surpass Dante (45). His *iter mentis* was also to lead to Paradise, but to a paradise that was given substance by Laura, not God. This paradise is, in fact, not much different from the kingdom of Venus found in the Triumph of Love, except that all is now truly eternal (46). It is a paradise of the eternal feminine, not of the Christian Trinity (45). Petrarch's religiosity is thus no longer a religion but rather a product of artistic taste (p. 46). The earthly poles that the poet cannot escape in the *Canzoniere* are sublimated in the *Triumphs*. There is no transformation of love into religious ecstasy as in Dante. Freed of earthly stain and elevated to an 'aestheticized paradise' which guarantees their perpetuation, Love and Glory triumph eternally. The *Triumphs* are like Elysian Fields in which are fused Petrarch's highly intimate love story and his humanistic concerns scattered throughout his Latin works (54).

All of this is mirrored in the very form of the two poems and in their general perspective. Whereas Dante's invention and use of the *terzina* is part of his concern with the Triune Almighty, Petrarch uses the metre only to provide an intricate veil designed to give the impression of a *lunga pittura*. This accounts for the greater difficulty one experiences in reading his *terzine*.

In effect, with respect to the allegorical implications of the two poems, we find in the contrast between the two poets a difference between the allegory of the theologian and that of the poet as developed by Charles S. Singleton.[3] Dante's poem calls for an acceptance of the literal sense, Petrarch's does not. This is why those literary historians are probably correct who argue that in his *Triumphs* Petrarch was really competing with the *Roman de la rose* (Goffis, 4–6). In both poems a poet–artist rather than a poet–theologian was at work. In both the stress was on the 'golden platter' rather than on the 'earthen vessel.'

In many ways, then, the allegory of the *Triumphs* reverses the method used by Dante. The poet takes abstract concepts (such as Love, Chastity, Death, Glory, etc.) and personifies them to convey a clearly defined intellectual and moral meaning. The historical personages of the *Triumphs* convey meaning only insofar as their relationship with these abstract

3 C.S. Singleton, *Dante Studies I; Commedia, Elements of Structure* (Cambridge, 1954), 84–94.

personifications is made clear. Dante's poem, on the other hand, takes
actual historical persons and events and makes them reflect abstract significations without losing their individuality. The resulting effect is a
surface which appears simple but is actually extremely complex. Petrarch's
surface, however, appears highly polished and complex, but the underlying meaning is rather simple. The metaphysical concerns of exegetical
interpretations were losing ground to the incipient humanism. The inherent lesson is a commentary on earthly life and man's role therein. As
Blackmur has pointed out, 'the secularization of literature destroyed the
usefulness of the conceptual and imaginative aspects of the technique of
scriptural interpretation ... what had been deeply useful in the understanding of life became a mere special competence and the competence
became ornamental and the ornamental became artificial with no longer
any grasp on actuality.'[4] In speaking of Petrarch's tendency to adorn the
truth, Cesareo remarks that 'for Dante the spirit of the thing sufficed;
Petrarch delighted in caressing it lovingly, developing it and illuminating
its form. Thus he gained in elegance what he had lost in immediate
efficacy.'[5]

To summarize briefly the basis for Petrarch's unenthusiastic attitude
towards Dante, one might generally assert that it was a deeply felt need
for balancing Classical and Christian literary ideals. We may see the view
expressed in *Sen.* 1.5, where by implication the reader recognizes that for
Petrarch the ideal man of letters 'knows what is due to Jupiter the adult-
erer, Mercury the panderer, Mars the manslayer, Hercules the brigand ...
and, on the other hand, to Mary the Virgin Mother, and to her son our
redeemer, very God and very Man.' The same view had appeared many
years before in the *Africa* where the poet defines the true poets of the
future as those

> Lofty intellects and noble spirits
> Who will combine within their minds
> The ancient love of the muses and Christian doctrine.

(IX. 459–61)

In his *Sen.* 1.5 to Boccaccio, Petrarch presents a staunch defence of
learning and literary values generally, pointing out how most of the
church fathers had indeed used the classics as a foundation for Christian
doctrine, how literature is a source of comfort and aid in the difficulties

4 R.P. Blackmur, 'Dante's Ten Terms for the Treatment of the Treatise,' *Kenyon
Review*, XIV (1952), 295.
5 G. Cesareo, 'Dante e il Petrarca,' *Giornale Dantesco*, I, 11–12 (1894), 507.

of the human journey, and how if learning had not been necessary for many saints, it never impeded anyone from becoming a saint. The journey to salvation is a blessed experience for all, but 'that journey is more glorious that achieves the summit accompanied by the loveliest light; whence the piety of an ignorant but pious man is inferior to the piety of a man of letters.'[6]

V

Turning once more from Petrarch the practicing poet to Petrarch the theoretician, let us now consider a document which perhaps affords the deepest insight into Petrarch's conception of poetry. This is the coronation oration delivered by Petrarch on that memorable Easter Sunday of 1341 before the Senate and the people of Rome upon receiving the crown of poet laureate on the Capitoline Hill. As Wilkins has stated and shown in his superb account of the ceremony, 'it was ... one of the most spectacular tributes to poetry ever paid and witnessed anywhere.'[7]

As we shall show later, there was something inherently poetic in the very manner in which Petrarch consciously lived his life. The two concepts of 'Parnassian Laurus' and of 'April 6,' as developed by Calcaterra, serve as the two poles of this poetic arrangement of his personal life.[8] It is therefore not surprising to find Petrarch continuing his poetic drama even during his coronation. His publicizing of the two invitations he had received simultaneously from Paris and Rome is by now too well known an episode in his life to dwell upon here. It is perhaps not as well known that the timing of his trip to Rome to receive the laurel crown was such that he was examined in Naples by King Robert on 6 April, was crowned in Rome on the morning of Easter Sunday, proceeded in solemn fashion to St Peter's to deposit his crown upon the altar, and presumably even wore one of King Robert's own robes which he had received as a gift.

Bearing all of this background in mind, let us now turn to the coronation oration delivered by Petrarch at the time of his crowning. The oration is divided into three parts. The first is introductory and deals primarily with the poet's drive to seek the laurel crown. The second deals with the 'nature of the profession of poetry.' The third part focuses on the character of the reward desired by the poet. The theme of the oration is taken

6 *Lettere senili di Francesco Petrarca*, tr. G. Fracassetti, vol. I–II (Firenze, 1869–70). The citation appears in vol. I, 48.
7 *The Making of the Canzoniere and other Petrarchan Studies* (Rome, 1951), 9. The text of the oration may be found in Wilkins, *Studies in the Life and Works of Petrarch* (Cambridge, 1955), 300–13.
8 C. Calcaterra, *Nella selva del Petrarca* (Bologna, 1942), chaps. I and VII.

from Virgil's *Georgics*, which Petrarch justifies with the following most significant opening sentence. 'Today, magnificent and venerable sirs, I must follow in my speech the ways of poetry, and I have therefore taken my text from a poetic source.' The Virgilian text is the following: 'But a sweet longing urges me upward over the lonely slopes of Parnassus' (*Georgics*, III, 291–92). The first portion of the oration is basically a commentary on these verses to indicate certain qualities which a poet should possess. These include the awareness of the difficulty of the poet's task, the eagerness of a studious mind, and the motivation for study which he compares with Cicero's definition of philosophy, poetry, and the other arts.

In addressing himself first to 'the inherent difficulty of the poet's task,' Petrarch indicates that, unlike the other arts, poetry cannot be attained through 'sheer toil and study.' There must be present in the true poet's spirit 'a certain inner and divinely given energy.' This is why Ennius and many other learned men were able to call poets sacred in their own right. Despite such inherent difficulties, as well as others that are peculiar to the times, Petrarch nevertheless would like to revive a custom 'that has long since fallen into desuetude.' He is not afraid to attempt climbing the lonely steps of Parnassus because 'the intensity of my longing is so great that it seems to be sufficient to enable me to overcome all the difficulties that are involved in my present task.' His motivations are three, the honour of the republic, the charm of personal glory, and the stimulation of other men to a like endeavour.

Turning in the second section to the nature of the profession of poetry, Petrarch assures his listeners that the poet's office and work are not what they are commonly believed to be. The office of the poet is to 'take things that have really come to pass and transform them by means of subtle figures into things of a different sort.' It is not therefore merely to invent subjects or stories, for only a liar does this. The poet's chief responsibility is to set forth truths, physical, moral, and historical, under the cloud of a poetic fiction. This would mean that there is little difference between the poet, the historian, and the moral or physical philosopher. The basic difference is similar to the difference between a clouded sky and a clear one, 'since in each case the same light exists in the object of vision, but is perceived in different degrees according to the capacity of the observers.' What makes poetry sweeter than the other disciplines is that 'a truth that must be sought out with some care gives all the more delight when it is discovered.' He himself would 'not wish to appear to be a poet and nothing more.' The obvious implication of this statement is that the poet should also reflect the truth reflected by the historian and the philosopher.

In section three, which speaks of the nature of the poet's reward, Petrarch indicates that if poets are not to fall into oblivion they must learn to express 'in the stable and enduring style of a true man of letters what it was that they really had in their minds and spirits.' Among the best rewards enjoyed by the great poet is his ability to give immortality to the names of great men of valour. This is why so many illustrious men and warriors of the past held poets in high esteem. And this is why the laurel crown is the due reward of both Caesars and poets. These two types of men also indicate that there are two ways of seeking glory, namely the way of the body and the way of the spirit. In many ways both Caesars and poets move toward the same goal, though by different paths. The laurel crown is appropriate for both for a number of reasons.

The shade afforded by the laurel tree symbolizes the resting place deserved by those who labour. The incorruptible leaves of the tree, which are said to be able to preserve from corruption those books and other things on which they are placed, symbolize the poet's power to preserve from corruption his own fame and the fame of others. Moreover, the laurel is a sacred tree, 'to be held in awe, and to be reverenced.'

Perhaps the most interesting observations on poetry appear towards the end of the oration. In speaking of the belief that a sleeping person touched with a laurel sees his dreams come true, Petrarch maintains that this really pertains to poets who are said to sleep on Parnassus. By this is meant that truth is indeed contained in poetic writings which fools may consider dreams but which are not, because the poet's head is symbolically wreathed with the leaves that make dreams come true. Furthermore, the fact that there is a close association between the laurel tree and Apollo implies that poetry promises foreknowledge of the future, Apollo being the god of prophecy and of poets.

In the same way the eternal verdure of the laurel is associated with Apollo and his love for Daphne and by extension with 'the immortality of fame sought through warfare or through genius.'

And finally the tradition that the laurel is immune to lightning is likewise an appropriate reason for its being worthy of poets, since a crown of laurel is given to those whose glory fears not the ages that like thunderbolts lay all things low.

Before leaving Petrarch's coronation it might be worth noting that the *Privilegium*, or diploma, given to Petrarch as part of the ceremony specifies the particular awards given to Petrarch on that occasion. Among these were the following: the title of 'Great Poet and Historian;' recognition of his being 'an outstanding teacher;' and recognition especially of his abilities as a poet but with the implication that it was just as applicable to his ability as an historian and as an interpreter of ancient and modern writings.[9]

Petrarch's coronation oration, therefore, was primarily a brief *Ars Poetica*. Petrarch's lofty conception of the poet and of poetry is apparent throughout. Not only must the poet guard against the excesses of the undisciplined imagination, but he must at all times base his poetry on reality. Poetry transforms this reality through symbols that the reader must penetrate through intellectual and emotional participation.

Once again, therefore, we have an extremely complex attitude towards the nature and function of poetry. By encompassing the rightful purview of history and philosophy, poetry as defined in the oration resembles the definition of literature rather than poetry as generally conceived. And it is here that the crux of the matter seems to lie, for such a definition had enjoyed a long tradition descending from both classical and Christian sources. If there was anything unique or original in Petrarch's position, it was in the highly personal manner in which he epitomized the concept in the image of the laurel. As we shall see, such a focus fully, and surprisingly, dominates the basic form of the vernacular *Canzoniere*. Meanwhile, the coronation oration has shown the extent to which for Petrarch the laurel crown, the ultimate symbol of reward for the great poet, reflects the rich traditions inherent in such names, words, and concepts as Apollo, Daphne, Caesar, History, Philosophy, Art, Truth, the Good, and the Beautiful.

VI

We find the same ideas permeating all of Petrarch's other works. In the *Africa*, for example, we find him quoting Lactantius who had written that 'whatever might be the work of history, or the practice of virtue, the lessons of life, or the study of nature befits the work of a poet provided that truth, nude elsewhere, is concealed under new garments, which like a thin veil, deceives the sight, making truth at times clear, at times hidden.'[10] Thus poetry is the most liberal of the arts, for it embraces them all. It develops the mind because it evolved from the attempts of primitive men to use lofty words of praise in worshipping their gods. Theology, in fact, is but poetry dealing with God; and the poet is divinely inspired, like the saint. As he states in *Epistolae metricae*, II, 11, 'Our madness is divine. Dreaming is a singer's right. Only when it soars can the soul, escaping mortality, sing of exalted things, leaving the vulgar mob far be-

9 Wilkins, *The Making of the Canzoniere*, 56.
10 F. Petrarca, *Africa*, ed. N. Festa (Firenze, 1926), Book IX, vv. 97–102.

low its feet ... If poets were mute, man would be mute also, and virtue would hide unknown, lovely only to itself, and all the great past would vanish, and even the fundamentals of our language!'[11] Even in the rather late *Sen.* XII. 2 he maintains that the poet's duty is 'to create by imagination, to treat of the nature or order of moral matters, to embellish truth with beautiful colors, and to cover it with a veil of pleasing invention.' The poet may alter facts to attain a higher truth, but the foundations must always be sunken in reality. Some poetry may have as its purpose beauty and delight; other poetry may have a highly civilizing function, such as the preservation of the sense of the past. Imitation of past greats is perfectly acceptable provided that only subjects and thoughts are imitated, not words. Like the bee, a writer may cull from the flower of a past great, but the honey he then produces must be his own. The writing of poetry calls for long meditation and the singing or reciting of the verses out loud and with detachment. Traditional rhetorical figures are not to be rejected. This includes the use of allegory which protects truth from becoming common and obvious. As for style, it should always be highly personal. 'Every man has by nature something individual and his own, in appearance, gesture, voice, and utterance and it is easier and better for him to develop and correct what he has than to try to change it.'[12]

The ultimate function of true poetry, then, is to take the very stuff of history and philosophy, recast it 'within a delightful and colorful cloud and thereby transform it into a goad for virtue.' By virtue Petrarch meant the ability to 'recte sentire de deo et recte inter homines agere.'[13]

Most of what has been said thus far implies of course a view of poetry as conceived by a highly learned man of letters. The remarks we have seen him make regarding Dante's *Comedy* would indicate that poetry in the vernacular would hardly qualify as great poetry. Yet we did note the attempt to make of the *Triumphs* a poem that would not only compete

11 M. Bishop, *Petrarch and His World* (Indiana, 1963), 300.
12 *Fam.* XII.2, in *Le Familiari*, vols. 1–3, ed. V. Rossi, and vol. 4, ed. Rossi and U. Bosco (Firenze, 1933–42). For bee image, see *Fam.* I.8.
13 *Fam.* XI.3. The following ending of *Fam.* I.9 is of particular interest in this regard: 'I cannot tell you of what worth are to me in solitude certain familiar and famous words, not only grasped in the mind but actually spoken orally, with which I am accustomed to rouse my sleepy thoughts. Furthermore, how much delight I get from repeating the written words either of others or sometimes even my own! How much I feel myself freed from very serious and bitter burdens by such readings! Meantime I feel assisted even more by my own writings since they are more suited to my ailments ... This I shall certainly never accomplish unless the salutary words themselves fall tenderly upon my ears. By arousing me through the power of an unsual sweet temptation to reread them, they gradually flow forth and transfigure my insides with hidden darts.'

with Dante, but that would presumably observe most of the qualities of the great poem. But what can we say about his *Canzoniere* which he took so many pains to complete precisely as he wanted? There are many critics who continue to hold the view that the promised masterpiece to which Petrarch so mysteriously and so often refers in his work was his collection of vernacular lyrics.[14]

VII

Before turning to the *Canzoniere* we might take a brief look at a letter which clearly indicates Petrarch's abiding concern for form. We have already observed that he worked on the collection of Italian poems throughout his life. The studies of Ernest H. Wilkins on the extraordinary care with which Petrarch developed the collection throughout the years, moving from one form to the next, have become milestones in Romance philology.[15] Ruth Phelps had already indicated the manner in which Petrarch attempted to inject variety in the ordering of the collection.[16] That Petrarch was mindful of the same concerns in organizing his collections of prose pieces as well may be seen in the prefatory letter to his principal collection of letters, the *Familiari*. In this letter to his beloved 'Socrates,' he recounts how he had decided to start collecting his letters as well as other writings and how he eliminated a sizable quantity by simply burning them. In speaking of the letters he alludes to the problem of giving them a tone and character that would be appropriate for a collection as distinct from individual letters. He acknowledges that in writing the original letters he had considered the variety of people to whom he had written. But in including them in a collection he was worried because 'the letters were so different that in rereading them I seemed to be in constant contradiction.' He accordingly had to make some changes in content and in style in order to avoid a kind of 'deformity' that could easily be discerned in the collection although it was hidden in the individual letters.

The same applied to highly personal matters which, while appropriate in the originals, did not warrant insertion in the collection. He also gave a great deal of thought to the title of the collection. The style, too, was of considerable importance. In rereading the letters he found that his style had moved from a strong and sober one in the early years to a weak and humble one in the later years. He is unhappy about this and urges Socrates to help him conceal this weakness. He gives a rather lengthy explana-

---

14 *Le rime di Francesco Petrarca*, ed. N. Zingarelli (Bologna, 1963), 17–28.
15 Wilkins, *The Making of the Canzoniere, passim*.
16 R.S. Phelps, *The Earlier and Later Forms of Petrarch's Canzoniere* (Chicago, 1925).

tion of why this occurred and assures Socrates that at the time of the prefatory letter he had become much stronger. He will, however, try to organize the collection in such a manner that the weakest part will be in the middle and the strongest parts at the beginning and end. The tone of these will be much more manly than the weaker ones. The collection therefore will appear 'woven with multi-colored threads.'

This very real awareness of structure and form inevitably affected Petrarch's vernacular works. In fact, in an early portion of this same letter he makes reference to his *Canzoniere* by way of contrasting this type of writing to his Latin works. In speaking of the overwhelming number of works he had unearthed as he searched for the letters, he says, 'part of the writing was free of literary niceties, part showed the influence of Homeric control ... ; but another part intended for charming the ears of the multitude relied on its own particular rules. This last kind of writing, which presumably arose among the Sicilians not many centuries ago, had briefly extended throughout the length of Italy and had once indeed been popular among the Greeks and Latins if it is true that the Attic and Roman people accepted only the rhythmic type of poetry.'

VIII

The vernacular lyrics of Petrarch seem to add an additional ingredient to this strong awareness of rules for the various genres and to the abiding sense of tone, structure, and general style. There is an equally strong awareness of the shortcomings and weaknesses of the vernacular as a medium for expressing certain sentiments that are particularly complex. While expressing this concept was a commonplace in both Latin and vernacular writing, the extent to which it seems to permeate so many of Petrarch's lyrics cannot be disassociated from his profound awareness of the difficulties of artistic creation.

As was previously stated, the *Triumphs* unfortunately remained unfinished, a fate they shared with a number of Petrarch's Latin works. In speaking of the *Triumphs*, Bosco has pointed out that Petrarch's Latin heritage had instilled in him a preference for the elaborately constructed work.[17] The vernacular, however, was more appropriate for the short poetic piece. This, in addition to his inability to construct elaborate structures as a result of his failure to give body to the abstract and an inspiration that had to move from the concrete, led Petrarch to his incomparable

---

17 U. Bosco, 'Francesco Petrarca,' in *Letteratura italiana, I maggiori* (Milano: Marzorati, 1956), 155–161.

success in the vernacular lyric. For Bosco, Petrarch the learned man and moralist appears in his letters, in his invectives, and in his essays; Petrarch the man appears most clearly in his *Secretum*; but Petrarch the poet is in the sonnets and in the *canzoni*. The *Triumphs* are really a systematizing of the *Canzoniere*. In it Petrarch seeks the unity of the learned man and the poet, but fails because he confuses erudition with poetry.

The lyrics of the *Canzoniere* on the other hand result from Petrarch's natural inspiration and ability. The organizing of the individual pieces into a collection encompassed a series of moments that are perhaps the clearest indicators of a kind of fusion between Petrarch's theoretical and applied poetics. As anyone familiar with the studies of Wilkins knows, the collection can be approached in a variety of ways. The first is the reading of the lyrics as independent pieces written at disparate times and having no necessary relation with their neighbours. Another possibility is to read the poems chronologically, following, wherever feasible, the sequence in which they were actually written. A third approach is to read them as they appear in the numerical order established by the poet and in the two parts into which they are divided. The fourth possibility stems from the monumental study of Wilkins which shows the various forms undergone by the collection over a period of more than thirty years.

The need for brevity makes it impossible to examine the making of the collection from each of these perspectives. For purposes of this paper the only logical approach would be to view the collection as the poet wished, in its final form. Our focus, however, will be on the collection viewed as a document representing a kind of portrait of the artist as a young man.

In a seminar which I gave recently at Johns Hopkins University, in which the approach was to examine the collection as it evolved from form to form, one of the students made some very significant inroads into the view that if taken form by form, the collection can indeed be considered a humanistic journal tracing the self-conscious development of an artist. Laura, as has been pointed out in the past,[18] could be seen as representing the new mode of poetry, one in which the poet self-consciously writes of his own craftsmanship. As he does so, she painfully reminds him of his inability to consummate fully his desire. But the poet must master his art or fear death, for each unsuccessful poem represents a moment, or better a day, closer to death, there being 366 such moments in the collection. Laura's ephemeral, shifting nature makes her identifiable only as a process undergone by the poet. She really plays a twin role, alluring him to externalize his own passions and moods and then guiding him in the craft

18 Zingarelli, *Le Rime*, 408.

of poetry. She reflects a kind of oscillating dialectic of the artist's personal development. Perhaps the most symbolic poem in the collection seeming to imply this is poem no. 23, in which the various transfigurations undergone by Laura ultimately lead to a vision in which the poet sees his beloved bathing naked in the fountain. As commentators have pointed out, this is but a version of Ovid's myth of Actaeon, the hunter who catches sight of Diana bathing nude in a sylvan grotto. As a revenge, Diana splashes water on Actaeon and turns him into a deer that is subsequently pursued and destroyed by his own hunting companions. The real point of the myth is that the transfiguration causes the hunter to lose his power of speech to identify himself. This is, in turn, the condition of the true poet in beholding the essential secrets of the poetic art or in beholding its innermost nature.

If we now turn to the collection as it stands in its traditional form, we do find the self-awareness of the artist emerging periodically. Unfortunately, we must restrict ourselves to only those examples that are perhaps the most significant as found in the first 50 poems of the collection.

In approaching Petrarch's *Canzoniere* as a finished artistic monument, however, we must constantly recall the incredible amount of labour spent by the poet in developing the collection over the period of almost 30 years and in ten different forms. One must further recall how at the very last moment Petrarch decided to change the order of the last 30 poems. The entire story, as recounted by Wilkins,[19] is in itself an indicator of the poet's deep concern for artistic balance and polish.

Another point to keep constantly in mind is the underlying assumption that everywhere, even in his most intimate poems, the poet must reflect the learned man familiar with the great minds of the past. To assume that the lyric qualities of Petrarch's poetry are strictly personal and bereft of all learned allusions is of course misreading the poetry as a collection. In point of fact, as I shall show elsewhere, the intent of the poet was to create a monument as much to poetry as to his beloved. The collection is basically encased in the framework of the Apollo–Daphne myth which in turn dramatizes the evanescence of truth and beauty as grasped by a poet and as present in the human condition.

The entire framework, therefore, derives from the learned tradition of Petrarch the scholar and humanist. But even more important is the manner in which such learning is enmeshed in almost every piece in such a way that it is barely recognizable. Thus, as many critics and commentators have indicated, the basic theme of the very first poem derives from Ovid

19 Wilkins, *The Making of the Canzoniere, passim.*

and Horace.[20] Similarly the figure of Cupid appearing in poem no. 2 is of learned origin, while the obvious references to the gospels of Matthew, Mark, and Luke found in poem no. 3 indicate the extent of the learned allusions. There are also many borrowings from the Provençal poets and other contemporary Italian and French sources. While Ovid and Horace lead the pack of Classical poets, it is not unusual to find references to prose writers such as Livy and Cicero. Assuming, therefore, that the very foundations of the collection reflect a high seriousness of purpose on the part of Petrarch, let us examine those moments among the first 50 lyrics that are most pertinent to our discussion.

Poem no. 1 of the *Canzoniere* already reflects a number of artistic awarenesses having to do with the nature of lyric poetry in the vernacular. In addressing the reader, or better the listener, the poet makes reference to 'the sound of scattered rhymes.' Obviously the 365 poems that follow are to be considered 'sighs' with which the poet 'nourished his heart' in his youth, when the poet was 'a man other than what I am.'

The second stanza similarly speaks of the poems as pieces in which the poet 'cries and reasons' in a variety of styles over his vain hopes and griefs. Obviously the composition of such poetry is appropriate only for a limited group, such as lovers, from whom the poet may expect some form of pity but not forgiveness. Poetry written in this fashion makes of the poet a kind of object of derision in the opinion of the greater part of the people. It is also obvious that the poems would sing about things that appear wonderful and exciting in the days of one's youth, but near 'vanity' when viewed through the eyes of a mature person.

Notwithstanding the tone of recantation that this first poem presumably sets for the entire collection, there is little question that the poet is presenting his poems fully aware of their highly sensitive nature. While there may not be actual expressions of artistic awareness in the verses of the next three poems of the collection, the manner in which they are placed in order to define the drama that is projected by the collection is in itself an artistic strategy. By setting his love experience within the framework of Good Friday with all its spiritual implications, the poet adds a dimension to his collection which will be felt throughout its unfolding.

Having set the foundations of the collection, the poet in poem no. 5 returns to the formal qualities of poetry. This is the poem in which the name of the beloved is eulogized in terms of the sounds emitted in pro-

20 Zingarelli, *Le Rime*, 283; see also the edition of G. Carducci and S. Ferrari (Firenze, 1943), *passim*.

nouncing it. The miracle of the name emerges from the poet's attempt 'to organize his sighs' in order to pronounce the name. To do honour to the name of the beloved requires more power than the poet can 'bear on his shoulders.' Ultimately the name itself teaches one 'to praise and revere' properly. It is at this juncture that the poet introduces yet another dimension, this time a classicizing one, by alluding to Apollo's laurel whose properties are such that 'a mortal tongue' may appear 'presumptuous' in its attempts to sing of it.

In poem no. 7 the poet is defined as someone who wishes to 'make a river spring from Helicon.' The implication is also present that poetry must involve philosophy in some manner.

In poem no. 12 the poet refers to his poetry as 'revealing his sufferings as they evolved over the hours, days, and years.' In poem no. 15 the poet–lover is indeed set apart as being exempt 'from all human qualities.' In fact, no. 17 indicates that because of his love the poet feels 'divided from the world.' Inspiration, according to poem no. 18, is like a 'light in the mind which burns and destroys.' In this same piece, the poems are referred to as 'tears' that the poet would like to shed privately. In no. 19 the inspiring light is so terribly strong that the poet is like that species of 'animals' that do not find peace until they are burning within the light. In fact the poet is perfectly conscious of the fact that 'I pursue what burns me.'

In no. 20 the labour of artistic creation involving the singing of beauty in rhyme is said to require a certain 'genius' rather than the actual physical labour of polishing or composing. This is because no 'sound' can ever fully achieve such heights.

In poem no. 23 the therapeutic value of poetry is touched upon for the first time. The poet makes reference to the fact that by singing one's 'grief becomes the less bitter.' This has led him to use more than 'a thousand pens' which have in turn enabled 'the sound of his sighs to resound in every valley.' In the second stanza of poem no. 23 Petrarch is transfigured into a green laurel tree, the symbol of poetry. Having become synonymous with poetry, the poet proceeds to be transformed into a swan in order to sing appropriately of his 'amorous woes.' In fact, the sounds of his poetry assume the colour of the swan as he finds himself helplessly singing whenever he tries to speak. The song results in sounds that are sweeter and more soothing than ever before. At this point a confrontation with the beloved occurs, which the poet says is beyond all power of words.

The poet alludes to the necessity of restricting himself to the most essential moments of his poetic experience, saying that the only points he would make are those that 'produce amazement in the listener.' Since he is in the figure of a stone, 'live words' were impossible for him and therefore he had to 'cry out with paper and with ink.' Finally he asserts that he had been like an eagle (the bird of Jove) raising as high as is possible his beloved who is herself referred to as the 'first laurel tree.'

Poem no. 24 indicates what the essence of poetry should be if the poet were worthy of cultivating it. The sonnet dramatizes this by speaking of the poet being denied the favour of Laura who once again is referred to as the laurel tree. In the second stanza the implication is clear that the poet must indeed cultivate not only the muses of Helicon but also Pallas, or the Cecropian Minerva whom Virgil referred to as 'Minerva Inventrix,' and whom Petrarch in poem no. 27 had identified with philosophy.

Poem no. 28 includes a highly significant and surprising conclusion that one would not readily connect with our main theme. But in speaking of the Crusade of 1333 and the need for serving mankind through courageous causes, the poet concludes the *congedo* or farewell by saying to the poem that it should not segregate itself from other poems simply because it is not a love poem. Rather it should keep in mind that love is much more inclusive than the love of a woman and its spirit may reside just as much in a poem dealing with a military exploit as with a moment of human love.

In poem no. 29 we once again return to a type of poetry which tries to incorporate into itself things that even one's memory cannot at times recall, especially in attempting to find appropriate comparisons for unique experiences. Thus in speaking of Laura and her effects upon him, Petrarch refers to her virtue, her beauty, and the power of her eyes which when put all together tax one's memory to the limit in trying to determine what is being beheld.

In the famous poem no. 30 the poet alludes to his inspiration (Laura) as his 'idol sculptured in a live laurel.' At the end of the poem the poet expresses the hope that his attempts to express his situation will perhaps have their effect on 'someone who will be born 1000 years hence,' who may feel some pity for him.

In poem no. 40 the art of poetry is equated with the art of weaving. The poem opens with Petrarch's announcement that if love or death does not interfere with 'the new cloth that I am weaving,' he will put together two kinds of truths, about whose identification critics have disagreed. Some identify them as historical as compared with imaginative or artistic writing, others believe that the reference is to the fusion of pagan and Christian values, still others consider the reference as applicable to philosophical and poetic truth. The image of weaving is continued in the second stanza where the poet announces a work which will be so sturdy as a result of being written somewhere between the style of the moderns and of the ancients that he feels it would bring his reputation as far as Rome. However, he is lacking certain books which he needs and which the poem is requesting. In referring to such books, he uses the expression 'blessed threads that were readily available to that favourite father of mine.' This reference to the art of weaving recalls other references to other arts, such as sculpture, painting, and music.

Scattered throughout the rest of the *Canzoniere* are examples of the poet's surprisingly modern awareness of the complexity of poetic composition. The references view the poet's craft and plight from an almost limitless number of vantage points, making an almost equal number of references to the moulding of language as to the nature of the inspiration. Thus in poem no. 155 words spoken by Laura are said to be sculptured in diamond in the midst of the poet's heart where love manages periodically to penetrate, enabling the poet to give vent to his tears and sighs. In no. 157 the sight of Laura weeping transmits to the poet's heart such a vivid image that no poetic skill or style can possibly reproduce it. No. 170 portrays passion as an emotion whose language can be understood only by the poet. Poems nos. 186 and 187 repeat a recurring motif but with the addition of a new dimension. Laura's beauty is such that it is truly worthy of the combined styles of Homer and Virgil, but this time the name of Orpheus is also added, thus introducing a magical dimension. No. 198 describes how the poet's intellect is literally overwhelmed by the sight of Laura's 'burning eyes and flashing hair.' No. 203 compares verses of poetry to sparks emerging from the poet's fire. The same image is continued in poem no. 217, in which the poet expresses his desire to be heard in his 'burning rhymes.' He also expresses his hope that his 'burning words' could dissipate the thick cloud that encloses Laura's heart. In no. 322 poetry is once again equated to music, while in no. 332 the poet confesses that all he has written is but a small distillation of infinite abysses that he has been trying to tap, and confesses that style simply cannot go beyond natural talent. Finally in no. 354 poetry is depicted as an arrow aimed at a mark which it must strike to qualify as art.

IX

In summary, then, Petrarch's poetics reflects a view of poetry that encompasses highly formal, intellectual, and exclusive elements. While the view does not depart radically from the tradition that was widely adhered to in fourteenth-century Europe, its application to a vernacular genre that Petrarch himself developed to perfection does incorporate a number of unique and original elements.

As we have seen, Petrarch's aristocratic view of poetry starts with the traditional concept that to qualify as great literature poetry must be highly learned, subtle, and consequently worthy of being written only in Latin. Poetry written in the vernacular could have important things to say to the general uneducated populace, but only poetry written in the style of a Virgil or a Homer and containing some of the truths of Christianity was worthy of the name. Most of what Petrarch has to say about either the content or style of such writing contains traditional echoes. To begin with, such writing must deal with 'first causes which rule and govern mortal things,' and must do so with words 'completely different from every day speech.' This kind of writing might provoke distrust of style, but this is irrational, for ultimately it is what such style does to the content that truly matters. To carry on a 'discourse different from the sense (literal) meaning' means essentially an intensification of such meaning.

The first surprise we encounter in Petrarch's attempts to define artistic literature raised to its highest potentiality is found in his letter to his brother in which a contrast is drawn between the 'hoarseness' of David's religious poetry and the beauties of the poetry of such classics as Homer and Virgil. It is here that we begin to feel a slight movement away from the tradition. It would appear that for Petrarch the single goal of Christian literature was too limited and even stultifying. The 'new poetry' must learn to wander away from the walls of the Little Jerusalem in order to get away from the tears and the hoarse voices of expiation and atonement. To deal with the exploits of the devotees of the Hebraic–Christian religion was indeed proper for the prophets and the testament writers. The new poetry must deal with outstanding human activity in its relationship to the evolution of mankind since the beginning of time. The focus must be on the active life although it may well touch upon the relationship to the problem and mystery of Christian salvation. Since its ultimate goal is truth, it too ultimately seeks to promote Charity but in a manner intended for lofty intellects. Petrarch thus calls for a sublimation of human experiences without clearly indicating their ultimate spiritual outcomes. Unlike the concern of religious writers, Petrarch's poet avoids mixing the Now and the Then. He does not try to reflect a view from God's eye, but rather from the eye of Man. And yet here too one must be careful, for this view does entail the Christian experience because the Man involved is the Fallen Man of Christianity. In short, Petrarch's poet does not avoid Christian doctrine; he simply uses it to achieve new artistic ends. Rather than a soul reaching for the transcendental, he portrays modern man's sigh for 'immortal beauty.' It is the desire for such beauty that indicates the divinity of Man, which becomes the theme of the new poetry, rather than the humanity of God.

It was in the coronation oration that we saw the clearest expression of Petrarch's traditional approach to poetry and literature. Perhaps the most important statement made there was Petrarch's awareness that the truly great poet must be consciously aware of the difficulties of his task. He must have a 'divinely given energy,' and he must possess the learning of the historian and the philosopher. The poet who wishes 'to appear to be a poet and nothing more,' is not a great poet. The context of this statement shows clearly that Petrarch means that concern for form or style in and of itself is not what makes the poet, but rather the extent to which he does have an historical and philosophical perspective. He must be able to express precisely what he had on his mind and in his spirit, but he must be able to do so 'in the stable and enduring style of a true man of letters.'

Perhaps the most direct application of the greater portion of the above principles may be seen in Petrarch's *Eclogues*, and in his *Africa*. Many of the principles are also contained in the *Triumphs*. Interestingly, however, while the *Eclogues* reflect a little more than thinly disguised allegories dealing with uncomplicated subjects, the *Africa* and the *Triumphs* attempt much more elaborate structures. The fact that the latter two were never completed supports the opinion that Petrarch was incapable of dealing with elaborately constructed works. On the other hand, his collection of lyrics, like the *Eclogues*, though on the surface resembling a work of sustained inspiration, consisted of 366 shorter pieces which could be placed like building blocks to achieve a structure of considerable complexity. It is in the *Canzoniere* that Petrarch's poetics seems to achieve real originality, despite the fact that he viewed the vernacular as a form of speech intended 'merely to charm the ears of the multitude.' This originality may be summarized in a limited number of basic concepts discussed, implied, or reflected in the content and/or form of the collection. The central concept is the use of the laurel tree with all its historical implications to epitomize the ambivalence and ambiguity of the poet's task. The very fact that the tree echoes the name of the beloved or vice versa and that its history is imbedded in what might indeed be called the 'first causes which rule and govern mortal things' provides the poet with a medium of expression which does indeed seem to do the many things that he says poetry should do.

The ambivalence or ambiguity provided by this central concept consists of the twofold theme that marks the collection. There is first of all the overriding theme of the love of the poet for a lady who clearly reflects all the qualities of 'immortal beauty.' Almost simultaneously, however, we feel the intrusion of the second theme, that of the complex significations implied by the interplay between the name of the beloved and the laurel tree. It is from this interplay that emerges the third central concept on which the originality of Petrarch's poetics rests. Its clearest expression is found in the myths of Actaeon and Orpheus both of which touch upon those magical aspects of poetry which have their roots in Platonic and Neo-Platonic circles but were not to be fully developed until the advent of the theoreticians of the eighteenth and nineteenth centuries. In the Actaeon myth we get a glimpse of the poet whose intuitive grasp of the essence of poetry is such that the necessary language to express his condition is fully understandable only to himself. Actaeon is transformed into a deer for having viewed the very essence of the hunt. He is then set upon by his companions because he can no longer speak their language in order to identify himself. The hunter has become the hunted. So is it with the poet.[21] He is set apart from the world, soars like Jove's bird, the eagle, produces utter amazement in his reader, and feels himself becoming one with poetry. He cannot rest until he is burning within the light of the beauty and the inspiration that it produces. He becomes like the phoenix (a concept that introduces a Christian dimension), and feels that his verses are like sparks from his fire. He feels in advance of his own age which is incapable of understanding him fully and thus most often addresses posterity rather than his contemporaries. By combining his great learning and wisdom with his new and strange form of expression, he produces a magical effect akin to the powers of Orpheus.

Perhaps the most original and modern quality that marks Petrarch's poetics is his profound awareness of his predicament. It is this awareness that defines the fundamental contradiction that for centuries has been recognized as an essential quality marking Petrarch's genius. It is the awareness of depicting a human experience that is infinite in its dimensions and the corresponding infinite struggle to convey the experience through the finite means of poetic language. It is also an awareness that the infinite dimensions involved are such because they involve that most complex of all human activity, Love, and that most elusive quality which alone can satisfy human longing, Beauty. But ultimately the awareness is

21 See opening lines of *Sen.* II.1 where Petrarch pictures himself as hunted by 'dogs.' Petrarch's sensitivity to the importance of the spoken word may best be seen in his numerous marginal notations referring to the sound of individual words as they appeared in earlier drafts of his poems. These may be seen scattered throughout *Vat. Lat.* 3196.

marked by the poet's confession or acknowledgment that after all his struggles and *recommencements* he has succeeded in giving only a 'distillation of the infinite abysses that he has tried to tap.' In one of the last poems added by Petrarch to Part 1 of the collection (no. 228) he seems to define such 'distillation' as 'Fama, Honor et Vertute et Leggiadria/Casta bellezza in habito celeste.'[22] The verses refer to Laura, but they also define Petrarch's ideal of poetry.

22 'Fame, Honour and Virtue and Charm/Chaste Beauty in celestial garb.'

LOUISE GEORGE CLUBB

The making of the pastoral play: some Italian experiments between 1573 and 1590

Una Maga prudente con liquori
Farà dormir ciascun, e de la notte
L'ombre faran sognar con finte larve;
E diverran tre bestie, tre animali:
Nel mezo, quattro miseri Pastori,
E quattro Ninfe, vi faran vedere
Come mal corrispondino i voleri
De gl'infelici, che son tutti Amanti
Ma l'una à l'altro di contraria voglia,
E come ragionando, di speranza
Vengon ripieni da la dolent'Echo;
Come fan sacrificio, e qual risposta
Hanno d'Amor nel Sacro Tempio havuta:
In fine, nel principio sentirete
Lunghe historie di pianti, e di martiri
Strane mutation, diversi casi,
Molte volubilita d'huomini e donne
E dal principio al fin burle vedrete
Assai nuove, e piacevoli: & io credo
Che non vi spiacerà d'haver il tempo
Speso in udir questa Intricata Selva
D'Amor, che porta d'Intricati il nome.

PASQUALIGO *Gl'Intricati*, Proemio[1]

THIS ARGUMENT INTRODUCES a five-act verse play in which there occurs, as promised, a constructive re-direction of affections among four pairs of shepherds and nymphs, whose names and concerns recall Montemayor's

---

A condensed version of a section from a work in progress on comic forms in Renaissance drama.

1 'A wise sorceress with liquors will put all to sleep, and the shades of night will

Diana. Caught in a maze of emotion complicated by a transvestite joke, they hold forth in various metres, singly, in duets, trios, and a final octet, on love, nature, illusion, love of nature, the nature of love, the illusion of love, the nature of illusion, and so forth. They are encouraged and deceived by the voice of Echo. The sorceress who puts them to sleep and sets matters right with her magic liquor and therapeutic dreams employs an infernal spirit, one Lucifero, functioning invisibly or in human form, as needed. He summons shadows of the night to make images, cracks Boccaccesque jokes at the expense of the mortals, and generally enjoys his work.

Also wandering the woods, bent on love, brawling with each other and ambushing nymphs, are a blustering Spaniard, Calabaza, a *villano* from the Maremma, and a Bolognese self-styled Doctor, predictably named Graciano. They join the refined shepherds for supper and singing, to which they contribute a clownish entertainment of their own: in parody of the shepherds' complaints, Graciano sings an insult to Love, likened to the braying of lovesick asses in May in the Maremma by the *villano*, who then offers a song about money, followed by Calabaza's Spanish 'Vellianico' (IV,4). These are the 'animali' who become beasts by being fitted magically with the heads of a ram, a bull, and an ass:

> GRACIAN. O cha ne i ved ben, ò cha un gran bech
> Spagnol ti è deventà, e ti Villan,
> A sidi un gran cornut, un gran boaz:
> Mo pian un poch, che quest nè al mie mustaz.
> VILLANO. Asino Gracian sei diventato.   (v,5)[2]

When the Maga restores and dismisses them with a condescending order to leave love to their betters, they depart muttering but with unimpaired self-confidence.

cause dreams of false spectres; and three "animals" will become three beasts: in the middle four unhappy shepherds and four nymphs will show you how ill-sorted are the desires of the unfortunate, for all are lovers, but no two in requited love; and how, discoursing, they are filled with hope by sorrowing Echo; how they perform a sacrifice, and what answer they have from Love in the sacred temple: in all, at first you will hear long histories of laments and sufferings, strange transformations, various cases, great inconstancy of men and women, and from beginning to end you will see very new and pleasing tricks: and I believe that it will not displease you to have spent the time in listening to this tangled wood of Love, that bears the name of *Intricati.*'

2 '*Gracian.* Either I can't see straight, or you've become a big buck goat, Spaniard, and you, peasant, are a great horned thing, a big ugly bull: Now wait a bit, this is not my face.
Peasant. Gracian, you've become an ass.'

Gl'Intricati is remarkable neither for its quality nor for the *commedia dell'arte* mask of Graziano, nor even for its resemblance to *A Midsummer Night's Dream*. It is remarkable, in fact, only for being so unremarkable an example of Renaissance Italian pastoral drama, a genre too often defined exclusively by Tasso's and Guarini's treatments of it.

Many of the pastoral ingredients used in *Aminta* reappear in *Intricati*, as they do in countless other pastoral plays: the arguments in various metres from several points of view for and against love, the *dubbi* posed in the spirit of courtly pastime, the attempted suicide, the oppression of nymphs by figures of lust (here the three clowns replace the more common satyr), the musing on time and mutability, the praise or abuse of the court, the appreciations of rural landscape of the Petrarchan stamp, the outbursts about the blindness of Cupid and of the human mind, the Ovidian reminiscences, and the hymeneal ending symbolizing reconciliation between Diana and Venus.

But *Intricati* moves at a considerable distance from *Aminta* by virtue of the shape and substance of its action, including the element attributed in another example of the genre to the inspiration of Apollo, moving the poet to

> ... mescer fra 'l pianto un breve riso
> Di semplici Villan sciocchezze, e scherzi
> Innestar anco fra dogliosi accenti
> (Castelletti, *Amarilli*, prologo)[3]

Castelletti's *sciocchezze* include a goatherd who tries to make love to a friend's wife and is turned into a tree and back again by a naiad into whose fountain he falls, and a third peasant who gets drunk in a tempest and imagines that he sees

> Cert'huomin, c'han l'orecchie lunghe, lunghe,
> Giungon da terra in fin sopra le stelle,
> Io non sò se sien asini, ò castroni.   (ii,6)[4]

The *pianto* and *dogliosi accenti* arise from the stock troubles that the god of Love, fleeing the court, visits upon Amarilli, her two suitors, and her lovesick friend. Again, as in Pasqualigo's play and in contrast to Tasso's, the action is complex and the coexistence of laughter and tears,

---

3 '... to mix with the tears the brief laughter of simple-minded peasants' foolishness, and also to include jests among the sorrowful accents.'
4 'Certain men with long long ears. They reach from earth up beyond the stars. I don't know if they are asses or geldings.'

as of fantasy and the plausible, is represented by juxtaposition of unmodi-
fied opposites. As for *Il Pastor fido*, which bears out its author's claim to
have diluted the extremes of two strains to produce a milder third, it would
seem on surface comparison that only its complication of plot makes for a
resemblance to pastoral plays of comic intrigue, buffoonery, and Ovidian
magic.

For all that contemporary criticism has revealed about the range of
correspondences between Arcadia and interior worlds of spirit, emotion,
and imagination, the serviceability of the pastoral in polar tension with
epic heroism as with urban mundanity, or the subtleties of the amatory
fixation distinguishing the Renaissance pastoral from the classical, knowledge of the dramatization of the literary pastoral has been left for the most
part in nineteenth-century formulations. Neither Empsonian soundings of
the pastoral mode in its most inclusive sense nor close analyses of a few
exceptional plays show how the pastoral tropes and types took the stage.

The undramatic character of *Aminta*, 'il più bel madrigale della letteratura italiana,'[5] has been remarked often. Compared with later pastoral
plays, for which it was a model of excellence and a quarry for song, senti-
ment, and situation, it seems a lyrical pageant of love, symbolic and stylized into hieroglyph, more tenor than vehicle. Insofar as it may be described as a dramatic genre, *Aminta* is a tragedy. More precisely, it is a
series of eclogues grouped around a single situation, leading to a simple
tragic denouement, on which a happy ending is superimposed. Italian pastoral drama in the mass, however, is essentially a comic genre, as appears
not only in the inherent happiness of the pastoral world observed by
Rousset,[6] but also in the theatrical articulation of the pastoral attitudes.
This is true of *Pastor fido* as well, despite Guarini's intention of raising the
pastoral drama to Aristotelian dignity with supports borrowed from
tragedy.

Were the commonly projected image of Italian pastoral drama to be
enlarged, the variety of contributing detail thus made visible might en-
courage further comparison with English drama. Richard Cody's recent
study of *Aminta* as re-enactment of Orphic rite and Neo-Platonic key to
three Shakespearean comedies[7] should be welcomed even by those hesitant to accept the rigorous hermeticism thereby imposed on the comedies,

5 'the most beautiful madrigal in Italian literature.' Umberto Bosco, 'Tasso, Torquato,' *Enciclopedia italiana di scienze, lettere ed arti* (Roma, 1937), 33, 313.
6 Jean Rousset, *La littérature de l'âge baroque en France.* Circé et le paon (Paris,
  1953), 33.
7 *The Landscape of the Mind. Pastoralism and Platonic Theory in Tasso's Aminta
  and Shakespeare's Early Comedies* (Oxford, 1969).

because Cody has understood that the effects of Italian pastoral drama may exist independent of Italian or of *pastori*. A clearer picture of the original genre would show that even the members of Shakespeare's audience with no head for esoteric Neo-Platonism could have recognized the pastoral inspiration of *A Midsummer Night's Dream*. The mere dilettante of literary fashion would have known, at least by hearsay, the more obvious features of a few kinds of pastoral plays being produced at Italian courts and academies. If modern scholars neglect some of the features and most of the kinds, it is because certain received ideas have long obstructed our view of the pastoral play.

The first of these is that *Aminta* and *Pastor fido* represent all there is to know about the genre. Long after the contributions of Carrara and of Violet Jeffery, this extraordinarily hardy simplification of Greg's conclusion has endured, explicitly in Gerhardt and in Orr,[8] implicitly even in Cody, although his thesis is profoundly contradictory of Greg in the large claim it makes for the importance to Elizabethan drama of the Italian pastoral play – indeed, Cody dismisses Guarini with a few words, regarding *Aminta* as a sufficient example of orthodox Italian pastoral.

The second idea to discard is that experimentation in pastoral drama ended with *Aminta*. No one doubts that long and deliberate cultivation produced the pastoral play, but although scholars from old Carrara to new Barberi Squarotti have recognized that the simple tragic form of *Aminta*[9] was not the structure used by Guarini, not to mention the intervening lesser dramatists, it is often contradictorily and mysteriously assumed that Tasso's pastoral marked the end of the trials, if not of the errors, that it determined the shape of the genre, in addition to its vogue and much of its matter, and that subsequent pastoral playwrights aimed no farther than at imitation or expansion, of the kind supposed to have produced *Pastor fido*. Had Greg actually read the plays of the 1570s and

8 Enrico Carrara, *La poesia pastorale* (Milano, n.d. [1909]); Violet M. Jeffery, *John Lyly and the Italian Renaissance* (Paris, 1929); W.W. Greg, *Pastoral Poetry and Pastoral Drama. A Literary Inquiry, With Special Reference to the Pre-Restoration Stage in England* (London, 1906), 176, 210; Mia I. Gerhardt, *Essai d'analyse littéraire de la pastorale dans les littératures italienne, espagnole et française* (Leiden, 1950), 94, 124–6; David Orr, *Italian Renaissance Drama in England Before 1625. The Influence of Erudita Tragedy, Comedy, and Pastoral on Elizabethan and Jacobean Drama* (Chapel Hill, 1970), 74–5.

9 Tasso, *Aminta. A cura di Giorgio Barberi Squarotti* (Padova, 1968). This editor speaks of Guarini's imitation of 'punti strutturalmente fondamentali' (6), referring to the Golden Age chorus as an example, but his discussion of the plot and its 'preteso "lieto fine" ' (18) states the essential tragedy of *Aminta*. On theories of origins see E. Bigi, 'Il dramma pastore del '500,' *Il teatro classico italiano nel '500* (Roma, Accademia Nazionale dei Lincei, 1971).

1580s which he mentions only to discount as not forming a link in a chain of organic development,[10] he would have observed in them a redoubled effort of experimentation with the same aims as that in pre-*Aminta* pastoral, with the added challenge of assimilating and rivalling Tasso's achievement.

Neither of these ideas should need refutation at this late date, for Carrara's encyclopedic work has long since supplied the information needed for an accurately revised view of the pastoral play. But Carrara himself, in the act of discarding such misleading simplifications, clouds the issue with his own categories, the 'satirico' of Giraldi, the 'comico' of Beccari and Lollio, the 'tragico' of Tasso, and the 'tragicomico' of Guarini, finally suggesting the possibility of a fifth type lost with the original version of Groto's *Calisto*.[11]

By way of a corrective I propose to survey a body of pastoral plays large enough to constitute a fair sampling, which were published between 1573, the year *Aminta* was composed and performed, and 1590, when *Pastor fido* was finally printed (actually issued in December 1589), five years after its completion. As far as can be determined, these plays were also written, or at least rewritten, between these dates. They are the works of writers of the academies and courts, at the centre of Italian literary life. The plays range in quality from deserving to undeserving of their common neglect, but in their time two-thirds of them went into more than one edition. Most of the authors wrote in other genres as well, some, like Groto, in many. Pasqualigo, Pino, Castelletti, and Borghini were highly regarded for comedy, and, fortuitously but significantly, the kind of *commedia erudita* they cultivated was the weighty, emotional, and intricately plotted *commedia grave*, with which many playwrights of academy or coterie in the second half of the sixteenth century hoped to give new aesthetic and moral seriousness to the genre.[12]

What is to be gained from the proposed reclassification of these twenty plays (for although Carrara mentions only about half of them, that half falls into his classifications given above) is not any permanent ordering system but a set of co-ordinates by which the path of the genre after Tasso may be traced, leading through a variety of experiments by writers who continued to search literary nature for the true shape of the pastoral play. Classifying the kinds with regard to mixtures of elements from diverse sources reveals something of the mutual attraction, largely under-

10 *Pastoral Poetry*, 210 ff.
11 *La poesia pastorale*, 344.
12 For discussion of the *commedia grave*, see L.G. Clubb, 'Italian Comedy and *The Comedy of Errors*,' *Comparative Literature*, xix,3 (1967), 240–51.

estimated by criticism, of courtly and popular traditions in Italian drama, and opens a new perspective on the distance between *Aminta* and *Pastor fido* and on some of the developments in drama contributory to that distance. Certain likenesses between the two also, especially the commitment to verisimilitude and the tempered single style, appear less inevitable and more deliberate in the light of dissimilar combinations which were being made by contemporary rivals. Moreover, classification of these combinations in the pastoral play during its phase of definition incidentally throws into relief some elements significant for Elizabethan drama.

A Antonio Ongaro. *Alceo: favola pescatoria*. Venetia, 1582[13] (dedicated 1581), 14 editions to 1722.

B Camillo Della Valle. *Fillide: egloga pastorale*. Ferrara, 1584 (perhaps written much earlier), 1 edition.

C Luigi Pasqualigo. *Gl'Intricati: pastorale*. Venetia, 1581 (published posthumously, probably written in late 1570's), 1 edition.
Cristoforo Castelletti. *L'Amarilli: pastorale*. Venetia, 1582 (first printed 1580, revised 1582), 9 editions including original and 2 revised versions.
Pietro Cresci. *Tirena: favola pastorale*. Venetia, 1584 (written 1584), 2 editions.
Cesare Simonetti. *Amaranta: favola boscareccia*. Padova, 1588, 1 edition.

D Luigi Groto. *La Calisto: nova favola pastorale*. Venetia, 1583 (written 1561, revised 1582), 3 editions, 2 in Allacci.
– *Il Pentimento amoroso: nuova favola pastorale*. Venetia, 1585 (performed 1575), 6 editions.
Diomisso Guazzoni. *Andromeda: tragicomedia boscareccia*. Venetia, 1587 (possibly first printed in 1574?), perhaps 3 editions, 2 in Allacci.
Raffaello Gualterotti. *La Verginia: rappresentazione amorosa*. Firenze, 1584 (performed 1581, revised 1582), 1 edition.
Gieronimo Vida. *Filliria: favola boscareccia*. Vinegia, 1587 (first printed 1585), 4 editions.

13 See L.G. Clubb, *Italian Plays (1500–1700) in the Folger Library* (Firenze, 1968), for further bibliographical details of the editions listed here, with the exception of Pescetti's *Regia pastorella*, to be found at the Vatican Library and included as the best-defined example of its particular and relatively rare type. The number of editions is taken from Lione Allacci, *Drammaturgia di Lione Allacci accresciuta e continuata fino all'anno* MDCCLV (Venezia, 1755) facsimile ed. Torino, 1961. The plays by Della Valle, Pino, Gualterotti, Vida, Lupi, and Pescetti are not mentioned by Carrara.

Pietro Lupi. *I Sospetti: favola boschereccia*. Firenze, 1589 (dedicated 1588), 1 edition, 2 issues.

Bernardino Percivallo. *L'Orsilia: boscareccia sdrucciola*. Bologna, 1589, 1 edition.

E Bernardino Pino. *L'Eunia: ragionamenti pastorali*. Venetia, 1582 (composed early, date unknown), 1 edition.

Camillo Della Valle. *Gelosi amanti: favola pastorale*. Ferrara, 1585, 1 edition.

F Orlando Pescetti. *La Regia pastorella: favola boschereccia*. Verona, 1589, 2 editions.

G Giovanni Donato Cucchetti. *La Pazzia: favola pastorale*. Venetia, 1597 (first printed 1581), 5 editions.

Gabriele Zinano. *Il Caride: favola pastorale*. Reggio, 1590(?) (first printed 1582, revised 1590), probably 3 editions, 2 in Allacci.

Angelo Ingegneri. *Danza di Venere: pastorale*. Vicenza, 1584 (dedicated 1583), 3 editions.

Raffaello Borghini. *Diana pietosa: comedia pastorale*. Firenze, 1586 (first printed 1585), 2 editions.

The features common to these plays reveal the conventions already accepted for the genre, with the sense thereby achieved of its being distinct from, if sometimes indebted to, other dramatic kinds in which pastoral and rustic elements also figure. No matter what the generic subtitle, they all have five acts and enjoy a fairly high degree of unity of time and of place. Eight of them are set in Arcadia (Greece or Magna Graecia not specified), two elsewhere in Greece, and the rest in Italy: Lyly's Lincolnshire, and Shakespeare's Arden are in the latter line of transplanted and rechristened Arcadias. All but Pino's are in verse, basically *endecasillabi, piani*, except for Groto's and Percivallo's *sdruccioli*, but with considerable metrical variation. Pastoral figures, names, song contests, love laments, praises of landscape, musing on the Golden Age, and comparisons with the court are ubiquitous, usually in the style of Tasso and of Sannazaro, often with evidence of direct recourse to the classical models of both. Montemayor also seems to be part of the common material, but his debt to Sannazaro makes for uncertainty in most cases. Differences in organization of the common material and introduction of other elements in combinations reminiscent of dissimilar pre-*Aminta* pastorals authorize the following divisions:

A Ongaro's *Alceo*, famed as 'l'*Aminta* bagnato,' is alone in a group reserved for pastorals in which the imitation of Tasso is carried out almost to the letter, in simple plot, single level of lyric style, the absence of low humour and unverisimilar elements other than the unexpendable figure of the satyr, who need not be represented more implausibly than as a hairy man, or, in *Alceo*, as a scaly one.

B Della Valle's *Fillide* illustrates the continuation of the court entertainment of the static recited eclogue with mythological tableaux. Cases of love, here set in slight motion with minor complications, stated as problems in the manner of court games, are demonstrated by a range of effects from tears to nymphs' practical jokes on an amorous old shepherd, resulting in Ovidian transformations into trees and streams and requiring the personal intervention of deities. As in *Aminta*, the sense of elegant pastime and probably of Neo-Platonic rite is strong, but both of these aspects are displayed in *Fillide* with uninhibitedly unverisimilar mythological representations. Its direct predecessors include Poliziano's *Orfeo*, Sabba da Castiglione's *[La Barona] Lamento del disgraziato pastore Clonico* (1528), and Epicuro's *Mirzia*, which, significantly, passed for new when published pseudonymously long after its author's death.[14]

C A combination of broad clowning along rustic lines as foil to the ideal manners and emotions of two or more pairs of shepherds and nymphs with free use of unverisimilar elements, including Ovidian transformations and magic from the *romanzo* tradition, is the distinguishing characteristic of this kind. Its forebears are less structured mixtures of coterie and folk types, such as Calmo's *Egloghe pastorali*, the rare *grottesca pastorale* occasionally cultivated by Mariano in the early days of the Sienese artisan plays,[15] and Iacomo Contrini's *Lite amorosa, comedia nova pastorale* (1568), in which nymphs, shepherds, a comic peasant, and two raucous Spaniards are entangled until a magician–hermit decrees a double wedding. Inevitably the combination suggests Lyly's *Gallathea*, his *Love's Metamorphoses*, and even more, *A Midsummer Night's Dream*.

14 Selvaggio de' Selvaggii, *La Martia, pastoral comedia* (Parma, 1582). The attribution of *Mirzia* to Epicuro, as well as its relation to *Martia* and to a still later version, *Trebazia*, are discussed by Parente, Marc'Antonio Epicuro, *I drammi e le poesie italiane e latine ... A cura di Alfredo Parente* (Bari, 1942), 233–52.
15 Andrea Calmo, *Le giocose moderne et facetissime egloghe pastorali* (Vinegia, 1553). For pastoral elements in the works of the Sienese Rozzi and their precursors, see Roberto Alonge, *Il teatro dei Rozzi di Siena* (Firenze, 1967), especially 47 ff.

D Plays in this group are differentiated from those in group c by the absence of the clown. Not that comedy is lacking to this kind – the lascivious cavorting of transvestite Jove and Mercury in Groto's *Calisto*, for example, is as broad as anything in the preceding group – but the peculiarly sharp contrast obtained by juxtaposition of the extremes, the farcical peasant or mechanical, whose language, manners, and grasp of life crazily reflect and comment on the shepherds, is missing. All the possibilities of fantasy and magic are left, however. Carrara classes Lollio's *Aretusa* (1564) and Beccari's *Sacrificio* (1555) together as simply comic, but Beccari's resolution of a love problem by transforming the blocking character into a wolf differentiates his view of the pastoral drama from Lollio's and links him with the later trials represented by this group. Lollio tailored the pastoral to meet the demands of *commedia regolare*, while Beccari borrowed comic structure to support pastoral actions alien to regular comedy.

E Some pastoralists tried to draw nearer to the plausibility expected of urban *commedia erudita* by banishing magic. The result is city comedy in the country. The most powerful immediate example for dramatists pursuing this line was Lollio's *Aretusa*, in which the conventional attempted suicide of the lovelorn shepherd leads to a Terentian resolution of what turns out in retrospect to have been a New Comedy situation. Casalio's *Amaranta* (1538), Rusante's *La Pastorale*,[16] and the *commedie villanesche* of the Rozzi's prime period have a less direct but still visible kinship with the type. The strongly comic flavour is not confined to a single social level. Della Valle's pranksters are refined shepherds, but Pino uses rustics. They are less like the abysmally crude *villani* of Rozzi farces than like the trim countryfolk of Lorenzo's *Nencia da Barberino*, closer to Jacquenetta of *Love's Labour's Lost* than to Audrey of *As You Like It*. Still, they are unconditionally rustic, designed not only in function but also in character as foils for the *pastori*.

F Rare, but not unknown to Italian literary drama, is the pastoral in which characters of a rank fit for epic and tragedy mingle with the lowest of clowns and in which the country is not a closed world to be measured against the spectators' extra-theatrical reality, but a place to visit and to leave within the fiction, if not actually with the represented action. The type owes something to Giraldi's earlier *tragedie di fin lieto*, and more to the *commedia grave*, but its true analogues are *As You Like It*, *Two*

16 For Ruzante, see Mario Baratto, *Tre saggi sul teatro* (Venezia, 1964), 11–68.

Gentlemen of Verona, and, above all, *The Winter's Tale*, which Pescetti's play also resembles not only in kind but in several details.

G Were *Pastor fido* to be included in the proposed classification, it would belong here, although none of these plays is labelled *tragicommedia* or depends on the material of classical tragedy as Guarini's play partly does. As in groups A and E, the supernatural element is rationalized as far as possible, and the worship of pagan deities conducted by priests with oracles is the fictive veil for late Renaissance Catholicism of the quietistic sort.[17] The didactic possibilities of the pastoral are more fully developed in this type than in any other, the dialogue tends to the overtly metaphysical and the action to the psychologically complicated. The impression of weightiness and of attention to Aristotle, with a pointed concern for decorum and verisimilitude is confirmed by the absence of clowns and of magic. The plots are all elaborate syntheses disguising the extremes of which they are formed. In the complexity of structure and in numerous vestiges of comic characterization and relationships lies the major difference between plays of this group and *Aminta*. These playwrights, like Guarini, used and modified results of other pastoralists' experiments with comedy, whereas Tasso sidestepped the genre almost entirely. The famous 'sorriso di Tasso' is only the mild light in which, as Toffanin has it, the *favola pastorale* looks into the mirror of Greek tragedy to see if there is a resemblance.[18]

Despite the differences represented by the above categories, these plays with one exception have more in common with each other than they have with *Aminta*. The point obscured by Carrara's divisions is that all of them but *Alceo*, including the 'tragicomico' *Pastor fido*, depend on the intrigue structure of regular comedy and are thereby separated from Tasso by their first principle. True, all twenty of them testify, by some borrowing or reference, to admiration for Tasso, and the generic subtitle most in evidence among them is his *favola boscareccia*, which had the virtue of being the least committing to an established form, the most hospitable to experiment. For the structural means of dramatizing the borrowed material, however, only Ongaro followed the master's lead, and even his watery copy is more dramatic than the original, in that Alceo and his Eurilla are

17 For a reading of *Il pastor fido* which emphasizes the contrast between the overweening human reason that misinterprets the providential oracle and the instinct that unwittingly acquiesces to it, see L.G. Clubb, 'Moralist in Arcadia: England and Italy,' *Romance Philology*, XIX,2 (1965), 340–52.
18 G. Toffanin, *Il Tasso e l'età che fu sua* (Napoli, 1949), 88.

brought face to face at least once (III,4). Tasso's purpose in avoiding a confrontation may well have been part of a Neo-Platonic design, as Cody asserts, but the omission increases his singularity among pastoral dramatists.

The other nineteen playwrights turn back before Tasso to the example of the pastoral experimenters who were in one way or another tapping the resources of the regular comedy, rooted in society, involving a larger number of people and their various concerns, drama in which love is not only divine furor, epiphany, or tragic obsession but also a motive in human relations adding to the complexity of ordinary life in which money, marriage, and family figure in an interplay of personalities, generations, and classes. The relations in which the characters stand to one another in most of these plays betray exposure to comic practices. Earlier, in both courtly eclogue tableau and popular semi-pastoral farce, there usually obtained a Saturnalian equality among mortals in common subjection to the sylvan deities, or a temporary juxtaposition of members of separate worlds, an extraordinary encounter of literary shepherds with local rustics and witches and gods, and perhaps burghers and princesses as well. But with attempts to make pastoral a regular dramatic genre came a sense of society within the play, of the social distinctions necessary to comedy and, under Guarini's influence, of the courtly hierarchy of tragedy. Pasqualigo's clowns represent a position of compromise. They are footloose on vacation in Arcadia, but they are snobbishly aware of social levels, urban ones at that, and Graciano claims a rank to which the *Maga* declares him not entitled (v,5).

Guazzoni's Panfila is identified as a servant in the *dramatis personae*, and although she comes in for her share of the amorous unrest suffered by the loftier nymphs, her task is to fetch and carry: she is, in short, a *fantesca* from *commedia erudita*. The distance that Guarini's Amarilli perceives between herself and the simple Arcadian shepherdess of her imagination (II,5, 627 ff.) is the semi-tragic version of the same social distinction.

Of the stock characters drawn from the comic stable for the making of the pastoral play the most versatile and catalytic is the *servo*, who in *commedia regolare* may be a dynamic element, acting as intriguer or go-between, or an ethical one, providing wit or absurdity, often borrowing characteristics from his fellows, the parasite and the braggart. Either way he functions in opposition to the sons, husbands, and fathers whose domestic conflicts constitute the *intreccio* – not in opposition to their plans, which he abets and often originates, but to their image of life. In the Arcadian social scale he is at the bottom and his tag in the *dramatis personae* is usually *capraio, pecoraio* (distinct from *pastore*), or *villano*. Occasionally, however, he is labelled *pastore* and only his behaviour identifies him as an underling. Sometimes he performs lustful acts associated with satyrs and sometimes, on the contrary, a satyr is assigned some aspect of a comic *servo* role. In the plays in group G the *servo* exists only vestigially, as in *Pastor fido*, where traces of him are visible in the Satiro, especially in his scenes with Corisca, echoing the exchanges of *servo–fantesca* and *servo–cortigiana* scenes of *commedia erudita*. The existence of such traces testifies to the history of this figure in the dramatization of the pastoral by Guarini's time, whereas Tasso's Satiro is not comic, and although his view of love is different from Aminta's and inferior to it, it is not complementary in any of the ways that the *servo*'s is to the *padrone*'s.[19]

The lumpishness of the clowns' lechery, incomprehension of love, or devotion to some gross object, edible, potable, or bestial, may simultaneously show off and show up the delicacy and intensity of the courtly shepherds.

In a single scene (II,3) Cresci's Orsacchio runs through a repertory of comic commonplaces proper to the *villano*. He begins with Terentian complaints about servitude, refers to his own love for the indifferent 'Smartilla,' in its brevity and infidelity a travesty of the pastoral ideal, likens himself to an ass[20] who carries wine but drinks water, gets drunk and has a song contest with his friend Corbaccio. They stagger off together, ending with a mock-Platonic reference to blindness, whereupon the Chorus with bland violence juxtaposes a serious observation on the timidity of true lovers and the coldness of beautiful women.

Guazzoni uses Montano, *capraio*, as a busy manipulating and tangling agent, bored by love, interested in food and drink, given to swearing by

19 In the *Compendio,* on the subject of mixing 'persone grandi' and 'persone vilissime' Guarini offers justifications which nullify each other, i.e., that humble characters are introduced only as instruments, not in order that their manners may be depicted, and that the confidants and 'nudrici' of noble persons are not really humble, but only less noble than the persons to whom they are attached. See *Il pastor fido e Il compendio della poesia tragicomica. A cura di Gioachino Brognoligo* (Bari, 1914), 256. In practice, Guarini's Satiro is a restrained delineation fit for the middle genre, but his ambiguous sharpness reflects the conventional presentation of the *servo scaltro.*

20 Images of asses and hallucinations are common in clown scenes, although only Pasqualigo amalgamates and expands them into a transformation like Bottom's. The deformation of the name Amarilli into 'Smartilla' is also used by Castelletti's Zampilla (I,4): mispronunciation of difficult words by the unlettered *servo* had by mid-century been used nearly to the point of exhaustion in *commedia erudita* and passed on to improvised comedy.

Mercury, god of thieves and, to Cinquecento audiences, god of *servi* by dint of his masquerade as Sosia in *Amphitruo* and its adaptations in *commedia erudita*. Speaking good Tuscan and never descending to slapstick, however, Montano also testifies to the gradual refinement of the rustic *servo* to fit him for the complex but homogenized pastoral drama of Guarini and the playwrights of group G.

Intrigue structure, as a means of translation into motion of matter, was definitive in making the pastoral play and is the characteristic shared by the greatest number of these samples. As a critical term in this connection, intrigue structure must be allowed no more than its literal significance of complex, involving a substantial number of characters with individual aims, whether or not their actions contribute severally to dramatic conflicts and resolutions. Dynamic use of intrigue structure was a comic ideal and is characteristic of many of these pastorals, including Castelletti's, Lupi's, Cucchetti's, and Guarini's, but static or expository handling of an intrigue situation also occurs. Instead of the single case of love proceeding along an episodic line to its end, as in *Aminta* and *Alceo*, all of the plays in groups B through G contain multiple love affairs. In *Fillide*, Della Valle presents three love affairs with three different obstacles, and tries to avoid simple parallelism by slightly intertwining the cases, using the comic devices of misunderstanding and mistaken identity. In his next pastoral, *Gelosi amanti*, he enlarges and twists his plot further in the direction of comedy and employs the trick of transvestism.

When Bibbiena established the device of transvestism onstage in *La Calandria* (1513), by merging the disguise of sex from medieval narrative with mistaken identity as used in New Comedy, he set a theatrical precedent for a trick which would flourish as well in Arcadian non-dramatic genres, *vide* Montemayor's *Diana*. By the time the dramatization of pastoral had become a serious concern, transvestism was an old theme with many variations. Pino denounced the device in comedy as worn-out and absurd[21] but his pastoral 'ragionamenti' include both a shepherd disguised as a nymph and a nymph disguised as her own brother, with results familiar to audiences of *La Calandria* and *Twelfth Night* alike. Either Pino wrote his pastoral play before tiring of the commonplace or he had different standards for verisimilitude in the pastoral, perhaps sharing Guarini's conception of the mode as the image of 'virgin human nature'[22] rather than a mirror of custom and daily life. The other pastoral dramat-

---

21 *Gli ingiusti sdegni* (Roma, 1553), Prologo.
22 Speaking of the eclogue from which the pastoral drama grew, Guarini says in *Il Verrato* (1588), quoted in Bernard Weinberg, *A History of Literary Criticism in the Italian Renaissance* (Chicago 1961), II,1082, n.15, that it shows 'la nostra na-

ists who used the sex disguise in the 1570s and 1580s apparently did not hold its familiarity against it. Characteristically, Guarini accepts but tones down the comic trick by keeping it offstage but making it the foundation of Mirtillo's narration of falling in love (II,1, 59 ff.).

With or without transvestites, static or dynamic, nineteen of the twenty plays under consideration reveal attempts to make multiple cases of love intertwine, depend on, or otherwise affect one another, and to achieve that integrated complexity in demand by writers and theorists of *commedia erudita*.[23] In addition to the tangle of misplaced affections which Beccari had borrowed earlier for *Il Sacrificio*, most of the commonplaces of situation and of action known to Italian comedy are annexed by these pastoralists: long-lost relatives whose recognition brings about the general resolution, disappearances, presumed deaths, vows taken or broken, mistakes in identity growing out of these past events, perpetuated and multiplied by disguises.

The roots of the action in Castelletti's *Amarilli* lie in a ten-year-old scandal involving supposed murder, madness, and the heroine's flight under an alias. Della Valle's Celio searches for his runaway sister, who masquerades as him. In Gualterotti's singularly inept play, Beatrice, disguised as Isabella, wants Verginia to be magically changed into a boy, until Verginia turns out to be Beatrice's missing husband in disguise. Pescetti's shepherdess is enabled to marry the prince of Lidia by the discovery that she is the long-lost daughter of the king of Caria. Such pressures from the past not only touch off individual actions at different moments in a play but also contribute to the tension of its action in a five-act present as a whole. A similar framing effect is sometimes achieved, as in comedy, through a motive more immediate in time, such as the determination of Guazzoni's Cupid to subjugate the elusive Andromeda, a purpose which agitates and unifies all parts of the play. Guazzoni's work, like Lyly's *Gallathea*, suggests the interest of dramatists in making internal action, involving specific characters in a comic movement of pursuit and evasion, out of Tasso's less dramatic use in prologue and epilogue of the ancient motif of the errant Cupid.

The complexity is great even in those plays in which the story seems

tura quasi vergine senza lisci, & senz'alcuno di quelli artifici, & di quelle finte apparenze che sono peccati propri della Città.'

23 Annibal Caro's boast in the prologue to *Gli straccioni* (*ca.* 1545) of the interdependence of his three 'casi ... intrecciati per modo che l'argomento è tutt'uno,' in Aldo Borlenghi, ed., *Commedie del Cinquecento* (Milano, 1959), II,126, is a representative statement of the preoccupation with intrigue structure of writers of regular comedy for the rest of the century.

to exist primarily in support of the kind of Neo-Platonism which Cody finds in *Aminta*. Ingegneri's *Danza di Venere*, short on low comic elements but full of the sort of Terentian echoes dear to *commedia regolare*, inherits from Boccaccio's tale of Cimone (*Decameron* v,1) its theme of love's power to refine and the lover's consequent power to act. The time setting is May Day and a dance is performed in the middle of the play (III,3), not as part of choral *intermezzo* but in the action proper, and is immediately followed by the abduction (a literal *raptio*) of the heroine. But for all the symbolism, the pattern of action is not that of *Aminta* but that of *commedia erudita* with its New Comedy heritage, its continual quarrying of *novelle*, its peripeties, recognitions, and large-scale final reunions. Although Groto's *Pentimento amoroso* also seems designed primarily to run a Neo-Platonic gamut of loves, its aim is achieved by employing a large number of characters in a complex design of cross purposes and motives typical of the comic structure most admired in the author's day.

All the standard comic features absent from *Aminta* are present, though blunted, in *Pastor fido*. Guarini's use of tragedy, specifically of Sophocles', was not a violent mutation in the comic evolution of pastoral drama. *Il Pastor fido* is undoubtedly a result of the confluence of comedy with tragedy characteristic of the period, but so is *commedia grave*. Although Guarini associates his curse framework with *Oedipus Rex*, the use of a framework giving dramatic action a past and a relation to time and futurity was a practice of comedy and was also used by more obviously comic pastoralists than Guarini. Commonplaces of situation and of action found both in New Comedy and in *Oedipus*, i.e., lost children, mistakes, linked recognitions, were developed in Cinquecento comedy with consciousness of both sources. Writers of *commedia grave* boasted of closing the gap between comedy and tragedy, and some invoked Sophocles without any apparent sense of incongruity: Maleguzzi's editor claims the pattern of *Oedipus* for *Theodora*, as Della Porta was said to have done for *La sorella*.[24] The phenomenon brings to mind, with due reservations, Northrop Frye's identification of New Comedy as a concealed 'comic Oedipus situation.'[25]

It was also possible to use intrigue structure as an expression of the ubiquitous late sixteenth-century theme of the discrepancy between appearance and reality by making metaphor of highly developed *intreccio*.

---

24 See Guido Decani's dedication to Flaminio Maleguzzi, *La Theodora* (Venetia, 1572) and Lucrezio Nucci's dedication to G.B. Della Porta, *La sorella* (Napoli, 1604).
25 'The Argument of Comedy,' *English Institute Essays. Edited by D.A. Robertson* (New York, 1948), 59.

With the precedent of occasional references in early Cinquecento comedies to the existence of a power higher than human foresight,[26] which arranges denouements while human beings think their entanglements hopeless, writers of *commedia grave* used their complex plots as illustration of the happily ironic truth that, when mortals, especially lovers, seem to themselves to be in unresolvable difficulties, they are in reality merely traversing the dark phase of a providential plan for their happiness. Commentaries placed in the last act as pointers to this truth, and the use of labyrinthine intrigue as structural metaphor of Divine Providence, attended by ironic peripeties and musings on human blindness to the ways of heaven were the hallmarks of the most elaborate and self-conscious kind of literary comedy during and preceding the decade in which *Aminta* appeared. Underlying the tendency was a general distrust of over-confidence in human reason, action, and ability to perceive truth. That Counter-Reformation quietistic moralism by which Matteo Cerini would distinguish Guarini from the 'Renaissance' Tasso[27] is, in fact, endemic in Italian drama of all genres after 1550, whether articulated in detail or merely gestured at in exclamations on the providential efficiency of love or some other benign suprahuman force.

The metaphoric use of intrigue plot was a practice ripe for exploitation in conjunction with such pastoral tropes and figures as the blind Cupid, the labyrinth of love, and love–death (symbolized in attempted suicide, or apparently fatal disappearance or transformation) causing changes or awakenings of heart. Tasso turns the commonplace of the shepherd's suicidal leap into a literally fortunate fall,[28] and his chorus comments on the discrepancy in knowledge which separates Love from his mortal victims on the 'ignote strade' to happiness (v,1, 1839–47). But Tasso limits application of this perception to the power of Love, Platonic without the Christian overtones it would have in *Pastor fido*, and uses it as ample declaration without benefit of support from a complex intrigue plot.

---

26 An example is the exclamation of Ariosto's Cleandro, 'E tu credi, Filogono, che così dal cielo ordinato era; che per altra che per questa via non era possibile che del mio Carino avessi mai ricognizione.' *I suppositi*, prose version (v,8) in Ludovico Ariosto, *Opere minori. A cura di Cesare Segre* (Milano–Napoli, 1954). Comments on unforeseen resolutions in Latin comedy are more casual and refer to chance rather than to providence. See Plautus, *Captivi*, prologue, and Terence, *Phormio* (v,757), for example.

27 'L'ombra di un capolavoro. Il "Pastor Fido" del Guarini,' *Letterature moderne*, VII,4 (1957), 459.

28 'fu felice il precipizio.' Quotations from *Aminta* are from the edition of Barberi Squarotti. In this speech Elpino goes on to say that under the sad image of death the fall brought life and joy to Aminta.

When Cresci paraphrases Tasso, however, he does so with specific reference to the resolution of the entanglement, and extends the range of his observation with philosophical generalization:

> Certamente la legge, onde governa
> Amore 'l mondo è cosi giusta, e retta,
> Che quando men si spera nel suo regno
> Haver del suo servire il guiderdone;
> All'hor piu si consegue, *ma l'humana*
> *Natura, ch'è imperfetta non discerne*
> *L'arti celesti sue*, e le maniere
> E gli incogniti modi, ond'egli pone
> I suoi seguaci in non sperata gioia.   (v,2 [italics mine])[29]

Ingegneri's Coridone, resolved on abduction but unwilling to presume on Venus' good will enough to seek sanctuary in her temple, marks the transitional phase in the gradual recognition of the pattern of his action when he recognizes that

> Non lece à noi d'interpretar la mente
> De gli alti Dei. Ciò forse ad alcun fine
> Venere volle, il qual è à noi celato.   (iii,1)[30]

Cucchetti's *Pazzia*, still closer to *Pastor fido* in this respect, is dominated by an emphasis on the worship of Jove, greater than other gods, to whom Christian-flavoured prayers are addressed (iv,5). Livia's bad advice to Alteria not to trust Fileno is based on the principle that one should never trust unless 'l'esperienza unica madre/ Della ragion, non se ne faccia certa,' to which Alteria answers that it is foolish to test basic things ordered by the 'sommo Dio de gl'altri Dei' (ii,7), and the unfolding of the plot proves her anti-empirical Counter-Reformation orthodoxy to have been right.[31]

At the end, the Corsica-like character of Branco, the deceiver, is forgiven for his machinations because the actions he did for ill turned out, as

---

29 'Surely the law by which Love rules the world is so just and right that in his kingdom when one least hopes for reward of his service, the more he then receives, but human nature, which is imperfect, does not discern his celestial arts and manners and the unknown ways by which he places his followers in unhoped-for joy.'
30 'It is forbidden us to interpret the mind of the high gods. That is perhaps willed to some purpose by Venus which is hidden from us.'
31 'experience, sole mother of reason, verifies it ... the highest god of all.'

heaven intended, to be for good, he the unwitting instrument, the others the surprised beneficiaries (v,3).

Pasqualigo's prologue emphasizes his play's need for explanation because of its being *intricato*; his Selvaggia observes that the lovers have been set at cross purposes by the 'disegni fallaci' of the 'cieche menti nostre' (I,2) and to the joint prayer 'O mostrane la via, ch'uscir possiamo/ Fuori di cosi oscuro labirinto' (IV,1),[32] a heavenly voice assents. The assent always comes, the conclusion is always hymeneal combination and pacification, a *discordia concors* which reveals love's providence (in plays of group G extending in the direction of Christian Providence), and the power of the providence and the wonder it arouses are in direct ratio to the complexity of the knot it unties.

Guarini's view is still more clearly Counter-Reformation Christian, allowing for the veil of pagan terms. The paean in *Pastor fido* at the moment of recognition includes a rehashing of the misunderstandings and confusions, all owed to the

> ... cecità de le terrene menti!
> In qual profonda notte,
> In qual fosca caligine d'errore
> Son le nostr'alme immerse,
> Quando tu non le illustri, o sommo Sole! (v,6, 1039–43)

Later in the same speech Tirenio apostrophizes heaven directly 'O alta providenza, o sommi dèi' (1117).[33]

While the image of blindness is probably the one most often used by Italian pastoralists to express the general difference between appearance and reality, especially in love, the image of the labyrinth also frequently and specifically underscores the function of the intrigue structure as the metaphor of human error. It was an image often employed in comedy, but one which pastoral drama could use more fully because of the half-articulated understanding that the subject of the pastoral in general was the mind or heart, and because the scene of the pastoral drama in particular included a wood. The *selva* and *prato* ordinarily specified in stage

---

32 'fallacious designs,' 'our blind minds,' 'Oh, show us the way out of so dark a labyrinth.'

33 'blindness of earthly minds! In what deep night, in what dark fog of error are our souls immersed, unless you illuminate them, oh highest Sun!' 'Oh, high providence, oh lofty gods.'

Quotations from *Il pastor fido* are from the edition of Luigi Fassò in *Teatro del Seicento* (Milano–Napoli, 1956).

directions are part of one set, but they are two different places. As the writer of comedy could make his characters wander the maze of a city represented by a few houses and three or four streets converging on a piazza, still more dramatically could the pastoral playwright render visible the erring of love by developing emotionally contrasting atmospheres for meadow and forest, without stretching the unity of place any more than it was stretched by the comedy set in which a neighbourhood stands for a whole city.

The dark wood confirmed by Dante as landscape for human error had also for the late Cinquecento poet the specific aspect of labyrinth of love, reminiscent of Horace and Petrarch but primarily identified with *Orlando furioso*, in which it is fictional 'fact,' principle of plotting, and, continually, simile.[34] Mario Praz' intuition of spiritual affinity between *Orlando furioso* and *A Midsummer Night's Dream*[35] merely omits the middle term in the process of transmission, the pastoral play in which the woods, the love errantry and its amazing effects take on the solidity of stage place, stage persons, and stage action. The playwrights' recognition of Ariosto's importance to the genre is expressed in their including him in prefatory genealogies and in their plundering of *Orlando furioso*. Della Valle places Ariosto with Petrarch in the first rank of pastoral authority by using them to make his plays partial centos: his rule in *Fillide* is 'E sempre obligo di chiudere il terzetto, e le stanze delle canzoni con un verso del Petrarca' (title-page),[36] and in *Gelosi amanti* he quotes Ariosto by the same rule in Acts I and III, Petrarch in II and IV, and both alternately, in Act V.

Even when not directly quoted, *Orlando furioso* is often evoked by the presence of didactic sorcerers resembling Atlante or Melissa, and by pastoral transformations, especially those of the loquacious arboreal variety, in which Ariosto's particular blend of the amorous cause from Ovid and Petrarch with the monitory effect from Virgil is dominant.[37] The Ariostean atmosphere is as natural to the pastorals of Pasqualigo, Guazzoni, and all the others in which magic or love madness occur, as it is alien to *Aminta*.

34 The most telling of which is, 'Gli [amor] è come una gran selva, ove la via conviene a forza, a chi vi va, fallire: chi su, chi giù, chi qua, chi là travia' (XXIV,ii 3–5). Ludovico Ariosto, *Orlando furioso. A cura di Lanfranco Caretti* (Milano–Napoli, 1954).

35 'Ariosto in England,' *The Flaming Heart: Essays on Crashaw, Machiavelli, and Other Studies in the Relations Between Italian and English Literature from Chaucer to T.S. Eliot* (Garden City, NY), 301–5.

36 'Each tercet (in the *terza rima*) and each stanza of the *canzoni* must end with a line from Petrarch.'

37 In *Orlando furioso*, VI,27–53, the voice of Astolfo speaks from a tree, describing his seduction and transformation by the Circe-like Alcina as a warning to Ruggero, a hero still more susceptible than Aeneas to distraction from his dynastic mission.

Like Beccari and Giraldi before him, however, Tasso uses the forest in
sinister contrast to the meadow or pleasance. The satyr's (narrated) attack on Silvia takes place in the woods, but not as part of labyrinthine
action. Many of Tasso's successors, on the other hand, use the woods for
visual demonstration of tragic error and complex action. In Groto's *Pentimento amoroso*, for example, tangled in love's deceits, Filovevia is lured
to the woods by a potential murderer (iv,3), while Dieromena wanders
(iv,3) in another part of the forest, beset with Dantesque thoughts of the
many shepherds who have there committed suicide (iv,4).

As it was not forbidden by rationalizing theory, Guarini also uses the
forest in opposition to the pleasance by making it the chosen ambience of
Silvio, the opposer of love, the place where he kills the boar and, ironically,
where he wounds himself with love by wounding Dorinda in her wolf's
disguise (iv,8). But Guarini does not develop the wood as a place of error,
because he did not need or wish to limit this kind of movement to a single
locus. His Arcadia does not include error but is itself in error, and not only
about love. When the oracle's truth is finally understood, providence
recognized, the general redemption is expressed in metaphor reminiscent
of Tasso's 'ignote strade':

> Eterni numi, oh come son diversi
> Quegli alti, inaccessibili sentieri,
> Onde scendono a noi le vostre grazie,
> Da que' fallaci e torti,
> Onde i nostri pensier salgono al cielo!   (v,6, 1207–11)[38]

But this perception of the common experience is preceded by individual recognitions of mistaken directions and providential actions in the
separate cases which go to make up the complex plot.[39] The metaphor of
the twisted paths is, in fact, descriptive of what the spectator has witnessed in the entanglements of the multiple plot.

Certain pastoral actions impossible to represent on the street set prescribed for *commedia erudita* without loss of the verisimilitude prized by
its practitioners were nevertheless naturally suited to articulation within
the comic intrigue structure of misunderstandings, cross purposes, mis-

---

38 'Eternal gods, oh, how different are those high, inaccessible paths by which your
grace descends to us from the erring and wrong ones by which our thoughts ascend
to heaven!'
39 See Coridone's recognition that his loss of Corsica was really a gain (iv,7). His
case is a minor eddy which repeats the major movement while contributing to it, an
example of the functional complexity Guarini boasts of in the *Compendio*.

placed affections, recognitions, reversals. One of these actions is sleeping, which occurs in ten of these twenty plays; another is dreaming, which occurs in eight. For authorized use of the commonplace of sleep, Italian dramatists needed to look no farther afield than Sannazaro's *Arcadia*. Uranio's sleep in the second eclogue, and Sincero's sleep and allegorical dream in the twelfth prose demonstrate the utility of these actions for contrast between the real and the apparent, the inner life and the outer. In drama, Beccari had used sleep in combination with a truth drug administered by the Satiro to Turico to discover the name of his love (*Il Sacrificio*, 1,5). Among early rustic dramas, the whole of *La Pastorale* is framed within the dream of Ruzante, who, unlike Shakespeare's Christopher Sly, is also an actor in his own dream. Still earlier, semi-dramatic use of the dream is recorded among the mimes and clowns prior to the flourishing of the proto-Rozzi, to follow no further the track of a very old *topos*.

The dreams are often compliments to patrons, like Glauca's panegyric of the Estensi in Percivallo's *Orsilia* (11,4), and even when not so locally applicable, are flexibly symbolic, providing the playwright with one more way to represent the effects of love. There was no rule against recounting dreams in *commedia erudita*. The phenomenon is rare, however, because in comedy the dream cannot be connected with sleep in the same organic way as in the pastoral, for simple lack of a locus, the comic street set affording no closer equivalent to places of rest than uncomfortable balconies and open loggias.

In the pastoral setting, on the contrary, falling asleep on grassy banks is a natural action which almost effortlessly makes for misunderstandings, deceits, and reversals desirable to the plot. It can be the occasion for attempted rape abridged into the stealing of a kiss, as in Guazzoni's *Andromeda* (1,8) or in Groto's *Pentimento amoroso* (111,1), where Menfestio finds Panurgia asleep and, acting on his impulse to kiss her, changes her love for him to a fury which begets further action. Or the rape may not be abridged, as in Groto's *Calisto*, in which case both the sleeping and its consequences occur offstage and are only narrated (v,1). The sleep of Ingegneri's Amarilli cures madness and engenders love in Coridone (1,1), converts Amarilli herself by means of a dream (11,5), and sets off several complications. Sometimes, as in *Intricati*, sleep is induced by magicians in order to pierce through illusion to reality, truth, and self-knowledge. Lyly's *Endymion*, as well as *A Midsummer Night's Dream* and *The Tempest*, suggests the range of variations this pastoral convention could support.

Il Pastor fido contains the distilled result of continued variation on the sleep–dream commonplace in Montano's prophetic dream (1,4,11, 790–

Giovanni Battista Guarini. *Il Pastor fido:*
tragicomedia pastorale. Venetia 1602. Act I

Vincenzo Panciatichi. *Gli Amorosi affanni: favola pastorale* [Venezia] 1606.
Prologue. Courtesy of The Folger Shakespeare Library

Vincenzo Panciatichi. *Gli Amorosi affanni: favola pastorale* [Venezia] 1606.
Act II. Courtesy of The Folger Shakespeare Library

Del Signor
TORQVATO
TASSO.

Qveste, che fur già noci a l'aria sparte,
E note incise in Faggi, & in Allori,
Mentre cantasti pastorali amori,
Qui raccogliesti poi, con sì bell'arte:
E ne vergasti sì lodate carte,
Che non pur tra Bissolchi, e tra Pastori;
Ma tra reali Alberghi eterni
Hauranno, e tra le Schiere alte di Marte.
Ciò che ammirò già Manto, e Siracusa,
Nè' duo famosi, e ciò che al mio uicino
Dettò già spirto di celeste Musa,
Puro in te trapasiò, qual matutino
Raggio in cristallo, ò in fonte onda trāsfusa,
Od Aura per sinirio alto camino.

Giovanni Donato Cucchetti. *La Pazzia: favola pastorale.* Venetia 1597.
Dedicatory sonnet by Tasso. Courtesy of The Folger Shakespeare Library

819), which Guarini uses in the oracular manner more common in tragedy and at the end dignifies with redefinition as 'sogno non già, ma vision celeste!' (v,6, 1160), in Tirenio's imagery quoted above,[40] and in Mirtillo's concluding speech describing the realization of his happiness as dream-like (v,10). In none of the Italian plays are sleep and dream used so insistently or made so encompassing as by Shakespeare or by Calderón, but the convention inviting such use owed its existence in considerable part to pastoral drama.

The pastoral device best suited to dramatic demonstration of the nature of love was one utterly forbidden even to the most romantic *commedia grave*. The magicians, alchemists, astrologers, and necromancers who turn up often in regular comedy, claiming many powers, including that of transforming people into other forms, invariably turn out to be charlatans. But, as several of these twenty pastoral plays demonstrate, real magic and Ovidian metamorphosis were stock elements of the genre. The transformations of clowns into animals and fountains constitute one example, and metamorphoses of the nobler characters are still more common.

The preferred sources include the Circe episode of the *Odyssey*, the Polydorus incident in the *Aeneid*, many stories of the *Metamorphoses*, and the Renaissance epic amalgams of them all, especially Ariosto's. In drama, on the courtly academic side, there was the precedent of mythological pageants and plays in which kaleidoscopic spectacles were standard features. Epicuro had turned a shepherd into a fountain and a nymph into a tree and had restored the latter onstage. The dominant Ferrarese line of pastoral drama produced examples which ran the gamut from prayers for metamorphosis in Lollio's realistic *Aretusa* through Beccari's offstage transformation of a troublesome character into a wolf, to Giraldi's, also offstage, of his entire female cast into woodland properties.[41] On the rustic side, the Rozzi also turned nymphs into fountains and trees,[42] and in his more academic but not much more dramatic *Egloghe pastorali* Calmo mixed Ovid with medieval magic: old Fondolo, for example, becomes a talking stone statue onstage (III,1), Clonico turns into a tree (III,2), and both are restored by the arts of the Maga and her familiar devil (III,3).

Cresci both transforms Dafne into a fountain (III,1) and back again (v,1), whereas Vida merely restores (v,7) a nymph who has been a foun-

40 'no dream indeed but a heavenly vision!' See p. 63.
41 *Martia*, III,2; II,9; III,3; *Aretusa*, IV,4; *Sacrificio*, v,6; *Egle, satira* (Florence, 1550?), v,5.
42 Alonge, *Il teatro dei Rozzi*, 53, 56.

tain since before the beginning of the play. Like Lyly's Fidelia in *Love's Metamorphoses*, Della Valle's Fillide appears first as a talking tree, but, more fortunate than Fidelia, she is restored by Cupid and bestowed on a shepherd (v,7, 8). A less spectacular kind of metamorphosis, one which, although hardly verisimilar, was closer to the practice of regular comedy, is the transformation of one nymph into another by Venus and Cupid in Della Valle's *Gelosi amanti* (iv,1). Groto has Jove and Mercury take on and put off the forms of Diana and her nymph Isse. These exchanges of identity and sex are radically different from those in comedy in being real instead of feigned. Although mere disguise became common in pastoral drama under the influence of comic practice, genuine transformation was never permitted in regular comedy.

Like stage sleeping and dreaming, stage metamorphosis can lead to and express perceptions of illusion, including love, and of truth, also including love. Occurring in pastoral drama, which is by its nature a means to such insights, metamorphosis can have the effect of a play within a play. Both the genre and the particular action belong to an inward movement in late Renaissance theatre, and metamorphosis was an action peculiarly effective for gaining distance from the external world of physical law and historical fact. It was part of continued experimentation towards the unverisimilar, the opposite direction from that which the Italian pastoral play would ultimately be made to take. In *Aminta*, as in *Pastor fido*, magic and metamorphosis are not admitted into the play proper except as psychological change. The supernatural and implausible are banished to the *intermezzi*. Only Tasso's lyrics are extant, but it is safe to assume that the spectacle accompanying Proteo's *intermezzo* included transformation, and Guarini's stage directions omit no technical possibility of metamorphosis: he specifies appearances of nymphs from trees and streams, satyrs from stones, and so forth, with admonitions to 'imitare il verisimile.'[43]

The non-magical Ovidian incident of Silvia's bloody veil and apparent death is imitated from Tasso by playwrights in different groups: Ingegneri, Pino, Lupi, Vida, for example. Apparently a reminder of Ovid together with an action symbolizing death or radical change seemed essential to some pastoralists, but an equally strong need for verisimilitude caused them to prefer the Pyramus–Thisbe story to those involving metamorphosis. Vida uses both actions, although without the Shakespearean irony of presenting the magical metamorphosis as real and the Pyramus and Thisbe episode as a play. Guarini, as usual, assimilates the experi-

43 Fassò, *Teatro del Seicento*, 319–22.

ments and rationalizes the results into verisimilitude. Dorinda's near-death in *Pastor fido* occurs while she is *disguised* as a beast.

Guazzoni combines supernatural effects of many sorts, a magician, a dragon, Cupid roaming in female, then in male, human form, Florido petrified into a statue (III,7) and restored (IV,4). But the eventual triumph of verisimilitude is, unexpectedly, forecast in this play: Florido's discussion of his transformation with Fillide reveals that it was effected by hypnosis (IV,4), was, in short, apparent, a deceit of the senses, pointing to the conclusion that human perception and human art are defective. The *mago* is benevolent and powerful but his art operates only to create illusion and to change Florido's exaggeratedly high opinion of human power. Like the magic rite in Lupi's *Sospetti*, which takes place offstage and, though effective, is strongly doubted by one of the characters, Guazzoni's use of metamorphosis is an approach to the plausible and natural, or at least to the debunking of magic, which, with the judiciary arts, was under Inquisitional ban. The scepticism of Lupi's doubter is an additional *sospetto*, working out the central theme of mistrust, but, like Guazzoni's treatment of metamorphosis, it also points towards Guarini's use of the pastoral to make orthodox comments about magic and divination, without altogether losing the attendant theatrical benefit. Guarini follows Tasso in neutralizing magic as medicine and goes beyond him in making pagan superstition a counter for true faith, the Arcadian oracle a veil for Divine Providence. At the moment of recognition, when blind Tirenio exclaims,

> O Montano, di mente assai più cieco
> Che non son io di vista,
> Qual prestigio, qual démone t'abbaglia   (v,6, 1049–51)

Guarini glosses the word *prestigio*, 'Voce latina, che secondo i teologi è un inganno che non ha la sua causa dalla parte della cosa che si trasforma, ma da quella di colui che vede o in quanto all'organo o in quanto alla potenza.'[44] The use of the idea of a demon, here merely part of a metaphor, but in earlier pastoral practice a member of the *dramatis personae*, and the careful explanation of the term *prestigio* as a defect in the eye of the beholder, the kind of hallucination, in fact, by which Guazzoni's magician accomplishes a metamorphosis, is a key to Guarini's realistic

---

44 'Oh Montano, more blind of mind than I of sight, what artifice, what demon dazzles you.'
  'A Latin word which, according to theologians means a deceit which takes its cause not from the thing transformed but from the person who observes it, with reference either to his organ of sight or to the power.' Fassò, *Teatro del Seicento*, 301.

adaptation of elements which elsewhere were used externally but for expression of the same inner states of blindness and confusion.

When the pastoral play was finally established by Guarini as a genre which could be defended in Aristotelian terms against stricter Aristotelians, all that was really left of metamorphosis was change of heart and maturing under the pressures of love. Development in character was uncommon in other regular genres of Italian drama, owing to the demands of unity of time and of the decorum regulating fixed types. It is rare in *commedia erudita* for characters to fall out of love or change their objects except when death, discovery of consanguinity, or some equally external event intervenes to rearrange the situation. The countless shifts and conversions of pastoral lovers, however, with or without magic and metamorphosis, opened new possibilities of characterization. And when magic and metamorphosis are subsumed into this more verisimilar psychological alteration, the impression of something like growth or at least mutability in character is heightened.

What happened to the Italian pastoral play is ironic. It seems to have been cultivated out of need for a genre which could deal, as the other dramatic genres in the sixteenth century could not do, with 'virgin human nature,'[45] with love and change, a genre which would, in its stylized way, probe rather than mirror reality. Their critical bias committed serious playwrights to imitation of life, however, and in seeking to make the needed genre respectable in terms of current theory, they tried to restrict the pastoral, with its vision for the mind's eye, to action which could not be rejected by the testimony of the senses.

The homogeneity of tone and style and the verisimilitude common to *Aminta* and *Pastor fido* gradually dominated the genre, without ever becoming a rule. When Castelletti revised *Amarilli* for the last time,[46] he cut his clownish rustics from four to one and did away entirely with the naiad and the Ovidian transformation. As a result, the comic discord of styles is reduced, plausibility is gained at the expense of charm, and *Amarilli* moves from Group c into Group e. Although even after *Pastor fido* was in print there still appeared pastoral plays containing magic, gods, and combinations of high style with low, clowning with idealized love,[47] such mixtures were more likely in *intermezzi, commedia dell'arte* scen-

---

45 Guarini's omission of the phrase when he revised *Il Verrato* and *Il Verato secondo* as *Il compendio della poesia tragicomica* may indicate belated recognition of how far from the simple eclogue and how near to the 'artifices of the city' his tragicomedy had taken the pastoral mode.

46 *Amarilli, pastorale. Nuovamente dall'istesso auttore accresciuta, emendata, e quasi formata di nuovo* (Vinegia, 1587).

47 For examples, see Carrara, *La poesia pastorale*, 367 ff.

arios or music drama derived from pastoral.[48] As the seventeenth century began, the literary pastoral play had years of life ahead, but in those years the imitations of *Pastor fido* would outnumber other types of pastoral, and the imitations would be closer to their original than *Pastor fido* had been to *Aminta*.

Tasso had rejected not only magic, metamorphosis, and clowns, but also intrigue structure and the other accoutrements of comedy. Guarini, on the contrary, expanded Tasso's speeches and situations, maintaining his verisimilitude and unified tone in a dramatic action which carried forward the series of attempts to match the pastoral milieu with the form of comedy, and vice versa. Guarini's baroque aim to establish a middle genre fusing tragedy and comedy, distinct from both, required

... dall'una [tragedy] ... le persone grandi e non l'azione; la favola verisimile ma non vera; gli affetti mossi, ma rintuzzati; il diletto, non la mestizia; il pericolo, non la morte; dall'altra [comedy] il riso non dissoluto, le piacevolezze modeste, il nodo finto, il rivolgimento felice, & sopratutto l'ordine comico ...[49]

But even the 'great' characters of *Pastor fido* bear the marks of comic ancestry, the verisimilar action was as much a demand of comedy as of tragedy, and both passions and danger had long been essential to the *intreccii* of *commedia grave*. The experiments in pastoral drama which continued until Guarini's synthesis finally established an orthodoxy for the genre help to identify and weigh the constituent elements of that orthodoxy. Prime among them is the *commedia erudita*, a source of structure and character types for the overwhelming majority of experiments and for Guarini as well.

When Jonard contrasts the play of love and change in traditional comedy, by which he means Attic New Comedy and its Renaissance continuation, with that of love and destiny in *Pastor fido*,[50] he makes a distinction which could as well serve to distinguish the regular comedy of the first half of the sixteenth century from its development as *commedia grave* in the second half. Guarini's synthesis of comedy and tragedy was made

---

48 For examples of special uses of pastoral elements in seventeenth-century *intermezzi* and *melodrammi*, see Beatrice Corrigan, 'Tasso's Erminia in the Italian Theater of the Seicento,' *Renaissance Drama*, VII (1964), 127–50.

49 'from the one (tragedy) ... great persons and not the action; the plot verisimilar but not true; the passions moved, but blunted; delight, not sadness; danger, not death; from the other (comedy) laughter not dissolute, seemly pleasantries, the fictional intrigue, the happy reversal, and above all the comic order ...,' *Compendio della poesia tragicomica*, 231.

50 Norbert Jonard, 'Le baroquisme du *Pastor Fido*,' *Studi secenteschi*, IX (1969), 7.

at a time when comedy was already imbued with certain tragic principles and practices, so that the division between his debts to the one or the other genre is not as sharp or the balance as equal as his own analysis would make them.

The elements which faded from the orthodox pastoral play, especially fantasy and the contrast between high and low styles, as they appear in the experiments of the 1570s and 1580s, also help to explain the difference between *Aminta*, where they are quite absent, and *Pastor fido*, where they exist vestigially. Moreover, these elements are to be found in English plays which give off pastoral vibrations but are rarely studied in connection with Italian drama, because they are not like *Aminta* and *Pastor fido*. The odd play of Fletcher or Daniel clearly inspired by Guarini is justifiably regarded as exceptional. The conviction that the work of Shakespeare and that of some of his contemporaries is more closely related to Italian drama than has yet been established awaits confirmation through increased knowledge of what that drama was. The range of comic possibilities, the mixtures of tones, ranks, and of the plausible with the fantastic displayed by the twenty plays examined here show that for a long time Italian dramatists entertained a very liberal idea of what a stage pastoral could be and do.

It is the effect of multiplicity achieved by juxtaposition of contrasting elements and levels of style that makes the many Elizabethan plays in which pastoral elements are used without declarations of form seem alien to the Italian genre as represented by *Aminta* and *Pastor fido*. Shakespeare's green world, in particular, seems to belong entirely to the immemorial English countryside, with its local folk customs, far from the literary Arcadia evoked for the court of Ferrara. Yet C.L. Barber himself, without breaking a Neo-Platonic code in order to do so, senses the aura of Arcadia in the wood outside Athens.[51] While native festivals and submerged memories of the primitive wild of romance, as they have been revealed in this context by Barber and by Frye,[52] respectively, surely provided Shakespeare with the manner of variation he would make on the conventions he chose, the conventions themselves belong to a more self-conscious and sophisticated art. *Aminta* and *Pastor fido* alone cannot tell the story of that art nor yield up that sense of the capacity of the pastoral dramatic genre shared by its Italian practitioners before Guarini and, I think, by many Englishmen, of whom Shakespeare was only the greatest.

51 *Shakespeare's Festive Comedy. A Study of Dramatic Form and its Relation to Social Custom* (Princeton, 1959), 145.
52 'The Argument of Comedy,' and in *A Natural Perspective. The Development of Shakespearean Comedy and Romance* (New York, 1965), passim.

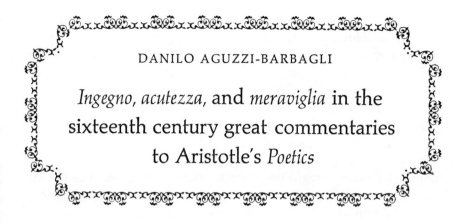

DANILO AGUZZI-BARBAGLI

Ingegno, acutezza, and meraviglia in the sixteenth century great commentaries to Aristotle's Poetics

IN HIS RECENT VOLUME for Vallardi's series on Italian literary history, Carmine Jannaco opens his presentation of the development of Italian literature during the seventeenth century with a lucid study of the origins of baroque poetics and of the new elements that become their inner motivations. Contrasting the idea of the marvellous in the critical literature of the Counter Reformation and the marvellous as it was understood by Marino and his followers and admirers, the critic states that in actuality they are two different things. 'The Cinquecento law of *admiratio* is in substance – and therefore in the artistic and pseudo-artistic achievements, which can be connected with it – something different from the Marinistic principle, remaining nevertheless its historical antecedent.'[1] Implicitly these words indicate a process of evolution. The writer, however, does not illustrate it to any considerable, or novel, extent, but limits himself to the conclusion that during the baroque age the marvellous strikes the senses and is at the same time a product of sensual psychology, instead of an appeal to the intellect. But, we might observe, something is obviously different from its former state at different levels of an evolutionary process. The point is to determine, first if something is in actuality the product of a certain evolution, and second how much of the former self is still a determining factor, once this entity has emerged into a new cultural and historical atmosphere. The vastness of his undertaking justifies Jannaco in not investigating to a fuller and original degree the impact of Counter-Reformation criticism on the poetics of the Baroque, mainly in relation to

1 Carmine Jannaco, *Il Seicento* (Milano, 1966), 9: 'Eppure la cinquecentesca legge dell'*admiratio* è nella sua sostanza – e quindi nelle attuazioni artistiche o pseudoartistiche ad essa collegabili – qualcosa di diverso dal principio marinista, pur costituendone il precedente storico.'

the central problems of *acutezza, ingegno,* and *meraviglia.* And we may note as one of his merits that he is aware of the fact that 'the impossibility to recognize with sufficient assurance a coherent graduality of elaboration and formation of aesthetical theories between the XVI and XVII centuries' may be imputable to deficiencies at the present stage of research on Renaissance criticism.

In an attempt to trace a gradual and coherent elaboration of the concepts of *acutezza* and the strictly related concepts of *ingegno* and *meraviglia* from their somewhat surreptitious beginnings in the Counter Reformation to their baroque triumphs, particular attention ought to be paid to the vastness and complexity of critical literature during the second half of the sixteenth century. We shall therefore examine here only the great commentaries on Aristotle's *Poetics,* which constitute to a large degree one of the points of departure for both the Aristotelian critical treatises, and the minor commentaries, now listed and discussed in Bernard Weinberg's *History of Literary Criticism in the Italian Renaissance.*

It is a well-known fact that the fusion of poetics and rhetorics, so evident in the literary theories of the seventeenth century is not a new departure, but rather the continuation of a process, which runs through the Humanistic movement and is actively developed in the critical literature of the sixteenth century.[2] An important aspect of this problem is the attempt to resolve the antithesis between the *prodesse* and the *delectare*: the sixteenth-century discussions of metaphor become an important part of this search for a new synthesis. All the late Cinquecento commentators of Aristotle's *Poetics* devote what seems at first an extraordinary amount of attention to chapters twenty-one and twenty-two, where metaphor is analysed with other figures of speech.[3] The first of the great commentators is Francesco Robortello, whose *In librum Aristotelis de arte poetica explicationes* appeared in 1548.[4] As we start to read Robortello's comments on

2 For the problem of the relationship between rhetoric and poetics during the Renaissance and the Baroque age, see the basic study of G. Morpurgo Tagliabue, 'La retorica aristotelica e il barocco,' *Retorica e barocco. Atti del III Congresso Internazionale di Studi Umanistici,* ed. E. Castelli (Roma, 1955), 119–95. Also: Franco Croce, 'Le poetiche del barocco in Italia,' *Momenti e problemi di storia dell'estetica* (Milano, 1959), I, 547–75. Seen in the light of these works, studies like: Giuseppe Zonta, 'Rinascimento, Aristotelismo e Barocco,' *Giornale storico della letteratura italiana,* CIV (1934), appear definitely dated.

3 *Poet.,* 1458a and ff.

4 By 1548 Vincenzo Maggi had almost finished the work of editing the commentaries, begun by Bartolomeo Maggi in 1541, and his own notes on the *Poetics* for the volume, published in 1550 with the title: *In Aristotelis librum de arte poetica communes explicationes.* For the problem of the chronological precedence of Maggi–

the chapters of the *Poetics* just mentioned we are impressed by the fact that the meaning of the original text is expanded through constant quotations from classical works on rhetorics, including Aristotle's own treatise on that subject. The commentator notes at the beginning of his discussion that the Aristotelian differentiation between current and metaphorical words is followed by Quintilian in the first book of the *Institutiones oratoriae* and by Cicero in the *De oratore*. Using the Ciceronian work as a starting point Robortello establishes for the first time in this section of his commentary a strong link between poetics and rhetoric.[5] As Robortello proceeds with the explanation of the four fundamental types of metaphors presented by Aristotle, he again introduces a passage from the *De oratore*, which was bound henceforth to be remembered in practically all the analyses of metaphorical style during the late sixteenth and seventeenth centuries. This is the paragraph where Cicero maintains that metaphors were originally invented to denote things devoid of a proper name and in the course of time began to be favoured, because of the intellectual stimulation and the consequent pleasure they provided; similarly clothes were first used to protect man from the cold and later were employed as ornaments of the body.[6] The tendency to read Aristotle in the light of classical rhetoric appears again when the Italian commentator proceeds to study the several types of metaphors. Showing a certain dissatisfaction with the conciseness of the text of the *Poetics* on that subject, Robortello observes that Aristotle imprecisely considers as metaphors figures that in Quintilian and Plutarch are defined as catachresis. And quoting again from Quintilian, Plutarch, Dionysius of Halicarnassus and the *Rhetoric* of the same Aristotle, the critic finds his master guilty of having described as a transposal of meaning from species to genus, what in reality is a synecdoche. Oversights of this kind cannot be forgiven among founders (or forerunners, if we will) of the cult of metaphor! In the next century Tesauro, a high priest of the same religion, will amply testify to the truth of this fact with long and subtle subdivisions of the metaphorical species.

Longer and more significant are Robortello's comments on the metaphor of analogy, the figure of speech destined to become a favourite

Lombardi over Robortello, see Bernard Weinberg, *A History of Literary Criticism in the Italian Renaissance* (Chicago, 1961), I, 373–4.

5 *Francisci Robortelli Utinensis in librum Aristotelis de arte poetica explicationes* (Florentiae, 1548), 245: 'Haec ille (Cicero) omnia referens ad oratorem ait; sed eadem ad poetas, quibus in hoc libello inservit Aristoteles, referri possunt; nam verborum propriorum et bonorum usus ac copia est quasi solum quoddam, in quo aedificet poeta et in quo adiungat artem.'

6 *De orat.*, III, xxxviii.

among baroque poets. The third book of Aristotle's *Rhetoric*[7] is liberally used to establish the principle that metaphorical style is more suited to the poet than to the orator.[8] The idea that metaphors provide pleasure is based instead on the *De oratore*. Robortello prefaces his discussion of Aristotle's exemplary metaphor: 'The cup may be called the shield of Dionysius' with a faithful summary of Cicero's opinion on the effectiveness of metaphors.[9] But he finds it necessary to dwell on the study of the power of metaphorical language and says: 'I add also for the sake of brevity that it is necessary that in a single metaphorical word be present many things, whereby the soul of the listener may be stimulated, delighted and filled with admiration, because with the strength of a single metaphorical word this quantity of things may be obtained.'[10] Students of baroque literature insistently repeat that seventeenth-century metaphorical poets (be they Marino, Góngora, or Donne) tend to stun their readers, to appeal to their senses and daze them with a voluptuous atmosphere, created by the magic of the word stretched to the limits of its expressive potentials. This is true indeed. We must not lose sight of the fact, however, that metaphorical expression demands first of all an acute and constant exercise of rational power by the writer and a corresponding amount of rational alertness by the reader. The exponents of late Renaissance and baroque 'wit' knew this very well themselves, but this kind of awareness begins to take consistency with Robortello. The study of his commentary reveals that the impact of metaphor on the intellect and subsequently on the senses is a discovery of classical rhetoric, revamped, accentuated, and at the same time popularized in the Italian Counter Reformation. Robortello's predilection for the metaphor of analogy is based on the fact that this particular figure of speech is charged more than any other with energy to affect the psyche of the readers. Consequently the critic is surprised to see Aristotle omit in the *Poetics* any reference to the type of metaphor κατὰ ἐνέργειαν, that is,

---

7 *Rhet.*, 1406b.
8 F. Robortello, *In librum Aristotelis de arte poetica explicationes*, 248: 'Metaphorae quidem et oratoribus et poetis conveniunt. Sed εἰκόνος, ut inquit Aristoteles, debent adhiberi raro ab oratoribus, quia ποιητικαὶ μᾶλλον εἰσίν.'
9 Ibid., 'Cicero ... facit ut verbum alieno in loco positum tamquam in suo si agnoscatur delectet. Quod si simile nihil habet repudiatur. Et certe ex notis rebus analogia seu similitudo dici debet in translatione facienda, nam duobus in primis de causis in translatione utimur, tum ut res clarior fiat, ut magis aliquid significetur, quod aliquoi satis exprimi non posset propriis vocabulis.'
10 Ibid., 249, 'Addo etiam propter brevitatem in translato enim verbo uno multa insint oportet, quae audientis animum pungant et oblectent, simulque admiratione afficiant, quod vi unius verbi translati potuerit tam multa proferri.'

according to the definition of Demetrius Phalereus and Quintilian, the figure wherein inanimate things are represented in a state of activity.[11] The commentator rapidly excuses Aristotle by saying that he possibly included this type among the metaphors by analogy, and then continues to study the relationship between metaphorical diction and sensuality.

The idea that metaphor is charged with power, affecting the intellect and the emotions by way of the senses, passes from Aristotle into the main stream of classical rhetoric.[12] According to Demetrius Phalereus, metaphor contributes to style both grandeur and pleasure;[13] Cicero maintains that 'metaphor is directed to the senses, especially the sense of sight, which is most acute';[14] Quintilian says that 'metaphor was established to move the soul, to express things and put them under the eyes.'[15] Robortello gives these theories new life, as he incorporates them in his conception of metaphor and categorically states: 'Things which are seen can be brought to the eyes of the mind more readily than those which are heard.'[16] Having thus clarified with the authority of the Ancients the particular nature of the power of metaphor, Robortello proposes it as a medium to elevate the poetical diction and help it attain the Aristotelian quality of magnificence. In his comments to *Poetics* 1458a, 15–23, he says:

If the poetical language is woven only with proper terms it will be humble and plebeian. That is the greatest vice, especially in the heroic poem, in the tragic and in many others that love the majesty of expression ... Proper terms must be retained, because they make the diction clear, but they have to be mixed ... with what is figurative and shuns the use of popular language ... This renders the oration sublime and lofty ... Aristotle declares all those things excellently and very abundantly in the third book of his *Rhetoric*, where he warns that orators should exercise restraint in these things, because they are the pertinence of the poet ... Strange and metaphorical words make the listeners wonder, therefore they give pleasure.[17]

---

11 Ibid., 242. Robortello insists on the fact that this type of metaphor is most poetical and is praised as such in Homer by Plutarch.

12 *Rhet.*, 1410b.

13 *On Style*, 78. See also G.M.A. Grube, *A Greek Critic: Demetrius on Style* (Toronto, 1961), 80: 'Metaphors ... contribute more than anything else to delight and impressiveness of style.'

14 *De orat.*, III, xl.

15 *Inst. orat.*, VIII, 6, 19.

16 F. Robortello, *In librum Aristotelis de arte poetica explicationes*, 252.

17 Ibid., 256, 'Si poeticus sermo ex propriis tantum verbis conficiatur, humilis fuerit ac plebeius, quod summum vitium praesertim in heroico poemate et tragico aliis-

In his treatise on style Demetrius Phalereus introduces a kind of classification by importance in the Aristotelian list of figures of speech. He maintains that 'some things are expressed with greater clearness and precision by means of metaphors than by means of the precise terms themselves.'[18] As an exemplification of this fact he quotes the Homeric image: 'The battle shuddered' and says that 'no change of phrase could, by the employment of proper terms, give the meaning with greater truth and clearness.'[19] Cicero also believes that the possibilities of building metaphors are practically numberless and that this figure brings to the oration a particular light.[20] Quintilian follows this line of thought and states that it is possible that the metaphorical expression may be better than the proper and can therefore be chosen for aesthetical reasons.[21] Having accepted these principles, Robortello is again surprised by Aristotle's observation that clearness of diction is best obtained through the use of lengthened, contracted, and altered words. The critic does not seem to accept this Aristotelian norm, since to him metaphor maintains supremacy over all other figures of speech.

Robortello's faith in metaphor is such that he suggests, as a kind of study most useful to poets of his time, that all methods of inventing this figure used by the Ancients be collected and assimilated, to the point of enabling a modern writer to use them as his own, whenever the opportunity arises.[22] This suggestion is certainly significant. In fact, the most vital type of humanistic imitation (the type already practised by Valla, Poliziano, and the most original among the fifteenth-century humanists) is here recommended as a method for becoming proficient in the art of metaphor. The suggestion of Robortello was welcomed, at least in part, by Emanuele Tesauro, whose *Canocchiale aristotelico* consists for the most part in a study of forms of metaphors, the examples of which are provided by both classical and Italian literature. And even Sforza Pallavicino de-

---

que multis, quae maiestatem amant. Sunt igitur propria quidem retinenda, quia perspicuum sermonem reddunt, sed immiscenda illis sunt peregrina et externa ... quicquid enim proprium non est reciditque a consuetudine loquendi popularis peregrinum et externum dici potest ... Sed optime et copiosissime rem hanc declarat Aristoteles ipse libro tertio *Rhetoricorum* ubi monet oratoribus modum in his esse adhibendum, quia ad poetas potius spectant.'

18 *On Style*, 82.
19 Ibid.
20 *De orat.*, III, xl.
21 *Inst. orat.*, VIII, 6, 4.
22 F. Robortello, *In librum Aristotelis de arte poetica explicationes*, 264, 'Nostra haec aetate putarim nihil utilius esse quam ex veterum libris, qui dicendi laude floruerunt, omnes translationum formas modusque colligere, ac animo ita complecti ut pro suis aliquis utatur, quando opus fuerit.'

voted six chapters of his *Trattato dello stile e del dialogo* to the problem of imitation from the Ancients and specifically to the problem of imitation in the art of metaphor.[23]

In the 1674 edition of the *Canocchiale aristotelico* Tesauro's definition of *ingegno* is validated in a marginal note by a quotation from the third book of Aristotle's *Rhetoric*, which reads as follows: 'In multo diversis perspicere ingeniosi est atque solertis. Decenter autem uti translationibus versatilis ingenii indolem praefert.'[24] Naturally the concept of *ingegno* is far from occupying in Robortello's whole system of poetics the central place it occupies in Tesauro's, and Robortello is too much of a humanist to try deliberately to squeeze out of an Aristotelian text a particularly favoured verbal correspondence. Nevertheless the classical texts, used by Tesauro to give his concept of *ingegno* the authority and the lustre of being a development of ideas already held, partially at least, by the Ancients, are precisely the same as those already explored about a century before by Robortello for practically the same purpose. In the commentary we find, at the germinal stage, an outline of the theory of *ingegno* as the element indispensable in the making of metaphors and responsible there-fore for the *meraviglia* resulting from the establishment of those rela-tionships and for the pleasure deriving from it. In his explanation of the passage in *Poetics* 1459a, 4–7, where Aristotle states that it is difficult to have a command of metaphor, Robortello says explicitly that the meta-phorical poet must be a man 'acri ingenio.' He qualifies this definition by describing *acutezza* as the capacity to know the nature and power of all things, how they agree, and how they do not agree, what are their simi-larities, their differences, their analogies. He makes a further qualification by stating also that *acutezza* is the capacity to weigh all those elements in order to make the proper transposal.[25] We may note here that the text of Aristotle barely justifies the employment of the expression 'acri ingenio' as the main quality of the creator of metaphor. In fact, the passage of the *Poetics* used by Robortello, and after him by a host of theorists of meta-phor, reads as follows: πολὺ δὲ μέγιστον τὸ μεταφορικὸν εἶναι. μόνον γὰρ τοῦτο

23 Sforza Pallavicino, *Trattato dello stile e del dialogo* (Torino, 1830), 100 ff.
24 Emanuele Tesauro, *Il canocchiale aristotelico* (Venezia, 1674), 55.
25 F. Robortello, *In librum Aristotelis de arte poetica explicationes*, 264: 'Metapho-ricum esse, cum ait intelligit aptum esse ad metaphoras effigiendas; ingenio acri enim opus est, nam cum ex similitudine et analogia, quae est inter res, ducantur, naturam omnium rerum ac vim nosse oportet, quaque in re conveniant et in qua non conveniant, saepe enim alia res maior altera, multae ab omni parte similes et aequales, rursus multae quae saltem ab aliqua parte sibi respondent. Haec igitur aliaque quam plurima diligenter sunt perpendenda, ut aliquis apte metaphoras confingat.'

οὔτε παρ' ἄλλου ἔστι λαβεῖν εὐφυίας τε σημεῖόν ἐστι· τὸ γὰρ εὖ μεταφέρειν τὸ τὸ ὅμοιον θεωρεῖν ἐστιν.[26] Demetrius Phalereus, Quintilian, and especially Cicero appear to be more directly responsible for suggesting the terms *ingegno* and *acutezza*, so widespread in the sixteenth- and seventeenth-century studies of metaphor. In the *De oratore* we read that there is a kind of wit (*ingenii specimen*) capable of transcending the pedestrian manner of expression and capturing distant relationships, without creating confusion in our mind.[27] Robortello knew well this passage. And he again expanded a Ciceronian thought in one of the conclusive statements of his study of metaphor when he said: 'Metaphors elevate the expression and (I do not know how) make it more full of movement, active and vigorous.'[28]

Though less elaborate than in Robortello, a very interesting discussion of metaphor appears in Bartolomeo Lombardi and Vincenzo Maggi's commentary on Aristotle's *Poetics*, in the course of their analysis of chapters XXI and XXII. The work of Lombardi and Maggi was published in 1550. Despite the fact that Maggi violently attacked Robortello,[29] indicating the omissions and mistakes in his work, the reading of his and Lombardi's comments on metaphorical language seems to reveal a certain continuity with the ideas already expressed by the rival commentator. Again Aristotle's *Rhetoric* and the treatises of Demetrius Phalereus, Cicero, and Quintilian are introduced to supplement the text of the *Poetics*. According to Lombardi–Maggi the first merit of metaphor, and one which is in total agreement with the general end of poetry as it is conceived in their system, is to teach. Proper terms, they assert, do not give us pleasure, but metaphors are most pleasing, because they reveal relationships not detected before.[30] In a somewhat more forceful way than Robortello, Lombardi–Maggi maintain that metaphors are the product of *ingegno* and that they

---

26 *Poet.*, 1459a, 5–8. S.H. Butcher translates this passage as follows: 'But the greatest thing by far is to have a command of metaphor. This alone cannot be imparted by another; it is the mark of genius, for to make good metaphors implies an eye for resemblances.' *Aristotle's Theory of Poetry and Fine Art* (London, 1923), 87.

27 *De orat.*, III, xi, 'Homines aliena, multo magis si sunt translata, delectant. Hic accidere credo, vel quod ingenii specimen est quoddam, transilire ante pedes posita, et alia longe repetita sumere; vel quod is, qui audit, alio ducitur cogitatione, neque tamen aberrat, quae maxima est delectatio.'

28 F. Robortello, *In librum Aristotelis de arte poetica explicationes*, 264: 'Translationes igitur ... exornant enim nimirum orationem, humoque attollunt, ac, nescio quomodo, nobiliorem vegetamque magis efficiunt ac nervosiorem.'

29 See Bernard Weinberg, *A History of Literary Criticism in the Italian Renaissance*, I, 374.

30 *Vincentii Madii Brixiani et Bartholomaei Veronensis in Aristotelis librum de poetica communes explicationes* (Venetiis, 1550), 225–6: 'Nomina vero propria nec ipsa nos de novo docent, quoniam ea scimus, at metaphora praeclare docet, quare merito iucundissima est.'

cannot be borrowed from others.[31] And again the metaphor of analogy is favoured among all others for its energy, for its capacity to give activity to inanimate things. The uniqueness of the talent of the *'ingeniosi et acuti hominis'*[32] is stated and illustrated with the help of the third book of Aristotle's *Rhetoric*. In their comments to *Poetics* 1459a, 4–7, Lombardi–Maggi insist on giving the concept of *ingegno* an Aristotelian paternity. Here they maintain that the study of the nature of things may indeed help the metaphorical poet, however 'to perceive similarity in dissimilar things is mainly the gift of nature and acute *ingegno.'*[33]

The main contribution of Lombardi–Maggi to the formation of the tradition of the theory of metaphor is their insistence on originality, on the necessity to discover metaphorically relationship between things, outside of the influence of other writers, trusting much more the natural power of the intellect, than the rather general rules of the rhetoricians. The stress placed by Lombardi–Maggi on the strict connection between the concepts of *ingegno, acutezza, meraviglia,* and the pleasure it affords, testify to the fact that the direction taken by Robortello in his interpretation of the passages on metaphor in the *Poetics* is not arrested, but continued and developed instead, even if this happens in a rather subdued fashion.

In a significant passage of his commentary to the *Poetics* (1560) Pietro Vettori maintains that the poetic art serves the opinion of those who listen, that it endeavours, in every way it can, to penetrate the soul of an audience, seizing all fit means for this purpose and rejecting those which are not. Therefore it is impossible to condemn the poet who takes what is suitable to his ends.[34] Here and elsewhere in his commentary Vettori reveals his fundamental rhetorical conception of poetry, which leads him to emphasize the necessity of a special poetical diction and the legitimacy to adorn it with 'flowers' and 'beauties.' If we bear in mind this pervasive tendency of the Florentine critic, we shall not be surprised to see how carefully he analyses and comments upon Aristotle's ideas on metaphor in the *Poetics*. Relying on his formidable knowledge of classical culture

31 Ibid., 227, 'Laudat (Aristoteles) preaterea eodem loco (*Poet.*, 1457b,6) metaphoram, quoniam ipsam aliunde sumere non possumus, sed ingenii nostri viribus ea nobis comparanda est.'

32 Ibid., 228.

33 Ibid., 246.

34 *Petri Victorii commentarii in primum librum Aristotelis de arte poetarum* (Florentiae, 1560), 291, 'Servit enim ars poetarum opinionibus eorum qui audiunt, studetque insinuare se omni ratione qua potest in animos eorum ipsorum, captans quidquid ad hoc aptum est, reiicensque contraria: accusari igitur non potest poeta qui arripit, quod sibi magis aptum esse intellegit.' On this problem, see also B. Weinberg, *A History of Literary Criticism in the Italian Renaissance*, I, 465.

Vettori outlines a history of the development of that figure of speech in the ancient world, which leads him to conclude that the best metaphors are those found anew by the poet.[35] As we can see the accent is again on the originality of the invention, as it was with Lombardi–Maggi. Like his immediate predecessors Vettori insists that the talent to discover relations between things is an extraordinary faculty (*eximia facultas*), which reveals the acuteness of the individual endowed with it and deserves the highest praise.[36] So the capacity to make new metaphors becomes one of the ways to attain poetical glory. Following the trend established by Robortello and Lombardi–Maggi, Vettori elaborates on the Aristotelian principle that the art of metaphor cannot really be obtained from others and that it cannot be taught by any teacher.[37] Really metaphorical is the poet, who, *ob ingenii acumen ... aut multarum rerum scientiam*,[38] is more able than others to detect similarities in things which are dissimilar and bring thereby pleasure to his audience.

The basic relationship between the concepts of *ingegno*, *acutezza*, *meraviglia*, and pleasure thus reappears in Vettori, who contributes to the formation of the ideal of the Marinistic poet mainly with his insistence on the singularity of the nature of the artist and on the glory, which he may

35 P. Vettori, *Commentarii in primum librum Aristotelis de arte poetarum*, 217: 'Eo magis ipsas (translationes) probari in oratione ac valere ad ingenium eius, qui ipsis utitur, commendandum, quod ad alio accipi non possunt, sed excogitentur oportet ab ipso, in mentemque veniant ei qui dicit aut scribit.'

36 Ibid., 'Hoc arbitror valere: proprieque illas esse translationes, quae occurrant alicui, nec ab alio unquam, quod ille sciat, usurpatae sint. Nam quamvis quae ab alio prius excogitata fuerint non omnino adhuc aequivoca sint, non tamen digna videntur quae plane metaphorae ipsius dicantur, qui illis postea utitur, nec eandem laudem ingeniique commendationem habent. Quod enim acumen ingenii ostendit uti verbo translato, quod aliunde sumpseris, exempli causa a Cicerone, Lucretio, Catullo, aliisque qui magnopere floruerunt ob facultatem eximiam translationum pariendarum et quis efficere non potest non magna etiam doctrina instructus.'

37 Ibid., 218, 'Non est proclivis videre quid similitudinis existat in rebus dissimilibus: qui autem hoc apte praestare possunt ob ingenii acumen, aut multarum rerum scientiam, ii multas elegantes translationes gignunt, ac vere μεταφορικοὶ nuncupantur, si toto animo incumbunt huic laudi seque aliquantum in hoc praeclaro opere exercuerint. Vera igitur translatio et quae proprie hoc nomine appellanda est, nisi fallor, vel potius ut mihi videor posse auctoritate gravium scriptorum affirmare, ea est quam significavi, id est quae primo ab aliquo excogitatur, ut ipse ante alios perspexerit similitudinem illarum rerum et unius nomen ad aliam ostendendam attulerit, quae tamen et ipsa suum ac proprium nomen haberet, si uti illo voluisset, sed ille exornandae orationis studiosus ipsum reliquit, ac pro illo alterum usurpavit, aptum sane illi rei propter similitudinem indicandae et simul animo eius qui audit oblectando.'

38 Ibid.

derive from his peculiar talent. Considering the frequently quoted lines of Marino:

> È del poeta il fin la meraviglia:
> parlo de l'eccellente, non del goffo;
> chi non sa far stupir vada a la striglia,[39]

the more sensitive among modern students of baroque literature[40] have called attention to the fact that the author of the *Adone* considers the art of *meraviglia* as the prerogative of individuals far above the average. The 'uncouth' may hope in vain to be able to astonish his public. But how, may we ask, does the poet acquire the refinement necessary to qualify as an 'eccellente' creator of metaphor? It is not our purpose here to try to answer this question in terms of the poetics of Marino, or of the theorists of the seventeenth century, for whom the problem is a vital one. We simply want to point out that the problem of nature and art, or if we prefer natural genius and doctrine, in the personality of the metaphorical poet, starts to be posited by the sixteenth-century commentators of Aristotle's *Poetics*. Vettori is aware of this problem and, although he does not try to solve it, he implicitly stresses its importance and its urgency.

The reader of Lodovico Castelvetro's explanations of chapter XXI and XXII of Aristotle's *Poetics*, in his famous *Poetica d'Aristotile volgarizzata et sposta* (the first vernacular commentary, published in Vienna in 1570), may at first gather the impression that the contribution of this critic to the development of the theory of metaphor is indeed very limited. Castelvetro accepts the idea, already popularized by the Aristotelians of his time, that the metaphorical poet is endowed with a superior and unique type of talent. In his opinion, too, only the poet is truly metaphorical who is able to detect, and render in the appropriate forms of verbal transposals, previously undiscovered relations among things. Like his predecessors he considers metaphor as the product of a 'greater acuteness of *ingegno*';[41] but he does exclude the possibility that some type of metaphor (for instance, metaphors from species to genus and from genus to species) may

---

39 'The end of the poet is the marvellous, I speak of the excellent poet and not of the uncouth one. Any poet who does not know how to astonish (his audience) deserves sharp criticism.'

40 See: Antonio Franceschetti, 'Il concetto di meraviglia nelle poetiche della prima Arcadia,' *Lettere italiane*, XXI (1969), 63–4.

41 Lodovico Castelvetro, *Poetica d'Aristotile volgarizzata et sposta* (Vienna, 1570), 271, 'Nella formatione delle translationi ... fa mestiere di maggiore sottilità d'ingegno.'

be borrowed from others.[42] He is even more daring when he speaks of compound words and suggests that in forming them the poet should feel as free as the classical and neo-latin poets. He actually coins some exemplary neologisms, like *Sylvicomus mons* and *Turricomi muri*, which undoubtedly would have sounded sufficiently seventeenth century even to Marino, or Tesauro.[43] But despite some overtones which may indicate a certain preference for pre-baroque modes of expression, despite the emphasis placed on *ingegno*, *acutezza*, and originality in the making of metaphors, the position maintained by Castelvetro on the general issue of metaphorical style and its prevalence remains somewhat ambiguous. This is not altogether surprising, when we frame Castelvetro's point of view of metaphor and *ingegno* in his general conception of the poetical work,[44] where the principle of verisimilitude acquires paramount importance, and when we keep in mind his naturalistic tendencies and his relentless rationalism. According to Castelvetro, metaphor must comply with the principle of *convenevolezza* (suitability), which determines the choice of diction according to the particular genre and the nature of the individual character. So Castelvetro maintains that metaphorical language is best suited to passionate persons,[45] who, in their frenzy, tend to synthesize in metaphors the extended terms of comparisons, figures more appropriate to calmer and more impassive individuals. And we might be tempted here to see a connection between Castelvetro's idea of metaphor and the theories on the basic sensuality of seventeenth-century metaphorical style. But that would be foolhardy perhaps, because we have to remember the continuous

42 Ibid., 'È cosa da stimar più il saper sciegliere la convenevole translatione, perciochè questa non si può prendere da gli altri, ma conviene che lo scrittore se la formi da se stesso per suo ingegno.' P.272, 'La translatione si può introdurre ne' nostri scritti per due vie: prendendola già formata da altri, o formandola di nuovo per nostro ingegno. Et ha gran differenza tra le predette vie, perciocchè se la translatione s'introduce come già formata e si prende da altri, non viene all'introducitore altra lode, che quella che gli può dare l'haverla usata a tempo, se vero sarà che l'habbia usata a tempo. Se s'introduce di nuovo formata d'ingegno dell'introducitore, gliene viene grandissima lode, non solo perchè l'habbia usata a tempo, ma anchora perchè l'ha formata di nuovo di suo capo, la quale formatione non si può fare senza sottile speculatione.' P. 272v, 'Queste translationi da genere a spetie e da spetie a genere non si possono formare senza speculatione. Perchè non si dovrebbono altresì prendere da altri?'
43 Ibid., 272, 'Se si poteva già comporre *aurum* e *coma* e dire *auricomus ramus*, si potrà altresì ora comporre *sylva* e *coma* e dire *sylvicomus mons*, ... sì come medesimamente potrei comporre *turris* e *coma* e dire turricomi muri.'
44 For a discussion of the poetics of Castelvetro, see Bernard Weinberg, 'Castelvetro's Theory of Poetry,' in *Critics and Criticism*, ed. R.S. Crane (Chicago, 1952), 349–71.
45 Lodovico Castelvetro, *Poetica d'Aristotile volgarizzata et sposta*, 275.

warning of Castelvetro that poetry imitates through 'harmonized words' a possible human action. This affords pleasure, not because of the brilliant acrobatics of metaphorical imagery, but simply because of the novelty of the case.[46] Castelvetro's constant preoccupation with the dependence of style on the nature of the action, his effort to maintain the mimetical relationship unaffected by the prevalence of rhetorical motivations may explain his limited enthusiasm for metaphor, as a medium to attain that clearness and magnificence advocated by Aristotle.

A confirmation of Castelvetro's guarded attitude in relation to the daring of metaphorical imagination is provided in practice by his criticism of Annibal Caro's canzone *Venite all'ombra dei gran gigli d'oro*. The frequent references to the pamphlets written on this occasion, which appear in the commentary to the *Poetics*, make the analysis of these works an integral part of the study of Castelvetro's theory of metaphor. Caro's canzone opens with the following image, where one can already feel the pomp and the intellectual mobility of the Baroque:

> Venite all'ombra de' gran gigli d'oro
> Care Muse, devote a' miei giacinti:
> Et d'ambo insieme avvinti
> Tessiam ghirlande a' nostri idoli e fregi.[47]

Without excessive consideration for the House of France (indicated by the *gran gigli d'oro*), or the Farnese (and their symbol the *giacinti*), and even less for Caro's *Muse* (wittily qualified with a baroque pun: *Caro-care*), Castelvetro opened his critical attack with the vitriolic observation that the Muses of Caro must have belonged to a pigmaic race, in order to fit in the shadow of lilies, however gilded.[48] Caro's answer to this acid application of rationalistic rigour (which incidentally could also be taken as a fine example of metaphysical wit) is worth noting as an antecedent of seventeenth-century libertarian positions. The poet reminds his censor that rational order manifests itself in particular ways in a poetical context: does Castelvetro think that poetry is mathematics? Does he not realize that poetry cannot be restricted within boundaries determinable by the

46 Ibid., 327, 'La dirittura della poetica consiste nel rassomigliare con parole armonizzate una attione humana possibile ad avvenire, dilettevole per la novità dell'accidente.'
47 'Come under the shadow of the great golden lilies dear Muses, sacred to my hyacinths and interlaced with both (of these kinds of flowers) let us weave garlands to our idols and ornaments.'
48 See Lodovico Castelvetro, 'Censura sopra la canzone precedente,' in *Apologia de gli Academici di Banchi di Roma contra M. Lodovico Castelvetro* (Parma, 1558), 15.

compass, that it must be considered according to the standard of things, which cannot be measured, of excesses and even of the impossible.[49] Indeed Castelvetro could not accept such criteria: to him the metaphors of Caro's canzone are faulty, because of *dissimilitudine, oscurità, sconvenevolezza.*[50] The first of these flaws is the lack of a proper degree of analogy between the terms of the metaphors: for example, the generosity towards poets of the kings of France cannot be related to the shadow cast by lilies. How many normal size ministers of the Muses could be accommodated under the shadow of a lily? Obscurity, according to Castelvetro, is generated when the metaphor is removed too far from the proper term and it does not contain the element which may lead to the gradual understanding of it. Finally *sconvenevolezza* consists in attributing to things or persons qualities of which they are devoid. For example, it is great *sconvenevolezza* to attribute to Cardinal Farnese the capacity to paint his name on lilies (be they the symbols of the king of France, or just ordinary garden lilies); it is also a *sconvenevolezza* just as unpardonable to overlook the fact that a lot of lilies, mainly those exposed to so much metaphorical sun, once they are cut and woven into garlands will just wither; 'il che,' adds Castelvetro with a kind of wit Marino would not have scoffed at, 'non si legge in historia o in favola essere operazione apollinea.'[51]

Despite his constant appeal to control, reason, verisimilitude, scattered throughout the pamphlets devoted to the controversy with Caro, the attitude of Castelvetro towards metaphor and its increasing popularity remains ambiguous and to some extent contradictory. Actually, in the *Ragione d'alcune cose segnate nella canzone d'Annibal Caro,* Castelvetro condemns the use of what he considers bad metaphor, rather than metaphorical style itself. Insofar as this is concerned he comes to the point of admitting that metaphor 'impresses in our mind the thing which it endeavors to express better than the proper term.'[52] We must conclude therefore that Castelvetro does not contribute too many new elements to the tradition of the theory of metaphor. Within the limits allowed by his general conception of poetry, he accepts the principles already established by the preceding commentators of the *Poetics.* But Castelvetro does not

49 *Apologia de gli Academici di Banchi di Roma contra M. Lodovico Castelvetro,* 59, 'Non vedete voi (Castelvetro) che havete presa la matematica in iscambio della poesia? Non v'accorgete che questra non va con la misura delle seste, ma con lo smisurato, con gli eccessi e con l'impossibile ancora, così crescendo come diminuendo e massimamente nel genere dimostrativo?'
50 (Lodovico Castelvetro) *Ragione d'alcune cose segnate nella canzone d'Annibal Caro Venite all'ombra de' gran gigli d'oro* (Kekrika, n.d.), 24.
51 Ibid., 46.
52 Ibid., 63.

oppose metaphorical style; on the contrary he implicitly admits that it can appear in the lyrical genre, provided that it is properly used. Given Castelvetro's reputation as a critic this admission is indeed relevant. And the more significant will it appear if we consider the fact that his position is one of the most important to our understanding of the crisis of Cinquecento Petrarchan lyric and its shift towards new forms of expression.[53]

By far the greatest contribution among the commentators on the *Poetics* to the establishment of metaphorical style is provided by Alessandro Piccolomini in his *Annotazioni nel libro della Poetica di Aristotile* (1575). This merit was already recognized by his contemporaries, as is shown by Scipione Bargagli, who in his *Imprese* says that Piccolomini treated metaphor with 'beautiful and appreciable abundance.'[54] Modern historians of literature have practically forgotten this aspect of Piccolomini's activity as a theorist of poetics, except for Giulio Marzot, who attributes to Piccolomini's treatment of metaphor 'an acuteness not to be found in any of his successors, not even in Tesauro, who copiously gathered, but did not discuss that matter too much.'[55] This judgment may appear somewhat exaggerated, the more so since Marzot does not study in any detail Piccolomini's discussion of metaphor. The fact remains, however, that in his commentary to chapters XXI and XXII of the *Poetics* Piccolomini gives a fundamental outline of the theory of metaphor, which could only be improved upon by seventeenth-century critics, but not basically changed.

Alessandro Piccolomini does not, as his predecessors Robortello, Maggi, and Vettori did before him, try to outline a history of metaphor, nor does he discuss in detail the view points of Cicero, Quintilian, and Demetrius Phalereus, although it is quite obvious that he is most familiar with the theories on metaphor both of the Ancients and of his contemporaries. The sole authority on which the Sienese critic relies is that of Aristotle. And

53 For the relevance of Castelvetro as a key figure in the crisis of Petrarchan lyric in the second half of the sixteenth-century see: *Le rime del Petrarca brevemente sposte per Lodovico Castelvetro* (Basilea, 1582); Pietro Mazzamuto, 'Lodovico Castelvetro,' in *Orientamenti culturali della letteratura italiana. I minori* (Milano, 1961), II, 1221–35; Luigi Baldacci, 'Intorno alla crisi del Petrarchismo,' *La rassegna della letteratura italiana*, VII (1954), 70 ff.; Ezio Raimondi, 'Gli scrupoli di un filologo: Ludovico Castelvetro e il Petrarca,' *Studi petrarcheschi*, V (1952), 131–210; Ettore Bonora, *Critica e letteratura nel Cinquecento* (Torino, 1964), passim; Riccardo Scrivano, *Il manierismo nella letteratura del Cinquecento* (Padova, 1959), 79 and passim. See also the important, but not complete, study by Benedetto Croce: 'La teoria della poesia lirica nella poetica del Cinquecento,' in *Poeti e scrittori del pieno e del tardo Rinascimento* (Bari, 1945), II, 108–17.
54 Scipione Bargagli, *La prima parte delle imprese* (Venezia, 1589), 81.
55 Giulio Marzot, 'Il tramite del Petrarchismo dal Rinascimento al Barocco,' *Studi petrarcheschi*, VI (1956), 130.

this to the degree that we could synthesize the viewpoint of Piccolomini on this matter with the following syllogism: Aristotle fully approves of metaphor, the metaphorical poet follows the teaching of Aristotle (doctored by the commentators ... !): ergo, to be metaphorical is to be Aristotelian. However strange this premise and the ensuing deductions may seem to us, we must remember that it would not have sounded in the least arbitrary to Emanuele Tesauro, who at the very beginning of his *Canocchiale aristotelico* states: 'Great courage and great hopes to investigate the fountainhead of this art (of *argutezza*) came to me from the divine Aristotle,'[56] and throughout his work quotes the authority of the Greek philosopher (*il nostro autore*, as he calls him) to support his opinions. We may notice here that, while it is quite correct to refer to Tesauro as 'the most Aristotelian'[57] among seventeenth-century critics, we must also remember that the genesis of Tesauro's particular blend of Aristotelianism is precisely in works like Piccolomini's *Annotazioni*. And perhaps it is important to remember that Piccolomini's study of metaphor, from the standpoint of the *Poetics*, was preceded by his commentaries on Aristotle's *Rhetoric*, just as Tesauro confesses that he worked on two volumes of *Osservazioni sopra tutta l'arte rettorica del divino Aristotile* before devoting his efforts to the *Canocchiale*.[58]

The basic principle that guides Piccolomini in his analysis of metaphor is the idea that only the poet who can detect previously undiscovered relationships between things can legitimately be called metaphorical.[59] The originality of the metaphorical language is strongly advocated with the authority of Aristotle, whose expression: μόνον γὰρ τοῦτο οὔτε παρ' ἄλλου ἔστι λαβεῖν εὐφυίας τε σημεῖόν ἐστι· τὸ γὰρ εὖ μεταφέρειν τὸ τὸ ὅμοιον θεωρεῖν ἐστιν, is translated: 'Essendo, questa cosa fra le altre tale, che da altri non si può imparare e fa inditio d'acuto ingegno.'[60] This quotation shows

56 Emanuele Tesauro, *Il canocchiale aristotelico* (Venezia, 1674), 2.
57 See Ezio Raimondi, *Letteratura barocca* (Firenze, 1961), passim.
58 Emanuele Tesauro, *Il canocchiale aristotelico*, 493. See also Ezio Raimondi, 'Una data da interpretare a proposito del *Canocchiale aristotelico*,' in *Letteratura barocca*, 53.
59 Alessandro Piccolomini, *Annotazioni nel libro della poetica di Aristotile* (Venezia, 1575), 327: 'Non s'ha da poter chiamare propriissimamente metafora quella che sia usata da chi non l'habbia da se stesso trovata, ma l'habbia tolta da qualcun altro, che prima di lui l'habbia posta in uso ... Et benchè dicendo Aristotile ch'ogni sorte d'huomini, fin nel parlar commune che tutto 'l giorno fanno, soglia usar parole metaforiche ... non impediscono le dette parole d'Aristotile che non s'habbia da stimar la verissima e legittimissima metafora quella che noi habbiamo descritta, cioè quando la parola metaforica non è tolta da qualch'un altro, da dallo stesso ingegno nasce di colui che l'usa.'
60 Ibid., 357.

clearly the transformation of the Aristotelian text, operated by an interpreter who is determined to see in the original a justification of his own pre-baroque tendencies. Having thus established his focal point in the understanding of the text of this section of the *Poetics*, Piccolomini proceeds to discuss the characteristics of metaphor. Under the general term of metaphor Piccolomini includes synecdoche, metonymy, antonomasia, and catachresis. He explains at length these figures and he mentions also the fact that allegory, proverb, epithet, and hyperbole can be considered forms of metaphor, as Tesauro amply demonstrated in the following century.

Naturally the major interest in this part of the study is devoted to the metaphor of analogy, of proportion. Piccolomini's definition of this figure is worth repeating, because of its accuracy and completeness. 'Metaphor of analogy,' he says, 'is a transposal of words, founded on similarity arising from quality, or other accident, which mutually and proportionally pertains to the thing, whence the word is transposed, as well as to the thing to which it is brought and placed.'[61] In his accurate study of the origin of metaphor Piccolomini analyses first the opinion of those who maintain that this figure was born out of necessity, to supplement the shortcomings of the language. Then he discusses the view of the theorists, who consider metaphor as a device invented to 'render things more clear,' by placing them visually in a rapid perspective before the intellect. The critic exemplifies this process as follows. When we make a metaphor like 'Desire spurs me to do some things,' we build this figure by transposing the verb *to spur* from the practice of horse riding to human activity. In doing so 'we present to the intelligence of the auditor not only the idea of incitement, but simultaneously the concomitant ideas of eagerness, vehemence, desire, determination.'[62] Finally Piccolomini discusses whether those who maintain that metaphor was born merely as ornament are correct. Rather than choosing any of these theories, the critic says that all

61 Ibid., 299, 'La metafora di proporzione è transportamento di parole, fondato in simiglianza, che nasca da qualità o altro accidente, che comunemente e proporzionalmente si truovi, così nella cosa donde si trasporta la parola, come in quella a cui si porta e si pone.'

62 Ibid., 319, '(Hanno) spessissime volte i nomi alieni, trasportati d'altronde, maggior forza a far conoscere al vivo le cose alle quali si portano, che non hanno li proprii nomi di quelle, mercè di quella somiglianza, che portano seco; la qual'è causa, che fra l'altre virtù e utilità che porta la metafora, una non picciola sia il render la locutione chiara ...' Se si dirà: 'Il desiderio m'inclina, o m'incita, a far la tal cosa, non sarà intesa se non quella pura inclinazione e incitazione; dove che se in luogo di quel verbo *incitare* userò il verbo *sprona*, trasportato dal pungere che facciamo il cavallo, e dirò che il desiderio mi sproni a far la tal cosa, subito s'offerirà all'intelletto di chi ode, non solo quella incitazione, ma la sollecitudine, et la vehementia del desiderio, e 'l dominio, che vi tien sopra.'

three are valid, since each one of them reveals a reason for the rise and the development of metaphor. In the concluding remarks of his analysis of the origin of metaphor Piccolomini makes a statement which is most important to the evaluation of his position as a forerunner of baroque sensibility. He says, in fact, that, 'moved by the desire to bring greater clarity and greater pleasure,' he would use a metaphorical image, regardless of the fact that the thing mentioned had a proper name, or it did not.[63]

After he has examined the final cause of metaphorical style, Piccolomini proceeds to study its efficient cause. This of course is *ingegno*, the marvellous faculty that permits man to find analogies and similarities among things. With a striking anticipation of Tesauro and the seventeenth-century metaphorical mentality, the Sienese critic does not limit the field of activity of *ingegno* in its process of association. For him the possibilities to present things in perspective, silhouetted against other things with the rigour of an arithmetic progression and yet initially mysterious, as forms suddenly appearing in a novel order, are practically infinite. Piccolomini in fact states that there is no thing so diverse, different and contrary to another thing, that someone who examines both in depth may not find some agreement, or similarity, or affinity between them, be they greater or lesser.[64] With reference to Tesauro, Ezio Rai-

---

63 Ibid., 322: 'Ma s'io vorrò trasportar a qualche cosa d'altronde il nome, non con altra intenzione, nè per altra causa, che o per farla più chiara e più manifesta, o per generar diletto, e in tal caso, a habbia quella tal cosa nome appropriato, o non l'habbia, non si potrà dire ch'a ciò m'induca la necessità di nominarla; et conseguentemente non sarà la necessità causa di tal metafora, salvo che per accidente, se la cosa non harà nome, ma si doverà dire che il voler io con questo nome metaforico e trasportato generar in colui che ode maggior cognitione d'essa cosa, o maggior diletto, sia la causa di tal metafora. Posciachè quando ben quella tal cosa non havesse appropriato nome, non per questo nascerebbe la metafora, ch'io uso in nominar, tal cosa da necessità, salvo che per accidente. Posciachè essendomi io nel trasportar il nome con qualche somiglianza o convenientia indotto, e molto principalmente dal voler cagionar maggior notitia, o maggior dilettazione, tanto la trasporterei se quella tal cosa havesse prima il nome, quanto se non l'havesse.'
64 Ibid., 322: 'Essendo dunque questa la forma delle metafore, facil cosa è di vedere che altra causa effettiva d'esse non si debba stimare, che quegli ingegni e quegli intelletti, che son habili a trovare nelle cose le convenientie e le somiglianze, che son tra esse; e trovate che l'hanno, le san ben accomodare in trasportar il nome d'una cosa all'altra, havendo già noi detto non si poter trovar cosa, tanto a qual si voglia altra cosa diversa, differente e contraria, che chiunque ben dentro le consideri e tutti li lor accidenti e tutti gli usi loro e rispetti esamina, non truovi qualche convenientia, o somiglianza, o affinità tra di loro, o maggiore, o minore, o in più numero, o in manco numero, secondo che più vicine e congiunte saranno insieme.' See also p. 359: 'Con tutto adunque che molti precetti e regole insegnar si possino per il conoscimento e per la formazione e per la fabrica delle buone metafore ... non si può nondimeno insegnare in particolare questa, o quella, o quell'altra meta-

mondi says that the seventeenth-century critic enriches the Aristotelian definition of metaphor with new values and, although guardedly, he makes of it a medium of 'associazionismo creativo e non mimetico.'[65] This observation is indeed acute and extremely relevant to the understanding of baroque poetry, and not only in Italy. But we must again stress that Tesauro's way was prepared for him by the sixteenth-century commentators of the *Poetics*. In his analysis of metaphor Piccolomini loses sight of the Aristotelian conception of the work of art as a likeness, or reproduction (ὁμοίωμα), of an original. If he is willing to choose the metaphorical image, even when something can be defined with its proper name, it is evident that he prefers to represent by association, rather than by similarity. Whether the critic is aware that in manifesting this tendency he is shaking some of the foundations of the Aristotelian system of aesthetics is a moot question.

As we mentioned before, for Piccolomini the principal merit of a metaphor (once it is constructed in obedience to the norms of correct correspondence and decorum) is its novelty. The main reason for this is the fact that only original metaphors can clarify something and at the same time bring pleasure. The relationship between the didactic power of metaphorical language and the pleasure that it provides to the reader is already expressed by Piccolomini in terms that will be developed later, but not basically changed, by Tesauro, and this *post factum*, that is to say after the experience of Marinistic poetry. According to Piccolomini the reader of metaphorical poetry is obliged to rapidly re-run the avenues, already treaded by the *ingegno* of the poet, and thus discover, as an almost autonomous act, particular characteristics of a given entity, fact, or action. So the pleasure experienced is in actuality the gratification of discovery and it is also the feeling of following the dynamics of creation in a fashion hitherto unsuspected. Thus a new, more intense, and more intimate relationship is established between author and reader.[66] It is precisely in order

fora; conciosiachè non possa qual si voglia precettore insegnarci come, volta per volta che ne faccia di bisogno, veggiamo e con l'intelletto penetriamo quello che sia di simile tra le cose fra di lor dissimili, com'è necessario che si faccia nel formar le metafore, non potendo un precettore antivedere e indovinare tutte le cose che nelle occorrentie del parlare ci siano per venir innanzi, che son quasi infinite.'

65 Ezio Raimondi, *Letteratura barocca*, 7–8.

66 Alessandro Piccolomini, *Annotazioni nel libro della Poetica d'Aristotile*, 325: 'Ben è vero che, quanto all'effetto che in coloro che l'odono suol far la metafora, la prima volta che viene all'orecchie loro, che è di recar loro chiarezza e diletto, quando avverrà ch'alcuno senta usare una parola metaforica, com'è a dir pastore in luogo di re, non più sentita da lui, il medesimo effetto farà rispetto a lui cotal parola, se colui che l'usa l'arà tolta da altri, che la farebbe s'egli fusse il vero inventor di quella ... Col frequentare d'udirsi e d'usarsi si vien tuttavia manco a con-

to maintain this active type of reading that Piccolomini warns against the danger of building metaphor on elements which are too distant, or too analogous, or obscene and offensive, or simply banal.[67] The origin of *meraviglia* is fully justified on the psychological level, as the natural reaction to active reading of metaphorical poetry, a type of exercise which involves a keener participation than the reading of self-evident images. *Meraviglia* then is the sense of surprise at having discovered something unknown and unsuspected before.

At the end of his discussion of metaphor Piccolomini seems to realize that in actuality it constitutes a long digression, which does not have much to do with the task of explaining Aristotle's *Poetics*. However, in a rather subdued fashion the critic expresses the hope that his work was not in vain and without purpose.[68] The rise of Marinistic poetry fully

siderare quella somiglianza, dove la detta parola metaforica è fondata e per conseguente si viene a far minore la maraviglia di quella novità e il diletto, che se ne suol prendere, essendo l'assuefazione e l'uso nemici della maraviglia e conseguentemente del diletto, che dietro segue all'ammiratione ... Tra le altre virtù che ha d'havere la buona metafora una è che dee recar chiarezza alle cose, per la notitia ch'ella genera, e per conseguente dee recar diletto, per la naturale inclinatione di sentir dilettatione delle cose che da lui nascono, amandole come cose proprie, il che consegue egli in udir la buona metafora, mentre che la somiglianza, che reca la parola trasportata, fa che nel concludere egli con veloce argomento la notitia della cosa di cui si parla, gli paia in un certo modo haver da se medesimo guadagnato cotal notitia e per conseguente ne prende dilettatione.'

67 Ibid., 356–7. Discussing the defects of metaphors and warning against the danger of superficiality, Piccolomini says: 'Comparationi ... fondate più tosto in medesimità, che in somiglianza ... non potrebbero far l'uffitio conveniente alle metafore, come quelle che, per la loro soverchia superficialità, non possono porre nell'animo di chi ode alcuna impressione di nuova notitia, o occasion alcuna di procacciarsela: per conseguente non lo commoverebbero, nè l'affettionerebbero di dolcezza alcuna.' In his definition of metaphor Tesauro says: 'Quinci ella (metafora) è di tutte l'altre (figure) la più pellegrina, per la novità dell'ingegnoso accoppiamento, senza la qual novità l'ingegno perde la sua gloria e la metafora la sua forza. Onde ci avvisa il nostro Autore (Aristotile) che la sola metafora vuol'esser da noi partorita, e non altronde quasi supposto parto cercata in prestito. Et di qui nasce la maraviglia, mentre che l'animo dell'uditore, dalla novità sopraffatto, considera l'acutezza dell'ingegno rappresentante e la inaspettata immagine dell'obbietto rappresentato. Che s'ella è tanto ammirabile, altrettanto gioviale e dilettevole convien che sia, perchè dalla maraviglia nasce il diletto, come da' repentini cambiamenti delle scene e da' mai più veduti spettacoli tu sperimenti. Che se il diletto recatoci dalle retoriche figure procede (come ci 'nsegna il nostro Autore) da quella cupidità delle menti umane d'imparar cose nuove senza fatica e molte cose in picciol volume, certamente più dilettevole di tutte l'altre figure ingegnose sarà la metafora, che, portando a volo la nostra mente da un genere all'altro, ci fa travedere in una sola parola più di un obieto.' *Canocchiale aristotelico*, 178–9.

68 Alessandro Piccolomini, *Annotazioni nel libro della Poetica d'Aristotile*, 366: 'Ma troppo forse mi son dilungato in questo, quantunque non in tutto, s'io non m'inganno, senza proposito, o inutilmente.'

proved that the direction taken by his investigation was not to be lost among his immediate successors.

Already in 1562 Francesco Patrizi da Cherso was protesting against the excesses to which the interest in stylistic complexities was leading his contemporaries. 'How blessed the world would be,' he exclaimed, 'had so many ornaments never been introduced, since they obscure the science of things.'[69] As we indicated elsewhere,[70] the Platonic philosopher accused the Aristotelians of his time of giving precepts for rhetoric, while thinking that they were teaching the art of poetry. Although himself a forerunner of seventeenth-century critical positions, Patrizi was correct, at least partly, in this accusation, as the tradition of the theory of metaphor is in itself sufficient to prove. What the philosopher did not foresee was the favour with which both the interest in stylistic ornamentation and the fusion of rhetorics and poetics was to be welcomed by the generations immediately following. The great commentators of the *Poetics* elaborated a theory of metaphor, which, in its basic structure, would only be amplified in the following century. The works of Robortello, Lombardi – Maggi, Vettori, Castelvetro, and Piccolomini provide a necessary and significant link between theorists like Tesauro and sixteenth-century critical literature.

69 Francesco Patrizi, *Della retorica dieci dialoghi* (Venetia, 1562), 31: 'Che beato il mondo s'egli non si fossero introdotti tanti ornamenti de' parlari, i quali ci hanno oscurato la scienza delle cose.' Quoted also in G. Morpurgo Tagliabue, *La retorica aristotelica e il barocco*, 127.
70 Francesco Patrizi da Cherso, *Della poetica*, ed. D. Aguzzi-Barbagli (Firenze, 1969), I, xiv.

C.P. BRAND

Tasso, Spenser, and the *Orlando Furioso*

THE RELATIONSHIP between *The Faerie Queene* and Italian romance has been the subject of an extensive critical literature and any further work in this field requires some justification.[1] The purpose of this article is not to reconsider the question of Spenser's indebtedness to Ariosto and Tasso, but to examine comparatively the reactions of the two later poets to the *Orlando Furioso* and to note en passant the extent to which their attitudes were in some cases already anticipated by Ariosto. So prominent indeed was Ariosto's poem in the eyes of critics and poets in the later sixteenth century that it could almost be said to have dominated Tasso's thinking and to a great extent to have conditioned the *Gerusalemme Liberata*; and we know, of course, that Spenser from an early date in the composition of *The Faerie Queene* was concerned to 'emulate and ... overgo' Ariosto. Both Tasso and Spenser inherited the attitudes of the latter sixteenth-century critics of the *Furioso*, and in three fields in particular their poems are closely affected by the current critical discussions.[2] These one could broadly categorize as relating to structure, style or tone, and morality,

---

1 The subject is so central that it enters most of the critical literature on Spenser. Apart from the standard works of Neil Dodge, S.J. McMurphy, E. Koeppel, H.H. Blanchard, and A.H. Gilbert, I have found much of interest in R.M. Durling, 'The Bower of Blisse and Armida's Palace,' *Comparative Literature*, VI (1954), 335–7; J. Arthos, *On the Poetry of Spenser and the Form of Romances* (London, 1956); G. Hough, *Preface to The Faerie Queene* (London, 1962); R.M. Durling, *The Figure of the Poet in Renaissance Epic* (Cambridge, Mass., 1965); A. Bartlett Giamatti, *The Earthly Paradise and the Renaissance Epic* (Princeton, NJ, 1966).

2 For the critical reaction to Ariosto in the sixteenth century, see especially G. Fumagalli, *La fortuna dell'Orlando Furioso in Italia nel secolo XVI* (Ferrara, 1910); Maxime Chevallier, *L'Arioste en Espagne* (Bordeaux, 1969); W. Binni, *Storia della critica ariostesca* (Lucca, 1951); R. Ramat, *La critica ariostesca* (Firenze, 1954).

and I propose here to consider, in turn, certain aspects of these which have generally been neglected by previous writers and to note how the two poets separately interpreted each problem and reacted to it in the composition of their own poems.

Problems of structure were among the most warmly debated topics in neo-Aristotelian criticism and it is unnecessary to stress the preoccupation of many epic theorists with Ariosto's apparent lack of any dominant single theme. Tasso's *Discorsi* and his *Allegoria* and Spenser's 'Letter to Raleigh' show their concern with this question,[3] and I do not wish to pursue this except to remark that it is already an important consideration for Ariosto and his predecessors. It is perhaps inevitable in the Renaissance treatment of romance. Pulci in the *Morgante* began with a disjointed romance to which he added in his later cantos an account of the defeat of Roncisvalles quite different in structure and tone; and Boiardo's first Book of the *Orlando Innamorato*, with its scattered adventures and serial technique, is similarly very different from the second, with its grand design of a united infidel attack upon France. So too the revision of the *Furioso* shows Ariosto's anxiety over questions of structure: the changes made for the 1532 edition, with the additional cantos concerning Ruggiero and Bradamante at the very end of the poem, established this as clearly the most continuous and dominant thread in his tapestry, and his other additions may well have been principally motivated by his desire to establish a better balance in the distribution of his material; and the *Cinque Canti* provide further evidence of Ariosto's concern for greater structural coherence – in the continuation of the Ruggiero story for example, and the emphasis on the large-scale or joint military venture rather than on the individual encounter.

One aspect of the structural problem which deserves greater attention is the relationship of the episode to the whole. It was much debated in the Cinquecento, particularly in the controversy between Ariostisti and Tassisti in the 1580s: Tasso himself entered the debate, as his letters to his revisers and his *Discorsi dell'Arte Poetica* show – in the latter, episodes are considered to be 'necessarissimi.' In the *Furioso* the episodes had tended to acquire an autonomy and independence of the main threads of the action: some are quite disconnected from the main themes, stories told by or about characters not involved in the rest of the poem (Norandino, Lidia,

---

3 On the composition of *The Faerie Queene*, I have studied particularly the arguments of W.J.B. Owen in 'The Structure of *The Faerie Queene*,' *PMLA*, LXVIII (1953), 1079–1100, and find the evidence still inconclusive. But it does not really affect my purpose here. See my *Torquato Tasso* (Cambridge, 1965), 230–2.

Adonio), or are self-contained adventures in which a leading character plays only a peripheral role (Ginevra, Ricciardetto, Marganorre). Tasso's reaction to this is to reduce very substantially the number of episodes, to give those few episodes relatively more space and prominence than most of Ariosto's and to integrate them in the action through a more thorough involvement of the major characters (Erminia, Armida). Spenser has no such radical approach – the episodes are not reduced in number, they are increased, but they are related explicitly to the moral/allegorical structure. Individual episodes tend therefore to merge into the overall theme. Those deriving from Ariosto may be simplified structurally, as in the adaptation of the Ginevra–Ariodante story which in Ariosto (IV,55) is both extraneous to the main action and complex in its implications. Whom is it about? It can be read as the story of the serving maid, or her false lover, or her wronged mistress or the mistress's lover. Spenser's version (II,iv) simplifies the structure of the episode: this is a tale of one person, the deceived lover and his intemperance; anything extraneous to that is excluded and in case we should mistake it, the Palmer tells us clearly its significance.

The Rocca di Tristano episode too, although extended by Spenser, is in effect simplified: in Ariosto (XXXII,65) it is quite involved: the obligation to fight for a place in the castle is a convention imposed as a result of a previous incident which distracts our attention from Bradamante's adventure, and it is complicated further by the intrusion of the messenger from the Queen of Iceland with her three suitors. Spenser (III,iv) adopts the central motif, the denial of hospitality because of jealousy, and discards the superfluous chivalrous tradition and Ullania; and he underlines the significance of the episode by showing the effects of excessive jealousy which drives the much-guarded Hellenore into the arms of Paridell and leaves her eventually with the Satyres: chastity is not to be enforced.

A further example of this disciplining of the Ariostesque episode is to be seen in the evolution of the Alcina story from Canto VI of the *Furioso*. Here it is a self-contained incident, a single adventure involving the seduction of Astolfo and Ruggiero that could be omitted without damaging the structure of the poem. It is comparatively brief and concentrated within the range of a few cantos; and it is split into two separate phases in the kingdoms of Alcina, representing lust or passion, and of her sister Logistilla, representing reason; the second phase is much briefer, less developed, and less interesting than the first. The allegory is itself episodic, not related to any larger purpose: while it might have been visualized as part of Ruggiero's schooling for his eventual role as founder of the Estense line, Ariosto clearly does not wish us to read this as a significant phase in his hero's development. It is significant that Ruggiero, having battled his way to the island of virtue succumbs almost immediately after this to the temptations of the naked Angelica.

Tasso's Armida clearly derives from Alcina (although there are other sources as well), but the story has evolved considerably, partly to respond to the desire for structural improvement. It has relatively greater prominence in the poem as a whole (it features significantly in four of the twenty cantos) and the repetition of certain motifs within it impress it more firmly on our imagination: we have first an account from a previous victim, Guglielmo, in Canto x; then an account from the mago of what the rescuing knights Carlo and Ubaldo must expect (Canto xiv); then the visit of the Christian warriors themselves. The enticing song occurs twice, the naked bathers appear twice, and the idyllic nature descriptions recur three or four times. The explicitly allegorical material is dropped but the episodicity is further reduced by the involvement of Armida in the siege of Jerusalem where she is reunited with Rinaldo; and the distracting and unconvincing rival realm of virtue is excluded.

Spenser's Bower of Blisse derives, of course, very largely from Tasso, but in certain ways his version is closer to Ariosto: in his use of allegory, here related to an overall plan; in his presentation of the virtuous counterpart, the House of Temperance, here expanded and developed poetically so that it balances the Bower in a way that Logistilla's kingdom certainly failed to do in relation to the island of Alcina; and in developing and repeating versions of the story Spenser goes further than Tasso. There are five phases here, spread over the whole of Book ii from Canto i to Canto xii. Thus, what had been an isolated self-contained incident in the *Furioso* is integrated by Spenser and Tasso in their different ways into the structure of their poems.

It is unnecessary perhaps to insist that the same trends are apparent in the canto-structure of the three poems. Ariosto's frequent change of subject was part of the romance tradition which he inherited from Boiardo but which he carried further than his predecessor and insisted on as a vital component of his narrative technique:

> ... perché varie fila a varie tele
> uopo mi son, che tutte ordire intendo. (ii,30)[4]

The effect is that brilliant kaleidoscope of changing patterns in which an overall design, if it is there, is forgotten. Tasso's canto-structure is less

4 '... since I need different threads for the different plots (fabrics), and I shall weave them all.'

complicated than Ariosto's, although it is clearly in the same mould, but there are fewer changes of subject within the canto and they are not highlighted as so often is the case in the *Furioso* (cf. Ariosto's abrupt 'Or lasciamo Rinaldo e torniamo a ...' with Tasso's insidious 'Tancredi intanto ...');[5] nor is the canto ending used so frequently to promote suspense. Spenser similarly tends towards a less broken canto-structure, even in the Ariostesque Books III and IV, where the cantos normally coincide with thematic divisions, and especially in the other books where the narrative thread is seldom broken and the cantos repeatedly end on a pause in the action rather than at a climax as in the *Furioso*.

This comparative lack of interest in suspense is apparent in other aspects of Spenser's narrative technique. Both Ariosto and Tasso are notably dramatic in their treatment of their material; this has often been pointed out with reference to Tasso who was enamoured of the spectacular and the theatrical and who often contrives his encounters in theatrical terms:[6]

> Degne d'un chiaro sol, degne d'un pieno
> teatro opre sarian si memorande;   (XII,54)

and a contrived word-order effects striking *coups de théâtre*, as when Erminia finds the wounded Tancredi:[7]

> Salta di sella e gli discopre il viso
> ed – Oimé (grida) è qui Tancredi ucciso.   (XIX,103)

In Ariosto the dramatic effect is not so recherché, but it is frequent and characteristic and it is alongside Spenser that it strikes us so forcibly. Consider the dramatic presentation of the Ariodante-Ginevra story, with Rinaldo's successive encounters with the monks, the would-be murderers of Dalinda, and with the serving-maid herself. Dalinda's account of the Polinesso–Ariodante conflict comprises effectively a play within a play with the dialogue between the two men followed by the tense balcony-scene; and this leads to two dramatic entrées at the Scottish court where Rinaldo interrupts the fateful duel, and finally the lost Ariodante, believed a suicide, reveals himself in a classic 'agnizione' scene, and the tragedy turns into tragi-comedy. A fine succession of dramatic incident is pre-

5 '... now let us leave Rinaldo and return to...,' 'Tancredi, meanwhile.'
6 'Worthy of a bright sun, worthy of a full theatre would such memorable deeds be.'
7 'She leaps from the saddle and uncovers his face and – Ah (she cries) here is Tancredi, dead.'

sented here with an eye to suspense, surprise, and involvement of the reader in the characters' feelings.

Spenser's version of this story in Book II of *The Faerie Queene* is strikingly undramatic. Guyon finds Phaon lying on the ground 'all soild with blood and myre' and Phaon then tells his tale in a long, measured narrative in due chronological order ending with his killing Claribelle, poisoning his friend Philemon, and attempting to murder the maid too, until the 'madman' beat him to the ground. But this tragic tale has no tragic tension in its presentation – even the grim murders do not disturb the even tempo of Phaon's narrative:

> I home returning, fraught with fowle despight
> And chawing vengeance all the way I went,
> Soone as my loathed love appeared in sight,
> With wrathfull hand I slew her innocent;
> That after soone I dearely did lament:
> For when the cause of that outrageous deede
> Demaunded, I made plaine and evident,
> Her faultie Handmayd, which that bale did breede,
> Confest how Philemon her wrought to chaunge her weede.
>
> (II,iv, 29)

The effect of this treatment, I think, is to reduce the autonomy of the episode: the direct speech of Rinaldo, Dalinda, Ariodante, and Polinesso creates effectively a separate play within the narrative: the reader is involved in their story and temporarily deserts the war of Charlemagne and the pursuit of Angelica. Spenser regains control for the narrative poet who disciplines the errant episode and brings it into the framework of the poem. The same effect is visible for example in the English poet's treatment of Ariosto's parody of chivalry in Canto xx of the *Furioso*. Here the dispute of two knights as to which of them should have to escort the ugly old hag Gabrina is conducted in a lively dialogue where Zerbino's mockery is matched by Marfisa's ingenious solution – the loser shall have the hag. In *The Faerie Queene* most of the parallel dispute between Braggadocchio and Blandamour is reported in Spenser's own words:

> But Braggadocchio said he never thought
> For such an Hag, that seemed worse than nought,
> His person to emperill so in fight.   (IV,iv, 10)

A similar effect is achieved by the substitution of indirect for direct speech in the comfort offered respectively by Angelica and the Palmer to the defeated knights, Sacripante and Guyon (*O.F.* I, 67; *F.Q.*, III,i, 11).

The effect of most of these changes in structure and narrative technique, I have suggested, is that the part is made more obviously subject to the whole. The strand in the plot, the episode, incident, or character loses something of its independence and merges, so to speak, into its background. Ariosto is content to let his separate episodes and incidents have their own autonomy; indeed his policy seems to be to juxtapose a succession of separate episodes or incidents in such a way as to create variety and suspense and thus illustrate his concept of the 'variabilità' of human experience. We cannot control our environment and the virtuous suffer no less than the vicious; we are plunged from fortune into misfortune and back again, and the consequences of intemperance or unchastity are not to be charted in any orderly fashion in the Spenserian manner.

This structural 'variabilità ' is paralleled in Ariosto's poem by a striking 'variabilità' of tone which was equally disturbing to many Cinquecento critics. Ariosto not infrequently leads us to the brink of tragedy and then skips away with a laugh; or he flies off in a fit of exuberant fancy only to plunge down into reality. Consider, for example, Bradamante's pursuit of the magician Atlante who, in order to safeguard Ruggiero, has constructed an enchanted castle on an inaccessible snow-clad mountain. As the enchanter flies down to the earth Bradamante seizes him and is about to cut off his head when she finds, not a threatening devil, but a cringing old man:

> Disegnando levargli ella la testa
> alza la man vittoriosa in fretta;
> ma poi che 'l viso mira, il colpo arresta,
> quasi sdegnando sì bassa vendetta;
> un venerabil vecchio in faccia mesta
> vede esser quel ch'ella ha giunto alla stretta,
> che mostra al viso crespo, e al pelo bianco
> età di settanta anni o poco manco.   (IV,27)[8]

Then we are off again into the realms of fantasy when the enchanter breaks his magic vessels and the castle vanishes into thin air. The incident

8 'Intending to cut off his head, she quickly raises her triumphant hand; but when she sees his face she holds back her blow, as though scorning so mean a revenge: she sees that it is a venerable old man that is so hard pressed, with a sad countenance, and wrinkled face and white hair which show he must be seventy years old or little less.'

is repeated by Spenser in Sansloy's pursuit of Archimago (I,iii, 37) but Ariosto's sudden change of tone is abandoned: before ever he sees Archimago's face, Una has warned Sansloy of his mistake.

There is a similar reaction by Spenser to the extraordinary episode in the *Furioso* where Astolfo fights with the invulnerable Orrilo who chases his own lopped-off limbs and replaces them on his mutilated body. From the realms of farce and fantasy we are suddenly plunged into a scene of macabre realism as Astolfo beheads Orillo and severs the fatal hair:

> E tenendo quel capo per lo naso,
> dietro e dinanzi lo dischioma tutto.
> Trovò fra gli altri quel fatale a caso:
> si fece il viso allor pallido e brutto,
> travolse gli occhi e dimostrò all'occaso,
> per manifesti segni, esser condutto;
> e 'l busto che seguia troncato al collo,
> di sella cadde, e diè l'ultimo crollo. (xv,87)[9]

There is a parallel incident in *The Faerie Queene* where Arthur fights the invulnerable Maleger and eventually drowns him in a lake (II,xi), but here too there is no attempt to reproduce the sudden fluctuations between fantasy and realism so characteristic of Ariosto.

The success of Spenser not merely in giving some structural coherence to Italian romance but also in achieving a very large degree of coherence of tone will be apparent to most readers – what C.S. Lewis called 'the seamless continuity of the whole.' This is effected by many different means, not least by what Coleridge called 'a marvellous independence and true imaginative absence of all particular space and time.' Commenting on this a recent critic notes that 'one feels no sudden jarring shift from the land of "mental space" back to the real world of history and geography, from the green world of Faeryland to the red and white world of Tudor history.'[10] It is remarkable that this should be so in a poem so closely involved with Italian romance. Ariosto's sense of 'geographical space' in the *Furioso* is acute: his hippogriph flies over much of the known world in a series of flights that must have been carefully planned with the aid of the maps and

9 'And holding the head by the nose, she shaves off the hair back and front: she found the fateful hair by chance among the others. The face then went pale and ugly, rolled the eyes, and showed clearly it had been brought to its death, and the body, which was following, lopped off at the neck, fell from the saddle and gave its last jerk.'

10 See T.P. Roche, *The Kindly Flame* (Princeton, NJ, 1964), p. 33.

globes of the Estense library, so that many of his remarkable adventures can be located by us quite precisely on the modern atlas. This confusion of fantasy and reality recurs also in the blurring of historical data with the fictions of the chivalrous tradition. There are, for example, five explicit parallels between events in the poem and the battle of Polesella (1509), in which a Venetian fleet in the Po was routed by a numerically inferior Ferrarese force: the fire-arms, personalities, tactics, and habits of Renaissance warfare recur repeatedly in the fairy-tale atmosphere of Alcina's island or Olimpia's Holland or elsewhere. Tasso's poem, while historically more homogeneous, repeats Ariosto's mingling of geographical reality with supernatural inventions. In the nineteenth century travellers to Jerusalem were known to carry their copy of the *Liberata* with them and identify the scenes described by Tasso. Spenser's rejection of both Ariosto's and Tasso's method of relating romance fiction explicitly to historical and geographical reality is a sign surely that he felt it had not proved successful, and artistically the discord between fact and fiction in the Italian poems has not been resolved satisfactorily in the view of many readers. Spenser's own solution, to separate romance and reality on the level of the narrative but to relate them at the level of allegory is, I think, one of the significant distinctions between his and Tasso's approach to the *Furioso*.

A further important distinction is in the reaction of the two later poets to Ariosto's style. Linguistically Ariosto inherits, partly from Dante, partly from the popular romance and lyric, a strain of forthright, blunt, and realistic diction which Tasso and his friends found crude and distasteful. Ariosto's style is varied, adapted to the constantly changing tone of his narrative, but there is a recurrently casual, conversational note, a use of popular, proverbial imagery, oaths, double-entendres, crude or obscene words. Tasso rejected this: the high tone of the epic was to be preserved and, to this end, pedestrian, realistic detail and prosaic, down-to-earth language are reduced. The task of the epic poet is to ennoble and heroicize human conduct, to raise it above the commonplace. The 'grand style' at which Tasso aims is a deliberate attempt to rival and if possible to surpass the classical poets, especially Virgil; and he inherits a vernacular which, in its attempt to prove its strength against Latin, cultivated a grandeur and a gravity which consciously reacted against the plebeian strains in Ariosto's diction.

Spenser did not share this aversion to the realistic and commonplace, to the concrete and crude detail. Classical culture had not yet established its hold on English education and English poets could write with their eye on the object rather than on the *Aeneid* or the *Metamorphoses*. Spenser is quite capable of grandeur but, as Graham Hough says, 'he is utterly remote from any neo-classical notion of continuous decorum' – witness the strange allegory of the human body in *The Faerie Queene* (II,ix), with Appetite and Digestion, the servants, removing scum, and the 'conduit pipes' removing 'fowle and waste liquor.' There is nothing remotely akin to this in the *Liberata*. Spenser replaces many of Tasso's vague, generic images with vivid, realistic detail: the sailing-boat, which Tasso rather suggests to ear and eye than describes,

> Biancheggian l'acque di canute spume,
> e rotte dietro mormorar le senti   (xv,8)[11]

becomes in Spenser:

> So forth they rowed, and that Ferryman
> With his stiffe oares did brush the sea so strong
> That the hoare waters from his frigot ran,
> And the light bubbles daunced all along,
> Whiles the salt brine out of the billowes sprong.   (II,xii, 10)

Indeed Spenser is sometimes more concrete and particular than Ariosto who is, already in 1532, steeped in the Latin poets, so that the attempt to seduce Ariosto's Ruggiero by softening him with 'una coppa di cristallo/ di vin spumante' (in Tasso even more generic, 'una mensa ... apprestata ... di cibi preziosa e cara') is carefully particularized by Spenser:[12]

> In her left hand a cup of gold she held,
> And with her right the riper fruit did reach,
> Whose sappy liquor, that with fulness sweld
> Into her cup she scruzd with daintie breach
> Of her fine fingers, without fowle empeach.   (II,xii, 56)

Not infrequently Spenser's derivations from the Italian poets reveal an extension or intensification of realistic detail, a closer and more attentive observation of a scene and an insistence on the crude detail: his Duessa, for example, with her 'sowre breath' and 'dried dugs' certainly outdoes Ariosto's Alcina in repulsiveness. And for his Fradubio, the man turned

---

11 'The waters whiten with hoary foam and roar as they are cleft behind them.'
12 'A crystal goblet, full of sparkling wine ...,' 'a bountiful and delightful table set with food.'

into tree, Spenser's method is more reminiscent of Dante's in the wood of suicides than to Ariosto's own ironical fantasy in treating Astolfo turned into the myrtle; after their painful conversation the Red-crosse knight

> The bleeding bough did thrust into the ground
> That from the blood he might be innocent
> And with fresh clay did close the wooden wound.   (I,ii, 44)

At a somewhat different level Spenser's reaction to Ariosto's Rocca di Tristano is quite uncharacteristic of Tasso in the tendency away from fantasy and towards a more earthy realism: in the *Furioso* Bradamante's duel for admission to the castle is motivated by an elaborate and fanciful chivalrous convention dating back to an adventure of Tristan; in *The Faerie Queene* the chivalrous paraphernalia are excluded and the disputes are all grounded on current, rational preoccupations: the newcomers need to get out of the rain, the castle-owner needs to safeguard his wife against the libertine wayfarers. Spenser adds to the Ariostesque original a swine-shed where the knights take shelter until it gets too crowded and they threaten to burn the castle down if they are not let in. The desire for verisimilitude is also seen in Spenser's adaptation of Ariosto's story of Ginevra and Ariodante where the serving-maid Dalinda's betrayal of her mistress is (perhaps consciously) rather unconvincingly motivated – she accepts her lover's patently false story that he hopes, through making love to her while she is dressed in Ginevra's clothing, to work off his foolish infatuation for her mistress. Spenser produces a more credible story: Pryene is persuaded to dress in Claribelle's clothes on the grounds that she is really just as beautiful as her mistress and that, bedecked in her finery, she would outshine Claribelle. (Shakespeare in *Much Ado* skated over this 'flaw' in the Italian story, insisting on Margaret's innocence, but neglecting to explain it.)

There is a further sense in which the tone of Ariosto's poem was distasteful to some late Cinquecento critics and notably to Tasso: it was too light-hearted, flippant, even irreverent in its treatment of traditional chivalrous motifs. The poet's attitude to the revered themes of love and war is so often strikingly ironical: he is sceptical about human nature and portrays the weaknesses and inconsistencies of his knights and ladies as readily as he does their heroism or devotion. He smiles at their gesturing and parodies their pretentiousness. While Ariosto's tone is so often gently mocking, Tasso's is quite the reverse: it is not merely that he excludes irony and humour from his poem; he goes further in underlining its seriousness, its magnificence. Where Ariosto smiles at the credulity of the 'volgo' with an occasional broad wink at the more knowing ones:[13]

> Se la fama dal ver non si diparte   (xii,49)

Tasso in all seriousness urges his readers to participate in his feelings of wonder, admiration, dismay: '... (o vergogna comune!)'; '(ahi stolta!)'; '(infausto annunzio!)'; '... (o meraviglia!).[14]

Spenser's reaction to Ariosto's irony is interesting. He is not impervious to the humour of the *Furioso*. On the contrary, a fair number of the derivations from Ariosto are from particularly amusing episodes in the *Furioso*, and I see no reason to doubt that Spenser smiled or laughed at them very much as we do. We cannot certainly equate Spenser with Tasso in the sequence: Boiardo laughed, Ariosto smiled, Tasso was not amused. The general tone of *The Faerie Queene* is, of course, far from light-hearted, but there are not infrequent instances in the poem, particularly in Books ii and iii, of an ironical humour quite close to Ariosto's: the prologue to Book ii, for example, with its insistence on the reality of Fairyland

> Who ever heard of th'Indian Peru? ...;

the apology at the beginning of Book iii, Canto ix, for the 'odious argument' he is about to embark on. The ironical tone of the episode where the Squire of Dames establishes the rarity of chastity is very akin to Ariosto's treatment of the same theme, and there are jests too, half at himself, half at his readers, about the progress of his tale, very much in Ariosto's style:

> But well I weene, ye first desire to learne,
> What end unto that feareful Damozell ...   (iii,vi, 54)

Ariosto's ironical presentation of the knights reluctant to duel in the rain is repeated by Spenser; so too is his scene of the lover who magnanimously allows his lady to choose between him and his rival and is then furious at the outcome.[15] From these and many other instances it is quite clear to us that Spenser understood and appreciated Ariosto's humour and that he was not averse to reproducing it in his own poem.

It is, however, also clear that Spenser did not consider an Ariostesque

13 'If report does not part company with truth.'
14 'Oh, common shame!'; 'Oh, foolish one'; 'inauspicious news'; 'Oh, marvel.'
15 Cf. *O.F.*, xxxii,65 and *F.Q.* iii, ix; *O.F.* xxviii, 107 and *F.Q.*, iv, v,27.

irony an appropriate tone for his poem as a whole and that he turns with Tasso towards a more serious interpretation of the romance tradition. For the conquest of Jerusalem by the crusaders irony would have been quite out of place; for the presentation of the 'twelve moral virtues' it was also out of place except that the fairy-land setting in which the virtues are enacted did not have to be taken quite so seriously. Spenser then is concerned to show that he means what he says and it is rarely that he permits himself such an open laugh as Ariosto. Where he uses Ariosto's comic material, the humour, as Dodge pointed out long ago, is notably tamer or toned down. But one can go further and show how several episodes where Ariosto mocks at the fragility of passions and principles are reconstructed by Spenser to emphasize a serious moral lesson. In the Ginevra story for example, the romantic devotion of Ariodante, which drives him to fling himself from a rock into the sea when he believes Ginevra unfaithful, does not survive the shock of his ducking and he changes his mind and swims out. Spenser ignores this and causes the unhappy Phaon in a fit of rage to murder his lady, his rival and almost murder the serving-maid in a tragic tale of intemperance.

Spenser also ignores another superb flash of Ariosto's irony in the scene where the pagan Ferrau courteously offers a lift to his rival Rinaldo so that they can both chase off after the fleeing Angelica:[16]

Oh gran bonta de' cavalieri antiqui!

The episode is characteristic of Ariosto – in Boiardo's poem in similar circumstances the Christian makes a smilar proposal and the pagan unceremoniously turns it down. Spenser repeats Ariosto's motif – he was surely charmed by its irony. But the theme is too serious for this near-parodying and his almost literal translation of the Italian has a different origin: two paragons of valour and virtue, Guyon and Britomart, come into conflict, and Guyon is unhorsed by Britomart's enchanted weapon; he is much disturbed at this but is persuaded to accept his defeat graciously by the Palmer who uses the arguments employed by Ariosto elsewhere with some irony (it was the fault of the horse). But the Palmer's reconciliation of the two knights in The Faerie Queene is a serious matter:

> Thus reconcilement was between them knit
> Through goodly temperaunce and affection chaste.   (III,i, 12)

16 'Oh what great virtue in those knights of old!'

and becomes an occasion for the celebration of the chivalrous ideal. The tone of the episode thus changes and the moral becomes dominant.

This adaptation of romance to the changed religious and moral temper of late sixteenth-century Europe is perhaps the most striking feature of Tasso's and Spenser's poems and it is hardly necessary to insist how they reflect Reformation and Counter-Reformation attitudes in their respective countries. Tasso's answer to the opponents of the 'licentiousness' and 'empty inventions' of the romances was to choose a religious and historical subject; Spenser's was to use the romance for moral and political allegory. In each case Ariosto's material and methods were adapted to different ends. The *Liberata* repeats Ariosto's pattern of a holy war complicated by love-adventures and enchantments; but the fighting is concentrated on the conquest of the holy city, the love-passions are the work of the devil who is trying to thwart the crusaders, and the 'enchantments' are largely the miracles worked by a Christian deity who surveys the scene from above with a Homeric grandeur. In both poems we have duels, sieges, knights seduced by wicked ladies in enchanted gardens, pastoral idylls, self-sacrificing lovers, glorious final victories delayed only by the machinations against the leading knights.

Spenser's intention is essentially similar, to exploit Ariosto's successful precedent but to use it for his own special ends. His method then is to allegorize the romance, not quite in the way the Cinquecento commentators had allegorized the *Furioso*, seeing in each of the incidents an *exemplum* of virtue or vice. Spenser does, of course, exploit Ariosto's explicit allegory (as in the Alcina episode) or elaborate the incipient or potential allegory of Ariosto's narrative (as in the story of Bradamante, who inspires Britomart). But often he adapts the Italian source to illustrate a moral clearly not applicable to Ariosto's material, or he inverts Ariosto's narrative as though to show, not what happened in the *Furioso*, but what in a more instructive poem might have happened.

To take the former procedure first, Ariosto's Rocca di Tristano is a story of ill-founded jealousy, where the suspicious husband is shown up for the fool he is and punished accordingly; in Spenser's version of the story the suspicions of Malbecco are only too well justified: no sooner does Paridell force his way in than Hellenore arranges to elope with him and she ends up as concubine to the Satyres. This is not, in other words, a story of ill-founded jealousy but of unchastity, which has no place in Ariosto's story. Similarly, in adapting another of Ariosto's tales of jealousy, that of Ariodante and Ginevra, Spenser changes significantly the moral significance of the episode: Ariosto shows how the senses can be deceived under the influence of passion: Dalinda believes Polinesso to be faithful when he is faithless; Ariodante believes Ginevra has deceived him when she has not. Love makes them prone to deception, as it does Phaon and Pryene in *The Faerie Queene*, but whereas Dalinda and Ariodante are ready to sacrifice themselves for their love, Philemon is driven into a blind rage that leads him to murder. It becomes a story of intemperate anger which has no place in the *Furioso*.

At other points in *The Faerie Queene* an Ariostesque situation is reversed: we are reminded closely of a precedent in the *Furioso* where the situation developed very differently. The unchaste Malecasta's intrusion into Britomart's bed recalls the seductive Alcina's arrival in Ruggiero's, but the outcome is quite different: Ruggiero yields to temptation while Britomart draws her sword on Malecasta.[17] The wounded Medoro and his nurse Angelica end up in an amorous idyll in a shepherd's cottage; but the wounded Timias cured by Belphoebe gets no encouragement at all from his chaste nurse.[18] Ariosto's Isabella in the robbers' cave is reminiscent of Spenser's Aemylia in the cave of the 'salvage man,' but while Isabella's downfall is caused by her lover's false friend Odorico, Aemylia's lover's friend ensures his release from captivity and happy reunion with his lady by his self-sacrificing impersonation of his friend in prison.[19] The situation in Ariosto where the brave Grifone is impersonated by the cowardly Martano, who steals the honour his companion has won in the tourney, is reversed in Spenser where Cambel puts on Triamond's armour in order to redeem his friend's reputation.[20]

A further example of Spenser's moralization of Ariosto's material is seen in his utilization of Angelica who, as Miss McMurphy pointed out,[21] reappears in several different guises in *The Faerie Queene*. There are obvious parallels in the situation of the two Florimells and of Belphoebe to that of Ariosto's character, but Angelica's situation is so to speak reversed in *The Faerie Queene* in Book I, where the lady asking for help is Una, representing truth and faith. Both she and Angelica have offered themselves as the prize, in each case we should note, before the poem begins, so that the first cantos open with the same situation, prepared in Ariosto's case by Boiardo and in Spenser's case by the 'Letter to Raleigh.' The lady is separated from her various escorts, flees when rivals fight over her; as Angelica nurses the wounded Medoro and takes him to the

17 Cf. *O.F.*, vii,26 and *F.Q.*, iii, i,62.
18 Cf. *O.F.*, xix,26 and *F.Q.*, iii, v,54.
19 Cf. *O.F.*, xiii,20 and *F.Q.*, iv, viii,56.
20 Cf. *O.F.*, xvii,110 and *F.Q.*, iv, iv,20.
21 S.J. McMurphy, *Spenser's Use of Ariosto for Allegory*, in University of Washington's *Publications on Language and Literature*, xxi (1924), 36.

shepherd's cottage, Una saves the Red-crosse knight from Despair and takes him to the House of Holiness; and the semblance of Angelica which deludes Orlando is paralleled by the semblance of Una which deceives St George. The narrative parallel is unmistakable, but the moral situation is reversed: Angelica is a distraction from the path of duty, and in any case her maidenly charm is a delusion. Who believes her when she swears she is a virgin? Not Ariosto:

> Forse era ver, ma non però credibile
> A chi del suo senso fosse signore.   (1,56)[22]

But Una escorted by St George is a serious matter, at whatever allegorical level you consider it, and no one doubts Una's chastity:

> At last it chaunced the proud Sarazen
> To meet me wandering, who perforce me led
> With him away, but yet could never win
> The Fort, that Ladies hold in soverayne dread.   (1,ii, 25)

It is not that Ariosto does not respect chastity, or chivalry, or friendship – he clearly does and he gives us some shining examples of all three. Ariosto cared about moral principles and contemporary social and political problems and his concern is apparent throughout his work; but he recognizes the fragility of human nature and he senses his powerlessness to change his fellowmen; his poem reflects in so many ways the moral temper of his environment and his age. Tasso and Spenser each lived in a different atmosphere, and each in his own way could raise his eyes beyond the imperfect human scene that confronted him: Tasso in a dream of a church militant where a heroic figure could fight and love in a blaze of glory; Spenser in a vision of another Christian ideal of 'vertuous and gentle discipline.' Each of them went back to Ariosto as his starting point and each refashioned the romance to meet his own artistic purposes and cultural situation. But so had Ariosto in his own way refashioned the romance in the hope of making it a worthy representative of *his* age. It proved a long and strenuous task for all three and it is small wonder that none of them succeeded in completing his ambitious work to his own satisfaction.

---

22 'Perhaps it was true, but not however credible to anyone who was master of his senses.'

Frontispiece of A.M. Salvini's *Il Catone*. Florence 1715.
Courtesy of the University of Toronto Library

HANNIBAL S. NOCE

Early Italian translations
of Addison's *Cato*

ADDISON's *Cato*, it will be recalled, was first performed at the Royal Theatre in Drury Lane on 14 April 1713, and within the week John Gay could write: 'Cato affords universal discourse, and is received with universal applause.'[1] That the applause was somewhat less than universal is demonstrated by the number of pamphlets provoked by the play.[2] Among the most censorious is John Dennis's *Remarks upon Cato*, published on 9 July 1713, in which the author sardonically observes that 'things have been carry'd to that amazing Height, either by French Extravagance or English Industry, that a Frenchman is now actually translating this Play into French, which is a thing beyond Example.'[3] The translator was Abel Boyer who affixes the date 'A Londres, ce 20–31 Juillet, 1713' at the end of the *Preface du Traducteur*.[4] That 'English Industry' was perhaps more

---

1 Peter Smithers, *The Life of Joseph Addison* (2nd ed. London, 1968), 259–78 and passim. Gay is quoted on 264. See also Bonamy Dobrée, *Restoration Tragedy 1600–1720*, (Oxford, 1929), Chapter IX and passim; *English Literature in the Early Eighteenth Century, 1700–1740* (Oxford, 1959), 248–9 and passim; and Allardyce Nicoll, *A History of Early Eighteenth Century Drama, 1700–1750* (Cambridge, 1929), 87–8 and passim.

2 Nicoll, *Early Eighteenth Century Drama*, 88: 'It produced a shower of pamphlets such as no other play had done.'

3 John Dennis, *Remarks upon Cato* (London, 1713), 3.

4 For Abel Boyer (1667–1729) see *Dictionary of National Biography*, II, 1015–16. The title page of his translation reads: *Caton-Tragedie-Par Monsieur Addison-Traduite de l'Anglois-Par Mr. A. Boyer ... A Londres-Chez Jacob Tonson ...* MDCCXIII. The *Preface du Traducteur* (pages unnumbered) is followed by the *dramatis personae* including the name of the actor for each role (repeats the cast names listed in the first editions of the *Cato*). Text pagination is 1–92. Quotations are from the *Preface* unless otherwise indicated by page numbers.
A *Caton d'Utique* by François Michel Chrétien Deschamps performed and printed in Paris in 1715 has, according to A.G. Hegnauer, *Der Einfluss von Addisons*

operative than 'French Extravagance' might be inferred from the fact that the translation was published by Jacob Tonson, Addison's and Boyer's publisher, and corroborated by references in the *Preface* to a 'Zoïle Anglois qui a eu l'Audace & la Presomption de se revolter contre le Goût de tout ce qu'il y a de Savant & de Poli dans la Nation Britanique' by attacking the *Cato*, a 'Censeur atrabilaire' whose name the translator will not rescue from the obscurity it deserves. In reality, polemical hyperbole aside, not such an obscure name, for this 'English Zoilus' can be identified with Dennis. It is therefore difficult to refrain from the conjecture that the translation was commissioned by Tonson to counteract, in part at least, Dennis's 'brutal mauling' of the *Cato* in his *Remarks*.[5]

But whatever the immediate cause of Boyer's translation may have been, his translation is pertinent to the discussion of subsequent Italian versions which, as we shall see, constitute a singular and significant achievement in Anglo–Italian literary relations in the second decade of the eighteenth century. Since Boyer's translation is apposite to our subject, we must begin with a brief comment on it. The translation is in prose, a choice Boyer justifies by stating: ''je m'apperçus qu' à la Verité *Caton* pourroit se soûtenir en François par les Caracteres, les Moeurs, & les Sentiments, mais qu'il perdroit beaucoup du coté de la Diction.' He explains this statement by contending that English is richer, more energetic, more permissive in its use of language, whereas French is more timid, more enslaved by rules and custom. Furthermore, English possesses a measured prose 'qu'on nomme Blank Verse' which can sustain itself 'sans le foible Appuy du Clinquant des Rimes.' To warrant his choice Boyer reiterates Madame Dacier's reasons for turning Homer's *Iliad* into French prose by quoting her verbatim – with the due substitution of Addison's name for that of Homer: 'Un Traducteur peut dire en Prose tout ce que Mr. Addison a dit, mais il ne peut le faire en Vers, sur tout en notre Langue, où il faut néces- sairement qu'il change, qu'il retranche, qu'il ajoûte.'[6]

Actually, the changes, cuts, and additions in Boyer's translation are kept to a minimum. There are in the *Caton* contractions, glosses, and interpolations which may be condoned because of the difference between

Cato auf die dramatische Literatur Englands und des Continents in der 1. Hälfte des 18. Jahrunderts (Hamburg, 1912), 62, nothing to do with Addison's play, though it may have been inspired by it ('der nichts mit dem Addison 'schen zu tun hat, obwohl einige Kritiker annahmen, es sei von dem Engländer inspiriert'). Xavier de Courville, *Un apôtre de l'art du théâtre au xviiie siècle, Luigi Riccoboni dit Lélio* (Paris, 1943–58), III (1958), 171, n.53, maintains that Deschamps 'fut à tort accusé d'avoir imité la tragédie anglaise.'
5 Dobrée, *English Literature in the Early Eighteenth Century*, 249.
6 Anne Lefebvre Dacier, *L'Iliade d'Homère* (Amsterdam, 1711), 38.

French and English syntax, but there is also the suppression of poetic images which, no doubt, Boyer found unsuitable to French taste. The following is a fairly typical example:

> His counsels bade me yield to thy directions:
> Then, Syphax, chide me in severest terms
> Vent all thy passion, and I'll stand its shock
> Calm and unruffled as a summer sea
> When not a breath of wind flies o'er its surface.   (182)[7]

translated by Boyer in this manner:

> Il me chargea de suivre les tiens, & deferer à
> tes Sentiments. Ainsi je te permets de me
> reprocher mes Defauts avec la derniere severité,
> & de donner un libre Carriere à tes Transports:
> & je t'assure que j'ecouteray tes Remonstrances
> sans la moindre emotion, & avec la derniere
> Tranquillité.   (16)

On the whole, Boyer can be said to be most faithful to the original in purely expository passages, and less so in emotional or in highly dramatic speeches. He has succeeded in transcribing 'tout ce que Mr. Addison a dit,' but he has done so in a style and manner diverging from the original, and this not merely because he chose prose to render Addison's verse, but because his prose is frequently uninspired and dull. Boyer was, to be sure, aware that in essaying a prose version some of the poetry of the original would be sacrificed, and he consoled himself by arguing that, if what Addison had thought and said would be expressed more simply and less poetically, a prose version 'vaut certainement mieux que tout ce qu'on seroît forcé de lui prêter en le traduisant en Vers.' It is disappointing to find that so much of Addison's poetic diction should be reduced to such pedestrian prose, and therefore Boyer's *Caton* can be characterized as being only a fairly faithful, literal, prosaic translation of the *Cato*. It might, nonetheless, have satisfied that public 'qui a fait paroitre beaucoup

---

7 Addison, *Cato, The Works of the Right Honourable Joseph Addison*, ed. Henry G. Bohn (London, 1871), I, 162–231. Quotations are from this edition. In order to avoid confusion arising from the numbering of scenes, which in the French and Italian versions do not correspond to the original because they follow the convention of dividing scenes according to the entrances and exits of characters, I have used page references throughout.

d'Impatience de voir *Caton* en François'; for us it is relevant because it led directly to the first Italian version of Addison's play.

Between 1713 and 1718 the *Cato* was translated into Italian six times; a remarkable number, especially if we remember that for the same period we have only one French version, while a German translation did not appear until 1735.[8] Two of the Italian translations have not been located, and consequently we know of their existence only through cursory contemporary accounts.[9] The other four are available in their original editions. Among these the first to be printed was *Il Catone*, translated into 'Tuscan prose' by an anonymous author.[10]

The anonymous *Catone*, printed in Amsterdam in 1713, is not a translation of the *Cato*, but rather a faithful rendering in Italian of Boyer's French version, from which it reproduces not only a word-for-word translation of the text but also of the *Préface du Traducteur*. The extent of its

8 A.G. Hegnauer, *Der Einfluss von Addisons Cato*, 96–137: A. Nicoll, *Early Eighteenth Century Drama*, 88. Of the Italian translations pertinent to the period we are discussing, Hegnauer lists Salvini's and mentions Valletta's, Nicoll only Salvini's. For the French see n.4 above. The first complete German translation is by L.A.V. Gottsched, *Cato, ein Trauerspiel*.

9 These are the translations of Nicola Saverio Valletta (1687–1717) and Rodolfo Aquaviva, s.j. (1658–1729).

Thomas Tickell in the introduction to Addison's *Miscellaneous Works in Verse and Prose* (London, 1726), xxiv, referring to the *Cato*, asserts: 'The translation of it into Italian, by Signor Salvini, is very well known; but I have not been able to learn whether that of Signor Valetta [sic], a young Neapolitan Nobleman, has ever been made public.' Further testimony to Valletta's translation is in *Notizie istoriche degli Arcadi morti*, ed. G.M. Crescimbeni (Rome, 1720–1), II, 350. Neither reference states whether Valletta's translation was in prose or verse. I have been unable to discover an extant copy of Valletta's translation either through my own efforts, or by means of the search made at my request by the *Centro Nazionale di Informazioni Bibliografiche* which included all Italian government libraries and the archives of the Accademia dell'Arcadia.

The only testimony to a translation by Aquaviva is that given by P.J. Martello, *Opere* (Bologna, 1723–35), IV (1723), 56, where he states that in the preparation of his own translation of the *Cato* he had consulted ('ho avuta sotto gli occhi') that of Aquaviva, 'literal, and in prose.' I have been unsuccessful in locating a copy of Aquaviva's translation. See also Gustavo Costa, 'Un avversario di Addison e Voltaire: John Shebbeare, alias Battista Angeloni, s.j. Contributo allo studio dei rapporti italo–britannici da Salvini a Baretti (con due inediti addisoniani,' *Atti della Accademia delle Scienze di Torino*, 99 (1964–5), 750, hereinafter referred to as 'Shebbeare.'

Addison's play was again translated, much later in the century and for the last time, by Gaetano Golt who published his translation in Rome in 1776.

10 The title page reads: *Il Catone-Tragedia-Dal Sig. Addison Inglese – composta nella propria lingua – in Verso, e transportata in Prosa-Franzese dal Sig. Abbate [sic] Bojer ... Stampata in Amsterdamo – da Iacomo Desbordes Librajo sul Ponte-della Borsa – E tradotta in Prosa Toscana.*

fidelity to its model can be measured by comparing the Italian to the French version of the lines above quoted:

Egli m'ingiunse di seguire i tuoi, e di condiscendere a' tuoi sentimenti; perciò io ti permetto di rimproverarmi coll'ultima severità i miei difetti, dando libera carriera al vivo tuo zelo; e io ti assicuro che ascolterò le tue correzioni senza il minimo risentimento, e con ogni possibile tranquillità. (14)

As translation of a translation it is peripheral to our subject, and it concerns us here purely as a chronological fact, namely that in the latter part of 1713 an Italian version, albeit once removed, of the Cato was available to Italian readers.

It was not long, however, before the anonymous Catone was replaced, and surpassed, by an Italian translation based on the original, executed with deliberate and careful respect for Addison's text by the author's friend – they had met in Florence – Anton Maria Salvini, eminent classicist, linguist, and academician.[11] Salvini tells us in his preface that he was moved to undertake the translation because the fame of the Cato had reached him from various sources, creating in him a longing to examine it in the original.[12] To do so he set about learning English – he was then in his sixtieth year – by employing a 'metodo etimologico,'[13] by means of which he was able 'in breve,' or, if we can credit another source, in two

11 C. Cordaro, Anton Maria Salvini; Saggio critico-biografico (Piacenza, 1906), includes a list of Salvini's translations: E.W. Cochrane, Tradition and Enlightenment in the Tuscan Academies, 1690–1800 (Chicago, 1961), passim: G. Costa, 'Shebbeare,' 727 ff.

12 A.M. Salvini, Il Catone – Tragedia – Tradotta – Dall'Originale Inglese (Firenze, Guiducci e Franchi, 1715): includes a prefatory letter by Salvini 'Al Benigno Lettore,' iii–vi; the list of characters in the play; a translation of Pope's prologue, 1–3; text of the play 5–80. It was reprinted ten years later with the English text on facing pages under the title Cato – a – Tragedy – By Mr. Addison. Il Catone – Tragedia – Del Signor Addison – Tradotta – da – Anton Maria Salvini – Gentiluomo Fiorentino (Firenze, Michele Nestenus, 1725). A letter of dedication to 'Enrico Mylord Colerane' (Henry Hare, third Baron Coleraine) is signed by Bastiano Scaletti, and is followed by an unsigned preface, 'Benigno Lettore,' which differs from that of the first printing. The rest of the edition reproduces the first with no significant variants. Quotations, except for those indicated from the preface of the first, are from the second edition.

13 Preface (1715), iv. Salvini defines it, rather cryptically, in these terms: 'metodo etimologico, che sulle origini, assonanze, o similitudini tratte da altre lingue, come sopra Luoghi, colloca le parole di quella lingua, che un vuole apprendere, come tante Immagini, da ravvisarsi dalla memoria' ('an etymological method by which the words of the language one wishes to learn are regarded in the fashion of a series of images to be recognized by one's memory, and are arranged, as though upon actual places, on the origins, assonances and similarities provided by other languages').

months,[14] to undertake his translation. He had, moreover, the help and encouragement of English friends living in Florence, for which he expresses his gratitude particularly 'al ... generoso ed ornato Cavaliere Sig. Giov: Moles–Worth, sotto i cui auspicij questa mia traduzione nacque, e al dotto Sig. Lockart, ambedue delle finezze della nostra lingua intendentissimi.'[15] The translation was completed prior to 10 October 1713. This he announced in a letter to Antonio Montauti bearing that date.[16] The following spring, during the carnival of 1714, Salvini's *Catone* was performed 'con bella maniera, e con decoroso apparato'[17] in Leghorn by the Accademici Compatiti.[18] The insistence of Daniel Gould and other English friends residing in Leghorn persuaded Salvini to publish his translation and it was printed in 1715. Daniel Gould was also responsible for forwarding copies of the translation to Addison who in a letter dated 13 July 1716 addressed to Gould writes:

I receiv'd your valuable present (for so I may venture to call it in S᷅. Salvini's incomparable Translation) and have disposed of those 50 copies by the help of my Bookseller, which are to be placed to that ingenious Gentleman's account.[19] I desire you will please to lett me know how I may transmitt to him the money or value of it. His version is wonderfully esteem'd in England by all who understand the Language. I must confess I did not think that a Diction so figured and metaphorical in the original could have run with so much Ease and Beauty in any Foreign Tongue. But when a writer possesses the whole compass of a language, I find he can speak what he will in it with the utmost propriety & elegance.[20]

---

14 Preface (1725), x.
15 Preface (1715), v. 'To the generous and endowed Sir John Molesworth under whose auspices this my translation was born, and to the learned Mr. Lockhart, both of whom fully understand the subleties of our language.' For the relations between Molesworth, who was British envoy to Tuscany 1710–14, and Salvini, see G. Costa, 'Shebbeare,' 728–33.
16 A. Graf, *L'Anglomania e l'influsso Inglese in Italia nel secolo* XVII (Torino, 1911), 261.
17 Preface (1715), v. 'In a fine manner, and decorously staged.'
18 M. Maylender, *Storia delle accademie d'Italia* (Bologna, 1926–30), II, 36–7.
19 Addison must have possessed other copies of this and of the second edition. When Addison's library was sold at auction by Leigh and Sotheby on Monday, 27 May, 1799 and on the four following days, the sale catalogue lists, for the second day's sale, lots 378 'Addison Il Catone Tragedia di Salvini' 4 copies (sold for two shillings), 379 the same 6 copies (two shillings three pence), 380 the same 6 copies (two shillings), and 381 the same 6 copies (two shillings). Since the catalogue reference does not indicate edition, it is impossible to determine which of the 22 copies sold were of the first or second printing.
20 G. Costa, who discovered and published the letter in 'Shebbeare,' 736.

High praise indeed, although one may demur at the precision of Addison's judgment on the 'ease and beauty' of the translation, if he had to rely on those 'who understand the language.'

Before, however, proceeding to a more objective evaluation of Salvini's *Catone*, we must consider his views on translation. Salvini not only extols the role of the translator, but goes so far as to equate it with original composition. When man exercises his faculty of speech he is *translating* ideas into the spoken language; when he writes creatively he does nothing more than express these translated concepts into a more refined and perfect language.[21] Moreover Salvini, consonant with his culture and times, conceived of translation in humanizing and humanistic terms. Not only is the act of translation a means of understanding, interpreting, and appreciating one's own linguistic patrimony, it also serves to enrich it. The translator, by studying a foreign culture, becomes the instrument by which his own national culture is amplified.

The seriousness with which Salvini approached translation, and the high standards he set for himself in accomplishing it are manifested in the statement:

Mi sforzai dunque, per quanto fare per me si potè, di rappresentar fedelmente in primo luogo i concetti degli autori, che io presi a tradurre; in secondo luogo, esattamente al possibile, le parole medesime, e l'espressione; e in terzo luogo, ciò che è il più malagevole, l'aria, il colore, e 'l carattere, che da' sentimenti insieme, e dalle parole, e da qualche altra cosa ancora, che non s'intende, risulta.[22]

This is a clear and concise expression of the criterion and method Salvini used in translating. Bearing it in mind, we can now examine how effective it was in his translation of the *Cato*.

---

21 A.M. Salvini, *Prose toscane* (Firenze, 1715), 535. 'Quello adunque, che noi chiamiamo parlare, non é in verità altro, che un tradurre, dal linguaggio de' pensieri, nel linguaggio delle parole. E quel che si dice comporre, non è altro, che un genere di parlare, cioè di tradurre più raffinato, e perfetto.' ('That, then, which we call speaking is in truth nothing more than a translation from the language of thoughts into the language of words. And that which one calls writing is nothing more than a kind of speaking, that is of translating in a more refined and perfect manner.')

22 A.M. Salvini, *Prose toscane*, 535. 'I endeavoured therefore, as far as I was able, to represent faithfully, in the first place, the ideas of the authors that I undertook to translate; in the second place, as exactly as possible the very words and the expression; and in the third place, that which is most troublesome, the tone, the color, and the character which result from the totality of the sentiments, the words, and of something else which is beyond comprehension.'

Salvini's choice of the unrhymed hendecasyllable as a vehicle for his translation was undoubtedly prompted by his desire to render Addison's blank verse as closely as possible.[23] True, the unrhymed hendecasyllable, more than any other Italian metric form, approximates English blank verse, although it must be remembered that it was also the traditional verse form for Italian classical tragedy. In choosing this particular form he is consistent with his aim of reproducing the expression of the original, or, to be more precise, the external mode of expression. The prosodic exigencies inherent in the verse form used by the translator may account for additions, deletions, and glosses; they may even be a determinant in the selection of a particular word, or in deciding the word order within the verse. All of this is inevitable, and acceptable, in the translation of poetry, provided that the sense and spirit of the original are not distorted. Alterations of this nature, once their existence has been noted, need not concern us further.

Besides fidelity to mode of expression, Salvini maintained that the translator should be faithful to the very words ('le parole medesime') of his original. This becomes an obsession with him with the result that the diction and style of the *Catone* can only be designated as contrived and convoluted. Salvini's translation of the English word used in its literal meaning can range from the right word, to approximation (e.g. 'Those hasty words' – 'le temerarie voci'), to nonsense (e.g. 'his grief / Swelled up so high' – 'E 'l gonfiato dolor'). He can also be misled by his search for cognate words (e.g. 'prompt' – 'pronto'; 'train of ills' – 'treno di guai'; 'grief'd' – 'gravato'), and he can distort the original by the use of learned words or neologisms (e.g. 'my forward cares' – 'l'ultronee mie cure').

If an obsessive preoccupation with the linguistic aspects of the original can lead Salvini into mistranslations of words, phrases, or passages used in their literal sense, he encounters further difficulties when confronted by Addison's metaphors and poetic images. Obviously the task of transposing figurative speech from one language to another is an extremely difficult one, and perhaps the dictum that only a poet can translate a poet is nowhere more applicable. Unfortunately Salvini – exceptionally conversant with classical and modern poetry, a sensitive reader of poetry – was not a poet, though like so many of his contemporaries he wrote verses

---

23 After the *Cato*, Salvini did a translation of Addison's 'Letter from Italy' in which he used the unrhymed hendecasyllable to render Addison's heroic couplets. A manuscript copy of the translation, with the author's emendations, is in the Marucelliana library in Florence, codex MS C 237. The translation was published in Florence (1754).

by the hundreds.[24] His translation, then, of figurative passages in the original are, at best, pedestrian; at worst, they dissipate Addison's poetic image. To illustrate the first category compare

> Thus o'er the dying lamp the unsteady flame
> Hangs quivering on a point, leaps off by fits,
> And falls again, as loth to quit its hold.   (205)

with

> Così cade, e risorge in un sol punto
> Stretta, e mal volentier suo posto lascia
> La tremolante e moribonda fiamma.   (101)

The second category can be exemplified by the concluding verses of the first act, where Addison introduces the highly lyrical image of the 'pure limpid stream' troubled momentarily and then repurified, an image resulting from a delicate poetical balance of realistic elements, contrasted with Salvini's version, where the image is destroyed by the introduction of gross terms logically strung together in discursive association. Another instance of a similar procedure is Syphax's simile which closes the second act. Syphax, the Numidian conspirator against Cato, vividly imagines Cato beset on every side by 'unforseen destruction' and in a simile that is both appropriate to his character and to the situation says:

> So, where our wide Numidian wastes extend,
> Sudden, the impetuous hurricanes descend,
> Wheel through the air, in circling eddies play,
> Tear up the sands, and sweep whole plains away.
> The helpless traveller, with wild surprise,
> Sees the dry desert all around him rise
> And smothered in the dusty whirlwind dies.   (200)

Salvini renders it in this manner:

> Così ne' vasti Numidi deserti
> L'impetuose subite bufere
> Van scherzando per l'aria in fieri giri,

24 *Sonetti di Antonmaria Salvini* (Firenze, 1728), more impressive as a beautiful example of eighteenth-century Italian typography than for the quality of the verses it contains. Quotations in the text are indicative of his limited ability at handling the unrhymed hendecasyllable.

Ravvolgono l'arena e portan via
Gl'interi campi: il viaggiante nudo
D'ogni soccorso con stupore orrendo
A se d'intorno l'arido ermo scorge
Levarsi tutto, e dentro al polveroso
Turbin rapito, ed affogato muore.   (87)

In this passage the translator dispels the sequence of emotions evoked in the original, which poetically prepare the reader for the tragic pathos of the conclusion. He does so by expressing them in terms that are all too prosaic, even sometimes, ridiculous (e.g. 'Van *scherzando* per aria in *fieri giri*': the contradiction created by 'Turbin rapito' (suggesting an ascending action) and 'affogato' (descending action) which depict the poor traveller in the ludicrous situation of being swept up by the whirlwind and drowned at the same time). Salvini, it would seem, was incapable of formulating poetical associations.

Judging the *Catone* on its own merits, apart and distinct from the original, Salvini can be credited with accomplishing a word-for-word, line-for-line translation that Dryden would have classified as a meta-phrase. Salvini was considered a master of prose style by his contemporaries. That his prose style could be alive, limpid, evocative, that it could communicate the author's enthusiasm for his subject can readily be seen by scanning the pages of the *Prose Toscane* or the *Discorsi Accademici*.[25] It is regrettable, therefore, to find the *Catone* so defective in this regard, for the Italian of the play reveals an artificially formal quality that can only be described, in Ciardi's term, as translatorese, a queer language-of-the-study that counts words but misses their living force.[26]

The unsuitability of Salvini's idiom in the *Catone* as dramatic dialogue, as living words that an actor could deliver and communicate to an audience, was soon detected by Luigi Riccoboni, actor-director-producer, theoretician and historian of the theatre, whose *nom de théâtre* was Lelio.[27] He knew that the *Catone* had been performed in Leghorn, but he was also aware that the performance was by amateurs for academicians and a select audience. Wishing to stage the *Cato* in Venice during the season of 1715, he felt compelled to prepare and publish his own version of the play.[28]

25 *Discorsi Accademici di Anton Maria Salvini* (3rd ed., Venice, 1735). See, for example, the prose of *Discorso* xcIII, 326–31, in which Salvini discusses and compares the suicides of Cato and Socrates.

26 John Ciardi, *Nation*, 178 (1954), 525.

27 See n.4 above for Xavier de Courville's authoritative study on Riccoboni.

28 L. Riccoboni, *Il Catone, Tragedia tradotta dall'Inglese* (Venice, 1715). Dedicated

Riccoboni had read the French version of the play and must above all have been excited by the character of Cato, for he was to write later: 'Caton est plus grand que tous les Héros des Tragédies anciennes, & modernes, & pourtant je le trouve toujours homme.'[29] A notable statement coming from an actor who, among other tragic roles, had played Britannicus and Oedipus; a declaration, moreover, which delineates the difference between the classical and eighteenth-century concept of the hero. Besides his enthusiasm for Cato, he admired Addison as a dramaturge and praised him for his ability 'de bien étudier ses spectateurs pour leur plaire.'[30] Riccoboni had started to translate the French version when Salvini's Catone came to his attention. He was about to abandon his own translation and produce Salvini's play when he was confronted by a great difficulty ('non poca difficultà'), namely that of Salvini's language. He found Salvini's Catone

così fedelmente dall'Inglese tradotto, e di così purgatissima Toscana lingua, che non così facilmente sarebbe dagli Attori stato concepito, e poco dagli uditori del basso volgo inteso, come non generalmente di questo studio di buona lingua instrutti.[31]

Both the statement on the 'purgatissima Toscana lingua' and the reference to the inferior knowledge of good Italian by the parterre are at least partially suspect: the first, notwithstanding the adulatory tone, will become evident in the discussion of the changes effected by Riccoboni of Salvini's language; the second, when we remember that a year earlier he had described the Venetian audience as making great strides towards perfection and good taste.[32]

to the Marquis Luigi Albergati, the preface, 'Al Cortese Lettore,' leaves no doubt as to the authorship. The text is also interesting because all verses cut from the actual performance are clearly indicated by quotation marks. A study of the cuts would in itself be relevant as evidence of Riccoboni's taste and of contemporary theatre practice. The largest number of cuts are to be found in the love scenes, but they are also used to avoid repetition and thereby tighten the action of the play, or when not in character.

29 L. Riccoboni, Histoire du théâtre italien (2nd ed., Paris, 1730–1), 317. Incidentally, the work is dedicated to Queen Caroline.

30 L. Riccoboni, Réflexions historiques et critiques sur les différents Théâtres de l'Europe avec les Pensées sur la Déclamation (Paris, 1738), 170.

31 L. Riccoboni, Catone, preface. 'Translated so faithfully from the English, and in so refined a Tuscan idiom that it would not easily have been learned by the actors, and little understood by that part of the audience belonging to the lower classes who are generally not instructed in this study of good language.'

32 Giulio Agosti, L'Artaserse (Venice, 1714). Riccoboni's dedicatory letter to Duke F.M. Pico della Mirandola: 'quanto gagliardamente, ed a gran passi s'incammina

To overcome the difficulty he decided to continue with his own translation, using the French and Salvini translations as models. Intrinsically Riccoboni's *Catone* is an adaptation of Salvini. Interventions from the French version are so negligible as to be almost imperceptible. Riccoboni uses the same verse employed by Salvini, the unrhymed hendecasyllable although he occasionally introduces shorter verses. His main concern is to render dialogue in as natural an idiom as possible without falling into common speech and at the same time maintaining a sustained nobility of tone proper to the subject of the play. And he succeeds. The means he employs to achieve his end are a linguistic reworking of Salvini's text. He simplifies Salvini's lexicon (e.g. abborre > detesta; agogni > brami; ermo > deserto); he rectifies his model's abuse of enclytic forms of the type 'honne,' 'dirammi,' 'presserotti,' 'leviamci'; and he reduces archaic expressions like 'Fisso in ismarrimento' to a more natural 'Sono fuor di me stesso.' Besides lexical and morphological changes Riccoboni (RIC.) also attenuates Salvini's (SAL.) sometimes involuted and often contrived periods. The following examples are representative:

> SAL. Non presserotti a cacciar tua passione (91)
>
> RIC. Io non ti chiedo a soffocar tuo affetto (49)
>
> SAL. non mai / Con tue mischiar le mie congiunte mani (95)
>
> RIC. Giuro, alla tua non mai unir mia destra (53)
>
> SAL. Con piacere e stupor io resto attonita (127)
>
> RIC. Cieli! stupor, piacer n'occupan l'alma (69)
>
> SAL. Vuoi ch'io con vil sommissione il numero
> Di schiavi a Cesar gonfi, e a Roma vinta
> Io dia la causa, ed un Sovran confessi? (133)
>
> RIC. Io salvarmi? e perchè? perchè Catone
> Di Cesare gli schiavi accresca anch'esso?
> Perchè con vile omaggio io dia per vinto
> L'onor di Roma, ed un Sovran confessi? (72)
>
> SAL. Son gli amici imbarcati? Puossi far
> Alcuna cosa ancor per lor servigio? (157)
>
> RIC. Son gli amici imbarcati? Altro ci resta
> A far per loro? (87)[33]

il nostro uditorio alla perfezione, ed al buon gusto' ('how valiantly, and with what great strides, our audience advances on the way towards perfection and good taste').

33 The corresponding verses in Addison are:

I would not urge thee to dismiss thy passion (201)
Never to mix my plighted hands with thine (203)

The naturalness of Riccoboni's dialogue is all the more evident when thus contrasted to the ponderous idiom of his model. By relying on his experience as an actor, on the actor's ear for the idiom most effective on the stage, Riccoboni produces a version of the *Cato* that is alive, modern, and eminently playable. That his audience thought so too can be gleaned from the comment that his *Catone* 'a été représentée sur notre Théâtre avec grand succès.'[34]

A quite different Italian version of the *Cato* from those examined is the *Catone* of Pier Jacopo Martello.[35] He was, not unlike Addison, esteemed by his contemporaries as a man of taste, a poet, and a playwright. The author of thirty-four plays, fourteen of which are tragedies (and of these, four deal with Roman subjects), he experimented with all dramatic genres. In a treatise, *Della tragedia antica e moderna* (1714), he demonstrates a sure and profound knowledge of tragic theories, as well as a deep insight into contemporary theatre conventions and practices. He had also introduced a new verse form for the theatre, a fourteen-syllable line in rhyming couplets, akin to the French Alexandrine. This is the metric form he uses for the *Catone*, and if it adequately imitates the rhythm of Pope's heroic couplets in the prologue, it is less successful with Addison's blank verse since the translator, for metric reasons, must needs have recourse to some deletions and a great many more additions.

Martello differs from Salvini not only in the prosody of their respective

With pleasure and amaze, I stand transported   (214)
Would Lucius have me live to swell the number
Of Caesar's slaves, or by a base submission
         – are my friends embarked?
Give up the cause of Rome, and own a tyrant?   (216)
Can anything be thought of for their service?   (225)

34 L. Riccoboni, *Histoire*, I, 317.
35 Bio-bibliographical information on Martello is contained in P.J. Martello, *Scritti critici e satirici* (Bari, 1963), 499–509. See also G. Costa, 'Shebbeare,' 743–51.

    Il Catone tratto dall'Inglese dell'Addison (sic) was first published in *Opere di Pier Jacopo Martello* (Bologna, 1723–35), IV (1723), 51–142. It is preceded by a dedicatory letter to the 'Principessa Panfilia' (Teresa Grillo Panfilia, Princess of Valmontone) and by a 'Proemio,' In this preface, which is not dated, the author tells us that he completed his version in Rome 'oggi ha un'anno' ('a year ago today'). Martello was in Rome as secretary to the Bolognese Embassy to the Holy See between 1708 and 1718. The translation could not have been finished before 1715 when two volumes of his plays (*Teatro italiano di P.J.M.*, Rome, 1715) were published without including the *Catone*, and for the additional reason that he refers to Salvini's *Catone* as a model. The *terminus a quo* for the translation is 1715, the *terminus ad quem* 1718.

    Three of Martello's plays, *L'Ifigenia in Tauride*, *La Rachele*, and *L'Adria*, were performed by the Riccoboni troupe, the latter in the same season with Riccoboni's *Catone*.

versions of the *Cato*, but more significantly he is diametrically opposed to him in his views on translation. Martello categorically states: 'Non da accorto, non da Maestro Traduttore è, parola per parola rendere fedel-mente.'[36] Moreover Martello asserts that his aim in attempting a new version of the *Cato* is very different ('diverso troppo') from Salvini's aim, acutely analysed by Martello in these words:

Il suo forse era (siccome io giudico) prestarci un'idea, non solamente del come pensisi, ma del come esprimasi un pensamento all'Inglese; di modo che non altro quelle formole di nostrale, se non i vocaboli, avessero. E in fatto, se a me accades-se di udire un Uomo così favellarmi, già indovinerei uno di quelli Oltramontani lui essere che l'Idioma nativo, comechè Italiane parole pronunziando, disimulare non sanno. Nè quel ch'io giudico è temerario, asserendosi dallo stesso Salvini nel suo Prefazio che l'Inviato Inglese alla Corte Real di Toscana, Cavaliere Gio: Moles Worth, quanto a straniero lice, della Toscana favella intendente, avea la sua versione approvata; il che certamente non sarebbe avvenuto, se Signore l'Inviato non avesse ravvisate le formole sue delle nostre parole vestite.[37]

The first part of this statement re-echoes Riccoboni's polite and encomias-tic appraisal of the Salvini translation ('così fedelmente dall'Inglese tra-dotto') which Martello elaborates with telling precision. The polemical barbs contained in the rest of the quotation have been recently explained on the grounds of literary rivalry, and ideological differences, between Salvini and Martello.[38] But this does non invalidate the basic correctness of Martello's judgment on Salvini's language.

Martello frankly confesses that he did not know English and, like Ric-coboni before him, admits, in spite of his strictures on Salvini's idiom,

36 P.J. Martello, *Catone*, 58. 'It is not like a wise, a master translator, faithfully to render word for word.' For a more complete statement on Martello's views on trans-lation, see H.S. Noce, 'Tre lettere inedite di P.J. Martello a Cornelio Bentivoglio,' *La Rassegna della Letteratura Italiana*, 64 (1960), 245–6.

37 P.J. Martello, *Catone*, 55–6. 'Perhaps his was (as I believe) to give us an idea not only of how one thinks, but of how one expresses a thought in an English manner; in such a way that those formulas should contain nothing of ours except the words. And in fact, if perchance I were to hear a man speak to me in such a manner, I would immediately guess that he was one of those ultramontanes who, while pro-nouncing Italian words, cannot hide their native language. Nor is my judgment foolhardy since the same Salvini in his preface states that the English Envoy to the Royal Court of Tuscany, Sir John Molesworth, who as far as it is possible for a foreigner, was proficient with Tuscan, had approved his translation. This certainly would not have happened if the Envoy had not recognized formulas familiar to him clothed in our words.'

38 G. Costa, 'Shebbeare,' 748.

that he has used Salvini's translation and another translation in Italian prose by a Father Aquaviva;[39] he further declares that he has not seen the French version. Like Salvini, Martello consulted English friends in Rome and was helped in the translation by his eldest son, Carlo, who knew English.[40]

Not only is Martello displeased with Salvini, he is also dissatisfied with Addison. He finds three main points to criticize in the *Cato*: the portrayal of Cato, the treatment of Caesar, and the on-stage death of the protagonist. Cato is too imbued with English spirit. The English face dangers in cold blood and with audacity, they neither exhibit too much pleasure in prosperity, nor too much grief in adversity. These qualities form part of Cato's character to be sure, but Addison has emphasized them to the detriment of Roman constancy. References to Caesar by Cato and his followers are too offensive and go beyond the just bounds of an heroic enmity. By presenting Cato's death on-stage, Addison has not been sufficiently circumspect in respecting the laws of truth, or, to put it in other terms, he has not adhered to the theatrical precept of the verisimilar, a precept tenaciously advocated by Martello.

The modifications that Martello introduces in the portrayal of Cato considerably change Addison's hero. Minor departures from the text of the original are the addition of encomiastic epithets found in the speeches of other characters in the play, but whether these have been inserted to emphasize Cato's nobility or merely added to fill out the verse is debatable. More significant is the interpolation of a verse or verses that serve to delineate a distinctive trait of Cato, or to introduce qualities not found in the original. An instance of this procedure is manifested in the dialogue between Portius and Marcus, Cato's sons, in I.i. Martello has Portius say:

> Fra le nubi de' mali, che il Padre ha intorno, e sopra,
> Quanto in lui più risplende da invidiarsi ogni opra!
> Incorona di gloria suoi anni il suo soffrire,
> Ed è martirizzato maggior del suo martire:
> Dì, che scemi la costanza nell'impugnar la spada,
> Perchè Onor, Virtù, Roma, e Libertà non cada.   (64)[41]

39 See n.9 above.
40 G. Costa, 'Shebbeare,' 749, correctly surmises that one of the two Englishmen who helped Martello with his translation was Richard Howard, Canon of St Peter's in Rome.
41 Addison's verses are:
> How does the lustre of our father's actions
> Through the dark cloud of ills that cover him
> Break out, and burn with more triumphant brightness!

By extending Addison's 'Greatly unfortunate' to 'Ed è martirizzato maggior del suo martire' Martello introduces the theme of psychological conflict in Cato, thereby attenuating, and humanizing, the stern character (according to Martello, the 'English spirit') of Addison's Cato. The addition in a speech by Marcus of

> Veggio il maggior de' Padri, che fesse mai Natura,
> Al più ingrato de' Figli mostrar la sua sventura,
> E lagnarsi, che sola non m'abbia, e che mentre ei
> Stette dall'una parte, stando dall'altra i Dei,
> E che quant' e' soggiacque alle Cesaree squadre
> Il Mondo inter, fuor che l'atroce alma del Padre.   (65)

is an obvious recourse to present a more traditional portrait of the hero. In 'che mentre ei / Stette dall'una parte, stando dall'altra i Dei' it is not difficult to discern a paraphrase of Lucan's 'Victrix causa diis placuit, sed victa Catoni,'[42] and in the last two verses Horace's

> Et cuncta terrarum subacta
> Praeter atrocem animum Catonis.[43]

There is, however, very little variation from the original in Cato's own lines, except, as we shall see, in the final scenes of the play.

The Martellian rehabilitation of Caesar who, it will be remembered, does not form part of the *dramatis personae* but is nevertheless the antagonist of the tragedy, is accomplished, not through the suppression of imprecatory epithets that Martello had found offensive in the original, but by inserting a long speech (thirty-six verses) in Caesar's defence. This occurs in Act II. Caesar has sent Decius, Cato's former friend, as ambassador to Cato and his Senate to offer terms. Cato rejects them; whereupon, in the original, Decius departs. Before Martello dismisses him he has Decius, in an impassioned speech, refute Cato's accusations by exalting Caesar as Rome's saviour, whose exploits have brought a greater measure of liberty to Rome than that which she had previously enjoyed.

> His sufferings shine, and spread a glory round him;
> Greatly unfortunate, he fights the cause
> Of honour, virtue, liberty, and Rome.   (173)

42 *Pharsalia*, I, 128.
43 *Odes*, II, 1.

It is in Act v that Martello deviates furthest from Addison. The opening scene, Cato's soliloquy on death and immortality, is faithfully reproduced. Even though Martello requires fifty verses to express what Addison had said in forty, he adds no new thought. He adheres to the original too in the scenes that follow, up to the final scene which Martello alters in order to avoid 'la stomachevole ed orrida morte di Catone medesimo in scena.'[44] Addison has Cato, who has stabbed himself, brought on stage by his servants. Cato inquires about the safety of his friends, disposes the future of his children, asks the gods to forgive him if he has 'been too hasty,' and dies. Martello changes and expands the scene in this manner. Portius hears his father's moans off-stage and rushes out to see what is the matter. A second moan is heard and Marcia too wishes to flee to her father's side, but Lucius, who thinks that Cato is crying out in his sleep, detains her by arguing that Portius is better able to reveal to Cato the impending doom whereas Marcia's weeping would only tend to anger her father and make him more steadfast in his hatred for Caesar because

> Nostra causa per quanto pugnare, e viver lice,
> Piaccia pur vinta a i Numi, piace a Lui vincitrice.[45]

Portius re-enters to announce Cato's fatal self-inflicted wound:

> Ei gode vedendo uscir la vita
> Per l'imo ventre aperto da cupa ampia ferita.
> Il brando ahi gli s'è tolto, ma tardi, e fra le ambasce
> Permesso ha il trattenergli per poco entro alle fasce
> Il sangue, e diferirgli la morte sol quel tanto
> Ch'ei vi riveda, e possa l'alma spirarvi a canto.[46]

Cato is brought in. He asks Portius about the safety of his friends (as in the original), and then, after Portius has assured him that they have been thought of and pleads with him to think of himself he replies:

---

44 P.J. Martello, *Catone*, 57. 'The disgusting and horrible death of Cato himself on the stage.'
45 A re-echoing of Lucan. See n.42 above.
46 P.J. Martello, *Catone*, 139. 'He rejoices in seeing his life exhale through the dark ample wound in his lower abdomen. The sword, alas, was removed from his body, but too late, and in his sufferings, he has permitted for a little while to let his blood be contained within the bandages, and defer death for only enough time to see you again, so that he may die near you.'

> Penso dalle catene fra poco ir liberato.
> Fu sicuro il mio colpo. Pochi momenti il lino
> Ed al sangue, ed all'Alma ritiene il lor cammino;
> E se più il ritenesse di quel ch'io voglio, in vano
> Atta a squarciar le fasce non serb'io questa mano.[47]

In the details here given, in those found in Portius' verses above cited, and particularly in Cato's threat of ripping the bandages from his wound should death be too late in coming, Martello closely follows the account of Cato's death in Plutarch.[48] Besides fidelity to a classical source, the details introduced by Martello have a technical function in that they render more verisimilar the time (note the several temporal expressions) that elapses between the actual stabbing and the death, especially when compared with Addison where the only detail given is 'Cato is fall'n upon his sword.'

Addressing Lucius, Cato continues his speech with a reference to Caesar's compassion: 'Sia virtute, arte sia la sua clemenza' ('His clemency may be virtue, or it may be cunning'). With an abrupt 'Ma torniam Padre' ('let us return to a father's cares'), Martello reverts to Addison's text to translate the verses on the arrangements Cato makes for his children's future. Sensing the approach of death, Cato bids his servants to bring him to his bed, and is carried off stage uttering the pious sentiments which are a paraphrase of Cato's last words in the original. All exit, except Lucius who soliloquizes on the sad event, laments the oppression of future generations, and concludes the transcription of 'What dire effects from civil discord flow,' the final verses in Addison's play. Lamentations are heard off stage, Juba enters and narrates the last moments of Cato's life:

> Con tutti al letto intorno
> Quasi il nostro sdegnasse cospetto, e quel del giorno,
> Comandò l'arretrarsi, perchè tratti in un canto,
> Ei, le man giunti al Cielo, sommesso orò sin tanto,
> Che squarciate le fasce, sì ch'Uom non se ne accorse
> Dall'aperta piaga, coll'alma il Sangue corse:
> Così cadde un Catone, lasciando ognun perplesso
> S'egli cadeo, o più a Giulio nemico, od a sè stesso.[49]

---

47 P.J. Martello, *Catone*, 140. 'I think that I shall soon be free of my chains. My blow was true. For a few moments the linen will impede its course to my blood, and to my soul, and if it should impede it longer than I desire, my hand will not be in vain to rip these bandages from me.'

48 *Lives*, Cato the Younger, ed. A.H. Clough (London–Toronto, 1912), III, 79–81.

49 P.J. Martello, *Catone*, 142. 'With all of us gathered around his bed he ordered us to

We note again in the first three verses of this narration the insertion of the verisimilar detail (e.g. at his command, we withdrew into a corner of the room), and in the next three the further insistence on the circumstantial facts of the situation with an emphasis on the awesome aspects of Cato's death. This is the technique Martello uses to produce an horrific atmosphere that is Senecan in tone, and an effective substitute for Cato's on-stage death. What is astonishing in the speech is the concluding couplet. By questioning the motivation of Cato's death, Martello not only, or merely, reiterates the theme of Cato's psychological conflict, but in effect casts doubt on the validity of his protagonist as a tragic hero and obviates thereby the possibility of catharsis in the play.

The mutations introduced by Martello do not necessarily improve the original, either as poetry or as dramaturgy. They do, however, reflect a very different approach to the translation of a dramatic text than that practised by Salvini and by Riccoboni. It is to Salvini's credit that he was the first to produce an Italian translation of the *Cato* based on the original, and one cannot discount the fact that both Riccoboni and Martello had his version to guide them with their own, though Riccoboni adheres to his model more closely than Martello does. Salvini is scrupulously faithful to Addison's text, but his translation is marred by the contrived style of his verse. Riccoboni succeeds in infusing life into Salvini's pedantic diction, and he produces an acting version of the play which, with minor linguistic changes, could still be staged today. Martello's adaptation, less pedestrian than Salvini's translation, reflects and incorporates the theories of 'modern' tragedy then evolving in Italy with its insistence on the verisimilar to conform with the rational aesthetic of the time.

If we can dismiss the anonymous *Catone* as being nothing more than a literal translation of Boyer's French version, we cannot do so for the three versions that succeed it, for they represent a significant and authentic contribution to the divulgation of Addison's play in Italy. They also enhanced his fame, although they did not generate it, inasmuch as Addison's Italian reputation predates the play, a circumstance that cannot be ignored in the attempt to account for the Italian versions of the *Cato*. Another contributory factor to the interest in the play can be related to the Orsi-Bouhours polemic, an earnest endeavour by the Italians to counteract the censure of Italian letters by French critics, which tended to foment in

---

draw back, almost as if he disdained our presence, and that of the day, therefore we withdrew into a corner, he, his hands joined in prayer, quietly prayed until he ripped the bandages in such a way that no one was aware of it, and from the opened gaping wound his blood, and his soul, poured out. Thus fell a Cato, leaving all in doubt if he fell more as an enemy to Caesar or to himself.'

Italian playwrights the desire to equal, if not surpass, the great French classical dramatists. In Addison they may have seen both an inspiration and an ally. The Roman subject of the play was, of course, appealing (Martello refers to Cato as a 'compatriota'). Italian enthusiasm for the *Cato* was assuredly stimulated by the neo-classical regularity of the play. Here, at last, was an English dramatist who, contrary to the current Italian ideas on the irregularity of English drama, could compose a tragedy according to the canons they themselves practised and consequently could understand and accept. Perhaps the most perceptive among them could even appreciate 'the atmosphere of truth, the feeling of purpose, which is in the *Cato*.'[50] Surely Salvini and Martello did, while Riccoboni could also be allured by the humanity of its hero.

These considerations, as well as the expressed motives of individual translators, can elucidate Italian interest in Addison's play. The number of Italian versions, performances, and editions of the *Cato* attest a sustained interest in an English play which was unique at that time. No other English play had previously received so much attention; none can be said to have been more effective in preparing the way for the eventual reappraisal of English dramatic literature by the Italians. Examined, moreover, in the larger perspective of the cultural climate then evolving in Italy, with its propensity to break away from narrow regionalistic concerns to a broader cosmopolitan view, the Italian translations of the *Cato* are exemplary contributions to, and an early manifestation of, the development of the Anglo–Italian literary relations in the eighteenth century.

50 A. Nicoll, *Early Eighteenth Century Drama*, 89.

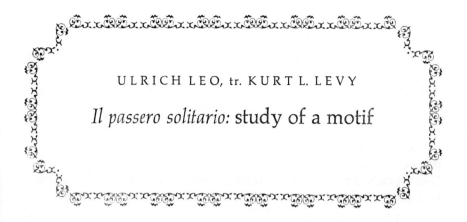

ULRICH LEO, tr. KURT L. LEVY

Il passero solitario: study of a motif

THE FOLLOWING PAGES are concerned with the title of the famous Leopardi poem and with nothing else. I have been puzzled for more than twenty years – perhaps for almost thirty, if truth be told – by the accepted interpretations of this title. Now I must come to grips with them, at least in a tentative fashion. Alberto Frattini,[1] the most recent editor of the *Canti*, is so far the last among those who do not feel that the title warrants even a note. S. Solmi, who, a few years earlier, edited the works in an ambitious series (which must perhaps still justify its existence[2]) reaffirms the abundantly known data: Psalm 102:8 was the first place where the motif occurred; the predecessors of Leopardi in making use of it were Petrarca and Pulci – a point on which we shall focus more detailed attention. Leaving the commentaries aside, the first treatment of the little motif which I have encountered is also of a quite recent date and stems from the pen of H. Rheinfelder. He introduces his sensitive analysis of two of Leopardi's poems with a discussion of the title, emphasizing that the correct interpretation of the title bears upon an understanding of the *passero* poem.[3] As far as the subject is concerned, however, he does not seem to get substantially further than did those who preceded him. He quite properly rejects the rendering 'the lonely sparrow' which is used

1 Brescia, 1960.
2 Giacomo Leopardi, *Opere* (Milano, 1956). (*La letteratura italiana. Studi e testi.* vol. 52, 1). Solmi mentions further Psalm 10: 2, but the latter does not have the slightest relation to our title. Psalm 102: 8 and Petrarca had been cited already by G.L. Bickersteth almost forty years ago (ed. *Canti*, Cambridge, 1923). There we find the additional note: 'the bird is not the English sparrow.'
3 'Two Poems by Giacomo Leopardi' (contained in the volume *Studi italiani*, VI, Cologne, 1961. pp. 76 ff.; regarding the title see pp. 77 f.). There is no reference to the title for instance in Emilio Bigi's fine book: *Dal Petrarca al Leopardi. Studi di*

even by so competent a scholar as Karl Vossler (compare the observation made by G.L. Bickersteth and cited in note 2).

How is it possible to speak of a 'lonely' sparrow? Actually, one of the distinguishing traits of the sparrow is the fact that it is not lonely. It is probably true to say that there is no more gregarious animal than the sparrow – a fact of which Leopardi was thoroughly aware (see note 3). A sparrow is, as everyone knows, gregarious even in the most ordinary sense of the word. It is quite possible, of course, that we are faced here with a paradox, namely with a sparrow that is lonely in defiance of all natural laws – much like the young poet who shuns his own kind without being able to tell us why he does so ('io non so come' ['Passero,' v. 22]). Yet solitude is not the only trait which distinguishes this *passero*; all day long it moves its listeners through the beauty of its song – 'ed erra l'armonia per questa valle' (v. 4). This, however, can, according to Rheinfelder, hardly be reconciled with a sparrow, just as it cannot be reconciled with a crow. It is conceivable that a sparrow may be lonely in defiance of its nature and for the sake of a lyrical paradox; but while it remains a sparrow it cannot possibly sing beautifully. It might chirp and warble; but this, of course, would clearly destroy the meaning of the comparison between bird and poet. The *tertium comparationis* used by Leopardi is precisely that both, bird as well as poet, *sing* in their chosen solitude, the bird physically, the poet psychologically.

There has been fairly general agreement therefore to translate *passero solitario* as 'blue-bird.' This was Paul Heyse's interpretation and H. Rheinfelder, too, resorts to 'blue-bird.' This position is based on the tacit assumption that something called *passero solitario* exists zoologically in

stilistica storica (Milano, 1954), 180 f. ('Il "Passero solitario" e il tema della solitudine'), nor is there any reference in K. Kroeber's 'The Reaper and the Sparrow' (*Comparative Literature*, x, 1958, 203 ff.). Even the meticulous Mestica [*Studi leopardiani* (Firenze, 1901), 210 f.] does not discuss the meaning of the title; unfortunately Mestica does not have an index. When Leopardi says 'passero' without supplement he is clearly thinking of the sparrow 'qual di passeri un groppo o di pernici / che s'atterri a beccar su qualche villa ...' (*Paralipomeni della Batracomiomachia*, vII, 39): 'un groppo'? The genuine sparrow as a gregarious animal! The 'musico augello' in the dense forest or 'nell'alto ozio de' campi ...' ('Alla primavera,' v. 69 ff.) is clearly the nightingale. Leopardi was an expert and a friend of birds. One of the very few occasions when the man who was forever morose, because he was incurably self-centred, put on a truly cheerful face was in his 'Elogio degli uccelli' (*Operette morali*, xvII). The French word 'moineau' (little monk) for sparrow must have been first of all a joke *e contrario*, in view of the conduct of the sparrow which is anything but monkish. (Gamillscheg does not comment on this is his *Etymologisches Wörterbuch der Französischen Sprache*, Heidelberg, 1928.)

real life, which means that syntactically *solitario* is not merely a descriptive epithet but rather an inherent component part of the bird name. However, is it not conceivable that the *passero solitario* and its more or less synonymous predecessors and contemporaries in other ancient and modern languages had originally not been zoological but rather *literary* creatures which reached the zoological realm only illegitimately as a bird term because of a syntactical error of the kind mentioned above? The following pages propose to examine whether or not this position can be substantiated. We shall be guided by two criteria: (I) What is the meaning of *passero*? and (II) What is its syntactical relationship to *solitario*?

II

Let us begin with the point from which Rheinfelder sets out in seeking to justify the consideration of the title in the context of his study. In his view, the 'sparrow' – gregarious, not lonely, by nature in contrast to the 'blue-bird' – constitutes an impediment to interpreting the poem as it was intended. Rheinfelder maintains that the 'lonely' blue-bird behaves in accordance with its nature, whereas a 'lonely' sparrow would clearly behave contrary to its nature. He implies that since the poet's human conflict with nature is contrasted with the conformity with nature on the part of a non-human creature, the 'blue-bird' must take the place of the 'sparrow.' This can hardly be accepted. It is not the fact that the 'lonely' bird lives in accordance with its individual nature, whereas the lonely youth does not, which in Leopardi's philosophy represents the difference between human and non-human creatures in their relationship to nature. Viewed in this manner, the bird might just as well have been a sparrow that is lonely contrary to its nature. 'Nature' in this context – and in Leopardi virtually always – is to be interpreted not individually but as transcending the individual, as the power which dominates *all* creatures collectively and which often represents God, or rather 'fate.' The contrast between 'civilized' man, the human being who has grown away from nature, and the non-human being which has remained close to nature, therefore consists for Leopardi in the fact that the latter submits without protest to every decree of 'nature,' including those which are not 'natural' to it. The former on the other hand rebels against them. What is involved, specifically and above all, is the natural fate of old age and death which all organic creatures must endure. Leopardi's teaching assigns the same fate to human beings and non-human ones. The difference is merely in the manner in which each group reacts to its fate.

The *passero solitario* is, of course, not the only illustration in Leo-pardi's verse of this fundamental contrast which is brought out when the poet addresses the bird almost with envy: 'Tu, solingo augellin, venuto a sera/del viver che daranno a te le stelle,/certo del tuo costume/*non* ti dorrai; che *di natura* è frutto/ogni vostra vaghezza' (thus also the seem-ingly unnatural 'vaghezza' of solitude [v. 45 ff.]). The broom too will soon succumb to 'the cruel violence of the subterranean fire' (of Vesuvius): 'E piegherai/sotto il fascio mortal *non* renitente/il tuo capo innocente'; it will not plead cravenly for its life, nor will it resist stubbornly: 'Ma più saggia, ma tanto/meno inferma dell'uom ...' (*La ginestra*, v. 300 ff.). The dying Brutus extols the 'fortunate *belve*,' because – innocent and ignorant of their own sufferings – their greater age leads them to the unforeseen step (death) (*Bruto minore*, v. 61 ff.). The shepherd on the Asiatic plain questions his flock: 'Dimmi, perchè giacendo/a bell'agio, ozioso/s'appaga ogni animale;/me, s'io giaccio in riposo, il tedio assale?' (*Canto notturno*, v. 129 ff.). Even in dealing with an aspect which is rare in Leopardi, namely that of activity as an answer to *noia*, we encounter the motif. Animals are no more predestined to be happy than are human beings; but they keep occupied attending to their daily needs and thus 'di noi men tristo/condur si scopre' (*e.g.* 'de'bruti la progenie') 'e men gravoso il tempo' (*Al conte Carlo Pepoli*, v. 37 ff.).[4] Besides, Leopardi surely did not

4 Reversing the 'homme machine' concept of the Age of Enlightenment, Leopardi carried the parallel between humans and animals to 'life after death'; notwith-standing his intellectual nihilism, it cannot be denied that the role which religious metaphysics played in his emotional life could not be eliminated. Thus he leads his readers – of course half jokingly and not without dantesque reminiscences – into the underworld ('inferno') of the animals (*Paralipomeni*, c. VII and VIII). Louis Fabre's poem 'Les canards sauvages' provides an echo of Leopardi's differentia-tion between human and non-human creatures in the pessimistic sense (cf. *Roma-nische Forschungen*, 73 [1961], 1 ff.). According to Leopardi, civilized man knows only during childhood ('fanciullezza') the blessings of 'ignoranza della morte,' the 'illusioni (errori),' the 'speme'; there was a time when the adult knew it too – in the Golden Age, the morning, the childhood stage of mankind: see 'Inno ai pa-triarchi' and, in greater detail, 'Storia del genere unano,' Part I (*Operette morali*, I). The statement 'di colpa ignare e de' lor proprii danni' which he applies to the animals ('Bruto minore,' v. 61) corresponds exactly to the remark 'di suo fato ig-nara / e degli affanni suoi' which refers to man of the Golden Age ('Inno ai patriar-chi,' v. 97 f.). Concerning the madrigal 'Imitazione,' which is cited at a later point in the text, I gave the little poem to the four members of my Leopardi Seminar (University of Toronto, 1961/62) for a strictly independent interpretation. The students were unanimous in taking the leaf to symbolize *human* destiny in keep-ing with Leopardi's pessimism. The opposite is true: in Leopardi it is only a non-human creature which can discuss its destiny with such light-hearted resignation – 'naturalmente.' 'Tutto l'altro ignoro': this is the very opposite of the insatiable and rebellious questioning of humans! In a paper entitled 'Intendimento di una

select arbitrarily for translation a delightful French madrigal in which the poet pityingly questions the *povera foglia frale*: 'lungi dal proprio ramo/ ... dove vai tu?' The leaf carried along by the wind does not answer plaintively, like a 'povera' and 'frale.' It is the poet who, on the basis of his own morose human nature, attributes such sentiments to the leaf. The leaf, quite on the contrary, answers cheerfully, unreservedly resigned to the natural course which its life is destined to follow: The wind tore me from my beech tree; I now let myself be carried wherever it wishes to carry me – '*e tutto l'altro ignoro./Vo, dove ogni* altra cosa,/dove naturalmente/ va la foglia di rosa/e la foglia d'alloro' (*Imitazione*, v. 1 ff.). The leaf, viewing the universe with the criteria of a leaf, is doomed to perish like beauty ('la foglia di rosa') and glory ('la foglia d'alloro), that is to say 'naturalmente' – 'in conformity with nature,' and above all, without seeking to 'know,' to understand anything (about death): 'tutto l'altro ignoro!' This is in striking contrast with the nagging questions posed by the *pastore errante.* Only man is unable to resign himself, either to the transience of beauty, or to that of glory, or to the inevitability of his own death. For this reason, a being that seems to him 'povero' and 'fragile' is in reality 'richer' and 'more resistant' than he himself, because it is carried towards death in a mood of cheerful resignation and not in one of despondent rebellion.

III

It would therefore *not* be necessary to object to the 'sparrow' because of the 'inner action' in Leopardi's *Passero solitario*. Our doubts are based rather on those reasons – both aesthetic and of subject matter – which were cited initially and which Rheinfelder had expressed in a similar manner. A sparrow as a lonely and melancholy singer comes closer to being a comic figure and certainly is not a lyrical one; as a lyric poet Leopardi could not possibly have had a sparrow in mind.

How did the sparrow come to form part of the title? It is difficult to refute conclusively the theory that the poet may have had a blue-bird in mind, although we shall, in the course of our reflections, encounter concrete arguments against this. At all events we are here concerned with the name and not with the subject matter. After personally consulting numerous Italians and Spaniards from different educational backgrounds I am able to infer that neither an Italian nor a Spaniard would say, on seeing any kind of a bird: 'Look at that *passero (pájaro) solitario.*' He

poesia leopardiana,' *Italica* 40 (1963), 35–51, I have discussed in a different context the subject of section II and this note.

would rather describe the bird, if it is a blackbird, as a 'merlo' ('mirlo'). As far as the Italian is concerned, and this is of most immediate interest to us here, we find a welcome confirmation in the *AIS* (*Atlante Italo Svizzero*), cards 488 ('passero') and 493 ('merlo'). On the former the sparrow appears almost invariably as passero (or its derivatives); on the latter, with even greater uniformity, the blackbird as merlo (with its derivatives). It follows from this that the common people in all parts of Italy, those who are untouched by literary influence and prejudice, do *not* refer to the blackbird either as passero (or as passero solitario) but rather as merlo.[5]

On the other hand it cannot be denied, that the lonely sparrow as a description of the blue-bird is found in countless Romance dictionaries and occurs even in specialized zoological vocabulary. To refer to the latter first, a fundamental manual such as Brehm's *Tierleben*[6] lists 'lonely sparrow' last among the seven German more or less popular names of the blue-bird. Yet a native German speaker would refer to a lonely sparrow only in joking paradox and, even then, certainly not as a name for a blackbird. This smacks of Berlin dialect. The Latin names, on the other hand, retain in part the epithet 'monticola solitarius'; 'turdus solitarius.'[7] As far as the dictionaries are concerned,[8] they list almost without exception –

5 I am indebted to my colleague Dr Luigi Romeo for calling my attention to the *AIS* in this context.
6 Fourth revised edition (Leipzig and Vienna, 1911/1920); particularly Vol. IX, 146. The entire volume IX deals with the category of 'passerines,' 'from the common raven to the gold-crest' (p. 1). The sparrows in the narrow sense form a subgroup of the finch family (pp. 365/376). But the Latin term 'passer' and the Italian word 'passero (-a)' refer only to this subgroup.
7 This is true for the Latin names which occur in Rheinfelder (p. 78) and Bickersteth.
8 *Italian*: Tommaseo, Rigutini-Fanfani, Zingarelli among others. The Crusca-Dictionary does not reach letter P. The new *Dizionario enciclopedico italiano* states under 'passero' among other things that the 'passero solitario' is able to live in a cage for 24 years. *Spanish*: Pagés (as well as Zerolo, Caballero etc.). Covarrubias does not have this entry. The Dictionary of the Spanish Academy is almost identical with Pagés; but the eighteenth edition (1956) describes the length of the 'mirlo' as 'dos centímetros' (instead of decímetros' which occurred in the seventeenth edition); this means that all of a sudden we are faced with a colibri which sings like a blackbird. *Spanish-French*: Domínguez indicates 'merle de roche, passereau solitaire.' *Provençal*: Raynouard has nothing to offer; E. Levy, in his *Provenzalisches Supplement – Wörterbuch* (Leipzig, 1894), quotes Mistral under 'pasera': 'passero: moineau femelle, ..., merle de roche.' He has three further references, among them a biblical 'pasera solitaria' to which I refer later on. *Catalan*: Alcover, vol. VIII, says under 'passara solitaria': 'en els dicc. antics aquest ocell (passera) es enomenat passara solitaria halcyo alcedo merula fusca'; *Dicc. catalá-castellá-llatí* ... (Barcelona, 1839), vol. II: 'passara solitaria, ... alción, martin

and frequently copying from one another – among the derivatives of the *passer solitarius* of the Latin Bible, to which we shall come shortly, a description of the blue-bird. Only Catalan asserts its independence: *passera solitaria* here has the meaning of 'king-fisher' (see note 8). I am led to wonder if this semantic detour may not go back to a confusion with the Latin *passer marinus*, 'ostrich' (gr. struthós), so called because it lives 'beyond the seas?'[9] We shall see that, also in the rendering of the under-lying psalm passage, Catalan deviates from its sister languages. Even a Biblical dictionary such as that of F. Vigouroux[10] favours 'blackbird' ('thrush'): 'le "passereau" qui passe la nuit solitaire sur le toit pourrait bien être la grive bleue.'

As far as the subject matter is concerned, it is quite conceivable, as I said before, that Leopardi's 'passero solitario' may well refer to a black-bird. The lonely melancholy, hesitatingly melodious singing of the latter in daylight would seem to fit splendidly the comparison with the young and misanthropic Giacomo. It is indeed a comparison which is preferable to that of a nightingale which bursts into song at night and with sparkling and untrammelled fulness.[11] But as far as the name is concerned, Leopardi compares himself to the poetically impossible 'lonely sparrow'; for *passero* in Italian means sparrow in the narrow sense. Why does he not say *merlo* or *tordo*? We therefore come back to our suspicion that *passero solitario* for Leopardi refers less to a zoologically defined bird species than to a literary motif. How did he arrive at this motif?

It has been mentioned above and is well known that the motif appears first in the Old Testament. Rheinfelder may be overly cautious when he remarks: 'It may well be that the term ... derives from a psalm passage in Latin ...'[12] There is no reason to doubt that Verse 8 of Psalm 102 (101 according to the old numbering)[13] introduced this literary motif into the Western world. On the other hand, the semantic road which the 'lonely bird' of the Hebrew original has had to travel, leading through the Bible

pescador.' However, one also finds 'passero' as equivalent of *Span.* 'pájaro soli-tario,' f.i. in the *Dicc. de la llengua catalana* ... , 9th ed. (Barcelona, n.d. [about 1920]), vol. II.
9 'Marinus auten quia peregrinus est et trans mare advehitur' (Forcellini).
10 *Dict. de la Bible* (Paris, 1928), IV, 2, col. 2176, under *Psalm* 102: 8.
11 'I sing like a bird ...' fits the nightingale; it fits neither the blackbird nor Leopardi.
12 Rheinfelder, p. 78. There is not more than a faint echo of a passage such as Virgil: *Aeneid* IV, 462 f: 'solaque culminibus ferali carmine bubo / saepe' (*scil.* visa) 'queri et longas in fletum ducere voces.'
13 The first psalm used to be regarded as an introduction to the entire Psalter; it merged with the second one, so that the second one appeared as the first one. Cf., for instance, *The Holy Bible with Commentary*, ed. F.C. Cook, IV (London, 1873), 149 b.

translations into medieval and modern (for us specifically Italian) literature, is a more winding one than it might appear, judging from Rheinfelder's few lines. As we follow this road, we shall understand more clearly
why it was precisely a sparrow to which the Italians (and not only the
Italians) attached, unrealistically and unlyrically, the epithet 'solitude.'

IV

The original Hebrew word costume, in which this animal of literary
renown first appears before us, is that of a *tsipor boded* ('bird lonely').[14]
The Hebrew word *tsipor* means 'bird' in general, but with a special
semantic emphasis on small birds. In this respect it approaches the Greek
struthíon monázon, which the Septuagint has seen fit to substitute for
tsipor boded instead of *orníthion monázon*. For *struthíon* by itself means
not only 'sparrow,' but generally the 'passerine species,' the sparrow
family, which designates, as has been pointed out,[15] a large number of
small and medium size birds, among them the blackbird.[16] It may therefore not be as surprising as it seems at first that the Septuagint used that
translation; however, it is the crucial happening in the semantic history of
our passage. The first translator of the Septuagint into Latin (*Vetus Latina*
[*Itala*]) substituted quite naturally the Latin *passer* (instead of *avis*) for
the Greek *struthíon*, the principal meaning of which is sparrow. *Passer*
however means sparrow in the narrow sense and nothing else.[17] And now
we come to the other crucial happening. As is well known, the *Vulgate* –
in contrast to the *Vetus Latina* – has not been translated from the
Septuagint but from the Hebrew original. Yet as far as the psalms are
concerned, the *Vulgate* does not use Jerome's new translation from the
Hebrew, but rather a revised version of the psalms from the *Vetus Latina*,
likewise done by Jerome (and now called 'Psalterium Gallicanum'). This

14 *Psalm*, 102: 8. I am grateful to my friend Dr Felix Eckstein (Toronto) for the Hebrew transcription; as for the translation, see Tarry Torcyner, *Die Heilige Schrift,
   neu ins Deutsche uebertragen* (Frankfurt a./Main, 1935), IV, 119. As for the meaning, see Wm. Smith, *Dictionary of the Bible* (London, 1893), III, 1364 f.; see also
   H. Guthe, *Kurzes Bibelwoerterbuch* (Tuebingen, 1903) under 'Voegel.'
15 See n.6.
16 With respect to *struthíon*, see for instance Stephanus, *Thesaurus L. Gr.* under:
   'pro qualibet avicula'; and perhaps John D. Davis, *A Dictionary of the Bible*, fourth
   edition (Philadelphia, 1927), 741 ('sparrow'): *struthíon* refers to smaller birds up
   to pigeon size, particularly warbling birds (which certainly does *not* fit the blackbird).
17 The *Thesaurus Linguae Latinae* by the German Academies has, after sixty years,
   not yet reached the letter P. The *Thesaurus* by Stephanus, as well as Forcellini,
   give 'sparrow' exclusively as the meaning of 'passer.'

revised version, which was based on the Septuagint and its *struthíon*, has retained the *passer*. There is interesting counter evidence to corroborate this: Jerome's new translation of the psalms from the Hebrew which has been mentioned before, though not found in the *Vulgate*, is nevertheless extant. And this translation from the Hebrew of our passage actually reads *avis solitaria* instead of *passer solitarius!*[18] If this translation of the psalms had reached the *Vulgate* along with Jerome's entire remaining text, we should have no problem with respect to the *passer solitarius*: Leopardi and those who preceded him in using the motif would have said 'avis solitaria' or 'uccello solitario!'

V

All this was destined to happen in order that western Christianity might be faced with a lonely sparrow as a symbol of desolate though musical isolation. Let us see now what western Christianity has done with this legacy.

It is most entertaining to follow the development. *Passer* meaning sparrow provided the point of linguistic juncture between the narrow and broad meanings – bird, passerine species, sparrow – in the history of the Hebrew–Greek development of our psalm passage. And *passer* in turn, starting down the road to the Romance vulgar tongues, can be seen to split up into the meanings which had just become joined. The etymon *passer* means bird in Spain,[19] Portugal, and Romania; sparrow in Italy, Northern and Southern France (Provence), and Rhetoromania; king-fisher (especially in conjunction with solitaria) in Catalonia. On the other hand, and contradicting in a way what has just been said, all the principal Romance languages, with the exception of Catalan, adopted the Latin etymon *passer* in translating the *Vulgate* verse in question, regardless of whether the meaning of the derivative in the individual languages was bird or sparrow. *The word form and not its meaning has been all important*: this must be

18 See *Liber psalmorum hebraicus atque latinus ab Hieronymo ex hebraeo conversus*, ed. Tischendorf, Baer, Delitzsch (Leipzig, 1874), p. iii f. As for the historical aspect, see for instance *Dictionnaire de théologie catholique* (Paris, 1936), xiii, col. 1108. The new Catholic rendering of the psalms into Latin does not give 'passer,' but 'avis': see *Breviarum romanum*, ed. amplif. (Taurini, 1957), 283. (I am grateful to my highly esteemed student, Father Sam Femiano, c.s.b., Toronto, for this reference.)

19 In modern Spanish: 'pájaro' (in contrast with 'ave') particularly for small birds which appears in flocks (like 'tsipor' and 'struthion'): see W. Beinhauer, *Das Tier in der spanischen Bildsprache* (Hamburg, 1947), 22 f. Beinhauer specifically cites 'un pájaro solitario' as a colloquial metaphor referring to a 'misanthropic, unsociable person' (ibid., 23).

borne in mind as we consider what follows.[20] Here are the Romance renderings of the passage (which, if no note is appended, have been taken from the current Bible translations:

Spanish: 'como páxaro solitario sobre terrado' (Juan de Valdés) ('bird').

Portuguese: 'como pássaro solitário no telhado' ('bird').

Catalan: 'com ocell solitario en el terrat' (not < *passer*).[21]

Provençal: 'com la pacera en mayson, que salutaria (1.: solitaria?) a non' ('sparrow').[22]

French: 'comme un passereau solitaire sur un toit' ('sparrow').

Italian: 'come passero solitario nel tetto' ('sparrow').

Rhetoromance: 'sco ün pasler soldan sün ün tet' ('sparrow').

Romanian :'ca pasărea singuralică pe un acoperiš' ('bird').

---

20 The English Bible translations, too – old as well as new, including the *Authorized version* – give 'sparrow.' The German translations, on the other hand, have given 'bird' since Luther.

21 *La Biblia* (Monestir de Monserrat, 1932), vol. x. Catalan is the only one among the principal Romance Languages which, in its translation of the psalm passage, uses 'ocell' (< avicellu-) instead of the derivative of *passer* (at least this is the case in the Bible edition of 1932, the only one which was accessible to me). I wonder if the special Catalan meaning of 'passera solitaria,' i.e. king-fisher, may have led to this special approach to its translation? A king-fisher after all is possibly even harder to reconcile with lonely song than a sparrow. This peculiar problem needs broader documentation for its solution. Some Catalan dictionaries give, by the way, also 'merlo' besides 'alción,' as the meaning of 'passera solitaria.'

22 I was not able, in spite of repeated efforts, to put my hand on a Psalter in Old (or Modern) Provençal, not even in the *Library of Congress* (see the end of this note). I therefore cite in the text the wording of the paraphrase of the psalm versified during the Middle Ages: there is no doubt that the editor took his *pacera* from his Bible, which applies also to the *passereau* mentioned in the cited (more recent) Old French verse paraphrases by Bèze and Desportes (see n.25 and pertinent text). The Provençal paraphrase quotes E. Levy, *Prov. Suppl. -Wb.* see 'pasera'; the complete text has been edited by G. Chabaneau, 'Traduction des psaumes de la pénitence en vers provençaux' (*Revue des langues romanes*, xix, 1881, 209 ff.). (Dr P.T. Ricketts, Provençalist at Victoria College, was kind enough to supply me with this reference.) Chabaneau attributes the text to the late thirteenth century (*Traduction*, p. 211); besides he has no doubt (p. 230, v. 28) that 'salutaria' (instead of 'solitaria') is due to a *lapsus pennae* on the part of the person who copied it. It is true, of course, that the first of the two prose translations to which I refer at the end of this note also gives 'salutari'! At the last minute I obtained through the *Société des Amis de la Bibliothèque Nationale* (Paris) two manuscript versions of the old Provençal translation of the Psalter. As was to be expected, the versified text does not differ essentially from these two prose versions. According to the information obtained from Paris they read as follows: (a) 'vellat he e son fet axi com a passera salutari ...' (MS. [French Collection], 2433, f. 124 vo. xv century, *Psautier en provençal*; as for 'salutari,' see above); (b) 'Jo veile e son feyt axi com lo passer qui esta tot sol el tet' (MS. [French Collection], 2434, f. 168, xiv century, *Psautier en*

As far as the French language is concerned, I have noted besides the Anglo-Norman form which occurs in the Oxford Psalter: 'sicume passer sultis (var. sultif) en maisun'; also, an Old French verse version of the Psalter, probably from the late twelfth century: 'cum passeres en maison seux,' where seux (< solus) is not attached as an attribute to passer (as would happen with a component part of the bird name) but performs a decidedly predicative (descriptive) function: 'a passer which is alone on the roof of a house.'[23] Finally we have the Lothringian form taken from the Metz Psalter: 'cum li passers ou li moixon (var. mouxon) solitaires on teit.'[24] Here the bird concept is linguistically doubled and there is something like a choice between passeres and moixon. The latter word is not mentioned by Godefroy, Littré, Meyer-Luebke, and Gamillscheg; Tobler-Lommatzsch and v. Wartburg have not yet reached the letter M. The only place where I found it was La Curne de Ste. Palaye, under 'moison 1.' La Curne cites as meaning 'moineau,' adding the following reference by way of documentation: 'tarins, arondes, moisons' (Modus, fol. 172). In discussing the translations of the psalm passage, reference has been made to a medieval verse version in Provençal (see note 22, also with respect to two prose versions in Provençal which reached me at the last moment).

And now we must turn to some direct echoes of the psalm passage from a later period. Marot and Bèze, in their sixteenth-century verse translation of the psalms, use passereau: '... comme durant son veuvage / le passereau sous l'ombrage / d'un toit ...' Philippe Desportes does the same in his translation: '... comme le passereau dolent et solitaire / sous un toit hébergé ...'[25] As can be seen, Bèze has sentimentalized the solitude motif into 'widowerhood' and has, in so doing, dispensed entirely with 'solitarius.' Furthermore, Bèze, as well as Desportes, turns the fact of sitting 'on a roof' into living 'under a roof,' or 'in the shadow of a roof'; this means presumably in the bird's nest (perhaps in the eaves trough). All this tends to do away more or less with the lonely–desolate condition of the

provençal). This second prose version contains, as does the verse version, the transformation of the epithet 'solitario' which performed a predicative function into a dependent relative clause; for further details see the text.

23 These are the two passages: Libri psalmorum versio antiqua gallica, una cum versione metrica ... , ed. Fr Michel (Oxonii, 1890), p. 146 (Anglo-Norman prose), p. 328 (Old French verse).

24 Le psautier de Metz, Texte du xive siècle. Ed. crit. Fr Bonnardot, t. 1 (Paris 1884), 282.

25 Cl. Marot and Th. Bèze: Les psaumes de David (La Rochelle, 1606, and later editions from which I was able to collate those of the years 1660, 1669, and 1672). Psalm 102 (101) has been translated by Bèze. Philippe Desportes, Cent psaumes de David, mis en vers françois. Avec ... (Paris, 1598).

bird. On the other hand, the word 'solitaire,' which had vanished completely in Bèze's 'veuvage,' becomes, in Desportes, detached from its noun 'passereau' through the insertion of a second epithet (*dolent*). With both translators then, the noun appears plainly alone *as the name of a bird*; solitaire (or its substitute) clearly appears as a supplement which only describes a condition (epi-theton!) and certainly not as a modifier of the bird name itself. The same happened in the Provençal verse-translation (see note 22) where, just as in one of the two Provençal prose translations (ibid.), 'solitarius' actually changed into a dependent relative clause. There is not the slightest suggestion of anything like 'the lonely bird (sparrow)'; it is quite clearly 'the bird (sparrow) which is lonely on the roof.' This and nothing else was the meaning of the original psalm passage in Hebrew and of its Greek and Latin reproductions. If those who used the motif and, above all, those who interpreted it had borne in mind that *boded*, *monázon*, *solitarius* and the greater part of their medieval echoes were to be understood as *detached* from the noun and merely as an adjective to the latter, there would have been no question of any misinterpretations because of 'lonely-bird' (in the case of Leopardi, 'lonely sparrow' and then 'blue-bird').

Wherever a particular Romance language refers to 'bird' with its *passer*-derivative, we arrive unexpectedly – provided *solitarius* is added – at the 'lonely bird' which occurs in the Hebrew original. Wherever the *passer*-derivative, has retained the meaning 'sparrow,' we are faced with the lonely sparrow though it is most improbable that this connotation, handed down through literature, should have denoted an actual sparrow. The special situation in Catalan (*ocell*, see note 21) confirms this assumption.

VI

Let us turn now to the non-biblical and specifically to the Italian versions of the Biblical motif. Leopardi is not the first one to bring the *passero solitario* into the post-Christian literary world, though he may actually have been the last one. Echoes of the Biblical motif go back to the first centuries of the Christian era. We must examine some of the references prior to Leopardi to find out whether in each case, as we stated above, *solitarius* was used as a modifier to the bird-name, resulting as it were in the birth of a completely new bird species, or whether – in the spirit of the underlying Biblical passage – it remains only a complementary adjective to the unchanging *passer* (or its derivative).

Paulinus Nolanus, one of the Church Fathers of the fourth century, provides us with an extensive allegorical interpretation of the psalm passage which he cites specifically. The Biblical 'passer solitarius in tecto' is interpreted here as being the soul which has reached the zenith of meditation: 'tunc in consummatione pedibus constitutis, super excelsa perfectae virtutis impositi ... efficiemur "sicut passer singularis (*var.*: unicus) super tectum." '[26] The poet of the psalm, in using his allegory, had almost the opposite in mind: not highest fulfilment, but rather deepest desolation. Paulinus applies his own interpretation to the passage without paying much attention to the meaning of the original. However, in substituting *unicus (singularis)* for *solitarius*, he shows, beyond the shadow of a doubt, his conviction that the adjective does not modify the meaning of the noun, but is merely appended (as a kind of general numeral). On the other hand, he hardly thought of a sparrow as the 'basic meaning' of his allegorical vision, but rather of a *bird*!

In the late Middle Ages, Albertus Magnus supplies a description of the 'passer solitarius' as a bird defined in the zoological and not the literary sense; in doing this he becomes formally the forerunner of the descriptions, more or less varying in content, which are offered by old and new dictionaries and by the zoological manual, as mentioned above (see notes 6, 7, 8, and pertinent text): 'De passere solitario: passer solitarius avis est nigra, *merula minor*, et est avis musica[27] et dicitur solitarius quia cum nullo sui generis unquam congregateur nisi tempore congregatioois (*sic!*). Habitat autem in parietibus, et *cum aliis passeribus se jungit*, et cum eis volat ad pastum, eos qui de sua sunt generatione omnino despiciens.'[28] With Albertus, therefore, it is not a question of a blackbird: his 'passero solitario' is 'smaller than the blackbird.' Nor is it a question of solitude: 'cum aliis passeribus se jungit ...': and the dwelling place 'in parietibus' does not correspond to the concept of 'lonely' life on the roof or in the forest, such as is cited in later dictionaries, etc. But, with Albertus, we do find *solitarius* not merely as a descriptive adjective to *passer*, but indeed fused with *passer* and essentially modifying its meaning: here the 'passer solitarius' appears specifically as a zoological species ('generatio'), in contrast with 'aliis passeribus.' (The reasons for Albertus' interpretation are another matter.)

The situation is different with Petrarca, who supposedly anticipated Leopardi's use of our motif in a passage which is cited in every Leopardi

---

26 Paulinus Nolanus: 'Epistola xL' (*P.L.* 61, col. 371 ff.); the quoted passage, col. 373. See also below G. Bruno's allegorical interpretation of one of his own sonnets (n.39 and pertinent text).

27 See 'musico augel' (nightingale) in Leopardi (see n.3).

28 *De animalibus*, 1. 23, 644b/645a (*Opera*, vi, Lugduni, 1651). Rheinfelder too cites and translates the passage (p. 78).

commentary. It may be worthwhile to take a closer look at this passage: 'Passer mai solitario in alcun tetto / non fu quant'io nè fera in alcun bosco.'[29] 'Never was there a "passer" on any roof as lonely – as I, nor a "fera" in any forest.' Here it is abundantly clear that the reference is not to a lonely sparrow and that solitario is not (as it was in Albertus) fused to passer as an attribute which cannot be detached. Instead solitario belongs to passer predicatively and descriptively; and not only to passer, but also to fera, which is contrasted isocolically with passer. From this contrasting with *fera* (wild beast) it follows furthermore that passer can hardly be meant as sparrow, or for that matter as any definite bird species. Evidently the generic term of wild beast can only be contrasted with the generic term bird. 'Never was there a *bird* on any roof as lonely / as I, nor a *beast* in any forest.' (With respect to Petrarca's absolutely synonymous 'augelletto,' see the relevant note.) In Leopardi we find: 'Ecco tra nudi sassi o in verde ramo / e la *fera* e l'*augello*' ('Bruto minore,' v. 91 f.).[30] On the other hand, it is unlikely that Petrarca would place his passero on a *roof* (instead of, for example, in a tree), had the passage from the psalm not fixed the 'bird on the roof.' This means, of course, that Petrarca's passero in sonnet 226 is a literary echo, a motif rather than a zoologically defined being. The meaning of the passer from the *Vulgate* has been broadened to refer to bird, by dint of its being contrasted with fera; in this way, and without the poet's intention, the passer has come to resemble again its Hebrew model 'tsipor.' The doubling – though antithetical in this case – by means of another image from the animal world (fera) brings to mind formally the above-mentioned 'passeres ou moixon' (see note 24), in so far as there too the meaning of passer was affected by the doubling. In Leopardi, there is neither the (antithetical) doubling, nor does his passero sit on a roof. He does sit on the old Recanati church tower. Evidently Petrarca's sonnet can hardly have served as Leopardi's model.

There is another pre-Leopardi passage which is frequently cited, namely one by Pulci. And once again we do not encounter the lonely bird (lonely sparrow), at least not conclusively: '... Poi in altra parte si vedea *soletta* / la passera *pensosa e solitaria* / che sol con seco stare si diletta, /

---

29 *Canzoniere*, no. 226.

30 Petrarca, as is well known, says on another occasion: 'vago augelletto che cantando vai' (no. 353). One might want to interpret the earlier mentioned 'passero' in this broader sense as 'augelletto'; yet, the *Vulgate* passage has exerted its influence only on sonnet 226 and not on sonnet 353: it is for this reason (and only for this reason) that we find 'passero' in no. 226. Leopardi, on his part, alternates between 'passero' and 'augellin' (see n.40 and pertinent text).

a tutte l'altre nature contraria ....'[31] These four lines occur among an almost unending enumeration of birds, in the course of the description of the tent which loyal Luciana had embroidered for Rinaldo who was not worthy of such a labour of love. The four walls of the tent are divided according to the four elements; the birds fill the second wall, that of air.[32] By far the majority of birds are merely mentioned, often two or three in one line: only the two which appear first – 'l'aquila' and 'la fenice' – are described in greater detail, more mythologically than naturalistically;[33] the 'tortoletta' (the same as the 'passera pensosa ...'[34]) receives four lines. Among those which are described more succinctly (two lines) we find, long before the 'passera pensosa e solitaria,' 'la passer ... maliziosa e cattiva / e par *sol* si diletti di far danno.'[35] We therefore have two references to 'la passer(a)' – first as a bird that is malicious, then as one that is melancholy and lonely. Whatever our interpretation of this double reference, we could not possibly suggest that two zoologically different birds are depicted here. It is simply a question of two 'passere,' each one described in more detail by two adjectives. In speaking of the first, the poet underlines its malice ('maliziosa e cattiva'); in referring to the second, he emphasizes its loneliness ('pensosa e solitaria'). It should be noted specifically that 'solitaria,' which had occurred also earlier in Desportes (note 24), is separated from its noun through an intercalated second adjective (pensosa), which means that it is not a modifier for the bird name. On the contrary, the echo-wise 'solinga' and 'sol' (the latter also in st. 54) reaffirm its status as descriptive (not modifying) adjective: the solitude motif fills half the stanza. On the other hand, it is not possible in this case to reduce one of the two 'passere' to the general meaning 'bird': for the two are actually links in a chain of individual bird species. Pulci here uses 'gli uccei'[36] to refer to the overall concept of bird. What kind of a 'passera' he had in mind in st. 60 (if the one mentioned in st. 46 is the ordinary

31 *Morgante*, 14, 60. Already in Latin and later in Old Italian, *passera* frequently appears as a variant for passer (o), without difference in meaning. With respect to *pasara, passero, passera*, see G. Rohlfs: *Hist. Gramm. der ital. Sprache*, par. 381.
32 *Morgante*, st. 46. The enumeration, or description, of the birds continues until st. 61.
33 Ibid., sts. 47 and 48.
34 St. 50.
35 St. 54. The two new Italian commentaries to the *Morgante* contribute little (Franca Ageno) or nothing (Giuseppe Fatini) towards clarifying Pulci's two 'passera.' Weston's edition has no commentary. The sparrow was one of the morally defamed animals of the Christian Middle Ages; this may have been due to the fact that it seemed to provide a tasty meal (*Luke* 12: 6).
36 St. 46 (cf. st. 61).

sparrow) remains a problem apart. Bearing in mind content rather than expression, one might endorse Rheinfelder's view that 'Pulci too ... is clearly thinking of the blue-bird.'[37] There is no doubt, however, that the 'passera' in st. 60 (and not the one in st. 46) was affected by the biblical model.

VII

However, the 'passero solitario' as a unified concept is found several times in Giordano Bruno's Italian writings; but it must be pointed out that, in content, the three passages which we propose to examine have nothing to do with the psalm excerpt, although in form they are closer to it than the majority of the passages which have been discussed so far. Bruno's 'passero solitario' neither sings, nor is it isolated (in spite of the term 'solitario'). It certainly does not embody melancholy, let alone despair. On the contrary, it appears once as one of the names of Christ, rejecting these names in a spirit of sarcasm: 'quante volte chiamano (*scil.* the Jews) ... il (Dio) novamente conosciuto da gli altri lor successori' (*scil.* by the Christians) 'Pellicano insanguinato, *Passare solitario*, Agnello ucciso ...'[38] The other two times, 'passero solitario' appears in two variations of one and the same sonnet. The initial lines in the first version read as follows: 'Mio passar solitario, a quelle parti / a quai drizzaste già l'alto pensiero, / poggia infinito ...'; and in the second version: 'Meo passar solitario, a quella parte / che adombr'e ingombra tutt'il mio pensiero, / tosto t'annida ...'[39] When the sonnet occurs for the first time, it appears with two others without commentary; when it occurs the second time, Bruno interprets the 'passar' as an allegory ('sotto forma d'un'altra similitudine descrive ...') 'per un cuor alato che è inviato da la gabbia, in cui si stava ocioso e quieto, ad annidarsi alto ...' This optimistic and idealistic approach brings to mind Paulinus Nolanus' interpretation which has been discussed before (see note 26 and pertinent text); the same as the latter, it is as remote as possible from the original, desperately sad meaning of the

---

37 Rheinfelder, p. 79 (cf. n.34).
38 'Lo spaccio de la bestia trionfante,' Diel. III, 2 (*Opere ital.*, a.c. di G. Gentile, 2. ed., Bari, 1925, II, 195).
39 'De l'infinito, l'universo e mondi,' Epistola proemiale, son. 1 (*Opere it.*, cit., I, 285); and 'Gli eroici furori,' III, 3, son. 2 (ibid. II, 377 f.). The editor, Gentile, quotes correctly Psalm 101 (= 102) v. 8 (in his note 2) in connection with the last-mentioned passage; however, he adds perplexingly: ' "passero solitario" è' (in the psalm!) 'imagine biblica per designare Dio.' Bruno in symbolizing the soul by means of a 'passer' (in the sense of bird), adopts the most ancient Christian symbolism: see G. Ferguson: *Signs and Symbols in Christian Art* (New York, n.d. [1955?]), 6.

lonely bird in the psalm passage. Also Bruno certainly does not mean a blue-bird, let alone a sparrow; he simply means a bird! As for the content, it is unlikely that Leopardi received the stimulus for his title from Bruno. But Bruno took the phrase naturally, the same as the other forerunners, directly or indirectly from the psalm.

From where did Leopardi get his 'passero solitario' which he elevated to the title of a poem, in which a youth, in dialogue with the bird and with himself, laments their mutual inability to enjoy their young days? In the course of his poem Leopardi mentions 'gli altri augelli' (v. 9) and he calls the bird which he addresses, once 'passero solitario' (v. 2), another time 'solingo augellin' (v. 45).[40] Drawing a parallel between the bird and himself, he says of his own person, 'io solitario ... uscendo' (the epithet here is predicative). Evidently he too is not concerned with depicting a zoologically defined bird species: the appearance and behaviour of his 'passero' are of no interest to him. We are told merely that it sings in solitude and that it, like its fellow creatures, obeys nature and therefore never, like the poet, will come to know the meaning of remorse. On the other hand, we may say, in spite of the title and of the first apostrophe, that Leopardi too regards the adjective 'solitario' as detachable from the noun 'passero' and not semantically joined to it. This is due to the loosening influence of the words 'solingo,' 'augellin,' 'io,' 'solitario,' which follow in short order and which prevent the word pair from congealing into linguistic rigidity.

Among all those who made use of the old motif and whom we have examined, Leopardi is the only one who has *himself seen* his 'passero solitario,' even though he does not describe its individual appearance. But he *did see* a bird, lonely, sitting not 'on a roof' but on the old Recanati tower; he heard it singing while the spring festival was in progress down in the town. Petrarca retained the 'roof' of literary tradition, whereas Leopardi replaced it with the 'tower' which he had seen. Leopardi, more than any of the forerunners, has personalized the traditional motif and, although he does not say anything about this and perhaps is not even aware of it, has done more than anyone before him to return the erroneous 'sparrow' to its original 'bird' status.

Is it actually necessary to search for Leopardi's source, apart from the knowledge of his having been inspired by a visual and auditive impression? Nothing in the poem is reminiscent of the psalm in the Bible; it is independent and self-contained, except for a small detail which does not fit and which therefore compels us to search for a source: and that small

40 See Petrarca's above-mentioned alternation between 'passero' and 'augelletto.'

detail is precisely the 'passero' in the title and in the first apostrophe. If 'uccello' or perhaps 'merlo' had been used in his title instead of 'passero,' nobody would have imagined that an 'outside' source might possibly have been involved in this poem. But he did say 'passero.' The earliest mention of the plan for the poem, which was discovered among his papers, consists only of the two words 'Passero solitario,' amidst other, laconically stated, work plans.[41] This earliest statement, in spite of everything that has been said so far, must surely be a quotation of the old psalm text from the *Vulgate*: a motif which he jots down for use on a future occasion. The occasion came when he *saw* the bird, perched alone on the old tower. This caused the poem to be born; but it retained its original title as planned, and did not succeed in shaking it off during its long years of maturing.[42]

The sequence of Latin, French-Provençal, and Italian passages which we have examined and which is far from complete does not under any circumstance permit a conclusive answer to the question of whether or not Leopardi followed a direct source. Like almost each one of these translators, prose writers or poets, we have conjectured that the motif did not pass from one to the other; it is more likely that each one independently seized the 'winged bible quotation,' using it and then allowing it to 'fly away again'! Paulinus Nolanus, Albertus Magnus, the Old French and Provençal Psalters, Bèze, Desportes, Petrarca, Pulci, Bruno, Leopardi himself – each gave a different treatment to the old motif. Variety marks its literary form. We find the attributive or predicative adjective which eventually turns into a dependent clause; we find complements to the adjective (other adjectives) to the point where the latter expand *leitwort*-wise; we find other animal names attached to, or contrasted with, the noun; indeed once we find 'unicus (singularis)' instead of 'solitarius.' Variety, too, marks its interpretation: the latter may be allegorical or ethical in the positive as well as in the negative sense; it may be applied in a zoological sense or appear as a symbol of some intimately personal lyrical emotion. The large majority of authors seemed to separate 'passero' from 'solitario' and paid little attention to the concrete meaning of the bird name; only Albertus Magnus and perhaps Pulci assigned a specific zoological meaning to the word. The others were guided more by the sound of the motif than by its specific content, more by the formal cliché

---

41 Printed in *Appendice all'Epistolario e agli scritti giovanili*, a.c. di P. Viani (Firenze, 1878), 238.

42 Every edition of the *Canti*, for instance that of I. Sanesi (Firenze, 1931), comments on the scantily documented history of the development of the *Passero solitario* from 1818 until its publication in 1835.

than by the animal name; and 'solitarius' in almost all cases was found to be semantically detachable from 'passero.'

In this sense all the literature passages which contain, in prose or verse, references to 'passero solitario' are *Bible quotations*. It is quite likely that even in the dictionaries which we have examined, as well as in the zoo-logical jargon since Albertus Magnus, 'the lonely sparrow' would not denote a separate bird species in all languages, if there had not been the psalm passage and the misleading *Itala*-translation which unfortunately crept into the *Vulgate*. Without the existence of that influential Bible passage the blue-bird would hardly be called lonely sparrow, and the king-fisher even less so. Blue-bird and king-fisher have as little connec-tion with that 'Passer solitarius,' Biblical-lyrical in flavour, as with the pelican or the owl which the psalmist cites in the preceding verse.

As far as Leopardi is concerned, I think I am in a position to state now that, in addressing the 'passero solitario' and even in endowing it with title status, he did not have a lonely sparrow in mind, or a blue-bird. He was merely thinking of a *bird* which he had heard singing on the old tower in solitude. To the latter he assigns the Bible term which he had jotted down earlier in his work plans, unconcerned with the concrete meaning of the word 'passer' in Latin and in Italian.[43] I am convinced, on the basis of the documentation which I have submitted in these pages, that the title of the Leopardi poem means precisely what the psalm denotes in the original Hebrew, namely: *the lonely bird*, and, more specifically, *the bird, lonely on the old tower*.

43 As for Leopardi's use of 'passer' without supplement, see n.3.

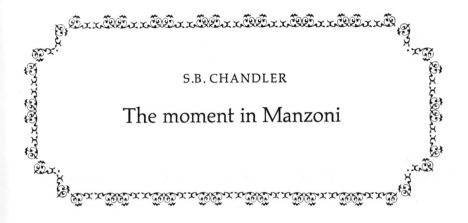

S.B. CHANDLER

The moment in Manzoni

IN A FAMOUS DISCUSSION in the eleventh book of his *Confessions*, St Augustine identified the present with a single instant and found a meaning for the terms 'past' and 'future' by enclosing the times thus denominated within the human mind. Life thus became a succession of indivisible present moments which could be anticipated as future or remembered as past. Through the centuries, this atomization of time has received varying developments from religious moralists and philosophical thinkers. In the thought of Alessandro Manzoni, the fundamental importance of the moment for the interpretation of the individual human personality first emerges in the *Osservazioni sulla morale cattolica* of 1819. The purpose of this study is to define the function of the moment in this interpretation and to show its realization in *I Promessi Sposi*; but first, I shall examine the elements on the basis of which Manzoni formed his viewpoint or against which he appeared to be reacting.

In the religious sphere, New Testament references to the uncertainty of the day and hour when the Son of Man will come were expanded in exhortations to be prepared for death and judgment at any of the continuous series of moments constituting a man's life. Manzoni's immediate sources here were the seventeenth-century French writers, Massillon, Bossuet, and the Jansenist Pierre Nicole, and also Paolo Segneri, all of whom he read in preparation for the *Osservazioni* and whose influence therein is manifest. A brief survey of their views will illustrate this point. On the possibility of death at any moment Massillon issued the clear warning: 'Faire toutes vos œuvres comme si vous deviez à l'instant en aller rendre compte; et puisque vous ne pouvez pas répondre du temps qui suit, régler tellement le présent, que vous n'ayez pas besoin de l'avenir pour le réparer,'[1] and he sums up: 'C'est-à-dire, pour recueillir toutes ces réflexions, qu'il en est de chaque moment de notre vie, comme de celui de notre mort.'[2] God's control of time allows no foreknowledge of our last moment: 'nessuno di noi non può mai promettersi un sol momento di vita (tanta è la gelosia con la qual Dio fra tutti gli altri domini ha voluto a sè riserbare quello del tempo)' contributes Segneri.[3] Each moment is equidistant from eternity or nothingness. According to Bossuet, 'Tout mon être tient à un moment; voilà ce qui me sépare du rien; celui-là s'écoule, j'en prends un autre: ils se passent les uns après les autres; les uns après les autres je les joins, tâchant de m'assurer; et je ne m'aperçois pas qu'ils m'entraînent insensiblement avec eux, et que je manquerai au temps, non pas le temps à moi.'[4] Each of us will be told: 'Il n'y a pas plus de tems pour vous,' says Nicole.[5] The concept of being standing out from nothingness and of the individual nature of death recall Heidegger. Life is complete at each moment and thus the individual is wholly himself at each in a moral sense and accountable for that condition alone: consequently, the moral condition of the soul at the point of death determines the nature of the divine judgment. Accordingly Massillon can affirm of the sinner at the Last Judgment: 'tandis qu'un seul moment consacré à un Dieu fidèle dans ses promesses eût pu lui mériter la félicité des saints'[6] and Segneri: 'A placar Dio non si richieggono molte ore; basta un momento.'[7] This point will be developed by Manzoni as will another concept, which is touched upon

1 Œuvres, I (Paris, 1877), 416.

2 Ibid., 466.

3 'None of us can promise himself a single moment of life (so great is the jealousy with which God among all his other supreme powers has wished to reserve to himself that over time)' in Opere, I (Milano, 1837), 14; see also 16. Cf. Massillon, Œuvres, I, 463: 'chaque moment que nous respirons est comme un nouveau bienfait que nous recevons de Dieu' and Nicole, Essais de morale, II (Paris, 1714), 326. In Opere III (Milano, 1838), 361, Segneri emphasizes the elusiveness of the present, which is like a point in a flowing river, the simile that goes back to Heraclitus and enjoyed great influence. The true present ('presente vero') is in God alone, that is, eternity is an 'eternal present.' Manzoni speaks of an endless moment as eternity in the Appendice al capitolo terzo delle Osservazioni sulla morale cattolica (1855) in Tutte le opere, a cura di Alberto Chiari e Fausto Ghisalberti, III (Milano, 1963), 218. Unless otherwise stated, all references to Manzoni's works are to this edition.

4 Œuvres, II (Paris, 1879), 500. It is interesting to read Erich Auerbach's comment on the procedure of Virginia Woolf, Marcel Proust, and James Joyce: 'there is confidence that in any random fragment plucked from the course of a life the totality of its fate is contained and can be portrayed,' in Mimesis, translated from the German by Willard R. Trask (Princeton, 1953), 547; cf. Rudolf Bultmann, History and Eschatology (Edinburgh, 1957), 108.

5 Essais de morale, 53 and 59.

6 Œuvres, I, 31.

7 Opere, I, 16. 'To placate God does not need many hours; a moment is enough.'

by Bossuet but assumes primacy in Manzoni, the heir to Condillac's and Rousseau's attempts to establish the individual personality. Bossuet observes that one sin will succeed another unless a person intervenes: 'Je veux dire, les péchés se succéderont les uns aux autres; et si vous ne faites quelque grand effort pour interrompre la suite de cette succession malheureuse, qui ne voit pas que d'erreur en erreur, et de délai en délai, elle vous mènera jusqu'au tombeau?'[8] Bossuet does not pose explicitly the question of cause and effect between sins. A final quotation will relate this succession of sins to a succession of moments: Massillon speaks of 'les emportements de la jeunesse, dont tous les moments ont presque été des crimes,'[9] an equating of moment and sin which recurs in the Innominato's contemplation of his past.

In philosophy, Descartes' theory of continuous creation deemed each moment distinct and indivisible and so non-continuous. Further, since no finite thing contains the reason for its existence, it, too, is non-continuous. Apparent 'continuous existence' is really God's repeated re-creation of the next instant and the finite object within it. For Descartes, therefore, change does not depend on a before–after relationship – the quality of one finite thing cannot be the cause of another. Thus moments themselves and time sequence stem from something outside them, infinite and eternal, i.e. God. No moment in a man's life determines the existence or quality of the next.[10] Leibniz's 'continual fulgurations of the Divinity from moment to moment' do not continually re-create monads but permit their continuance and development according to their own nature.[11]

It was the sensationalists, however, especially Condillac, and Rousseau, who associated the moment with the individual personality, as Manzoni does in a different sense. Condillac agrees with Descartes that the moment precedes duration.[12] A man is, if he feels: feeling distinguishes him

---

8 Œuvres, ii, 149.

9 Ibid., i, 30. The Night Thoughts of Edward Young, which were very well known in Italy in the last thirty years of the eighteenth century, continually link the moment to the transience of life, but, in their 'Pre-romantic' melancholy, are completely at variance with Manzoni's outlook.

10 Cf. the opening pages of the Introduction of Georges Poulet, Studies in Human Time, translated by Elliott Coleman (Baltimore, 1956) and Norman Kemp Smith, New Studies in the Philosophy of Descartes (New York, 1963), 202–7.

11 Monadology, par. 47; see The Monadology and Other Philosophical Writings, translated with introduction and notes by Robert Latta (London, 1965, reprint), 243–4. In his Rêve d'Alembert, Diderot speculates that everything changes and passes away and that the world begins and ends at each moment; see Ernst Cassirer, The Philosophy of the Enlightenment, translated by F.C.A. Koelln and J.P. Pettegrove (Boston, 1955), 91–2.

12 Cf. Poulet, Studies in Human Time, 20.

from non-being. The depth of his feeling of existence is governed by the intensity of his sensations and, since feeling is momentary, the more the sensations, the stronger the sense of duration. A man is only what he is at any moment, but this personality is composed of a succession of past moments, identified by the feelings that marked them. The statue of Condillac's *Traité des Sensations* is merely the sum of all it has acquired, for the mind contains only a collection of ideas formed from sense impressions; thus existence at any instant is equivalent to being one's present and past in themselves and as recalled in the memory. If the memory of a past experience is strong enough, it can become a present sensation or *imagination*. At the beginning of his *De l'esprit*, Helvétius asserted 'puisque se ressouvenir, comme je vais le prouver, n'est proprement que *sentir*.' In Italy, Pietro Verri followed Condillac in defining life as 'una serie di momenti' and time, in its relationship to us, as 'la successione delle nostre sensazioni.' Life is a series of momentary sensations, pleasant or unpleasant, with Verri, like Maupertuis, according predominance to the latter. As for religion, it assures us of a time when 'saremo capaci d'una serie non interrotta di purissimi piaceri, della quale frattanto portiamo inerente a noi stessi il desiderio.'[13]

Rousseau equates existence and feeling: 'Exister, pour nous, c'est sentir; et notre sensibilité est incontestablement antérieure à notre raison.'[14] Life is composed of a series of feelings 'la chaîne des sentimens qui ont marqué la succession de mon être.'[15] He can forget the events of the past, but not the feelings – a position against which Manzoni may be consciously reacting in his analysis of the Innominato. The only liaison in our existence is 'une succession de moments présents dont le premier est toujours celui qui est en acte. Nous naissons et nous mourons chaque instant de notre vie.'[16] The association of feelings and moments is emphasized at the beginning of the seventh book of the *Confessions*.[17] We should accept the instant and our experience therein and thus participate

---

13 'We shall be capable of an uninterrupted series of purest pleasures, a series of which in the meanwhile we bear inherent in ourselves the desire,' in *Del piacere e del dolore ed altri scritti di filosofia ed economia*, a cura di Renzo De Felice (Milano, 1964), 49, 63, and 33. The Helvétius reference is in *De l'esprit*, introduction et notes par Guy Blesse (Paris, 1959), 77.
14 Quoted from the *Lettres morales* by H.G. Schenk, *The Mind of the European Romantics* (London, 1966), 4, and Pierre Burgelin, *La philosophie de l'existence de J.-J. Rousseau* (Paris, 1952), 124.
15 *Les Confessions suivies des Rêveries du promeneur solitaire* (Paris, 1961), 414.
16 Quoted by Burgelin, *La philosophie*, 142.
17 *Les Confessions suivies des Rêveries*, 347.

in eternity through a feeling of self-fulfilment and should be totally present, at all times and places, to what befalls us.[18] Self-identity is established by the series of past feelings and moments held in the memory: 'Ce que je sais bien, c'est que l'identité du moi ne se prolonge que par la mémoire.'[19]

Rousseau, then, yearns to eternalize himself in the present and contract out of time: he can reduce life to a sensation of pure existence or assert that days of pleasure and glory, too fair to perish, were concentrated by a sweet ecstasy into a moment like to eternity, but this eternity of happiness was indeed but an instant of his life and then time resumed its slow course.[20] This attitude foreshadows the Romantic craving to reconcile dualities, to embrace all experience, to attain the infinite by grasping the moment, because, with all idea of continuity gone, only the moment remains and each passing emotion is of equal value, even the fleeting succession of them in the Protean Tieck. Schleiermacher's stress on feeling in religion leads to a similar conclusion, for religion can unite a man with the infinite and eternal in one moment.[21] The ecstasy of love can produce a moment of the blissful harmony of Paradise.[22] Goethe's Egmont can ask why the enjoyment of the present moment should be foregone to secure the next, but his Faust learns that the hour should *not* remain, no matter how sweet, for, if it did, constant striving and seeking, in which lies the value of life, would be nullified. As Emil Staiger observes, in Goethe's present moment, being appears as becoming and becoming as being.[23] Finally Schiller, in addition to his concept of a moment of decision in a man's life in a political sense, as Illo brings home to Wallenstein in *Die Piccolomini*, II 6, and Countess Terzky to Wallenstein in *Wallensteins Tod*, I 7, conceives of moments dominated either by passion or tranquil-

---

18 Cf. Burgelin, *La philosophie*, 136 and 119.

19 *Rêveries du promeneur solitaire*, Quatrième promenade (Genève, 1948), 70.

20 Quoted from *La Nouvelle Héloïse* by Mark J. Temmer, *Time in Rousseau and Kant* (Genève et Paris, 1958), 44.

21 *Reden über die Religion an die Gebildeten unter ihren Verächtern*, in the second Rede: 'In the midst of the finite to become one with the infinite and to be eternal in one moment, this is the immortality of religion.' See Schenk, *The Mind of the European Romantics*, 115.

22 Foscolo, *Ultime lettere di Jacopo Ortis* (1802) in *Opere*, Ediz. nazionale, IV (Firenze, 1955), 199–201, speaks of 'questo momento di paradiso,' 'quell'istante divino,' and his mind as being all beauty and harmony.

23 *Goethe* (Zürich, 1959), Bd.3, 479. Faust is finally reconciled to the flow of time and the angels proclaim 'Wer immer sich bemüht, den könen wir erlösen' ('He who ever strives, him can we redeem'), in Part II, act v, 936–7. Cf. Goethe to Eckermann on 3 November 1823.

lity which affect decisions and, inevitably, presuppose the notion of an unstable personality. These decisions of a moment govern the content-ment or misery of a person's future states of mind.[24]

The foregoing paragraphs present some considerations relating to the background of the importance of the moment in Manzoni. In the first four *Inni sacri* he had considered the intervention of the eternal in history through the Incarnation. He stresses the historical character of the events of Christ's life as recorded constituents of the human past, yet shows their enduring effect, in that Christ as Man–God was both temporal and eter-nal: the Church, existing in this world as the Body of Christ endowed with the eternal functions of the Holy Spirit, must continually re-create and re-enact in its festivals these events in their deepest significance – a view that delivers them from historical relativism. Yet, despite their con-tinuing significance, these events remain historical[25] and in no sense are we considered contemporary with them, as for Kierkegaard,[26] nor do they constantly recur within the individual Christian soul, as in the existential concept of Rudolf Bultmann,[27] but, in his participation in the liturgy by an act of faith, man does transcend his present to share a living exper-ience with past generations who have transcended their present.[28] The only explicit coupling of the 'moment' with circumstances reaching beyond it occurs in an early draft of *La Risurrezione*: 'Egli è il fin d'ogni desiro. / Tanto secolo di sospiro / Un momento pareggiò.'[29]

Manzoni devoted himself to the first part of the *Osservazioni sulla morale cattolica* in 1817–18. This part was published in Milan in July 1819 and, for a year or so thereafter, he bestowed perfunctory attention on the second part, but despite the promptings of Monsignor Luigi Tosi, his spiritual director, he never finished it. A revised version of part one appeared in 1855. My concern being with Manzoni's thought up to and including *I Promessi Sposi*, I shall deal mainly with the 1819 edition. The starting point of the work is the Christian conviction that this life is in-

24 E.g. Shrewsbury's words to Elizabeth on her decision for Mary Stuart's execution in *Maria Stuart*, IV 9.

25 Cf. Luigi Derla, *Il realismo storico di Alessandro Manzoni* (Milano-Varese, 1965), 163. St Augustine had made this point vividly: 'Christ died and rose from the dead only once; he will not die again,' quoted from *De Civitate Dei*, XII 14 by Erich Frank, *Philosophical Understanding and Religious Truth* (New York, 1966), 69.

26 *Der Augenblick*: see Oscar Cullman, *Christ and Time*, translated by Floyd V. Filson (London, 1951), 146 and 168 ff.

27 *History and Eschatology*, 153.

28 Alan Richardson, *History, Sacred and Profane* (London, 1964), 264.

29 'He is the goal of every desire. One moment equalled so long an age of sighing.' (Cf. Herbert Butterfield, *Christianity and History* (London, 1954), 121); from *Tutte le opere*, I, 33.

complete and meaningless in itself, but forms one complete whole with the next life. Man was created for an order of perfection, to be begun in this world, though its fulfilment must await the next (1,13, 385).[30] Religion offers assistance in our progress towards this perfection (1,14, 390) – indeed, the maxims of the Gospel make sense only if all does not end with this mortal life (II,2, 506). Completeness in the next life consists of a happiness which itself forms part of moral perfection – the two rarely go together here below – a repose deriving from being absolutely in order, of loving God fully and having no will but his, of freedom from sorrow because bereft of inclination to evil and of any spiritual conflict. This life is a becoming (for each individual, not in the Hegelian sense for mankind, a concept which abolishes individual value, as Kierkegaard noted), whose direction and impetus depend on ourselves, and everything extraneous to preparation for the future life or which makes us forget we are on a journey is vanity and error (II,2, 504). We are allotted a period of time to prepare for eternal life: so this life has positive value, 'le seul moyen de notre salut éternel,' as Massillon had put it.[31] Our motive force is 'l'idea sempre viva di perfezione e di ordine che troviamo egualmente in noi' (Al lettore, par. 21, p. 268),[32] accompanied by a faith in its promised attainment. If this life is a time of trial and our reward or punishment depends on our performance herein, 'l'uomo che al finire della prova è in istato di giustizia, dev'essere in istato di salvezza' (1,9, 349).[33]

Like Massillon and Bossuet, Manzoni recalls the Church's warning to sinners of the uncertainty of the moment and manner of death: consequently, a reasonable man – for, like all true doctrines, the Christian religion addresses itself to the reason – will grasp the single essential point that we should be ready, since the Son of Man will come at an hour we do not expect. Thence Manzoni concludes 'Dunque è ragionevole di vivere in ogni momento in modo che si possa con fiducia presentarsi a Dio; dunque la conversione è necessaria in ogni momento ai peccatori, la perseveranza ai giusti (1,9, 351),[34] a statement that shows, by underlining the dynamic life of the just, that a character like Lucia is far from inactive spiritually. The idea of conversion naturally includes its possi-

---

30 Quotations from *Tutte le opere*, III (Milano, 1963).
31 *Œuvres*, I, 462.
32 'The ever existent idea of perfection and order that we find equally within us.'
33 'The man who at the end of the trial is in a state of justice, must be in a state of salvation.'
34 'Thus it is reasonable to live at every moment in such a way that a man can present himself to God with confidence; thus conversion is necessary at every moment for sinners, perseverance for the just.'

bility at each moment of life (1,9, 348) and the Church makes this declaration, but its difficulty increases as time passes, as sins pile up, as vicious habits grow, and as God is wearied by deafness to his calls. The difficulty is greatest at the moment of leaving life, a point reinforced by quotations from the impressive array of Bossuet, Bourdaloue, Massillon, and Segneri. Sinful habits contracted during a whole lifetime cannot be destroyed in the single moment of death, Bourdaloue had said. Against the Pelagian position that, at any moment, the will is independent of all past choices, Manzoni follows the Pauline view that the sinner is hindered by the past self he has constructed (in John 8:34, Jesus had said that every man who commits a sin is a slave to sin), whereas the righteous man is free in Christ who, by divine grace, sets him free for freedom (Gal. 5:1), free from his sin and his past self, uninhibited by any limits (1 Cor. 3:21–3). Though the final moment of sinner and righteous is a consequence of their lives, this conclusion is not inevitable: at any previous moment a choice was possible between the voices within them of God and of sin – indeed, only death can close off all possibilities. Unfortunately, man's inner ear hears only too often, not a distinct and certain answer, but the confused sound of a sorrowful conflict (1,5, 307): this is the precise situation of the Innominato, whose internal dialogue can be resolved only by its externalization and the introduction of Cardinal Borromeo as an interlocutor. Even a righteous man needs divine help at each moment since his total moral condition is present at each (1,12, 377).

The moral state of a man at the moment of death results from all previous moments and represents his complete self, as did all of those moments in their turn. How can a person be other than what he is at the present? He could scarcely petition for judgment on the basis of some past moment of his own choice. Awaken now, do not say you will repent some day, Bossuet had sternly warned, 'car quelle autre heure voulez-vous prendre? En découvrez-vous quelqu'une qui soit plus commode ou plus favorable?'[35] If judgment is made on the basis of the moment of death, other moments are irrelevant because a man is no longer such,[36] a point not appreciated by Dante's Francesca, but which saved Buonconte da Montefeltro with his final tear of repentance. Man *is* what he decides and, as an autonomous spiritual personality, is wholly responsible for his decisions: there are no 'off-moments' outside the moral reckoning, nor can a balance be struck of good and bad moments to see which predominates,

35 Œuvres, II, 148.
36 Cf. Romano Amerio's edition of the Osservazioni (Milano-Napoli, 1965), III, 195–200.

nor can a good moment cancel a bad. When a man approaches Scripture with heart and intellect, he at once feels that he should employ according to God's law 'ognuno di quei momenti, dei quali si darà conto a Dio; che non ve n'ha uno in tutta la vita per il peccato' (I,9, 355–6).[37] We must always walk carefully, not as foolish but as wise men, buying back time by good deeds, words of St Paul which recur in Borromeo's admonition to don Abbondio. There is no leeway for sin and the blood of a single man spilled by his brother is too much for all centuries and for the whole earth (I,7, 316) and an entire life of merits does not suffice to cover one violent deed (I,7, 328), that is, to sponge the record clean as if nothing had happened. Berdyaev styled 'a great injustice' the imputation to a person of eternal responsibility for actions performed in a brief space of time,[38] but, as Amerio observes,[39] actions are good or bad according to the eternal law, not to time and this world. Bossuet replied to a supposed objection from a sinner on this score: 'n'est-il vrai que, lorsque tu te livres aux objets de tes passions, tu veux pécher sans fin?'[40] Manzoni refutes Sismondi's suggestion of an element of chance deciding the everlasting fate of a dying man's soul: being in a state of grace or otherwise depends, not upon chance, but on the man's properly directed or perverted will, and thus dying at one moment rather than another cannot be construed as ill fortune (I,12, 376–7).

Man's incentive to use each moment positively is fortified by the knowledge that, whenever he turns to religion, it will console him with the assurance that he may still enter on the only way necessary for true and perpetual happiness.[41] Christianity maintains its validity at every moment and is not subject to the assertion that everything has its own time and that it is absurd to preach in society (II,2, 527). As a result, any criticism that religion played an excessive role in the world as dramatized in *I Promessi Sposi* would have appeared to Manzoni illogical and unrealistic.[42] In the novel he did not narrowly apply the doctrines of the *Osservazioni*; with his keen awareness of the individual and his typically Romantic in-

---

37 '... every one of those moments, for all of which account will have to be rendered to God; since there is not one in the whole of life for sin.'
38 *Christian Existentialism. A Berdyaev Anthology*, selected and translated by Donald A. Lowrie (New York, 1965), 171 and 216.
39 *Osservazioni*, III, 200.
40 *Œuvres*, IV (Paris, 1877), 768.
41 *Frammenti relativi alla seconda parte della Morale cattolica*, in *Tutte le opere*, III, 559.
42 E.g. Giovita Scalvini in his essay on *I Promessi Sposi* of 1831: see Mario Marcazzan, *Foscolo Manzoni Goethe* (Torino, 1948), 221; and Croce in his essay of 1921, now in *Alessandro Manzoni*, 6th ed. (Bari, 1969), 7–9. Cf. Amerio, *Osservazioni*, I, cvii.

terest in historical events and situations as unique and unrepeatable, he recognized that men exist at specific times and places and cannot escape their impact, even Federigo Borromeo himself. He investigates the feelings, motives, and reactions to historical events of the individual, since man is partly temporal, but also his attitude to life, that is, his relationship with God, since the eternal and temporal elements unite in man to form the human person. Manzoni's preferred situation is of a character coming to an understanding of reality, in the Christian sense, and consequently transforming his way of life and himself.

In presenting Padre Cristoforo, Manzoni adopts the analytical method of Condillac and Destutt de Tracy[43] by going back to his basic character in order to show and explain its development up to the present, but Rousseau, too, had remarked at the beginning of the Confessions that to know him in advanced age presupposed knowing him well in youth. The point of interest for us, however, is the climactic moment of choice, when Lodovico rejects his previous way of life and makes a decision which governs his future life as Padre Cristoforo, the 'new man.' His upright and violent character had led him to defend actively the weak and wronged, but perforce by the same deceitful and violent methods as his adversaries; hence spiritual conflicts and an occasional desire to enter a monastery. Looking at the body of a nobleman slain by him after a quarrel arising from a point of honour, Lodovico had a 'revelation' of feelings unknown to him before: 'Il cadere del suo nemico, l'alterazione di quel volto, che passava, in un momento, dalla minaccia e dal furore, all'abbattimento e alla quiete solenne della morte, fu una vista che cambiò, in un punto, l'animo dell'uccisore.'[44] A moment suffices for the passage from life to death, from time to eternity, and for the transformation of a man's moral outlook, as it must since life consists of moments: the subsequent decision actually to become a monk is merely the formal completion.[45] He assumed the name Cristoforo, which

43 For the whole question of Manzoni and the *Idéologues*, Elena Gabbuti, *Il Manzoni e gli ideologi francesi* (Firenze, 1936) remains indispensable; but see also A. Leone de Castris, *L'impegno del Manzoni* (Firenze, 1965), 3–28.
44 'The falling of his enemy, the transformation in that face, which was passing, in a moment, from threat and fury to the prostration and solemn quiet of death, was a sight which changed, in an instant, the mind of the slayer.' In *Tutte le opere*, II, tomo I (Milano, 1954), 63. Cf. Nicole, *Essais de morale*, IV, 2. Alberto Chiari, *Rileggendo il Manzoni* (Roma, 1967), 40, stresses the point of the moment opening upon eternity, but takes no account of the relevant passages in the *Osservazioni* and so misses the real point.
45 For such an instant change in a man, Erich Frank cites Augustine, *Sermo* 362, 17, 20, and 277, 11, 11: *Philosophical Understanding and Religious Truth*, 84, n.47.

had belonged to a servant killed in the affray, to remind him every moment of what he had to expiate, of the need, therefore, to buy back time.

The treatment of Gertrude's character is far more complex. Her life is fragmented into moments of disparate moods and resolutions, at some of which she could have made decisions for her whole future, whereas, in fact, she avoided them by acceding to suggestions or pressure from others; however culpable her father and daunting the circumstances, she herself sinned by not using her reason and will to reject a life unsuited to her. Like the sinner of the *Osservazioni* and of its precursors, each successive fall confirms her downward path.[46]

Placed in the convent at the age of six and destined for the veil, Gertrude at first found the moments of her present dominated in turn by two visions of the future: the pleasures of worldly life according to other girls and the joys of convent life as painted by her parents. These alternations became her past, so that the present always resembled the past. Her visions grew more sentimental at adolescence and she regarded them at some moments as desirable, and also attainable since her consent was needed for becoming a nun, and at others as sinful. At one of the latter she was persuaded to petition for examination before the Vicar of the nuns by calculating sisters who were watching her closely. She repented, counter-repented, and sent her father a letter of withdrawal.

The same process continued after her return home for a period of one year after the petition, as prescribed by the rules. Coldly received and excluded from domestic and social activities, she lived an intense inner life. She set sensations of present objects against visions of future happy situations, so divorcing her imagined future from all contact with the present, without whose direction it could never exist. Her liaison with a page marked a hopeless attempt to transfer an imagined future into the present, as would happen later with her far closer relationship with Egidio. She seemed, says Manzoni, like one who had found something of importance and wished to contemplate it at every moment, unknown to others. On the discovery of this liaison, she was closely imprisoned, with a hint of an undefined, hence more fearful, punishment to come. This hint ensured her continued dwelling in an imagined future away from the past whose comprehension was needed before any change was possible in the present. Filled with remorse and terror for the future, she could not return even for a moment to previous fleeting satisfactions without recalling their consequence in her

46 Cf. Giovanni Getto, 'I capitoli "francesi" de *I Promessi Sposi*,' in *Studi in onore di Carlo Pellegrini* (Torino, 1963), especially 588 and 598–9.

present sorrows: past visions of future joys had determined her present – in fact, she had never lived consciously in the present. She finally transferred her imagined future satisfaction to the respected and influential condition of a nun. Lifelong thoughts opposed this step, but times were changed and she yielded to her father's will. It was not times, of course, but she who had changed, her will weakened by previous moments of failure to make a decision. Fashioned by her past and not understanding it, she was unable to control its projection into the present from which her future would flow.

A crucial moment has been reached, one, says Manzoni, when the youthful mind will respond to any appeal having an appearance of good or sacrifice, moments for which scheming craft watches. Moved by an instantaneous tenderness and a desire for human companionship and acceptance, coupled with fear and prepared by a sense of shame, Gertrude assents to her father's assurance that the world contains too many dangers for her.

At this stage, Gertrude finally attempts to review her past, an essential preliminary to a positive attitude to the future, and to ascertain her own will, but the machinery now set in motion was proceeding at breakneck speed: in other words, she is postulating the existence of an impersonal, irresistible force to cover her failure to pause for a moment and to assume responsibility with a decision, no matter how uncomfortable the result. She realizes that withdrawal now would require much more strength and resolution than a few days before when she had already felt her store insufficient, but does not perceive that this gradual erosion derives from her repeated surrenders. The same comment applies to her self-promises to be stronger in future as she counted the occasions remaining for retraction during the return from Monza, where she had formally requested entry after wavering, typically, between the moment of seeing her father's eyes and another of catching sight of one of her former companions, with the opposing resolutions generated by each.

The irony of Gertrude's self-deception emerges at the next major crisis. The Vicar of the nuns, who is charged with testing the depth and sincerity of new aspirants, unconsciously refers to the whole pattern of her past oscillation by his warning that a momentary cause can produce an apparently enduring impression, yet, with the cessation of the cause and a change of mind ... Ultimately, after a year's novitiate studded with repentances and counter-repentances, the series of surrenders ends in an automatic and inauthentic 'yes' at the moment of profession.

Thereafter, Gertrude continued to waver between the fleeting moods and attitudes of different moments. As she declined to overcome her fate by accepting it and making it part of herself, her present could not be thrust towards any future, a highly abnormal situation from which the advent of Egidio delivered her with an immediate future of a certain kind. Until that moment, she had sought to compensate for her closed future and abhorrent present by undoing a thousand times in thought what she had done in action. Her present lacked meaning through the absence of a true awareness of past and future.

The moments of every human life are not equally visible in each. In the consistent, smoothly flowing life of Cardinal Borromeo they are indistinguishable from each other, like the drops of water in a stream; but Gertrude's failure to attain an interpretation of life and self-discovery leaves her a prey to easily discernible moments of contrasting feelings. The root of her sin is grounded in the mind and will wherein lies the power of self-determining choice: threats and perils are irrelevant to this choice. The achievement of salvation without suffering cannot be guaranteed, uniting man with the suffering Christ, a lesson Borromeo recalls to don Abbondio. Every man lives out his life within limits (Sartre's 'facticity') and these very limits both engender and restrict his choices. Gertrude concentrated on finding expression and satisfaction in this life alone, without reference to its completion in the next. For Manzoni, any earthly tranquillity depends on supernatural principles, and two of God's greatest gifts are hope and the resignation stemming from it.[47] After her profession, Gertrude could have looked to an assured and tranquil future but, instead, she lingered negatively over moments of the past.

It is the episode of the Innominato, however, which best exemplifies the function of a series of moments in the construction of personality and the power of the will to change the direction of development; but it also illustrates the existence of the self, the solid identification of which exercised Locke,[48] Rousseau, Condillac, and the Idéologues, while Kant proclaimed a timeless, logical, and moral self which observes its changing empirical counterpart immersed in moments of time. Manzoni, however, sees man as belonging both to the finite order of successive interrelated moments and to the universal order where such interrelationship does not apply.[49] In this episode are dramatized some of the fundamental ideas of the Osservazioni.

Soon after promising don Rodrigo to kidnap Lucia, the Innominato feels annoyed at his promise and appears to enter a period of movement

47 Opere inedite o rare di A.M, pubblicate per cura di Pietro Brambilla da Ruggero Bonghi, III (Milano, 1887), 196, 197–8.
48 Essay concerning Human Understanding, Book II, chap. 27.
49 See Amerio, Alessandro Manzoni. Filosofo e teologo (Torino, 1958), 81.

from one momentary viewpoint or feeling to another, in the manner of Gertrude; but, unlike her, he is making conscious efforts to restore the old self against the emerging new self. For some time he had felt a certain vexation and discomfort at his crimes and now a certain repugnance to them which he had conquered long before returned, at a time when the long, unlimited prospect of the future and a feeling of vigorous vitality filled his mind with unthinking confidence.[50] Now, however, it was thoughts of the future that rendered the past more irksome: 'Grow old! die! and afterwards?' Death was not an external enemy susceptible to superior weapons, but was born within him and, however much he strove to put away the thought of it, it advanced a step every moment – a motive common in Manzoni's seventeenth-century religious writers.[51] One can speak here of a general anxiety or *Angst* rather than simple fear of a discernible object which could be met with courage: indeed, the Innominato's effort to find such objects is irrelevant and thus vain, though he views death as the prelude to a continued future, not as the non-being or *Nichtigkeit* of the existentialists. His self-discovery will bring a realization of his autonomous personality, a kind of *Selbständigkeit*, but he does not create his own individual meaning: the essential difference from modern existentialism is that he penetrates to a pre-existing meaning, universally valid and incontrovertible. Thus his anxiety, originating in the inadequacy of his vaunted power, suggests something beyond it, an individual judgment, God, ignored by him though never denied. In moments of unexplained dejection and terror, God seemed to cry within him: 'I am, however.' He sought to suppress his anxiety by a display of fierceness, envying the times when he could commit iniquities without remorse (whether these are his or Manzoni's terms is not clear) and striving to recapture his old will in order to convince himself that he was still the same: but he is already changed, though he must still achieve a new consistency to carry over from one moment to the next.[52]

The appearance in the valley below his castle of the carriage bearing Lucia heightens the Innominato's anxiety because it symbolizes the imminent decisive moment whose inevitability he has yet to admit, the climax and resolution of his waverings. As he tells his old servant woman, the carriage advances with the step of death. As yet, the direction of his future

50 Cf. Bossuet, *Œuvres*, II, 149, of 'pécheurs endormis': 'et comme ils veulent se persuader, malgré l'expérience et tous les exemples, que leur vigueur présente les en garantit, ils découvrent toujours de temps devant eux.'
51 E.g. Massillon, *Œuvres*, I, 411; Bossuet, *Œuvres*, II, 148; Nicole, *Essais de morale*, II, 2; Segneri, *Opere*, I, 14, and especially II, 193.
52 For Manzoni on anxiety ('inquietudine'), see also *Opere inedite o rare*, III, 196–7.

is uncertain: as Bossuet had observed, 'Si notre salut s'approche, notre damnation s'approche; l'un et l'autre marche d'un pas égale.'[53] Weakened further by his bravo il Nibbio's extraordinary talk of compassion, he orders him to hurry to don Rodrigo, then at once countermands the order, compelled by an imperious 'no' within him: that is, like Gertrude, he postpones the moment of decision.

Lucia's subsequent words to him penetrate to the heart of his problem since they embody two fundamental Christian theses: God forgives so much for an act of mercy and it does not profit a man who must die one day to make a poor creature suffer.[54] Her image dwells in his mind during the night to personify faith, innocence, and goodness and so represent one of the two opposing poles of his mind; in this respect, Lucia precedes the Cardinal, perhaps as feeling before reason and rational clarification. His past crimes, present in his memory, since memory is contemplation of the past through the present,[55] aroused not the feelings of those moments, but a kind of terror and a certain fury of repentance. All seemed changed to him, but the change was in himself. No other thought could displace his problem, all his activities had lost their former meaning. The lack of meaning in his past drained all meaning from his future, for the past should direct the future and be unified with it through the present moment: a decision in the present is also a decision of how the past is to determine the future. The Innominato is moving towards the necessary assumption of responsibility for his past and of a consciousness of guilt which will lay upon him a responsibility for the future, to be discharged in the actions of present moments.[56] Though his past cannot be deleted, he can attain a freedom to advance from his inescapable point of arrival towards a goal different from that to which his past had previously tended. This is the Christian freedom of St Paul. A transformed relationship to God and self must precede a corresponding attitude to other men.

As his new self emerged to judge the old, the Innominato could not explain his acceptance of don Rodrigo's commission. It had been an instantaneous movement of his mind obeying long-standing, habitual feelings, a consequence of a thousand preceding actions, Bossuet's 'suite de cette succession malheureuse' which took possession of Gertrude.[57] Thus

53 Œuvres, II, 151.
54 Segneri, Opere, I, 164, notes that God kept Sarah, Rebecca, Susanna, and Judith inviolate since they were in peril either through his will or that of others.
55 St Augustine, Confessions, XI, 18. The position is close to Freud's and Bergson's view of memory as the possession of past events by present ones.
56 Bultmann, History and Eschatology, 141 and 109.
57 Bossuet, Œuvres, II, 149.

the memory of one crime led him back over the whole series, each identified with the time of its perpetration: 'd'anno in anno, d'impegno in impegno, di sangue in sangue, di scelleratezza in scelleratezza.'[58] Each reappeared, shorn of its motive feelings, with a hideousness those feelings had concealed – sins seen in their true nature as in the *Inferno* of Dante.[59] We are far from the affective memory of Rousseau. These crimes were his, they were himself. He was the aggregate of his past, the product of sinful decisions and actions. Despair at this realization led to thoughts of suicide because he did not yet perceive the possibility of becoming a new product of new decisions and of buying back time through grace. He could think only that, if the next life existed, death itself could offer no escape. He continues to veer towards opposite courses in succeeding moments, from a moment of relief in remembering Lucia's assurance of God's forgiveness and a resolve to release her next morning, to an apprehension of the emptiness of the future. Flight would provide no escape as it could not deliver him from himself.[60] A moment of decision must follow, a *Kairos* in which the eternal will enter the temporal, when the Innominato will accept the gift of grace and begin a series of unbroken moments on the path of righteousness. Manzoni overcomes the difficulty of presentation by introducing, to welcome Federigo Borromeo, the sound of bells pealing, which conduct the Innominato to a dialogue with this unique representative of the Church. The problem can thus be posed and resolved in terms of Christian teaching. During the dialogue, the Innominato acknowledges his transformation in the words: 'Dio veramente grande! Dio veramente buono! io mi conosco ora, comprendo chi sono; le mie iniquità mi stanno davanti; ho ribrezzo di me stesso; eppure ...! eppure provo un refrigerio, una gioia, sì una gioia, quale non ho provata mai in tutta questa mia orribile vita!'[61] His sins exist within his mind, not as a series of individual moments, but as a unified mass which defines him. Since he looks at them in a new light, however, he is a different personality, bound for a future influenced by the past, yet in a direction of his own choosing. His task is

58 'from year to year, from undertaking to undertaking, from bloodshed to bloodshed, from crime to crime' in *Tutte le opere*, II, t.I, 365.
59 Cf. Jacques Maritain, *Existence and the Existent*, translated by Lewis Galantiere and Gerald B. Phelan (New York, 1966), 79.
60 Cf. Massillon, *Œuvres*, I, 13. Unlike Massillon, Manzoni does not admit occasional bouts of soul-searching, anxiety, and near-despair in the sinner's past life.
61 'God truly great! God truly good! now I know myself, I understand who I am; my iniquities stand before me; I have a disgust for myself; and yet ... ! and yet I feel a solace, a joy, yes a joy, such as I have never felt in all this horrible life of mine!' II, t.I, 387–8.

only beginning, but, like Christ, the Cardinal receives him for his faith alone, before any reparation.

Each man, therefore, must come to a realization that this life is a time of trial which is completed in the next and given meaning thereby. Unlike so much eighteenth-century thought, Manzoni does not regard happiness as life's goal; rather, he looks to the moral expression of the individual personality through an understanding and acceptance of reality, though happiness is the eventual reward. Each person must assume responsibility for the conduct of his life, whatever the social or historical context. A prerequisite is the perception of himself in the general scheme of things, of his position within time while linked to the eternal. Time and human lives are composed of moments, at each of which man is his complete self and accountable as such; each moment requires a decision whether for perseverance or change, but such change grows ever more difficult as habit is hardened and personality forged, yet is always possible since, in this respect, a before–after relationship is not causal. A different evaluation of one's past precedes change in the present towards a new future. Like the Romantics, Manzoni recognizes a struggle for individual freedom, but a freedom attained in the originally Pauline sense, not by excessive assertion in a realm empty of content,[62] where self-destruction is reckoned a victory: and from his struggle man returns with a new assurance to a life of reconciliation with his companions in time.

62 Cf. Paul Tillich, *The Courage to Be* (New Haven and London, 1952), 87.

GIOVANNI CECCHETTI

Verga and *verismo*: the search for style and language

OF THE VERGA STORIES collected in *Primavera ed altri racconti* ('Springtime and Other Stories'), 'La coda del diavolo' ('The Tricks of Life') was probably the weakest. It was also the last to be written and the one to close an era in the author's personal history. After January 1876 Verga did not appear in print until August 1879, when he wrote 'Fantasticheria' ('Images'), chronologically the first of the pieces to be included in *Vita dei campi* ('Life in the Fields'). In the intervening years he suffered some severe family losses. In 1877 his sister died, and in 1878 his mother followed her to the grave. He had been deeply attached to both, and their disappearance plunged him into periods of depression and extended meditations on human destiny. While we cannot prove that this appreciably darkened his vision of life, we may safely infer that it brought it into sharper focus. For, if no one can possibly maintain that personal experience automatically produces intense works of art, everyone must acknowledge that at least in general terms the roots of a work of art and of the particular conception of life it implicitly postulates unfailingly lie in personal experience. Circumstances also forced Verga to spend a great deal of time in Sicily, and his Milanese friends began to intimate that he had given up writing altogether.[1]

We cannot forget, however, that the meditations determined by family losses must have simply compounded and deepened a crisis Verga had been experiencing for some time. Ever since he had completed 'Nedda' in 1874, he had become more and more detached from the world and characters of his early novels and, as a result, had been seeking a more strenu-

---

1 *Corriere della sera*, 9–10 September 1877. Quoted in A. Navarria, *Lettura di poesia nell'opera di Giovanni Verga* (Messina-Firenze, 1962), 70.

ously realistic approach to life. Immediately after 'Nedda' he announced to his publisher, Emilio Treves, 'Padron 'Ntoni,' a 'bozzetto marinaresco.'[2] But he never sent it. He kept writing and rewriting it for five or six years, until the end of 1880, when it finally turned into *I Malavoglia*.

Those years of trial and error in the pages of 'Padron 'Ntoni' are of great significance in the sense that during this time Verga became conscious of his new characters and of the necessity of creating a style that should be one with and the same as their daily existence. It was then that he reached his maturity. Towards the end of that period he began to use the interludes and the empty spaces born of his own dissatisfaction with 'Padron 'Ntoni' to experiment with his new concepts in a series of short narratives that were to rate with the best produced in Europe during the second half of the last century. 'Fantasticheria,' the first of those narratives, is not a story but, as the title suggests, a series of images. It must be read as both an introduction to Verga's most original work and a statement of transition. Its substance clearly anticipates the plot of *I Malavoglia*. Yet the writer is mainly interested in deliberately contrasting the sophisticated and parasitic world of the rich with the unvarnished, and poor, surroundings he had known in Sicily during his youth. Only in the latter does he feel he can find human drives in their unmarred nudity and, thereby, rediscover life as it is. In *Eros* (1874) he had stated that 'tutta la scienza della vita sta nel semplificare le umane passioni, e nel ridurle alle proporzioni naturali.'[3] Thus he had indicated his awareness of the psychological complications and falsifications which are typical of the idle, the vain, and the self-centred. But he had not expressed a rejection, for 'reducing' human passions to 'natural proportions' implies starting from their most ornamented and most sophisticated (most unnatural) state, and then, by scratching and scraping, finally uncovering their native essence. This was substantially the method he had used in 'Nedda' (a contemporary of *Eros*), where the frequent social polemics betrayed, among other things, the avowed intention of retracing one's own steps, without being quite sure that it could be done successfully.

With 'Fantasticheria' Verga tells us that he knows he has found an environment where those 'natural proportions' are instinctive and vital, and that from now on he intends to adhere to it. Before the fishermen's hovels, when his lady companion says that she does not understand how

---

2 This 'novelette about fishermen' is said to be close to completion in a letter of 1875 to Emilio Treves, published by Lina e Vito Perroni in 'Storia de *I Malavoglia*,' *Nuova Antologia*, 16 March 1940.
3 'All the science of life consists in simplifying human passions and in reducing them to natural proportions,' *Eros, Il marito di Elena* (Milano, 1946), 165.

anyone can live there, he remarks that, notwithstanding all hardships, these people may even have fuller lives than the rich of the cities: 'Così poco basta perché quei poveri diavoli ... trovino in quelle casipole sgangherate e pittoresche ... tutto ciò che vi affannate a cercare a Parigi, a Nizza e a Napoli.'[4] These people, he admits, have chosen an oyster's life: like oysters, each one clings stubbornly to his rock. Yet they are at least as respectable as those who find them ridiculous. The various members of a family stick together and work together as if guided by inviolable sacred principles, the principles of the 'religione della famiglia.'[5] Their wisdom is the product of the experience of an untold number of generations, and their human feelings are sound and natural, not spoiled by fictitious yearnings. Not only cannot their life be sneered at, but it can even be quite desirable. Thus Verga announces his choice of characters, but at the same time he is convinced that he has to create an expressive medium, a language and a style perfectly suited to the reticent but extremely resonant medium of those characters.

If in its entirety 'Fantasticheria' must be considered a statement of transition and a conscious return to the poor of the Sicilian villages, 'L'amante di Gramigna' constitutes an effort to carry out what we may vaguely call the ideal of the logbook,[6] that is to say, an effort to present

4 'Very little is necessary for those poor devils ... to find in their dilapidated and picturesque' hovels what you anxiously seek in Paris, in Nice, and in Naples,' *Tutte le Novelle* (Milano, 1940), I, 146.

5 'The religion of the family hearth.' This formula was quoted and developed by L. Russo in the *Malavoglia* chapter of his well-known essay, *G. Verga* (4th ed., Bari, 1947), and later picked up by most Verga critics.

6 Refers to an incident of which Verga spoke towards the end of his life: 'Avevo pubblicato qualcuno dei primi romanzi. Andavano: ne preparavo altri. Un giorno, non so come, mi capita fra mano una specie di giornale di bordo un manoscritto discretamente sgrammaticato e asintattico in cui un capitano raccontava succintamente di certe peripezie superate dal suo veliero. Da marinaio: senza una frase di più del necessario; breve. Mi colpì, lo rilessi; era ciò che io cercavo senza rendermene conto distintamente ... Fu un fascio di luce.' ('I had published some of my first novels. They were selling. I was planning others. One day I happened to lay my hands on a logbook. It was a rather ungrammatical and asyntactical manuscript, in which the captain succinctly related certain difficulties his ship had faced – in a sailor's style; without a word more than necessary; briefly. I was struck. I re-read it. It was what I had been unconsciously looking for ... A flood of light.') Riccardo Artuffo, 'Interviste siciliane. Con Giovanni Verga,' *La Tribuna*, Roma, 2 February 1911. Also B. Croce, 'Dalle memorie di un critico,' *La Critica*, 20 January 1916, reported the story, and it has subsequently been repeated by many Verga scholars. We do not know when the incident took place. What we do know, however, is that the logbook cannot be held responsible for Verga's style. Very probably the anecdote indicates a point of consciousness – the moment when the writer clearly realized that to be himself he had to conquer a personal realm of words and a personal syntax, at once simple and rich in underlying tension.

human events with the rich essentiality Verga thought he had finally discovered.

'L'amante di Gramigna' ('Gramigna's Mistress') first appeared as 'L'amante di Raja' in the February 1880 issue of *Rivista minima*, a periodical edited by Salvatore Farina. It acquired the present title later the same year, when it was rewritten, and included in *Vita dei Campi*. The story proper is preceded by a letter to the editor, which is of extraordinary significance both for what it explicitly says and for what it implicitly suggests. In it Verga shows that, after having long pondered narrative problems, he has now reached some unshakable convictions. At the same time he proves an old truism: that to create a masterpiece one must be, among other things, deeply aware of what he is doing and of all the intricacies of his chosen art form, to the point of being able to discuss it competently even on a theoretical level.

The opening paragraph reads as follows:

Eccoti non un racconto, ma l'abbozzo di un racconto. Esso almeno avrà il merito di esser brevissimo, e di essere storico – un documento umano, come dicono oggi ... Io te lo ripeto così come l'ho raccolto pei viottoli dei campi, press'a poco con le medesime parole semplici e pittoresche della narrazione popolare, e tu veramente preferirai di trovarti faccia a faccia col fatto nudo e schietto, senza stare a cercarlo fra le linee del libro, attraverso la lente dello scrittore.[7]

'Storico' ('factual') and 'documento umano' ('human document') are further developed by Verga when he mentions the 'studio delle passioni umane' ('study of human passions') and the perfect novel of the future:

Ogni sua parte sarà così completa che il processo della creazione rimarrà un mistero ..., il suo modo e la sua ragione di essere così necessarie che la mano dell'artista rimarrà assolutamente invisibile ... allora avrà l'impronta dell'avvenimento reale; l'opera d'arte sembrerà essersi fatta da sé.[8]

---

7 'Here is not a story but the sketch of a story. It will at least have the merit of being very short and of being factual – a human document, as they say nowadays ... I shall repeat it to you as I picked it up along the paths in the countryside, with nearly the same simple and picturesque words characterizing popular narration, and you will certainly prefer to find yourself face to face with the naked and unadulterated fact, rather than having to look for it between the lines of the book, through the lens of the writer,' *Tutte le Novelle*, I, 203.

8 'Its every part will be so complete that the creative process will remain a mystery ... its manner and its reason for existing so necessary that the hand of the artist will remain absolutely invisible ... ; it will have the imprint of an actual happening; the work of art will seem to have made itself,' ibid., 204.

All this has a familiar ring, for it repeats some of the fundamental tenets of French naturalism as they were assimilated by the writers of the Italian *verismo* school.

The importance of *verismo* cannot be exaggerated – not only for Verga but for all modern Italian writers. The word itself occurs in all histories of Italian literature and in all essays and articles devoted to Verga's works. However, at least to my knowledge, its origins and its nature have never been clearly and concisely explained. Critics have generally contented themselves with merely mentioning the existence of the phenomenon, in the belief that every reader knew exactly what it was. Here I shall try to give very succinctly the origins of this literary school, to present its principles, and then to show how Verga applied them.

Verismo was the new name given to traditional realism for the purpose of revitalizing it; it simply meant 'true to life,' and stood in opposition to the meaningless, worn-out fantasies of late Romanticism. While Verga was not the founder of the school (at one point he even denied belonging to it), he was profoundly affected by it; in fact, his masterpieces are hardly conceivable without the premise of *verismo*. All the most significant Italian writers of the second half of the nineteenth century and of the beginning of the twentieth century were deeply influenced by the principles of *verismo*. They provided the artists with the necessary freedom to explore all human fields without fear or hesitation. Even Pirandello and Svevo (to mention the least obvious cases) can be historically justified only if we do not lose sight of the fact that they initially followed the theories of *verismo*. The same must be said of Giovanni Pascoli who, because of those theories, initiated contemporary Italian poetry by finally throwing open the doors of the inexhaustible storehouse of everyday language and by striving for a direct, pre-rational rendition of man's emotional world.

Historically and generally, realism may be viewed as either a philosophical doctrine or as literary method. In both cases it has a fairly long history. As a philosophical doctrine, it gained its greatest ascendance in the eighteenth century, mainly in England and in France, and in the nineteenth century, mainly in Germany. As a literary method, it goes back to the Greeks of the Alexandrine era, and to the Latins of the silver period – notably Petronius Arbiter – but it flourishes in the works of Boccaccio, and, later, in many writings of the Italian Renaissance. It is difficult, for instance, to conceive of anyone more deliberately realistic than Pietro Aretino, at least in the general interpretation of the term.

During the middle of the nineteenth century, realism became popular in various European countries, especially in France and in Italy, where, in spite of the Romantic movement (or perhaps because of it), the continuing tradition of set literary rules had become a stifling trap. In Italy, Manzoni might be defined as a realist, but his followers and imitators stressed his so-called moral ideals. The Milanese *scapigliati*, who had some influence on Verga and Capuana, chose 'realistic' principles that actually inter-mingled with the weaker manifestations of late Romantic psychology.

Strangely enough, in Italy the one who was chiefly responsible for promoting a new narrative approach to life and literature was the Neapoli-tan scholar and critic, Francesco De Sanctis. While profoundly familiar with the culture of the past, he was also a man of his time, up-to-date on everything published and ever ready to offer his own comments and personal conclusion. He was familiar with the philosophical trends of the day, including positivism and determinism, and could write essays on Darwin as well as on Zola. In September 1868 De Sanctis published in the influential *Nuova Antologia* an article entitled 'Petrarca e la critica francese' (later reprinted as an introduction to his celebrated *Saggio critico sul Petrarca*), which reads like a profession of faith in the principles of realism. After painting a rather dismal picture of contemporary writing, he came out with a statement perfectly epitomizing the substance of the essay: 'Cosa resta a fare? ... dov'è scritto "ideale", metterci "reale".' We may contend that in De Sanctis' mind this statement must be connected with Vico, whom he defines as 'il vero padre di questa nuova arte,'[9] and with a rejuvenated Faust, the symbol of science, searching for truth through the study of nature, but it is unquestionable that the great critic sees in realism the rebirth of literature, as is clearly proven by his rambling and surprisingly out-of-focus study on Zola (written in 1877). Inci-dentally, until late in life De Sanctis avoided the newly coined word *verismo*, but opted for the traditional *il reale*.

If De Sanctis' enthusiasm for realism surprises those who associate his name merely with the rigorous critical principles by which the value of literary works must be judged only on their own merits, it can be under-stood and justified in the framework of an era when the need for renewal was deep-seated and widely felt. But we cannot overlook the fact that the

---

9 'What is there to be done now? ... To replace the "ideal" with the "real." ' ('The true father of the new art.') Of the works of F. De Sanctis there are many excel-lent editions. The first of the two quotes will be found a few pages before the end of the 'Introduzione' to *Saggio critico sul Petrarca*, and the second in the last page of 'Zola e l'*Assommoir*,' *Saggi Critici*, III. This essay is the stenographic text of a lecture delivered in 1879; in it De Sanctis reiterates ideas he had stressed several times in the past.

young writers grouped in Milan found more direct and more immediate encouragement to try different avenues in the ideas coming from France. There the theories of Comte's positivistic philosophy were given new relevance in the teachings of Taine and were being integrated with the sociological applications of Darwin's recent scientific discoveries. This was rapidly producing the so-called school of naturalism. A generation of writers looked to Balzac as the forerunner of a new literary method and to the novels of Flaubert as its possible examples. In an unceasing effort to keep his Romantic temperament in check, Flaubert had, in fact, declared that he aimed at reproducing 'things' in such a way that they could be touched, and had lent credibility to the theory of 'impersonality.' Yet the one who became not only the master, but the personification, of naturalism in France was Emile Zola.

The bridge between traditional realism and the explicitly proclaimed naturalism of Zola and his followers can be found in *Germinie Lacerteux*, published in 1864 by the De Goncourt brothers. If Zola's *Thérèse Raquin*, published in 1867 and reprinted in 1868 with an important preface by the author, became the mother of all subsequent naturalistic novels, the De Goncourt work certainly influenced Zola and helped him to discover his own inclinations. In the 1870s many writers looked to Zola as the initiator of a new literature. In Italy what De Sanctis was saying and the *scapigliati* were unconsciously looking for was thought to have finally been accomplished by the dynamic young French novelist.

According to the principles of naturalism, the writer must study his human subjects with the scientific objectivity of a physiologist or a physician, and must present them with equal detachment. It was, in fact, from a treatise on experimental medicine by Claude Bernard that Zola said he had derived his theories on the novel.[10] Human reality must further be viewed from the standpoint of its own irreversible deterministic laws of heredity and environment. In practice this is done by seeking out the people of the city slums, the corrupt and the degenerate, by observing how they act and react, and by ascertaining how their degeneracy passes from generation to generation. The novel is the result of this observation. It is, consequently, 'plotless,' and almost writes itself through the characters' actions and reactions.

10 Claude Bernard's book is the well-known *Introduction à la medicine expérimentelle*, published in 1865, and Zola's declaration can be found at the beginning of *Le Roman expérimental*. Although written many years later, *Le Roman expérimental* presents substantially the same theories Zola had first developed in the 1868 preface to *Thérèse Raquin* (cf. John C. Lapp, *Zola before the 'Rougon Macquart*,' Toronto, 1964, 89).

Italian *veristi* believed in some of the principles of naturalism but, with the possible exception of the theory of impersonality, or detachment, they did not make any special attempt to apply them. They did not purposely seek out the corrupt and the degenerate, and on the whole they rejected the deterministic law of heredity. It is interesting that they did not even call themselves naturalists, but simply 'neo-realists' (which may be an accurate translation of the term *veristi*). Verga denied being one of Zola's followers, and Zola rightly rejected him as such. It is a matter of record that soon after the two writers had finally met, Zola, upon realizing that Verga was in substantive disagreement with several naturalistic tenets, said to a common acquaintance: 'On me dit que votre ami Verga est un grand écrivain, mais il n'a que des idées très arrêtrées.'[11]

The *veristi* looked for the reality of human passions in the eternal interplay between man's actions and man's aspirations. They did not go to the slums in search of characters, but to the far-away provinces, where they thought man to be more genuine, not yet psychologically complicated or deformed by the 'civilization' of the big cities. They stressed the inner world of their people by bringing to light their incessant impulse for life and their innate morality. Of course, the fact that Italy offered so many different regional environments made their task easier. Yet we must remember constantly that the *veristi* unfailingly found their characters in the regions of their youth. This would have made it impossible for them to look at those characters with the clinical eye of the scientist, even if they had chosen to stick to the letter of naturalism. Their acceptance of the theory of impersonality, on the other hand, helped them to get rid of superficial subjectivity and excessive sentimentality.

The works of the *veristi* turned out to be so different in spirit as well as in form from those of Zola that his actual influence on them was rather limited. A few decades ago, P. Arrighi wrote two bulky volumes in support of the thesis that *verismo* was totally dependent on French naturalism.[12] The truth is that a compelling need for renewal was being experienced in Italy before Zola appeared on the horizon, and that naturalism represented an important means by which the writers found their own way to satisfy such a need. *Verismo* must then be defined as the offspring of the marriage between pre-existing realism and naturalism. Like all offspring, it soon showed its independence from the parents, even if its personality con-

---

11 G. Prezzolini, 'Giovanni Verga,' *Nosotros*, XLI, 7, quoted in T.G. Bergin, *Giovanni Verga* (New Haven, 1931), 58.
12 *Le vérisme dans la prose narrative italienne* and *La poésie veriste en Italie* (Paris, 1937).

tinued to be marked by some of the most conspicuous characteristics of both.

Since his early years Verga had studied his men and women very carefully and tried to present them with objectivity. In a letter to Felice Cameroni, dated 18 July, 1878, he asserted: 'Ho cercato sempre di essere *vero*, senza essere né *realista*, né *idealista*, né *romantico*, né altro, e se ho sbagliato, o non sono riuscito, mio danno, ma ne ho sempre avuto l'intenzione – in *Eva*, in *Eros*, in *Tigre reale.*'[13] Thus he took himself out of contemporary discussions on naturalism. It is doubtful, however, that he would have consciously recognized the aims of his own past works had it not been precisely because of those discussions. If anything, in his mind he was fusing traditional realism with naturalism. In reference to 'Nedda' we can mention some of the tenets of naturalism, and in an analysis of *Eros* we must stress that in that work Verga follows the positivistic and deterministic principles of cause and effect. It is true that he does not adopt Zola's 'scientific' method, and never will, but how could he have followed those principles without being aware of the emerging new European literary trends? The introduction to 'L'amante di Gramigna,' written about a year and a half after the letter to Cameroni, confirms this contention. Verga regularly brushed aside classifications and labels. He considered schools of secondary significance and insisted on works of art: 'c'è posto per tutti e da tutti può nascere l'opera d'arte. Che nasca, questo è l'importante.'[14] But this does not exclude his acquaintance with naturalism, his direct collaboration on the development of *verismo*, and all the benefits of self discovery he derived from it.

The main spokesman of *verismo*, Luigi Capuana, expressed in theory what Verga managed to achieve in practice. In the preface of *Profumo* (1890), looking back to his young years when he had not yet understood the principles of the new literature, he stated that then he, as well as many others, had not realized that '*il vero ideale è la realtà* che si attua e si trasforma'[15] – which is amazingly similar to what De Sanctis had written in 1868, in the preface to his *Saggio critico sul Petrarca.*

13 'I have always attempted to be true to life, without being either a realist or an idealist or a Romantic or anything else, and if I have made mistakes and if I have not succeeded, too bad for me, but such was always my intention – in *Eva*, in *Eros*, in *Tigre reale*,' in 'Lettere inedite di Giovanni Verga, raccolte e annotate da Maria Borgese,' *Occidente*, 20 May 1930.
14 'There is room for all trends and for all writers, and everyone can produce a work of art. What counts is that the work of art comes into being,' Ugo Ojetti, *Alla scoperta dei letterati*, a cura di Pietro Pancrazi (Firenze, 1946; 1st ed., Milano, 1895), 117–18.
15 'The true ideal lies in reality itself, as it happens and as it changes.'

Verga's terminology in the introduction to 'L'amante di Gramigna' must then be read in the literary climate of *verismo*, as it developed in Italy during the 1870s. 'Storico,' in the sense of 'factual,' the reference to the fashionable definition, 'documento umano,' 'fatto nudo e schietto,' the artist remaining 'assolutamente invisible,' and the work of art that 'sembrerà essersi fatta do sè,' are all expressions pertaining to specific contemporary theories of fiction. Most of them come from French naturalism, but they are absorbed into an independent context, as demonstrated by the phrases referring to language: 'come l'ho raccolto pei viottoli dei campi, press'a poco con le medesime parole semplici e pittoresche della narrazione popolare.' This statement springs not only from Verga's own intention to write straightforward and naked prose, similar to the prose of the logbook, but also from the then generally accepted belief in popular literature, or folklore, conceived by many as a fresh and powerful manifestation of human creativity and, therefore, as an unparalleled model, as well as an inexhaustible source, for writers.[16] Such a belief became a logical component of the *verismo* theories. A number of authors explored the lower levels of the social ladder in the conviction that the tales and the language uncoverable there bore the imprint of unsurpassed originality. The case of Verga is, of course, much more complex. But he too drew from local tales and characters. We know, for instance, that 'L'amante di Gramigna' and 'La Lupa' (The She-Wolf) are based on stories of real people and were inspired by Capuana, who spoke to his friend of the adventures of the two Sicilian women. Later on, when Capuana himself

16 Many studies of the psychology of the masses, or, as they called it, of demopsychology, were then being made. They were generally works based on a tremendous amount of documentary material gathered directly in the provinces with the intent of preserving, and emphasizing the importance of, popular traditions. The greatest scholar in the field was the Sicilian Giuseppe Pitré, whose 1872 *Storia della poesia popolare* exerted considerable influence on the literature of the time. Pitré collected documents of popular traditions and folklore to fill twenty-five volumes. A novelist who was also a scholar, Girolamo Ragusa-Moleti, exploited Sicilian folklore themes for his tales. He is considered significant in the development of the local aspects of *verismo* (L. Russo, *I Narratori* [Milano-Messina, 1951], 145). On *verismo* there exists a fairly large bibliography, but there are very few works combining good information with reliable criticism. I shall quote only three: L. Russo, 'Introduzione,' *I Narratori*; Giulio Marzot, *Battaglie veristiche dell'Ottocento* (Milano, 1941); Mario Marcazzan, 'Dal romanticismo al decadentismo,' in *Letteratura italiana. Le correnti* (Milano, 1956), 663–896. The last of the three is by far the best and most comprehensive treatment of the subject. After this paper was completed, I read two brief but good chapters on Verga and *verismo* and on Verga's poetics in the preface to 'L'Amante di Gramigna,' by Francesco Nicolosi, *Questioni verghiane* (Roma, 1969), 61–76.

wanted to pay 'L'amante di Gramigna' his highest tribute, he said that Verga had re-created the events with an artistic power rivalling popular narration.[17]

With Verga, however, we should not be misled by his statement – 'come l'ho raccolto pei viottoli dei campi, press'a poco con le medesime parole semplici e pittoresche della narrazione popolare' – into thinking that he intends to transcribe directly what he hears. The dense spontaneity of a text cannot be improvised, nor can it be found in someone else's schematic recounting of an event. Verga knew that he had to conquer it for himself with long and unceasing labour. In fact, he wrote and rewrote until he had found a satisfactory mode of expression. Of 'L'amante di Gramigna,' for instance, even without taking into account all the probably discarded versions, we have no less than three different readings, and all three are totally divergent, in both presentation and narrative details, from the 'real' story, as it was later told by Luigi Capuana. 'Narrazione popolare' represents, then, nothing more than the name Verga is giving to his own ideal of narrative prose. Through it he can attain 'il fatto nudo e schietto'; he can fulfil, in other words, the illusion of complete objectivity, in accordance with the principles of *verismo*.

As implied in what he wrote to Cameroni, Verga was conscious that in most cases his previous works were approximate and ineffectual because they had been written in a style lacking firmness and power. His phraseology had been drawn from the average literary bourgeois language and was, consequently, made up of expressions that had been worn out and rendered nearly meaningless by continuous usage. The characters clothed in that language were equally superficial, often even without a semblance of really profound life. Thus when he speaks of the sea captain's log, as well as when he says that he is relating the story with the simple words characterizing popular narration, on the one hand he admits the shortcomings of his previous writings and on the other he declares his determination to abandon empty literary methods and forms in favour of fresh and unadorned expressive patterns.

It is precisely with this in mind that we must read a statement he made to Ugo Ojetti in 1894, where he maintained that the study of the vocabulary is of absolutely no help to an author who wants to acquire a measure of originality, for 'ascoltando, ascoltando si impara a scrivere.'[18] He in-

---

17 In the lecture, 'La Sicilia, nei canti popolari e nella novellistica contemporanea' published in the miscellaneous volume, *L'Isola del sole* (Catania, 1898).

18 'It is only by listening and listening that we learn how to write,' Ojetti, *Alla scoperta dei letterati*, 116.

ferred that an author finds within himself the personal impact of his own words after he has heard them from the lips of those people for whom they carry a profound individual weight, and not by merely looking them up in the dictionary. For in the last analysis, everyone has to create for himself a language perfectly suitable to the environment and the inner world of his characters.

Verga looked for this suitable language in the very environment and in the very lives of his characters. It was partly the natural result of his constant effort to be 'true to life' (to quote his 1878 letter to Cameroni once more). In such novels as *Eros* this effort had persuaded him to adopt some of the sophisticated phraseology of spoken Florentine. Now he had to find an expressive medium fitting the unsophisticated world of Sicilian peasants and fishermen. In 'Nedda' he had not been able to do so. In the few cases when he had felt the necessity to stress the local social milieu, he had resorted to the photographic reproduction of dialect phrases and expressions. It was like abruptly inserting dissonant and shrill notes into the midst of a conventionally smooth musical score.

Those who are familiar with Italian dialects know that some of them are actually languages in their own right, with a vocabulary and syntax of their own. The reasons for this phenomenon lie in historical factors of long standing, and it would be out of place to discuss them here. But people who have grown up with a dialect could not express their emotions with equal energy and directness were they forced to speak the national language. Verga's Sicilian fishermen and peasants did not know standard Italian at all. Had he translated them into the shallow bourgeois idiom of the time, he would have destroyed the intensity of their feelings. And since he could not write in Sicilian dialect, he was forced to create a medium in which those poor and illiterate people could live and express themselves with fully personal implications.

For the purpose he adopted a great many local expressive patterns and grafted them on to the old trunk of standard Italian. Thus, with the few exceptions I have mentioned, every word of the mature Verga can be found in a common Italian dictionary. Certain cadences and certain rhythms, which evoke an environment and a way of life belonging only to those characters, are not, however, always standard Italian. The phraseology itself is often translated from the Sicilian. The syntax is extremely simple, spoken; and its structure consists chiefly in a seemingly unending sequence of co-ordinate clauses linked together by the conjunction *e* (and).

Once the expressive choices were made, the same effort to achieve total objectivity led Verga to a technical discovery of fundamental importance. He began to narrate in the words of the characters. Until then, even the most poignant stories carried in every sentence the obvious imprint of the author, and the reader, as Verga himself would say, had to look at them 'through the lens of the writer.' His own stories, on the other hand, sound as if they were related mainly by an invisible popular narrator who belongs to the same social milieu as the protagonists and who has witnessed the events. While this method justifies the original language mixture, it makes it almost natural to introduce the comments and thoughts of the characters into the narrative stream. Reading Verga, we are often under the impression that the characters are narrating themselves, in their own peculiar terminology and that, therefore, they are painting their own portraits. This has caused some critics to speak of 'racconto dialogato,'[19] and of free indirect speech. In reality we are confronted with an embryonic form of interior monologue, which Verga attained simply because of his compelling desire to be 'true to life.' He stated that all he had aimed at was to put himself 'nella pelle dei miei personaggi, vedere le cose con i loro occhi ed esprimerle colle loro parole.'[20] He did not realize that in the process he had initiated the techniques of modern narrative prose – at least to a considerable extent.

From 'L'amante di Gramigna' on, Verga strove for the greatest possible economy of words and for maximum condensation. Not only did he refrain from any direct intrusion into his texts, but eliminated everything that could be suggested between the lines. Above all, he avoided traditional descriptive passages. For most writers, past and contemporary, descriptions were often pretexts to show off their embroidering ability and virtuosity and had very little to do with the characters' emotional vicissitudes. But the very fact that he was narrating with the words of his people forced Verga to be unceasingly intent upon their individual reactions. As a result, he could mention external elements only when those people mentioned them, that is to say, when they found them relevant to their everyday lives. Thus in I Malavoglia the sea of Aci-Trezza is not

19 'Dialogued narration,' Russo, Giovanni Verga, 409.
20 'In my characters' skins, to see with their eyes and to speak in their words,' Lettere al suo traduttore, a cura di F. Chiappelli (Firenze, 1954), 130–31. On Verga's 'free indirect speech,' see L. Spitzer, 'L'originalità della narrazione nei Malavoglia,' Belfagor, xi (1956), 37–53, and especially the first part of my article, 'Aspetti della prosa di Vita dei campi,' Italica, xxxiv (1957), later reprinted in Leopardi e Verga (Firenze, 1962) and now in Il Verga maggiore (Firenze, 1968 and 1970), 27–46, whose conclusions have been widely accepted by subsequent critics, often without quoting the source.

Romantic, but is looked at with the very eyes of the fishermen who find in it their means of subsistence, and sometimes their death. A storm, or even the changing voice of the tide under a gloomy sky, are significant only insofar as they become both the repositories and the projections of human hopes and fears.

On 10 July 1879, Francesco De Sanctis proclaimed: 'il motto di un'arte seria è questo: poco parlare di noi, e far molto parlare le cose.'[21] This was exactly what Verga was beginning to do in a much bigger way than the great critic could have anticipated. Verga's highest and most consistent accomplishment in this sense is represented by the entire novel, I Malavoglia. But for perfection and originality, his Sicilian short stories should not be placed on a much lower level.

In 'L'amante di Gramigna' Verga tells of a girl who falls in love with a bandit without having ever seen him and cannot help going after him and making him her only reason for life, as if blindly submitting to an irresistible spell. Peppa leaves her home and her fiancé, follows the bandit as he is hunted by the police, is wounded by a gunshot, and finally, when he is caught, she becomes a cleaning woman in the barracks adjoining the jail and is filled with admiration for the carabinieri, who had proved even stronger than her man.

The theme itself is rather unexciting, for it is grounded on some very common and basic principles of feminine psychology. But, as with all artistic products, what makes the story outstanding is the way the theme is treated and how it finds concrete life in the style. In the first page Verga creates a vast atmosphere, filled with the most diverse people, all busy either pursuing or discussing the same man, and then places him at the centre, like a giant, a legendary figure, alone against a thousand. In comparison, all those who are chasing him appear ridiculously small. No one has seen Gramigna, but everyone is constantly aware of his presence and is totally overwhelmed with admiration for him.

Parecchi anni or sono, laggiù lungo il Simeto, davano la caccia a un brigante, certo Gramigna, se non erro, un nome maledetto come l'erba che lo porta ... Il prefetto fece chiamare tutti quei signori della questura, dei carabinieri, e dei compagni d'armi, e subito in moto pattuglie, squadriglie, vedette per ogni fossato, e dietro ogni muricciolo; se lo cacciavano dinanzi come una mala bestia per tutta

21 'The motto of serious [literary] art must be this: let us not talk, but let us make things talk,' in the closing lines of 'Zola e l'Assommoir.'

una provincia, di giorno, di notte, a piedi, a cavallo, col telegrafo ... Nelle campagne, nei villaggi, per le fattorie, sotto le frasche delle osterie, nei luoghi di ritrovo, non si parlava d'altro che di lui, di Gramigna, di quella caccia accanita, di quella fuga disperata. I cavalli dei carabinieri cascavano stanchi morti; i compagni d'armi si buttavano rifiniti per terra, in tutte le stalle; egli solo, Gramigna, non era stanco mai, non dormiva mai, combatteva sempre, s'arrampicava sui precipizi, strisciava fra le messi, correva carponi nel folto dei fichidindia, sgattaiolava come un lupo nel letto asciutto dei torrenti. Per duecento miglia all'intorno, correva la leggenda delle sue gesta ... lui solo contro mille, stanco, affamato, arso dalla sete, nella pianura immensa, arsa, sotto il sole di giugno.[22]

Throughout the passage we immediately sense a deliberate popular, somewhat aliterary tone. The constant movement and activity are obtained with the simplest expressive means. Incidental comments, obviously repeating remarks by the various observers, are inserted into the narrative stream with the greatest ease (e.g. 'un nome maledetto come l'erba che lo porta' – *gramigna* is the Italian for crabgrass). The same tendency to tell the story in the words of the villagers is evident in the alogical use of mixed metaphors which are often intended to reproduce an impression of emphatic awe ('sgattaiolava come un lupo'). The syntax is mostly based on an elementary sequence of quick, identically structured phrases. On the surface this prose looks very unsophisticated, yet it communicates with great immediacy and without distractions. After such an opening we are ready for the story, whose real protagonist is not Gramigna, but his mistress.

Peppa, one of the most beautiful girls in Licodia, with a rich dowry, and engaged to be married to a well-to-do and strong young man (who

22 'Several years ago, down there along the Simeto, they were chasing a bandit, a certain Gramigna, if I am not mistaken ... a name as cursed as the grass that bears it ... The prefect sent for all those gentlemen of the police department, the *carabinieri* and the soldiers; patrols and squads were immediately in motion, sentries were placed along every ditch and behind every wall; they drove him before them like an evil beast, over the whole province, by day, by night, on foot, on horseback, and by telegraph ... In the fields, in the villages, on the farms, under the tavern boughs, wherever people met, they spoke only of him, of Gramigna, of that relentless chase, of that desperate flight. The *carabinieri*'s horses dropped dead tired; the soldiers, exhausted, threw themselves on the ground in every stable; the patrols slept on their feet; he alone, Gramigna, was never tired, never slept, always fought, climbed on cliffs, slipped through the wheat, ran on all fours in the thick of the cactuses, slunk like a wolf down the beds of dry creeks. For two hundred miles around ran the legend of his deeds, he alone against a thousand, burning with thirst, in the immense burnt plain, under the June sun,' *Tutte le novelle*, I, 204–5.

'portava lo stendardo di Santa Margherita come fosse un pilastro, senza piegare le reni'),[23] is the envy of all the women in town; she is considered so fortunate that her mother weeps with joy. But she wants the bandit, Gramigna, of whose fearless exploits she has heard so much: 'quello sì, ch'era un uomo!' ('That one, that one was a man!'), says the narrator in the very words Peppa would say only to herself. She had never seen Gramigna, yet 'pensava sempre a lui, lo vedeva in sogno, la notte, e alla mattina si levava colle labbra arse, assetata anch'essa come lui.'[24]

At the end of the first page Verga had stressed one main characteristic the townfolk used to single out when speaking of Gramigna: his thirst ('sete'). Now he sees it grow in Peppa's imagination, for whom it becomes so all exclusive as to turn into the very essence of the bandit's difficult life. Soon, through a direct psychological transference, the girl identifies herself with Gramigna to the point of experiencing the same thirst and the same need to satisfy it. But then we understand that the thirst she feels, when she gets up in the morning with her lips burning, is both the image and the counterpart of another, and deeper, personal need. Thus this elementary factor, in an equally elementary human context, must be viewed as much more than analogy, for in it we find the substance of a psychological identification.

Peppa discovers where Gramigna is hiding and goes to him. She meets him 'nei fichidindia di Palagonia ... lacero, insanguinato, pallido per due giorni di fame, arso dalla febbre, e colla carabina spianata.'[25] At first he does not want to have anything to do with her, but then he tells her to go and get some water. While she is gone, the bandit hears some gunshots, and then sees her come back 'lacera, insanguinata.' Now her process of identification with the man is complete; like his, her clothes are torn, and like him, she is bleeding from gunshots. Now she will follow Gramigna everywhere, suffering the same hunger and running away from the same police bullets.

In a story of only a few pages Verga manages to create a highly poetic character. His stylistic compression, rather than preventing, helps him to evoke some profound human associations. A few words, or the repetition of a key phrase, are often enough to bring to the surface what lies

23 'Carried the banner of St Margaret without bending his back, as straight as a pillar,' ibid., 205.
24 'She was always thinking of him, she saw him in her dreams at night, and in the morning she got up with her lips burning, and felt as thirsty as he was,' ibid., 206.
25 'In the cactuses of Palagonia, his clothes torn, bleeding, pale after two days without food, burning with fever, his rifle ready,' ibid., 207.

hidden in the subconscious. What could have easily resulted in a weak and sentimental romantic story has become a powerfully new personal creation. With 'L'amante di Gramigna,' Verga shows that he has definitely opted for certain characters and has conquered a prose which is born of their inner world. Now he is finally proving to be the true artist who can open unsuspected vistas with an unmistakably original expressive medium. We know that his long search has come to an end and that he is finally ready for his masterpieces.[26]

26 This paper is part of a chapter in a book on Verga, which the author is now in the process of completing.

MADDALENA KUITUNEN

Ibsen and the theatre of Roberto Bracco

THE UNFAVOURABLE CHARGES levelled against the theatre of Bracco originate principally from critics who insist in considering him a follower, or at least, a poor imitator of Ibsen. Judgments have been passed and conclusions very often drawn, based on the similarity of certain personages and situations in the production of both playwrights. It was rather a fashion for critics at the end of the nineteenth century to see the influence of Ibsen in all the Italian plays written at that time, as Stäuble has pointed out in his study of Bracco.[1] Giacosa, Praga, D'Annunzio, and Pirandello, to mention only a few, seem to have undergone more or less the same fate, but Bracco was the one who suffered most from a comparative association with the Norwegian. Ibsen's popularity can be best summed up in the following statement by Bradbrook: 'He was the first, and perhaps the only writer to achieve as a dramatist the kind of European fame which now belongs to film stars. The nineteenth century dramatic tradition is Ibsen.'[2] Two leading Italian theatre critics expressed reservations about Bracco and assigned a higher place to Ibsen; D'Amico noted: 'Bracco, dopo aver letto opere di Ibsen si credette un pensatore e si mise ad escogitare una serie di casi patologici';[3] and Apollomio wrote: 'Bracco è vita seconda di Ibsen, polemica aggiunta alla verità.'[4]

Unless otherwise identified, translations in the footnotes are by the author.

1 A. Stäuble, *Il teatro di Roberto Bracco* (Torino, 1959), 44.
2 M.C. Bradbrook, *Ibsen the Norwegian* (London, 1948), 77–8.
3 S. D'Amico, *Il teatro del '900* (Milano, 1932), 40. 'Bracco, after reading Ibsen's works, considered himself as a thinker and began composing a series of pathological cases.'
4 M. Apollonio, *La storia del teatro italiano* (Firenze, 1938), IV, 297. 'Bracco is a repetition of Ibsen, polemics added to truth.'

The few who praised Bracco without these reservations were often moved by sentimental reasons rather than by objective and sound analysis, as one can gather from Villanova D'Ardenghi's introduction to his *Teatro neo-idealistico*: '... salvo rare eccezioni, per i lavori e per i personaggi che esamino partitamente io dimostro una grande simpatia, spesso un grande entusiasmo ... vi è poi una ragione speciale di sentimento che giustifica l'insistenza della lode in questo caso.'[5] More sympathetic and complimentary was Parisi who felt entitled to begin the appraisal of his fellow Neapolitan with this melodramatic statement: 'L'idea di comporre un libro sulla sua vita e sulla sua arte ... è nata dal grande affetto e dalla grande devozione per il Maestro. Senza questo assillo sentimentale, confesso che il solo proposito di scrivere di lui ... mi avrebbe sgomentato al punto di rinunziarvi.'[6]

It is the aim of this paper to examine Bracco's debt to Ibsen, his treatment of similar themes, and to reassess the position of the Italian dramatist in relation to his times, background, and culture. When his plays began to be performed in Naples, in the last decade of the nineteenth century, Bracco was in his late twenties and Ibsen's fame was establishing itself on the Italian scene for the first time, thanks to the interpretations of Eleonora Duse and Ermete Zacconi and through translations from the French version of Count Prozor, the only translator from the Norwegian authorized by Ibsen.[7] This was more than mere coincidence because it put the two playwrights on a direct level of confrontation in Italy, and the sensation stirred by the social and pathological implications of the plays of the Norwegian was bound to relegate Bracco to a secondary role

5 B. Villanova D'Ardenghi, *Teatro neo-idealistico* (Milano, 1907), 6. '... with few exceptions, I show great sympathy for the works and the personages I examine in particular, often great enthusiasm ... there is also a special sentimental reason which justifies my insistence in praising in this case.'

6 P. Parisi, *Roberto Bracco* (Milano, 1923), 7. 'The idea of composing a book on his life and art was inspired by my great affection and devotion for my teacher. Without this sentimental stimulus, I confess that the idea of writing of him, ... would have embarrassed me to the point of giving it up.'

7 The first drama by Bracco, *Una donna*, was presented in Naples at the Fiorentini theatre on June 5, 1893. Ibsen's plays were performed for the first time in Italy in the following order: *A Doll's House*, Filodrammatici, Milan, 9 February 1891; *The Wild Duck*, Manzoni, Milan, 26 September 1891; *Pillars of Society*, Filodrammatici, Milan, 24 November 1891; *Hedda Gabler*, Comunale, Trieste, 2 April 1892; *Ghosts*, Manzoni, Milan, 22 December 1892; *The Master Builder*, Della Valle, Rome, 18 March 1893; *Rosmersholm*, Gerbino, Turin, 8 January 1894; *The Woman of the Sea*, Filodrammatici, Milan, 3 February 1894; *An Enemy of the People*, Manzoni, Milan, 22 February 1895; *Little Eyolf*, Manzoni, Milan, 22 February 1895; *John Gabriel Borkman*, Bologna, October 1898; *When We Dead Awaken*, Manzoni, Milan, 2 May 1900.

since he failed to arouse discussion as spectacularly in his own works. An echo of the uproar caused by Ibsen is thus viewed by Lorenzo Gigli:

Casa di bambola fu nell'estremo Ottocento il grido della donna, la grande polemica femminista. Nacque e si diffuse il 'Norismo.'[8]

Gli Spettri non furono altro che un manifesto a disposizione delle leghe europee dell'antialcoolismo, al fine di mettere sotto gli occhi delle folle atterrite gli spaventosi fenomeni del 'delirium tremens.'[9]

Ibsen was a pioneer of the neo-idealistic theatre and Bracco a prominent Italian exponent of it, and, as such, they observed contemporary society, adopting moral and social topics for their theatrical works, which would show a certain degree of involvement with the problems of their times. Both of them turned their attention to the soul, to the interior life, to the observation and probing of the subconscious, and above all to the role of women in the family and society. If they are generally classified as belonging to the wide movement of neo-idealism, the terminology 'theatre of ideas,' adopted for Ibsen, and 'theatre of thought' for Bracco, is not sufficient to define the differences between them.[10] Their dramatic techniques were different, their use of the principles of the naturalistic school varied; the worlds they drew their characters from were basically different, almost as opposite as were their views on the problems of emancipation of women. These are fundamental elements to examine in order to prove that in their approach to art the two should not be judged on the same level.

Ibsen created the middle-class tragedy that develops out of social problems and issues, retaining the principal divisions of classical tragedy such as: introduction, rising action, climax, and falling action, and at the same time liberating it from the conventional formality and restrictions of the five acts. This dramatic structure is perfectly recognizable in *Ghosts*, *Rosmersholm*, *The Master Builder*, and is impervious to basic change in the other more domestic tragedies, where some stages of the process may

8 *Ibsen, I capolavori* (Torino, 1946), series directed by Lucio Redenti with an introduction by Lorenzo Gigli, 319. 'At the end of the nineteenth century *A Doll's House* was the outcry of women, the great feminist polemic. "Norismo" was born and spread.'

9 Ibid., 369. '*Ghosts* was only a manifesto in the hands of European leagues against alcohol with the purpose of exposing to frightened crowds the dreadful phenomena of "delirium tremens." '

10 Stäuble, 261.

not be represented openly, but nevertheless are communicated to the audience by implication and flashback. As Gosse says: 'Each of Ibsen's plays presupposes a long history behind it; each starts as an ancient Greek tragedy.'[11] The only relevant divergence from the classic falling action is found in dramas like *A Doll's House* and *The Woman of the Sea* with the final unravelling of the plot which replaces the catastrophe or death of the hero. One of Ibsen's greatest accomplishments in dramatic technique remains his change from verse, used in his early production, to prose, abandoning thus 'the language of the Gods' and portraying truthfully the human beings he dealt with in his works.

In Bracco's case, although complete independence of the five-act structure is also exercised, no dramatic work of his complies in following the traditional stages necessary for the moulding of a tragedy. He writes independently of any organized procedure that might add more pathos to his scenario and makes great use of the scenes, a division less scientifically systematic. He achieves outstanding success in a dramatic form not practised by Ibsen, the one-act play. Bracco's highly flexible technique was at its best in this genre, where he could answer the demand for unity of effect, vigour of dialogue, and stressing of character, given the economy of narrative material. Such a change in dramatization is in accordance with the following definition of Arthur Miller: 'The dramatic form is a dynamic thing.'[12] It is most significant that Jean Dornis who criticizes Bracco as an unsuitable southern student of Ibsen's Nordic school, has words of praise for *Le maschere*, 'sa première pièce originale,' and *Don Pietro Caruso*, that 'petit chef-d'œuvre.'[13] These are the two one-act plays performed respectively in 1894 and in 1896 in which Bracco limits the dialogue and condenses in a few scenes the dramatic passions of his main characters, who dominate the whole drama and succeed in conveying to the audience the feeling of their tragic experience. It is not appropriate to say like Dornis that Bracco in these two plays avoided creating 'les types exceptionelles à l'imitation d'Ibsen,'[14] because it is rather through the efficaciousness of the short dramatic form of the one-act play that criticism can better evaluate Bracco's art and originality.

The preparation Ibsen and Bracco had for the stage is also particularly linked to the results achieved through their different dramatic techniques. For Ibsen it was a lifelong training that began in 1851, when he was only twenty-three years old, with his apprenticeship at the Bergen National

---

11 E. Gosse, *Henrik Ibsen* (New York, 1908), 240.
12 Arthur Miller, *Collected Plays* (New York, 1965), 10.
13 Jean Dornis, *Le Théâtre Italien Contemporain* (Paris, 1904), 241, 250.
14 Ibid., 261.

theatre, continued when he became director of the Christiania Norwegian Theatre, and was encouraged by a travelling grant he received for the purpose of studying the European stage. He focused all his efforts on his dramatic production, taking care of the smallest details, even to the matter of lighting and contemporary stage machinery.

The gloomy Norwegian landscape, which is almost always perceived through windows and doors, also constituted the most suitable setting for events taking place on the stage. As Heller says:

By the social background of his plays we are perpetually reminded that he came from a smallish country ... And just as this oppressive social environment ... is essential to a satisfactory understanding of Ibsen's people, so again the strictly natural setting of the locality, the Norwegian landscape, is inseparable from their meaning.[15]

In *Ghosts*, Ibsen's most moving tragedy, the natural background plays a role equal to that of the main characters. The landscape of the fjords, discernible through the large glass panes, half obscured by the rain and mist, looms as a shadow in the three acts. It stands, heavy with sadness and evil omen, as a silent witness to the tragic happenings of the Alving family. Even the early morning sunlight that appears at the conclusion of the play helps to produce a tragic impact on the audience when Oswald, overcome by the darkness of his delirium, shouts 'Mother, give me the sun,'[16] and repeats the cry, motionless, until the curtain falls.

Bracco's creativity was not exclusively confined to the theatre, but manifested itself in different fields, since he was a reporter, a literary and a music critic, a vernacular poet, and a short-story writer. In the theatre he was not limited to the tragic form, but achieved success also in farces. His versatility made it impossible for him to devote himself systematically to his dramatic production. Rather than striving to master the dramatist's craft to enhance the structure of his plots, Bracco focused his attention on depicting Neapolitan life as it was, in all its multiple aspects. A basic trait of the city he was portraying was the use of songs and motifs that his personages would often hum, even on their way to committing suicide, as in the case of Don Pietro Caruso in the play by the same name.

Ibsen himself must have been fascinated by this Neapolitan peculiarity and he proved it by including part of a tarantella tune in the second act of

15 O. Heller, *Henrik Ibsen* (New York, 1912), 12.
16 All quotations from Ibsen's plays, with the exception of *Little Eyolf* are taken from *Eleven Plays of Henrik Ibsen* (Random House, n.d.), with an introduction by H.L. Mencken.

A Dolls House. The long sojourn of the Norwegian dramatist in Rome lasted from 1864 to 1868 and later from 1878 to 1884 with the interruption of several trips to the region of Naples. That period is considered to be his most productive and it coincided with the composition of *A Doll's House,* written in great part at the Hotel Luna in Amalfi in the summer of 1879. The tarantella Nora dances so frantically in the second act is not only a reminder of her trip to Southern Italy but also her farewell to the unreal life of 'a little lark.' Soon after the tarantella, her husband will become aware of her unconscious forgery and he will finally reveal himself in all his rigid narrow-mindedness. Music in this drama, as in Bracco's, as in Neapolitan life, represents a world in which sunshine and tragedy are tightly interwoven.

Nature, described in the bright Neapolitan landscape, stands as a symbol of cheerfulness and gaiety. The gay atmosphere, far from creating a striking contrast to the personal drama of Bracco's characters, is a most fitting background for understanding it. It is not surprising, therefore, to read this luminous description in the first act of *La piccola fonte:* 'In fondo, la linea d'un parapetto di pietra taglia l'azzurro chiarissimo e brillante del mare ... il sole splende dovunque un bagliore abbagliante. L'aria è piena di gaiezza.'[17] The existence of Teresa, the protagonist of *La piccola fonte,* is intimately associated with this sight because her role in the play is developed in accordance with a poetical concept. Her desire for a life of love and dedication plunged her into insanity when she realized it was not reciprocated by her husband in his selfishness and vainglory. Only in her cheerful surroundings, however, is she capable of detaching herself from reality by constantly clinging to her happy past through her memories and her attachment to those objects constituting a meaningful part of that past.

A leading principle of the naturalistic school such as the role played by pernicious hereditary factors in human life is closely connected to Ibsen's most outstanding plays. Ibsen analyses as a psychoanatomist the physical and mental suffering of some of his protagonists and relates it to the dissolute behaviour of their fathers. Oswald Alving's sickness in *Ghosts* is a living accusation of his father's dissipated life, and Mrs Alving's anguish and remorse reach their climax when she becomes aware of this shattering reality. In *The Wild Duck* little Hedvig's lingering

---

17 All quotations from Bracco's plays are taken from the 1922 Sandron edition. 'In the background, the line of a stone parapet cuts the very light and bright blue of the sea ... Sun diffuses everywhere a dazzling brilliance. The air is full of gaiety.'

Emma Gramatica in the role of Nora in Ibsen's *A Doll's House*.
Courtesy of the *Enciclopedia Biografica Italiana*, Series 9

Ermete Zacconi in Roberto Bracco's *Don Pietro Caruso*.
Courtesy of Cappelli editore, Bologna

Ermete Zacconi in the role of Oswald in Ibsen's *Ghosts*

blindness serves to reveal the identity of her real father from whom she had inherited it. This circumstance was of primary importance in the development of the play since it pushed little Hedvig to suicide. Dr Rank in *A Doll's House* has to admit before dying from his incurable disease: 'My poor innocent spine has to suffer for my father's youthful amusements' (Act II).

The relevant implication of hereditary diseases was sustained by the science of the time and was adopted by a wide range of writers with too much insistence and a certain degree of exaggeration, as Cesare Lombroso, a leading psychiatrist and anthropologist of the last century, pointed out:

Ibsen, per esempio, negli *Spettri* ha fatto il quadro più esatto della paralisi generale progressiva frequente appunto, come nel suo eroe, in uomini di grande attività mentale che abusarono dei piaceri o del lavoro intellettuale, sopratutto se hanno un fondo ereditario ... solo che egli ha il torto di accumulare in un solo soggetto i fenomeni di una grande quantità di malati, esagerandone quindi le linee ...[18]

Bracco had the benefit of about fifteen years from the time of Ibsen to the beginning of his productive period and therefore dealt with the problems of heredity factors more cautiously. For the Neapolitan it was not a profoundly accepted belief on which to base the unlucky existence of some of his characters. The best known reference to it is found in *Don Pietro Caruso*, when the protagonist points out to count Fabrizii the reasons for his personal misconduct: 'Signor conte, io sono stato sempre una persona squilibrata e spregevole, poichè fin dalla mia prima giovinezza si svilupparono in me i tristi germi che avevo ereditati nascendo.'[19] Although this situation was not emphasized unduly in Don Pietro's tragedy as it was in the case of Oswald in *Ghosts*, it contributed, however, to Don Pietro's decision to commit suicide. It is particularly significant that Ermete Zacconi, who excelled in pathological roles, achieved one of his greatest suc-

---

18 Cesare Lombroso, 'Il delinquente e il pazzo nel dramma e nel romanzo moderno' in *Nuova Antologia*, CLXIII (1899), 665. 'For example, Ibsen in *Ghosts* has given the most exact picture of progressive general paralysis, common, as in the case of his own hero, to men of great mental activity who have abused pleasures and intellectual work, above all if they have an hereditary background ... except that he is wrong in accumulating in one person alone the phenomena of a large number of illnesses, thereby exaggerating a little.'
19 'Sir, I have always been an unbalanced and contemptible person, because since early childhood the evil germs I had inherited, when I was born, have been developing in me.'

cesses in Paris in January 1911 in the interpretation of both *Ghosts* and *Don Pietro Caruso*, for which the French government awarded him the Cross of the Legion of Honour.

A turning point in Bracco's attitude towards naturalism's fundamental doctrines is well demonstrated in his last and most debated play, *I pazzi* (1922). If the playwright does not openly attack naturalism, he does so indirectly by criticizing positivism, its philosophical counterpart, in connection with the science of psychiatry. In *I pazzi* Bracco deals exclusively with the problem of madness in all its aspects, and is opposed to the application of scientific rules that would explain causes and consequences of this so-called sickness. Francesco, the protagonist of *I pazzi*, opens a clinic to treat alienated people with a more personal and spiritual method rather than to apply exclusively the rules of official science. To his doubts about the success of his mission, Professor Bernardi, his colleague, answers that: 'Il positivismo applicato alla psichiatria è un ammasso di preconcetti cristallizzati, i quali danno sempre ai fatti le medesime fisionomie, false e bugiarde.'[20]

Another dogma of naturalism emphasized the effects of the environment on the conduct of individuals. It was accepted in 1908 by Bracco in *Nellina*, a drama about a young girl who found it impossible to run away from a life of corruption that had surrounded her since her early childhood. The same situation had been presented earlier in *Sperduti nel buio* (1901) with Paolina who leaves Nunzio, the only person who could love and respect her, because she is unable to abandon an easy life of vice and expediency. So detrimental to her behaviour had her environment been that she does not even possess the judgment of a moral conscience but acts only according to instinct.

In *I pazzi* Bracco adopts a reverse solution with Sonia, a patient in Francesco's clinic. She too comes from a corrupt world but she has the force of character to abandon it, unlike Nellina and Paolina. She is capable of redemption through love and comprehension. The new attitude developed by Bracco in his last play does not go counter to his preceding work, but helps to clarify the author's conception of art, clearly specified in his preamble to *I pazzi*: 'L'Arte non offre, non indica, non suscita soluzioni di problemi che anche la Filosofia invano affisa o sviscera o espone scevri di scorie. Al più al più, si sforza di tradurli in visioni che parlino alla sensibilità, senza troppo incomodarme la mente.'[21]

20 'Positivism applied to psychiatry is a mass of crystallized preconceptions, which give always the same false and deceiving aspects to facts.'
21 'Art does not offer, does not indicate, does not inspire the solution of problems

If the world from which Ibsen and Bracco drew their characters is carefully examined, one realizes that for them it was not only a case of portraying two different nations, geographically apart, but two societies founded on basically different structures. By the middle of the nineteenth century, Norway already had a stable bourgeoisie, and it is from this class that Ibsen chooses his main characters, his doctors, magistrates, well-to-do people, completely remote from a life of material misery and starvation. The working class appears indirectly in a secondary role through house-keepers and carpenters. In showing how these people's problems were unimportant to him or at least to his art, Ibsen was quite explicit in *The Wild Duck*. The starving people of Ekdal's household, rather than expos-ing some deplorable social conditions, make the author muse over an odd combination of Bohemianism and starvation on the fringes of the middle class. This is how Hjalmar answers little Hedvig who is waiting for some leftovers from a dinner party which he was invited to attend alone:

HJALMAR. No, I positively forgot to get anything. But wait a little! I have some-thing else for you, Hedvig ...
HJALMAR (with a paper). Look, here it is.
HEDVIG. That? Why, that's only a paper.
HJALMAR. That is the bill of fare, my dear; the whole bill of fare. Here you see: 'Menu' – that means bill of fare.
HEDVIG. Haven't you anything else?
HJALMAR. I forgot the other things, I tell you ... Sit down at the table and read the bill of fare, and then I'll describe to you how the dishes taste. Here you are, Hedvig. (Act II)

What Ibsen exposes in his social dramas is a solidly established society whose main problems arise out of domestic life. G.B. Shaw sees this class as the only possible source of Ibsen's social theatre:

And here let it be said that the comparative indifference of the working class to Ibsen's plays is neither Ibsen's fault nor the fault of the working class. To the man who works for his living in modern society home is not the place where he lives, nor his wife the woman he lives with ... It is in the propertied class only that two people can really live together and devote themselves to one another if they want to.[22]

which Philosophy, too, vainly fixes or uproots or exposes without dross. At the most, it attempts to translate them into forms that may speak to one's sensibility without overly upsetting one's mind.'
22 G.B. Shaw, *The Quintessence of Ibsenism* (London, 1913), 129.

Woman's freedom, woman's role in her family and in society are problems better understood in an environment that has already achieved higher standards of living. Ibsen was adamant about this point, as can be deduced from the statement he made in 1898 at the general convention of the Women's Rights League of Norway: 'It is for the mother by strenuous and sustained effort to awaken a conscious feeling of culture and discipline. It is the women who are to solve the social problem. As mothers they are to do it and only as such can they do it. Here lies a great task for women.'[23]

Bracco, on the other hand, besides being, at the height of his dramatic production, 'the embodiment of Naples, city of colour and sound,'[24] was also the playwright that brought upon the stage the sordid conditions of the people of his city, especially with *Una donna, Nellina, Sperduti nel buio*, and *Don Pietro Caruso*, so continuing the tradition of Romantic realism as Beatrice Corrigan has pointed out in a recent study.[25] Special attention to this problem was also devoted by the Neapolitan novelist Matilde Serao who published in 1903 *Il ventre di Napoli*, a vivid sociological study about the shocking state of her city. The book contains two sections, written twenty years apart, and from the beginning of its introduction shows the author's concern for the stagnation of social conditions which had not improved since the period of her first investigations.[26] Bracco's people range in variety from a dissolute, aristocratic world, consisting of selfish, useless individuals, to a destitute one, crowded with the underprivileged, foundlings and prostitutes who are not only poor, victimized, and exploited, but the very dregs of Neapolitan society: a subsocial, rather than a social class. It is in describing this class that Bracco is most convincing. A married status, far from being a barrier to personal freedom and independence, as in the case of Nora in *A Doll's House*, is a coveted dream for many of Bracco's heroines. An attractive Neapolitan woman of the lowest class must resign herself to be the mistress of her lord who discards her as soon as he finds a younger and prettier substitute, as in the case of Gigetta in *Nellina*.

It is on the issue of woman's role that Ibsen and Bracco take different stands. For the Norwegian dramatist, as we have seen, women were simply a means to achieve social goals. Bracco's women are represented instead

23 Heller, 137.
24 R. Altrocchi, 'Bracco and the Drama of the Subconscious' in *North American Review*, ccxxiv (1927), 151.
25 Beatrice Corrigan, 'Neapolitan Romanticism and the Social Conscience' in *Studies in Romanticism*, v (1965), 120.
26 Matilde Serao, *Il ventre di Napoli* (Napoli, 1906).

as mothers, mistresses, lovers, instinctive in their affection, jealousy, dedication, and all those attributes most becoming to the sentimentality of Bracco who 'difese la donna per ciò che più amò in lei: la gentilezza, la squisitezza, la semplicità, l'amore.'[27] Ibsen claims freedom and independence for his women; Bracco asks for protection and respect. Bracco did not hesitate to speak openly in their defence, in lectures and meetings, reaffirming publicly what he had advocated in art.[28] Ibsen placed woman's freedom before her duties towards her children, as in the conclusion of *A Doll's House*. This play's particular ending caused such a strong reaction in Germany that in 1880 he, much against his inclination,[29] was forced to write for his German audiences a new conclusion with a submissive Nora choosing to remain with her children.

Ibsen's neglect of children in his dramas does not end with *A Doll's House* but is carried to more shattering conclusions in other plays which followed. In *The Wild Duck* little Hedvig's happy world collapses when she becomes aware of her father's growing indifference towards her. She could not possibly understand Hekdal's well-founded suspicion that she was not his own daughter; she was only conscious of her father's sudden revulsion from her. Gina, her mother, is too concerned about concealing her past and trying to give a normal appearance to her conjugal life to realize how deeply her fourteen-year-old daughter is hurt by the new feeling of uneasiness developing in their household. Hedvig feels alone and neglected, caught as an intruder between her parents, and her suicide is caused by a hidden wish to re-establish between them that normality which her presence would undermine. Hedvig, besides being a victim of human misunderstanding, with her self-sacrifice becomes the most complete feminine character of Ibsen's women, because 'he made of little Hedvig Hekdal a pure embodiment of other-love and self-immolation.'[30]

The child as an unsurmountable barrier between parents was a theme with which Ibsen had already experimented in the impressive poem *Brand* (1866). Like the great dramatists of the past, he was too devoted to the effectiveness of his tragic art to indulge in praise of maternal love. Bradbrook explains the lack of it in Ibsen: 'Unfortunately, the maternal

27 M. Gastaldi, *Una coscienza* (Milano, 1945), 29. 'He defended women because he appreciated in them: kindness, sweetness, simplicity, love.'
28 Two important lectures by Bracco on this topic were 'La donna napoletana' given at a private club in 1901 and 'Le evoluzioni della donna' given for the first time at the Minerva Theatre in Trieste, 11 November 1901 and then repeated, with some modifications, in other cities. Both of them are included in a collection of Bracco's writings *Tra gli uomini e le cose* (Napoli, 1921).
29 P. Watts, *Introduction to A Doll's House* (London, 1967), 18.
30 Heller, 218.

passion is not a subject for drama. The Greeks and Shakespeare drew only unnatural mothers (except Constance in *King John*, and Hecuba in *The Trojan Women*). Mother love is too simple and inflexible for the basis of drama.'[31] The correctness of the above assertion is demonstrated in *Little Eyolf* (1894), a tragedy intimately connected with the sad mood of isolation of the Norwegian people and their doom to a life of monotony and alienation. Rita's love for Allmers, her husband, is terrifying in her predatory way of expressing it. She has lost her power of alluring him and she feels the spectre of loneliness gradually overpowering her. Little Eyolf, their lame son, instead of drawing the two closer, is considered by Rita an obstacle to her exclusive possession of Allmers' love:

ALLMERS.   No, I can't. I must share myself between Eyolf and you.
RITA.   But if Eyolf had never been born? What then?
ALLMERS (evasively).   Well, that would be another matter. Then I should only have had you to be fond of.
RITA (in a low trembling voice).   Then I could wish I'd never borne him.

(Act II)[32]

The catastrophe of little Eyolf's death which happens soon after, does not fulfil her dreadful wish but widens the gulf already existing between her and Allmers. Rita gives up fighting to keep him, and her son's tragic end will haunt her final loneliness with remorse.

By the time Bracco starts his career as a playwright, concern for children had replaced woman's freedom as a subject for the European stage, as may be deduced from the following statement by Scheifley: '... But the child came to the dramatist's rescue ... It is natural that he should not have realized at once the value of the child; for what the child had gained, the mother lost ... And so the campaign of liberation, ... at whose head was Ibsen, came to an end, in the drama, about 1895.'[33]

Besides this historical change in the mood of European plays, Italian commentators at large were not enthusiastic about Ibsen's women, who lacked the ideal femininity they believed in. The critic Boutet attacked Nora as a person without a soul in his review of *A Doll's House* which appeared in the theatrical periodical *Carro di Tespi*, after the first Italian performance of the play.[34] Dismay at the total lack of feeling in Ibsen's women was expressed in a booklet about Ibsen published in Milan in 1893.

---

31 Bradbrook, 90.
32 H. Ibsen, *The Master Builder and Other Plays*, with an introduction by Una Ellis-Fermor (Penguin Books, 1958), 236.
33 W.H. Scheifley, *Brieux and Contemporary French Society* (London, 1912), 258-9.
34 Gigli, 319.

Its author concludes, astonishingly enough, with an exhortation to young Italian dramatists to study Ibsen and not to imitate him, so that they might avoid the unpleasant influence deriving from his feminine characters.[35] Bracco certainly accepted and put into practice this message. He not only foresaw 'the value of the child' but extolled it with sentimental and moving eloquence. One of his first dramas presented in Naples in 1893 bears the title *Una donna* and develops the theme of woman's regeneration through motherhood. Clelia, the protagonist, does not renounce her debased way of living even when Mario, a poor young man, falls in love with her. As soon as she realizes she will be a mother, however, everything acquires a new meaning for her and her only concern is that her child may have a father, a home, the normal upbringing that had been denied to her. Her son could have all this, Mario's mother suggests, provided Clelia gives him up entirely. She consents, placing her son's happiness before her own, but the sacrifice and implications of this choice are too heavy a burden for her and she prefers suicide to a life deprived of her child. Stäuble judges the conclusion of *Una donna* to be in sound agreement with Bracco's defence of women: 'La rigenerazione morale di Clelia, acquista un rilievo più spiccato, e la morte mette ancora più in risalto, la responsabilità dell'uomo, che di questa rigenerazione, non aveva compreso la sincerità.'[36]

Ten years later, in 1903, Bracco treated the same theme of motherhood, more idealistically, in *Maternità*. Claudia has been living with her husband Alfredo for ten years, without really knowing him completely, but when she realizes she is going to be a mother, she wants to know objectively the man she married. She hides in the house of a friend and listens to a conversation in which Alfredo reveals himself in all his abjectness, and it is here that some parallels might be drawn with the heroine of *A Doll's House*. Claudia too decides to leave her husband when she discovers her real self: 'Ho saputo ciò che desideravo di sapere. Ho saputo che mio marito è molto più vile, è molto più volgare di quanto mi era parso sinora ... Io mi preparo a vivere della mia felicità, d'una felicità che è soltanto mia' (1,6).[37] In a similar way Nora had expressed her disenchantment about the man she had married: 'It was tonight, when the wonderful thing did not happen; then I saw you were not the man I had thought you' (Act III).

---

35 A. Boccardi, *La donna nell'opera di Henrik Ibsen* (Milano, 1893), 51.
36 Stäuble, 77. 'Clelia's moral regeneration stands out more prominently and her death focuses the responsibility of the man who did not understand the sincerity of this regeneration.'
37 'I found out what I wanted to know. I found out that my husband is more cowardly, more vulgar than he appeared to me up to now ... I am preparing to enjoy my happiness, my own personal happiness.'

And the laws compiled by men, that judge only mechanical facts, without taking into consideration any intimate reason, suggest a bitter criticism in both Nora and Claudia. When Krongstad had made Nora aware of the seriousness of her forgery and of the insensibility of the law before any justification except a legal one, she had answered '... it must be a very foolish law' (Act I). Likewise Claudia, in view of future legal complications in taking away her child from its father, exclaims: 'Che importanza ha il codice nel caso nostro? Tu vuoi accettare una paternità di cui non sei convinto per carpire del danaro a un parente milionario. Ecco la profanazione alla quale mi oppongo' (II,4).[38]

Motherhood is, however, the motive that differentiates Claudia from Nora. Claudia in fact has been pushed into all this turmoil exclusively for the sake of her child, and suicide will end her life because she is told it will never be born alive. This conclusion produced some astonishing comments about Bracco's excessive concern with maternal feelings: 'Dramma audace, di alto significato morale. Svolge il tema che il figlio appartiene alla madre, se non esclusivamente alla madre. Il sentimento della maternità sale al fanatismo.'[39] If Bracco went to an extreme, it was because he wanted to demonstrate that femininity finds its epitome in the fulfilment of maternity.

The attitude of Ibsen's and Bracco's heroines towards fate also helps to widen the dissimilarities already described. In Ibsen there is found the struggle of the hero who refuses to resign himself to his destiny, but tries, even though he is doomed, to escape from the world of utilitarian order into which he has been cast. What Stäuble defines as the 'violente ribellioni ... titaniche aspirazioni verso l'alto'[40] of Ibsen's personages, is the result of his conception of tragedy. As Sverre Arestad sums up in a specific study on this topic: 'An Ibsen tragic hero stands forth as a living testimonial to the powers of human will ... In the process Ibsen depicted man's attempt to achieve the unattainable and to will to rise above circumstances to complete freedom. But man was denied success, and therein lay his tragedy.'[41]

Helen Alving in Ghosts is devoured by hatred in her helpless rebellion

38 'What does the law matter in our case? You want to accept a paternity of which you are not convinced to extort money from a wealthy relative. Here is the treachery I oppose.'
39 C. Antona Traversi, La verità sul teatro italiano dell'Ottocento (Udine, 1940), 205. 'Daring drama of high moral significance. He develops the theme that a child belongs to its mother, if not exclusively to its mother. The feeling of motherhood reaches fanaticism.'
40 Stäuble, 60: 'violent rebellions, unattainable titanic aspirations.'
41 S. Arestad, 'Ibsen's Concept of Tragedy' in PMLA, LXXIV (June, 1959), 297.

against the unjust laws of society. It is not only an unhappy married life that is the cause of her torment but also her past submission, her failure to stand up and fight for her rights when it was necessary: '... I must struggle for my freedom ... I ought never to have concealed what sort of a life my husband led. But I had not the courage to do otherwise then – for my own sake either. I was too much of a coward' (Act II). Her past failure turns her present futile struggle into vengeance. She is almost monstrous in her readiness to accept her son's love for Regina, the girl she knows is his half-sister. This is her last challenge to her cruel destiny which crushes her even more with the revelation of Oswald's illness. Boredom and emptiness envelope the life of Hedda Gabler, that other towering virago of Ibsen's plays. She is surrounded by people who do not measure up to her ideal and therefore Lövborg's suicide becomes for her a coherent act that predicts her own death: 'a deed of deliberate courage, ... a deed of spontaneous beauty.' How could her own suicide be visualized otherwise than as her bold defiance of human fate?

Bracco's figures, on the contrary, do not fight against adverse forces but bow their heads in acceptance of them. Stäuble explains this fatalism as typically Southern,[42] but it is rather the logical behaviour of gentle and humble creatures. Giulia Artunni in *I fantasmi* is Bracco's answer to Helen Alving. A past of devotion to a husband who jealously loved her prevents her psychologically from associating herself with a new life of love and companionship. There is no self-recrimination, or feeling of vengeance for the promise her husband Raimondo had obtained from her on his death bed. The only outlet for her intimate suffering is expressed in her wavering approach towards Luciano, the young man who loves her, in order to dissuade him from his plans. Her resigned conclusion is that she will never be able to reciprocate his love, and her explanation is a sub-dued cry: 'Non posso, non posso.' Teresa in *La piccola fonte* is the noblest example of love, devotion, and self-abnegation. She meekly accepts a secluded and unassuming way of living so as not to interfere with her husband's presumptuous and vain plans. His lack of consideration and neglectfulness will cause her insanity, only then will he fully perceive what Teresa's submissive love meant to his life and work.

Bracco was coherent in his mission of elevating women to a high moral level. If he focused his attention on them, after the stormy uproar provoked by the Norwegian, it was not to obtain a futile and absurd parity of rights and sex, but to uphold feelings and qualities pertaining to their nature.

Ibsen's inimitable art, instead, did not need to give proof of any coherent

42 Stäuble, 60.

mission or purpose. To those who question this point, surprised like Mencken because Ibsen had asked different questions in *A Doll's House* and in *Ghosts*, but had been unable to give any answer in *Hedda Gabler*,[43] the best response comes from the great dramatist himself, who admitted a few years before his death: 'Whatever I have written has been without any conscious thought of making propaganda. I have been more poet and less social philosopher than people generally seem inclined to believe.'[44]

43 Mencken, 14.   44 Heller, 137.

A scene from 1956 Rome production of *La patente*

OLGA RAGUSA

Pirandello's *La patente*: play and story

PIRANDELLO'S ONE-ACT PLAY *La patente* (The Licence) has enjoyed a theatrical history of uncommon success, not matched however by an equally rich, varied, and perceptive history in Pirandello criticism. It was first performed at the Teatro Alfieri in Turin, on 23 March 1918, but this performance has gone almost completely unnoted.[1] It is more usual instead to hear of the Rome performance of 19 February 1919, in a Sicilian ver-

The play *La patente* was first published in *Rivista d'Italia*, 31 January 1918. Shortly thereafter it was issued together with *Lumíe di Sicilia* (Sicilian Limes) and *Il berretto a sonagli* (Cap and Bells) as Volume III of the first collection of *Maschere nude* (Naked Masks) (Milano: Treves, 1920). Together with *L'imbecille* (The Imbecile), *Lumíe di Sicilia*, and *Cecè* (Chee-Chee), it later formed Volume XX of the second collection of *Maschere nude* (Firenze: Bemporad, 1926; Milano: Mondadori, 1933). It is now in *Opere di Luigi Pirandello* (Milano: Mondadori), *Maschere nude* (1962), II, 601–18. All quotations in the present essay are from this edition. The first English translation, by Elizabeth Abbot, appeared with the title *By Judgement of the Court*, in Luigi Pirandello, *One-Act Plays* (New York: Dutton, 1928). It has more recently been translated by William Murray with the title *The License*, in Pirandello's *One-Act Plays* (Garden City, NY: Doubleday Anchor Books, 1964; New York: Funk & Wagnalls, 1970).

The short story by the same title, first published in *Corriere della sera*, 9 August 1911, was included in the collection *La trappola* (The Trap) (Milano: Treves, 1915) and later in Volume III, *La rallegrata* (The Caper), of *Novelle per un anno* (Firenze: Bemporad, 1922; Milano: Mondadori, 1934). It is in Volume I of the 'Omnibus' collection of *Novelle per un anno* (Milano: Mondadori, 1937), with minimal notes giving the variants. Like the play, it is now in *Opere di Luigi Pirandello*, *Novelle per un anno* (1966), I, 512–19. According to Frederick May (Luigi Pirandello, *Short Stories*, selected, translated and introduced by Frederick May [London: Oxford University Press, 1965]), there is no English translation of the story.

1 Leonardo Bragaglia lists it in the chronology of the play in his *Interpreti pirandelliani* (Roma: Trevi, 1969), 96, with the erroneous information that it was given at the Teatro Carignano. However, in the body of his discussion he fails to mention it and gives the 19 February 1919 performance as the première. Luigi Ferrante, both

sion, '*A patenti*,[2] prepared by Pirandello himself and with the famous character actor Giovanni Grasso junior as Chiàrchiaro, or of the Milan performance of the following year with the even more famous Angelo Musco in the same role. The two interpretations represented, in Leonardo Bragaglia's broad synthesis, the two faces of Sicily and the two faces of the Sicilian theatre – the Sicily of knives and duels against the Sicily of broad humour and folklore, and the Sicily of Greek tragedy against that of the puppet stage.[3] *La patente* was later performed in a Roman dialect version (with Ettore Petrolini as Chiàrchiaro), a Genoese one, a Venetian one, and a Neapolitan one (with Peppino De Filippo always in the same role). The 1953 film adaptation, one of four Pirandellian episodes consti-tuting *Questa è la vita* (This is Life), is remembered for the tense and lugubrious interpretation of the great dead-pan comedian Totò,[4] while

in his *Pirandello* (Firenze: Parenti, 1958), 96, and in *Pirandello e la riforma teatrale* (Parma: Guanda, 1969), 109, cites only the 19 February 1919 Rome performance, as does M. Lo Vecchio-Musti under the heading 'Prime rappresentazioni,' in his Bib-liography in L. Pirandello, *Saggi, poesie, scritti vari* (Milano: Mondadori, 1960), 1276. The anonymous review which appeared in Turin's *La Stampa*, 24 March 1918, reports that the performance was given in honour of the actress Jole Campagna and that Angelo Musco took the role of Chiàrchiaro. (Jole Campagna belonged to a well-known family of Sicilian actors and in September 1917 she had played in '*A vilanza* [*La bilancia*; The scales], the dialect comedy written in collaboration by Pirandello and Martoglio.) In summarizing the plot, the *La Stampa* reviewer men-tions that the job Chiàrchiaro lost was that of teacher. This detail, reminiscent of the figure of Toti in *Pensaci, Giacomino!*, differs from what we have in the printed text, but it need not surprise us, for dialect comedies followed many of the tradi-tions of *commedia dell' arte*, including improvisation. In commemorating Musco's death, for instance, Silvio D'Amico spoke of 'the eternal phenomenon of the popular comic and dialect theatre where in the beginning is the actor and not the author,' and of Musco's 'fatal lack of discipline, his congenital faithlessness as far as the texts were concerned, his physical need to betray and remake them,' so that he never rose to the level of 'interpreter' but always remained an actor and a clown (*Nuova antologia*, CCCXCIV [1937], 111–13). But the nature of Musco's art must not be misunderstood: perhaps a traitor to the author, but for E. Gordon Craig he was the greatest actor in the world and for Antoine 'an overflowing comic energy' such as had never been seen on the stage before. Both these opinions were recorded by Silvio D'Amico in *Tramonto del grande attore* (Milano: Mondadori, 1929) and are now quoted in D'Amico's *Cronache del Teatro*, E. Ferdinando Palmieri and Sandro D'Amico, eds. (2 vols., Bari: Laterza, 1963–4), II, 457, n.16.

2 The manuscript of the translation is extant and is scheduled for publication in the forthcoming new edition of Pirandello's *opera omnia* under the editorship of Giovanni Macchia.

3 L. Bragaglia, *Interpreti*, 69. On Pirandello's own feelings regarding the contrast between Grasso and Musco, see his 4 February 1917 letter to Martoglio, published by Sandro D'Amico in 'Itinerario di Pirandello al teatro,' *Il Veltro*, 8 (1968), 93.

4 Vito Pandolfi, 'Quattro atti di Pirandello,' *Il dramma*, no. 94 (May 1956), 18.

the 1959 television play was distinguished by the 'brilliant, grotesquely modern' interpretation of Mario Scaccia.[5]

In criticism, on the other hand, the work has been pushed to the side, caught among a crowd of more significant three-act plays that preceded and followed it chronologically, and subordinated in the one-act category to the variously more striking *Lumie di Sicilia* (Sicilian Limes), *La giara* (The Jar), *All'uscita* (At the Exit), and *L'uomo dal fiore in bocca* (The Man with the Flower in His Mouth). Thomas Bishop, for instance, calls it 'a short, inconsequential play' of some interest only because of its treatment of illusion, and invokes the name of Kafka to characterize its kind of absurdity.[6] Ferrante groups it with *Il berretto a sonagli* (Cap and Bells) and *Bellavita* (Bellavita) as a folk comedy on the theme of the revolt of the underdog offended in his sense of honour.[7] J.-Th. Paolantonacci, J. Chaix-Ruy, Aldo Borlenghi, Sandro D'Amico, Benvenuto Terracini, and Giuseppe Giacalone fail to mention it or the short story on which it is based entirely.[8] Leone De Castris does no more than name Chiàrchiaro in passing as one of the lesser brothers of Ciampa, Baldovino, Leone Gala, Martino Lori, and Fulvia, all of them troubled and disturbed persons in search of something, in whom Pirandello discovered the underlying human condition and the grotesque conventions by which they live.[9] Tilgher, with considerable felicity but understandable brevity, inserts *La*

5 L. Bragaglia, *Interpreti*, 70.

6 Thomas Bishop, *Pirandello and the French Theater* (New York: New York University Press, 1960), 19.

7 L. Ferrante, *Pirandello*, 97. See also Ferrante, *Pirandello e la riforma*, 109, where the *scalognati*, 'the unlucky ones,' of *Giganti della montagna* (The Mountain Giants) are added to the category of social victims.

8 J.-Th. Paolantonacci, *Le Théâtre de Luigi Pirandello* (Paris: Nouvelles Editions Latines, n.d.); J. Chaix-Ruy, *Pirandello: Humour et poésie* (Paris: Del Duca, 1967); Aldo Borlenghi, *Pirandello o dell'ambiguità* (Padova: R.A.D.A.R., 1968); Sandro D'Amico, 'Itinerario'; Benvenuto Terracini, 'Le *Novelle per un anno* di Luigi Pirandello,' 283–398 in *Analisi stilistica* (Milano: Feltrinelli, 1966); Giuseppe Giacalone, *Luigi Pirandello* (2nd ed., Brescia: La Scuola Editrice, 1969). Of the commonly used reference works there is no entry for *La patente* in *Dizionario Letterario Bompiani* (Milano, 1947–68) which otherwise covers the works of Pirandello rather thoroughly, nor is the play discussed by Giovanni Macchia in his chapter on Pirandello in Vol. IX of the Cecchi-Sapegno *Storia della letteratura italiana* (Milano: Garzanti, 1969). In *Enciclopedia dello spettacolo* (Roma: Le Maschere, 1961) Alberto Spaini groups *La patente* with *L'altro figlio* (The Other Son) and *Bellavita* (Bellavita) as works which consist of a series of monologues, with the 'chorus' represented in turn by a judge, a doctor, and a lawyer: 'The antagonist has not yet been born.' My view of *La patente* in part challenges this judgment.

9 Arcangelo Leone De Castris, *Storia di Pirandello* (Bari: Laterza, 1962), 170.

patente in his schematization of the whole of Pirandello's work, by seeing it as a central link in the thematic development of the clash between Life and Form.[10] Pasini discusses it together with *La giara*, *L'altro figlio* (The Other Son), and *Lumíe di Sicilia* under the heading of 'Cose minori. Alla maniera antica' (Minor Things. In the Old Manner) and summarizes it following the schemes of *L'umorismo*, Pirandello's essay on humour, as a drama of 'illusion creating reality.'[11] Although Janner finds that, together with *Il berretto a sonagli*, *La patente* is one of the two most original of Pirandello's early plays, he also feels that it does not go much beyond the story from which it is drawn, a judgment he then seems to contradict with his rapid enumeration of the characters and scenes that *have* been added to heighten the 'widespread atmosphere of grotesque terror' so necessary to the situation.[12] Starkie uses the play to illustrate the Sicilian character of Pirandello, especially insofar as his style, 'full of jerks and jolts,' is concerned.[13] More recently a critic who describes his approach as a combination of literary criticism and stage directing has pointed out that Chiàrchiaro with his sunken cheeks, his dark-rimmed glasses, and his gravedigger's garment was visualized in terms of the contemporaneous expressionist theatre.[14] A students' guide to the work of Pirandello includes the short story though not the play in its analysis of the major works, but its discussion is marred by an overemphasis on the moral and psychological at the expense of the formal.[15] More perceptive and incisive are the observations on the relationship between the play and the story in Giuseppe Morpurgo's annotations to his school edition of the *Novelle*.[16] But the two best readings that have come to my attention are Franz Rauhut's in his 'Pirandello als Sizilianischer Mundartdramatiker' (Pirandello as Sicilian Dialect Dramatist) and Domenico Vittorini's in *The Drama of Luigi Pirandello*.[17] Rauhut's insight into the character of Judge D'An-

10 Adriano Tilgher, *Studi sul teatro contemporaneo* (Roma: Libreria di Scienze e Lettere, 1923), 192.

11 Ferdinando Pasini, *Luigi Pirandello (Come mi pare)* (Trieste: Biblioteca di cultura de 'La Vedetta italiana,' 1927), 293–4.

12 Arminio Janner, *Luigi Pirandello* (Firenze: La Nuova Italia, 1948), 291–2.

13 Walter Starkie, *Luigi Pirandello* (3rd ed., Berkeley and Los Angeles: University of California Press, 1965), 88.

14 Maurizio Del Ministro, 'Lettura di testi pirandelliani,' *Letteratura*, no. 94–6 (1968), 135.

15 Gaetano Munafò, *Conoscere Pirandello* (Firenze: Le Monnier, 1968), 147–8.

16 L. Pirandello, *Novelle*, a cura di Giuseppe Morpurgo (20th ed., Milano: Edizioni Scolastiche Mondadori, 1946), 106–17.

17 Franz Rauhut, 'Pirandello als Sizilianischer Mundtartdramatiker,' 148–72 in *Der Dramatiker Pirandello*. Zweiundzwanzig Beiträge herausgegeben von Franz Norbert Mennemeier (Köln: Kiepenheuer & Witsch, 1965); Domenico Vittorini, *The*

drea is truly exceptional, for in the literature on *La patente* this second protagonist (or antagonist) almost never comes in for mention.[18] For Rauhut, instead, he is like Professor Toti in *Pensaci, Giacomino!* (Think It Over, Giacomino!) one of the Pirandellian philosophers of 'love of neighbour,' opposed to Chiàrchiaro who is seen by Rauhut as a Pirandellian philosopher of 'hatred of neighbour.' Vittorini, who calls the play 'a little jewel of its kind,' does not overlook D'Andrea either, but places him next to Chiàrchiaro as one of the *two* protagonists that carry the meaning. Yet both Rauhut implicitly, by discussing the play in the context of Pirandello's dialect theatre, and Vittorini explicitly, by classifying it with the naturalistic drama which is seen as treating 'humble themes of Sicilian life,' end up by limiting its wider implications. In conclusion, however, we must add to Vittorini's special credit that, no more than Leone De Castris, did he miss the resemblance of Chiàrchiaro to other Pirandello characters: 'Chiàrchiaro is the first character that gives evidence of traits which, enriched and deepened, will blossom into more complex personalities in later plays.'

Of course, the proverb says 'Del senno di poi son piene le fosse' (It is easy to be wise after the event) – and to no one does hindsight offer greater satisfaction than to the critic who turns back from his vantage point to consider earlier appraisals of an artist's work. Yet a measure of surprise at finding *La patente* so generally slighted may be permitted. Not that its first reviewers, working under the peculiarly awkward conditions of journalism, could have been expected to transcend the dialectal dress in which it first appeared[19] in order to relate it to its author's broader message in *Così è (se vi pare)* (Right You Are [If You Think So]), by common agreement the work that marks the turning-point in Pirandello's development and which was already well-known. But surely in retrospect

---

Drama of Luigi Pirandello (Philadelphia: University of Pennsylvania Press, 1935; New York: Dover Publications, 1957), 54–7.

18 Only one of the drama reviews I have seen even mentions the role of D'Andrea: Vito Pandolfi in *Il dramma*, May 1956, speaks of the actor Mario Siletti who played the Judge with 'pathetic resignation,' giving him an air of 'disconsolate and good-natured' gentleness.

19 Some of the early reviewers, such as Eugenio Cecchi who wrote for *Il giornale d'Italia* under the pseudonym Tom, were unable to understand Sicilian and objected vigorously to plays in dialect (see L. Bragaglia, *Interpreti*, 27 and 41–2). Moreover, there was considerable antagonism elicited by the provincial Musco among sophisticated intellectuals, as can be seen, for instance, in Piero Gobetti's 'Pirandello e il buffone Angelo Musco,' *Energie nuove* (Torino), 1–15 December 1918 (now in *Le riviste di Piero Gobetti* [Milano: Feltrinelli, 1961], 90–1). Pirandello's own feelings regarding the dialect theatre were ambiguous, as is apparent from his 1909 essay 'Teatro dialettale?'

the play should more readily have been seen to fall within that period of extraordinary activity which witnessed the composition of more than twenty plays in six years, some of them written with amazing speed in a matter of weeks, if not days. The rapidity with which Pirandello was able to write at that time is naturally not significant in itself but because it offers concrete proof of his intensified creativity, of that fire which in a short span of time refined his ideas to their essence and concentrated them in ever more readily perceivable and recognizable concepts and images. Composed between *Pensaci, Giacomino!*, *Liolà*, *Così è*, *Il berretto a sonagli*, and *Il piacere dell'onestà* (The Pleasure of Honesty) on the one hand, and *Il giuoco delle parti* (The Rules of the Game), *Tutto per bene* (All for the Best), *Sei personaggi* (Six Characters), *Enrico IV* (Henry IV), and *Vestire gli ignudi* (To Clothe the Naked) on the other, *La patente* belongs by chronology and conception to that centrally important group of plays analysed by Leone De Castris as embodying the progressive unfolding of the character without an author. In this connection, one of the purposes of the present essay is to show how at the confluence of Pirandello's Sicilian and Italian experiences, and under the compelling impact of his sudden discovery of the dramatic conventions as they operate on the stage,[20] Chiàrchiaro, the character who was to become the protagonist of the play, burst into full theatrical life. Moreover, since *La patente*, like many others of Pirandello's plays, is derived from an earlier short story, the essay also aims at being a contribution to the so far all too brief tradition of the close study of the transformation of narrative into drama within the Pirandello corpus.[21]

Inasmuch as the play is available in English translation whereas the story is not, it seems advisable to begin the discussion with an analysis of the

20 Leone De Castris (*Storia*, 111–15) has spoken of the dramatic dimension of certain stylistic procedures in Pirandello's short stories. But there is a difference between drama in narrative and drama on stage, something Giovanni Macchia saw clearly when he gave the title 'Teatro e palcoscenico' (Theatre and stage) to one of the subdivisions of his chapter on Pirandello (Cecchi-Sapegno, IX, 467–70). What I have in mind here, however, is specifically related to the context of Pirandello's working with dramatic techniques in the first part of *La patente*.

21 Occasional references to this whole area of Pirandello studies abound, but only two thorough explorations of particular relationships between stories and plays have come to my attention: Ulrich Leo's seminal 'Luigi Pirandello zwischen zwei literarischen Gattungen' (Luigi Pirandello between Two Literary Genres), *Romanistisches Jahrbuch*, XIV (1963), 133–69, which deals with *L'uomo, la bestia e la virtù* (Man, Beast, and Virtue), *O di uno o di nessuno* (Either Someone's or No One's), and especially *Così è*; and J.H. Whitfield's elegantly executed analysis of *Tutto per bene* (All for the Best), 'La metamorfosi della novella,' in *Atti del Congresso internazionale di studi pirandelliani* (Firenze: Le Monnier, 1967), 735–42.

play. What first strikes the reader is that the work is a well-made problem play, both terms being understood here in the technical meaning they have for late nineteenth-century realistic drama. The author's mastery of his craft is evident in the ease with which one scene leads into the next, climaxing in an effective and striking *dénouement*, which is followed, somewhat exceptionally, by a second and lesser falling action, the clinching demonstration in this cold blooded dialectical encounter that, regardless of the facts of the case, Chiàrchiaro and not Judge D'Andrea was correct in his interpretation of the practical aspect of the existential situation presented. Though both characters are non-conventional in their attitudes and are thereby antagonists of society, faced by a common social problem to be solved, their distance from their fellow-men creates no solidarity between them but opposes them in a duel in which the realist defeats the idealist and the irrational forces win out over the rational. The two-step *dénouement* is thus the logically necessary conclusion to the full unravelling of the action – but Pirandello did not hit upon it at once.

Greater clarity can be achieved, I believe, by breaking up the single and compact act into its component scenes, a division which does not, of course, occur in the printed version where no separations are indicated when there is a change of characters on stage. Yet it is obvious that, in distributing the action, Pirandello was thinking in terms of scenes, just as though he had been working in the more usual three-act format.[22] Thus Judge D'Andrea's initial solo appearance with the business of the two bird cages and the papers on his desk (sc. 1) is followed by a short scene with the usher, Marranca, whom he sends to get Chiàrchiaro (sc. 2), and Marranca's exit coincides with the entrance of the Three Judges for a choral scene, in which talk of D'Andrea's goldfinch, of Chiàrchiaro, and of the administration of justice in general serves to reveal preceding circumstances important for understanding the Judge's *forma mentis* and the paradoxes of the case to be tried (sc. 3). Marranca's return from his errand, accompanied not by Chiàrchiaro but by the latter's daughter Rosinella, is the cue for the departure of the Three Judges and for a change of focus from the case as a legal and social problem to the case as a human one (sc. 4). Rosinella's pleading with D'Andrea to try to convince Chiàrchiaro to withdraw his accusation provides information about the family background and foreshadows in the most explicit manner so far the grand entrance that Chiàrchiaro will eventually make (sc. 5). The entrance

22 The fact that Pirandello thinks in terms of scenes does not preclude the experimentation with respect to this very point which takes place in the trilogy of the theatre within the theatre: the ingenious way, for instance, in which *Sei personaggi*, although only 'a play in the making,' is divided into acts through the accidental lowering of the curtain at the end of what thereby becomes a *de facto* Act 1.

is delayed by a short scene in which Marranca announces Chiàrchiaro's arrival and D'Andrea helps Rosinella escape by a back exit (sc. 6). The rest of the play is given over to the confrontation between Chiàrchiaro and the Judge and this ends with the *coup de scène* of the goldfinch's death: 'as though pushed by a gust of wind,' Pirandello writes ambiguously in the stage directions, a window opens and knocks the cage from its stand (sc. 7). At D'Andrea's outcry, the Three Judges and Marranca run in again, thus bringing all characters except Rosinella on stage for the finale (sc. 8).

But though the play falls easily into its component scenes and divides further into two balanced parts, of which the first finds D'Andrea on stage without Chiàrchiaro while the second unites the two protagonists, there is no break in the action rising to its climax and resolution, and each scene contributes to the continuity of the whole, not only in terms of plot and characterization but specifically in the observance of the basic dramatic rule of showing rather than telling. Thus, up to Chiàrchiaro's entrance we have a series of reiterations and variations through which he and the other characters in relation to him are defined; after his entrance we have on stage, *coram populo*, the two opposing and contradictory views of the man, so similar to the unsettling effect created in *Così è (se vi pare)* by the successive 'explanations' of signor Ponza and signora Frola.

In first introducing Chiàrchiaro Pirandello has recourse to descriptive epithets in the mouths of those who speak of him and to gestures of reaction to the mention of his name. 'Benedett'uomo!' (That tiresome man!)[23] D'Andrea exclaims impatiently at sight of the documents on his desk (sc. 1). And Marranca, when he hears the Judge pronounce Chiàrchiaro's name, makes a sign of exorcism of the evil eye (sc. 2). The Judge comes to Chiàrchiaro's defence, calls him 'un pover'uomo' (a poor devil of a man), but Marranca is unconvinced of his innocuousness: three times he avoids saying his name. In scene 2 he hesitates a moment before coming upon the expression 'questo galantuomo' (this gentleman) with which to refer to him; in scene 4 he reports on his errand by using the emphatic '*Lui*' (He – Pirandello's italics); and in scene 6 he ushers in Chiàrchiaro with 'Eccolo!' (Here he is!). Each one of these moments, beyond being the faithful rendition of carefully observed superstitious behaviour, increases the sense of Chiàrchiaro's exclusion, of his absolute difference from others which robs him even – as it will later rob 'Enrico IV' – of the right to his name. And it is a measure of Pirandello's deftness at rapid characterization and of his unerring attention to telling detail that he has not over-

23 All translations throughout the essay are mine.

looked these almost imperceptible opportunities for creating suspense but has known how to exploit fully the possibilities offered by an essentially functional character like Marranca. Later, when D'Andrea speaks to the Three Judges of the unjust trial which as public prosecutor he must institute, he again refers, generically this time, to 'un pover'uomo' who is also 'una vittima' (a victim). But when the Three Judges learn that the 'pover'uomo' is none other than Chiàrchiaro, they too jump back in alarm and, like Marranca, make signs against the evil eye (sc. 3). D'Andrea's next use of 'pover'uomo' refers directly to Chiàrchiaro, '*questo* pover'uomo' (*this* poor devil of a man – italics mine) who is also 'un disgraziato' (an unfortunate wretch of a man). And though the Second Judge concedes that 'disgraziato' is descriptive of Chiàrchiaro's plight, he repeats at the same time what the First Judge has already said, 'E un pazzo!' (He's a madman!). The connotation of 'disgraziato' used in conjunction with 'pover'uomo' is, of course, different from that of 'disgraziato' used with 'pazzo,' insanity being by itself the ultimate social exclusion. Two additional attributes are assigned to Chiàrchiaro in this important scene (still sc. 3): violence and a kind of awesome frightfulness – the violence of his protests against those who have given him the reputation of having the evil eye, and the terribleness of his supposed power and perhaps even of his physical appearance.

So much for the effectiveness on stage of words and gestures. Rosinella's scene (sc. 5) brings about a change in perspective. While characterization through epithets continues ('fustigato da tutti, sfuggito da tutto il paese come un appestato' [scourged by everyone, avoided as though he had the plague], 'E come impazzito mio padre' [He's like a man gone mad, my father], Rosinella says of him), the audience now moves closer to Chiàrchiaro. There is no need, of course, for the Judge to do so, for he has stood by Chiàrchiaro all along, although, as the action will show, he has been mistaken in his estimate of how to help him. And indeed it is not D'Andrea who summons Rosinella, but it is she who comes running to him in apprehension for her father. Is Rosinella's scene expendable? In a certain sense it is, and the fact that there is no place for her in the final choral grouping is a hint that her presence continues in some ways to be felt as an intrusion. Moreover, all the information that she gives – and it is considerable – will be repeated in a more direct form by Chiàrchiaro himself. We learn, it is true, that there are four persons involved in the family tragedy, that Chiàrchiaro has been unemployed for a year, that he is the object of a heartless persecution. And we learn most importantly that there is nowhere for his family to go, for his reputation would follow them like a second skin: 'Ce la portiamo appresso la fama,' Rosinella says, 'dovunque andiamo. Non si leva più neppure col coltello' (We'd carry this reputation with us wherever we'd go. We couldn't get rid of it even by cutting it off with a knife), and in her expression the coalescing of mask and being is forcibly implied. The audience learns all this and, what is especially useful in terms of drama, learns it in a manner particularly favourable to Chiàrchiaro. Rosinella is an appealing intercessor for her father. Her youth, her evident poverty, her decency elicit sympathy on basic human grounds, something, it will be seen, that Chiàrchiaro has little use for, but which is a *sine qua non* in the direct encounter between fictionalized world and spectator in realistic drama. Thus Rosinella's scene is a bridge in more ways than one, but principally in containing a description of the change that has come over Chiàrchiaro and a recital of some of the reasons for it: the most important reason will be told later by Chiàrchiaro himself. Yet the scene is also a postponement, part of a fundamental strategy in drama, where time no less than space must be treated differently than in narrative. So that it is this aspect rather than its content, which, together with its function in generating audience sympathy for Chiàrchiaro, stands out when one considers Pirandello's theatrical know-how.

All is ready now for Chiàrchiaro's entrance, prepared for, as we have seen, in dramatic terms by showing the reaction both of those who feel pity for him and of those who fear him, and by having a person close to him, especially invented for the purpose, tell facts about his background which only she can know. But Chiàrchiaro has not yet spoken for himself; he has not yet presented his own case. There is one passage in scene 5 in which something of his inner torment, of that life of feeling which appears to the outside world only in the actions and attitudes to which it gives rise, appears to shine through. It is the important exchange between the Judge and Rosinella:

ROSINELLA.   ... Per carità, signor giudice: gliela faccia ritirare codesta querela! Gliela faccia ritirare!
D'ANDREA.   Ma sí, carina! Voglio proprio questo. E l'ho fatto chiamare per questo. Spero che ci riuscirò. Ma voi sapete: è molto più facile fare il male che il bene.
ROSINELLA.   Come, Eccellenza! Per Vossignoria?
D'ANDREA.   Anche per me. Perché il male, carina, si può fare a tutti e da tutti; il bene, solo a coloro che ne hanno bisogno.
ROSINELLA: E lei crede che mio padre non ne abbia bisogno?
D'ANDREA.   Lo credo, lo credo. Ma è che questo bisogno d'aver fatto il bene,

figliuola, rende spesso cosí nemici gli animi di coloro che si vorrebbero bene-
ficare, che il beneficio diventa impossibile. Capite?
ROSINELLA.   Nossignore, non capisco. Ma faccia di tutto Vossignoria![24]

But it is obvious that in its statement of a fundamental paradox the passage is essentially generic: that it refers more to the difficulties of helping
any poor devil of a man rather than this particular one; that the insight
that those most in need of help are often the least willing to accept it, that
their would-be benefactor is more often proudly rejected than gratefully
acknowledged, is the consequence of D'Andrea's tendency to ruminate, to
'philosophize,' a tendency only briefly referred to in scene 3 when the
First Judge says to him: 'Sèguita, sèguita, mio caro, con codesta filosofia,
e vedrai come finirai contento!' (Just keep on with that kind of reasoning
of yours and you'll see how happy it'll make you!) but more fully developed in the story. The insight is of course applicable to Chiàrchiaro's
case, but it is not yet Chiàrchiaro's case itself. The Judge for all his understanding of Chiàrchiaro cannot tell us his *ragione* (reason). It is Chiàrchiaro himself who must do so, and he must do so with the intense and
desperate anguish to which there is no answer, not with the calm reason-
ableness of conviction that can issue into the optimistic rhetorical question, 'Capite?' (You do understand, don't you?).

I have spoken so far only of the first part of the play, pointing out elements of continuity, contrast, and suspense in its inner dynamics and
devoting some attention to the two functional characters, Marranca and
Rosinella, for one of whom there is no counterpart in the story and for
the other only a very shadowy one. There is in other words an usher in
the story whom D'Andrea sends out to get Chiàrchiaro, but he is name-
less, featureless, and lacks speech. As far as Rosinella is concerned, one
may wonder whether to the reasons for her invention already discussed

---

24 ROSINELLA.   ... Please, Your Honor, have him drop this case! Have him drop it!
D'ANDREA.   But, of course, my child. That's exactly what I want. And that's why
I've had him come. I hope I'll be able to convince him. But, you know, it's much
easier to do harm than to do good.
ROSINELLA.   No, Your Honor! For you too?
D'ANDREA.   Yes, for me too. Because harm can be done by anyone and to anyone,
but good can be done only to those who need it.
ROSINELLA.   And do you think that my father doesn't need it?
D'ANDREA.   I know he needs it. But it is this need, my child, that so often embitters
the hearts of those we would like to help so that we can do nothing for them. Do
you understand?
ROSINELLA.   No, sir, I don't understand. But please do everything you can, Your
Honor.

there should not also be added a possible practical one – in terms of production of the play – the need for a role for a female character to accommodate the leading lady of a troupe of actors.[25] Obviously, without Rosinella, the play would have an all male cast, something which would not at all be unsuited to the nature of its story, but which would be contrary to normal theatrical practice. There are three other characters who have roles in the play while their counterparts were only briefly mentioned in the story. The transformation of what were originally some vague colleagues of D'Andrea into the Three Judges offers a fascinating insight into Pirandello's workshop. In the story D'Andrea seeks advice on how to handle Chiàrchiaro's case from his colleagues: 'ma questi, appena egli faceva il nome del Chiàrchiaro ... si alteravano in viso e si ficcavano subito una mano in tasca a stringere una chiave, o sotto sotto allungavano l'indice e il mignolo a far le corna, o s'affervavano sul panciotto i gobbetti d'argento, i chiodi, i corni di corallo pendenti dalla catena dell'orologio.'[26] In this passage the number of colleagues involved is unspecified but their reactions upon hearing Chiàrchiaro's name are three-fold: they either slip their hands into their pockets to touch 'iron,' or they make signs of exorcism with their fingers, or they grasp the talismans hanging from their watch chains. In the play, the stage directions – 'i tre Giudici ... danno un balzo indietro, facendo scongiuri, atti di spavento e gridando ...' (the Three Judges ... leap backward, making signs against the evil eye, making gestures of fright, and shouting ...) – are much less explicit, eschewing all reporting of the specific signs against the evil eye, but the judges are three. For each type of gesture a character has emerged!

Aside from the intrinsic interest of these observations regarding the minor characters of *La patente*, there is also the fact that they all belong to the first part of the play. For one of the striking aspects of the transformation of story into play in this case is that the work of re-elaboration required for the first part was quite different from that required for the second. Though the story is divided asymmetrically into three sections, the balancing of its action is very similar to that of the play, Parts I and II corresponding to scenes 1 through 6 and being dominated by the presence of D'Andrea; Part III corresponding to scene 7 and consisting exclusively

---

25 The fact that this play in which the woman's role is so very minor should have been chosen for a performance in honour of a leading actress is not irrelevant in this connection.

26 'But they, as soon as he would mention the name of Chiàrchiaro ... blanched and either stuck a hand in their pockets to touch a key, or with their index and little finger made a sign against the evil eye, or grasped the silver hunchbacks, the nails, the coral horns hanging from their watchchains on their waistcoats.'

of the meeting and clash of D'Andrea and Chiàrchiaro. There is nothing in the story to balance scene 8 and we shall return to this point later. It is a fact of considerable interest and well worth noting that the meeting of D'Andrea and Chiàrchiaro presented itself to Pirandello from the beginning in dramatic form. From the moment that D'Andrea catches sight of him in his office to the end of the story practically everything is in dialogue. In reworking this section Pirandello therefore had little to do except transfer the dialogue almost *verbatim* to the play and permit the connecting narrative material to be absorbed into stage directions. The procedure is a common and familiar one in Pirandello's adaptations of his stories for the stage and need not be further illustrated here: a rapid glance at the two texts side by side will show what has happened.[27] The problem was different for the first part. In that instance a play had to be fashioned out of descriptive, narrative, and *style indirect libre* passages. It was in fashioning this play that, as we shall see, Pirandello took a radical step in displacing D'Andrea and in shifting the determining weight of protagonist to the shoulders of Chiàrchiaro.

In turning from Pirandello's dexterity in the medium of drama to the emergence of Chiàrchiaro as the play's protagonist, we move from an area in which Pirandello has much in common with other playwrights to one in which he is quite unique. For the Pirandellian character is different from other characters not only because his perception of reality is a distinct and recognizable one, but also because he imposes himself upon author, fellow characters, and spectators in a characteristic and unusual manner. This is already true of the Chiàrchiaro of the short story whom Judge D'Andrea finds standing in front of him when he raises his eyes from his desk: '... Chiàrchiaro che gli era entrato nella stanza, mentr'egli era intento a scrivere' (... Chiàrchiaro who had come into his room while he was busy writing), Pirandello writes. The important words here are 'che gli era entrato nella stanza,' for the expression unmistakably echoes the 'mi trovai davanti' (I found in front of me) repeated twice of the Six Characters in the Preface to that play, the 'me lo vidi entrare in camera' (I saw him coming into my room) which announces the arrival of Icilio Saporini in *La tragedia di un personaggio* (A Character in Distress), and the 'vi trovai un insolito scompiglio' (I found an unusual fuss there), which signals the presence of dottor Fileno among Pirandello's Sunday

---

27 Useful observations on the relationship between stage directions and parallel passages in the stories are found in Aldo Vallone, 'Le didascalie nel teatro,' 501–7 in *Atti ... studi pirandelliani*.

morning habitués in the same story. In each case the character imposes his presence decisively and palpably upon a passive (at least at that moment) and helpless receiver. The reaction of the latter is not always the same. Pirandello accepts Saporini and finds a place for him in a story (although, as he adds wryly, he is to die there). He refuses to satisfy Fileno and drives him into non-being. What he does with the Six Characters is too well-known to warrant repeating here. Judge D'Andrea also reacts to Chiàrchia-ro's appearance:

Ebbe uno scatto violentissimo e buttò all'aria le carte, balzando in piedi e gridandogli:
– Ma fatemi il piacere! Che storie son queste? Vergognatevi![28]

The violence of his reaction and his indignation are not dissimilar from the impatience expressed by other Pirandello characters in comparable situations. As a matter of fact, a case might be made for seeing in Judge D'Andrea's reaction an abbreviated model for the long and varied tug of war beween characters (specifically the Father and the Step-Daughter) and *Capocomico* (director) in *Sei personaggi*. The licence which Chiàrchiaro demands would thus become the material and therefore ludicrous equivalent of the artistic form which other of Pirandello's characters plead for, the stamp of reality and identity – someone else's or more broadly speaking society's – conferred on an individual who has lost his own sense of it because his personality has in some way been mutilated.[29]

But while it is true that a close reading already shows traces of the character without an author in the story, it is only in the play that Chiàrchiaro makes the fully prepared grand entrance of which we spoke earlier. To appreciate what has happened to Pirandello's conception of him, three

28 'He was violently startled and throwing the papers off his desk leaped to his feet, shouting:
– What do you think you're doing? What nonsense is this? You should be ashamed of yourself!'
29 In her 'Pirandello and the Theatre of the Absurd' (*Cesare Barbieri Courier*, VIII, Spring 1966, 6), Beatrice Corrigan says on this point: 'Pirandello holds that the individual cannot feel secure in his illusion unless he can persuade others to share it.' Pushed to an extreme this is the strategy and the anguish of the schizophrenic; Pirandello's characters stop short of complete disintegration, but they express their desire for consistency with the intense and desperate desolation which appears on Fileno's face when Pirandello rejects him: 'una cosí intensa e disperata angoscia si dipinse sul volto del dottor Fileno, che subito tutti quegli altri [i miei personaggi che ancora stavano a trattenerlo] impallidirono e si ritrassero' (an anguish so intense and desperate appeared on Dr Fileno's face that immediately all those others [my characters who were still trying to hold him back] grew pale and retreated).

texts must be placed next to one another at this point: the story, the play, and the play as it reveals itself in performance. In the story the famous description of Chiàrchiaro's transformation from 'povero disgraziato' (a poor devil of a man) to 'jettatore' (man who has the evil eye) follows immediately upon the passage quoted above in the preceding paragraph:

Il Chiàrchiaro s'era combinata una faccia da jettatore, ch'era una meraviglia a vedere. S'era lasciata crescere su le cave gote gialle una barbaccia ispida e cespugliuta, s'era insellato sul naso un pajo di grossi occhiali cerchiati d'osso, che gli davano l'aspetto d'un barbagianni; aveva poi indossato un abito lustro, sorcigno, che gli sgonfiava da tutte le parti.[30]

In the text of the play the sequence in which D'Andrea's reaction and Chiàrchiaro's appearance are recorded is reversed. According to the usage which places the description of a new character immediately after his first entrance on stage, the equivalent of the passage just quoted precedes D'Andrea's reaction and his exclamations of annoyance and disgust. In performance, of course, this temporal dimension is lost, for the spectator perceives visually what in narrative or stage directions can be told him only by the author. The visual perception makes present what in the story was past. 'Chiàrchiaro gli era entrato nella stanza' (Chiàrchiaro had come into his room), says the story. 'Tiene una canna d'India in mano col manico di corno. Entra a passo di marcia funebre, battendo a terra la canna a ogni passo, e si para davanti al giudice' (He carries a bamboo cane with a handle made of horn. He walks in funereally, tapping the cane on the ground at every step, and takes a stand in front of the Judge's desk), say the stage directions. As can be seen, there is in the play, in addition to the change in tense, the introduction of a detail of Chiàrchiaro's 'masquerade,' which in the story had been postponed to a later moment.[31] The cane

---

30 'Chiàrchiaro had fixed himself up to look like a "jettatore" and he was a wonder to behold. He had let a rough, bushy beard grow on his sunken yellow cheeks, had put a pair of thick, horn-rimmed glasses on his nose, which made him look like an owl; then he had put on a shiny mouse-coloured suit which hung around him on all sides.'

31 In the story the cane appears only when Chiàrchiaro is already seated and is rolling it back and forth along his thighs as though, Pirandello writes in one of his arresting comparisons, it were a rolling-pin. The episode is transferred without change to the play where, however, coming after the initial visual and aural impressions of Chiàrchiaro's entrance it acquires a more threatening resonance than it had originally: the domestic object, one suddenly remembers, has often figured prominently in acts of violence. But the pleasure of this discovery is reserved for the *reader* of the play only, for when stage directions are translated into actions they lose the specific values and connotations of the words in which they are

beating rhythmically on the ground accompanies the impression of black magic made by Chiàrchiaro's costume with an ominous aural undertone. The Chiàrchiaro, who in the story had come into D'Andrea's study almost surreptitiously, in the play strides across the stage attracting a strange hypnotic attention to himself.

I should like now to examine some of the reasons which may account for the greater forcefulness of Chiàrchiaro's entrance in the play, and turn then to Pirandello's final rounding out of his figure in the course of the rest of his encounter with D'Andrea.

But there are two anecdotal explanations of the origin of the play which must first be dealt with. One occurs in Musco's memoirs *Cerca che trovi* ... ; the other is reported as having been given by Pirandello himself.[32] In recalling moments of his long and fruitful association with Pirandello, Musco speaks of an encounter which he says occurred on the day after the Rome première of *Liolà*. He was walking with Pirandello and Rosso di San Secondo, the other important dramatist of those days of Sicilian origin, in Piazzi Poli, the little square behind the Galleria Colonna in the heart of Rome, when they witnessed an attack by two brutes upon a poor ragged wretch of a man. Upon asking what had happened, they were told that the man who was being mistreated had the reputation of being a fearsome bearer of bad luck, a 'jettatore.' Thereupon talk turned to this superstitious belief and, Musco concludes, the first idea for *La patente* came to Pirandello. The story attributed to Pirandello, though not identical, bears a strong resemblance to Musco's. According to it, Pirandello, who did not himself believe in the evil eye, had met a man in Rome who was reputed to have that magic power and was as a result so thoroughly shunned by others that he was forced to live alone, a social outcast. Overcome by pity for him Pirandello wanted to befriend him, but he was warned against doing so by his acquaintances. It then happened that in a minor street accident Pirandello was hit by a car and thrown into the arms of this very man who saved him from harm. 'And that was the first germ of *La patente*,' he is quoted as having said, 'which I then forthwith wrote.' In spite of the slight variations, the two stories may very well refer to the same incident. We can be sure, however, that the first idea for *La patente* did not come to

couched. Another instance of a strong, commonplace comparison in the transformation of narrative into drama is the 'sfagliò come un mulo' (he started back like a mule) said of Chiàrchiaro in the same scene and which is replaced in the stage directions by the colourless 'tirandosi indietro' (stepping back).

32 Angelo Musco, *Cerca che trovi* ... (Bologna: Cappelli, 1929), 169. Pirandello's own story is told by Ottavio Profeta in *De Roberto e Pirandello: Note* (Catania, 1939); I have not been able to see this work and derive my information from Rauhut, 'Pirandello als ... Mundartdramatiker,' 165.

Pirandello after the 4 November 1916 performance of *Liolà*, for the story
by that name on the same subject had been in print since 1911. Yet something may very well have happened on the day remembered by Musco to
revive the original idea in Pirandello and to suggest how this story too
could be changed into a play for the Sicilian comedian.[33] At any rate, the
version of the play which was published in *Rivista d'Italia* in January 1918
is described in the subtitle as a *novella sceneggiata* (dramatized short
story), and it can be presumed that it was this text which served as the
basis for the 23 March 1918 Turin première. The fact that the anonymous *La Stampa* reviewer referred to earlier makes no mention of the
play being in dialect may point to one of two alternatives: either the performance was in Italian or the principal actor or actors improvised a dialect
translation as he or they went along. This latter possibility may account
for the fact that in the extant dialect text only the part of Chiàrchiaro (but
I am almost positive – as positive as one can be without having actually
seen the evidence – also the part of Rosinella) is in dialect.[34] But it is not
so much this matter which is of significance here as the light the two anecdotes shed on the primacy of the theatre for the growth of Pirandello's
reputation. It is fully understandable that, when Musco first played the
role of Chiàrchiaro, he was not acquainted with the details of the play's
history and pre-history, and that as a result the encounter on Piazza Poli
and the emergence shortly thereafter of the character of Chiàrchiaro
seemed to him incontrovertible proof of the inevitableness with which the
raw materials of life are turned into art. As for Pirandello, there is in point
of fact nothing in the anecdote as he told it to suggest, as critics have implied, that it was the play he was thinking of as the work directly inspired
by his meeting with a real life and blood 'jettatore.' It might just as well
have been the story. In any case, it is in the two texts, play and story, more

---

33 Pirandello had already written in Sicilian or translated the following plays for
Musco: *Lumìe di Sicilia, Pensaci, Giacomino!, Il berretto a sonagli, Liolà,* and *La
giara.*

34 Rauhut, 166, reports that Sandro D'Amico showed him the manuscript of the Sicilian version and pointed out 'that only Chiàrchiaro as a man of the people uses
dialect; the others speak Italian because they belong to a higher class.' I am quite
sure that a closer examination of the manuscript would show that Rosinella too
speaks dialect. Rauhut also mentions (361, n.31) Pirandello's interview in *Corriere della sera,* 10 October 1923, where he spoke of two of his regional plays
translated into Sicilian by Musco. Rauhut supposes that if Musco actually translated any Pirandello works into Sicilian, these have not yet come to light. On the
basis of the evidence presented in this essay, however, I would propose that *'A patenti* may very well be one of the two plays Pirandello had in mind: the circumstances reviewed here suggest that a translation of *La patente* was extant prior to
the official one performed in February 1919.

than in any possible effects of contingent circumstances, that we must seek evidence for Pirandello's artistic creativity. And yet the fact that the anecdote exists, that it was transmitted, and that it is mysteriously suggestive, by itself tells something about the strongly haunting quality of the figure of Chiàrchiaro.

In looking now for the internal reasons that determined the evolution of Chiàrchiaro, we must consider first of all the different development given D'Andrea in the play and in the story. Put very briefly, in the story D'Andrea is presented more fully than in the play. His role in terms of plot is the same, but Pirandello tells more about him, details of his appearance, of his life, of his feelings, which in the play are omitted altogether. While in the play we learn that D'Andrea has the reputation of being an eccentric, nicknamed Giudice Cardello (Judge Goldfinch) because of his habit of taking his goldfinch with him to the office every day, in the story we are told of the sleepless nights he spends gazing at the stars, establishing geometric relationships between them, and sending his soul wandering among them 'like a little lost spider.'[35] While in the play we hear him discussing the case with the Three Judges on the day that he has called Chiàrchiaro to his office, in the story we learn of the long period of indecision that has preceded his calling Chiàrchiaro, of his frequent attemps to draw advice from his fellow judges, of his particular dislike of the two opposition lawyers, Grigli who has the profile of an aged bird of prey, and Manin Baracca who bought an enormous talisman against the evil eye for the occasion and wears it on his fat belly, 'ridendo con tutta la pallida carnaccia di biondo majale eloquente' (laughing with all his overflowing pale flesh which made him look like an eloquent blond pig).[36] Finally, while in the play we are given no physical description (the spectator, it is true, *sees* D'Andrea step on stage and thereby receives an immediate physical impression of him, but that is the doing of actor and director and not of Pirandello), in the story there is an elaborate one which tells of his age, his thick woolly hair, his broad bulging forehead, his wrinkles, his small leaden eyes, his crooked stooped shoulders on which he seemed to carry an unbearable weight. In the story, in other words, we get one of 'those minute pedantic portraits' which are so common in Pirandello's stage

35 The image of the spider as an emblem for man already occurs in a letter of Pirandello to his sister, 31 October 1886. 'Luigi Pirandello, Lettere ai familiari,' presentazione di Sandro D'Amico, *Terzo Programma*, no. 3 (1961), 273–80.

36 In contrast to what happens to the anonymous judges in being transferred from story to play, these two very 'real' lawyers are reduced simply to a name (Lorecchio).

directions and which he was in the habit of simply lifting from his stories: 'fine psychological indications,' as one critic has said, 'most precious for his future interpreters, but extending to physical particularities with which no make-up man would ever be able to endow an actor.'[37] But in the case of D'Andrea, Pirandello did not follow the usual procedure and by the time he came to the play he let this part of the characterization drop completely.

What induced Pirandello to suppress other aspects of D'Andrea as well? As we have already seen, scenes 1 through 6 were fashioned with material from Parts I and II of the story, reorganized in such a way as to fit the new medium. Characters were created and scenes devised so that what was important to the plot and to characterization could now take place on stage. The many paragraphs devoted in the story to D'Andrea's attitude to his work and to his struggle with the case of Chiàrchiaro are reduced to a few quick notations (some of them invented for the play): his walking on carrying a tiny bird cage in his hand, his words to the bird, his exclamation of impatience at sight of the papers of the case on his desk, and later, in conversation with the Three Judges, his recollection of the 'court' game of his childhood and its relation to the 'game' he is forced to play now. The narrator's voice, which in the story had expressed that deep identification between author and character which lies at the root of Pirandello's penetrating attention to D'Andrea, is now silent. The action on stage, with its quick give and take, its entrances and exits, its mounting expectation of the direct confrontation with Chiàrchiaro, leaves little room for a more leisurely and thorough presentation of D'Andrea.

But it is not only the play in contrast to the story that minimizes the role of D'Andrea. In the course of the story itself a shift of emphasis from D'Andrea to Chiàrchiaro was already apparent. For while it is the Judge who there, as later in the play, takes the initiative of calling Chiàrchiaro to his office to discuss the merits of his case, it is Chiàrchiaro who once in the office does most of the talking. It is as though, in the very act of writing, Pirandello, beset by the urgency and oddity of Chiàrchiaro's plea, found it more and more difficult to permit D'Andrea to dispute his views. The tables are subtly turned. No longer is it the Judge who tries to convince the plaintiff to withdraw his case because it is contrary to his interests, but the plaintiff pressing the Judge to institute the case so that he can the more rapidly lose it, and thereby win it! For the paradox of the

---

37 Alberto Spaini, 'Pirandello autore drammatico,' in *Enciclopedia dello spettacolo*, VIII, 156.

situation is that Chiàrchiaro has understood something which D'Andrea, in spite of his inclination to reflection, his indignation at the injustice done Chiàrchiaro, and the long hours spent pondering a course of action, has not. What Chiàrchiaro has understood is that there is no way back to a *status quo ante*.[38] Nothing will ever convince, not just the two men against whom he has brought proceedings, but the whole town including lawyers and judges (with the exception of D'Andrea) that he is not a 'jettatore.' Therefore, D'Andrea's sympathy is of little use to him. D'Andrea's rationalistic impatience with the ignorance which lies at the basis of superstition can find no answering chord in Chiàrchiaro. Chiàrchiaro lives under pressure: he must find a solution to his plight immediately and cannot wait for the rosy morrow which the dream of progress through education and enlightenment promises. He must transform ignorance not into knowledge, as D'Andrea would like to do, but into salvation for himself. Thus, instead of fighting against the reputation that has blighted his life, he will now strengthen his claim to it. If he has been unjustly accused of being a 'jettatore,' he will show his accusers that he is indeed the bearer of bad luck and that his power is more deadly than they had supposed. To achieve this, he has already clothed himself in a new uniform and he comes now to demand a certificate. He argues his case lucidly, with a disconcerting logic which rests on an absurd notion of the social meaning of a legally conferred privilege, in which a high level of abstraction and a shrewd understanding of the world of practice mingle. Just as the Judge had to earn his degree to exercise his profession, so he too, the outcast, is applying for the right to collect a fee for a service rendered. In his case the service will be withholding his supposed but firmly believed-in influence of evil. In the story Chiàrchiaro foreshadows what he will do: 'Mi metterò a ronzare attorno a tutte le fabbriche; mi pianterò innanzi a tutte le botteghe; e tutti mi pagheranno la tassa, lei dice dell'ignoranza? io dico della salute!'[39] In the play he goes further and mimics the scenes that will ensue:

CHIÀRCHIARO.   Mi metterò a ronzare come un moscone attorno a tutte le fabbriche; andrò a impostarmi ora davanti a una bottega, ora davanti a un'altra. Là c'è un giojelliere? – Davanti alla vetrina di quel giojelliere: mi pianto lí,

---

38 The theme is a familiar one in Pirandello from *Il fu Mattia Pascal* (The Late Mattia Pascal) to *La nuova colonia* (The New Colony), but as far as I know it has never been studied as such.

39 'I'll start hanging around all the workshops. I'll take up a stand in front of all the stores. And everyone will pay my tax. You call it the tax of ignorance? I call it the tax of my salvation!'

eseguisce

mi metto a squadrare la gente cosí,

eseguisce

e chi vuole che entri più a comprare in quella bottega una gioja, o a guardare a quella vetrina? Verrà fuori il padrone, e mi metterà in mano tre, cinque lire per farmi scostare e impostare da sentinella davanti alla bottega del suo rivale. Capisce? Sarà una specie di tassa che io d'ora in poi mi metterò a esigere!

D'ANDREA.   La tassa dell'ignoranza!

CHIÀRCHIARO.   Dell'ignoranza? Ma no, caro lei! La tassa della salute![40]

This is the argument which in the story, as in the play, bit by bit reduces D'Andrea to silence. It is driven home by Chiàrchiaro's insistent tapping of his cane on the ground, by his repeated threats, and by his calling D'Andrea more than once his bitterest enemy. It is an argument, however, which leaves the Judge intellectually unconvinced. Even the great self-revelatory statement which occurs in both story and play: 'Perché ho accumulato tanta bile e tanto odio, io, contro tutta questa schifosa umanità, che veramente credo, signor giudice, d'aver qua, in questi occhi, la potenza di far crollare dalle fondamenta una intera città!'[41] is powerless to move D'Andrea from his position. Chiàrchiaro's lines parallel 'Enrico IV', 'capii ... che sarei arrivato con una fame da lupo a un banchetto già bell'e sparecchiato' (I understood that I would be arriv-

---

40 CHIÀRCHIARO.   I'll start buzzing around all the workshops like a blue bottle fly. I'll take up a stand in front of this store and that store in turn. Is there a jeweller's there? – I'll take a stand in front of his shop window (*he does so*). I'll look people straight in the face (*he does so*). Who do you think will still want to go in there to buy a jewel in that shop, or to look at the window? The owner will come out and will place three, five coins in my hand to have me move on and to take up a stand in front of his competitor's window. Do you get it? It'll be a kind of tax that from now on I'll start collecting!

D'ANDREA.   Sure, the tax of ignorance!

CHIÀRCHIARO.   Of ignorance? No, sir! The tax of my salvation!

41 'Because I have heaped up so much bitterness and so much hatred against this loathsome human race that I really think, Your Honor, that here in my eyes I have the power of shaking a whole city to its foundations!'

Chiàrchiaro's lines as they appear in the play (the version quoted here) are only slightly different in the story. I have not examined the two texts for stylistic divergences of this kind, or indeed have I stopped to consider the evidence which the available intermediate text of the *Rivista d'Italia* brings to this point. Yet one example among many might be cited. In the passage in which Chiàrchiaro describes how he will go about collecting the tax, the *Rivista d'Italia* text reads: 'Mi metterò a ronzare come un *calabrone* attorno a tutte le fabbriche; mi *stabilirò* ora davanti a una bottega, ora davanti a un'altra: mi pianto cosí (*eseguisce*), e mi metto a *guatare* la gente cosí (*eseguisce*); e chi vuole che entri piú in quella bottega? Vien fuori il padrone, e mi *mette* ...' (I'll start buzzing around all the workshops like a wasp; I'll establish myself first in front of one store and then in front of another;

ing with ravenous hunger at a banquet which had already been cleared off the table), and permit a glance at the inner abyss that the cruelty of man to man has created. They are the sudden illumination which makes an apparently insane decision appear to be the most rational, the only rational, in the world. In the story D'Andrea is overwhelmed by pity at this point and embraces Chiàrchiaro. In the play he is similarly touched but his reaction is more restrained: he gazes at Chiàrchiaro stunned. The hesitant and perplexed question, 'La patente?' with which in both instances he answers what is no longer Chiàrchiaro's request but his command to get on with the trial – 'Istruisca subito il processo' (Get on with the case at once) are Chiàrchiaro's words in the story, and 'Si metta a istruire questo processo' (Get down to this case) in the play – is an indication not of his having been won over, but of his having been hammered into psychological exhaustion. And if there should be any doubt about this reading of D'Andrea's reaction, Chiàrchiaro's line in the play, 'Lei è rimasto come una statua di sale!' (You're struck dumb like a pillar of salt!), to which there is no equivalent in the story, is enough to dissipate it. The direct encounter with Chiàrchiaro has shown D'Andrea that it is not only difficult to help this man in distress but that it is downright impossible.

But for the situation to be pushed to its logical conclusion it is not enough for D'Andrea to have been reduced to silence. He must also be destroyed. For to Chiàrchiaro's single-mindedness, even if only one individual survives who does not believe in his power, there is danger that in

this is how I'll do it [*he does so*]. I'll stare at people this way [*he does so*]. And who do you think will still want to go into that store? The owner will come out and put ...). I have italicized only those words of Chiàrchiaro that are different in the two versions, but a comparison between the passage as quoted here and as quoted earlier will show in the later version the insertion of whole new phrases as well. Some of the changes between the *Rivista d'Italia* text and the definitive one were no doubt the results of experiences during rehearsals and performance. The difficulties encountered by Pirandello with the actors who interpreted his works are well known, but it might not be inappropriate to refer here to a letter he wrote Martoglio (12 February 1917) apropos differences that arose during Musco's rehearsing of *Il berretto a sonagli*. Musco had complained about lines he considered difficult and contorted. Pirandello wrote: 'Words must be given a soul if they are to live. It is the soul that was lacking during the rehearsal of Musco and the others. Lacking the soul, the actors found themselves embroiled in long sentences full of parenthetical expressions which they didn't know how to recite to the end! Why is it that all those long sentences, those parenthetical expressions were not noticeable when I said the lines? Because I gave a soul to the characters; in reading, I communicated to them their spoken action. Because this is the characteristic of my dialogues: they are made not of words but of psychological feelings' (S. D'Amico, 'Itinerario,' 94). A stylistic study of the transformation of the story into the play, especially insofar as the dialogue passages (second part of *La patente*) are concerned, would involve a careful examination of at least four texts, the three already available and the text of the Sicilian version soon to come.

the end no one will. It is here that the play goes further than the story and by doing so brings to full light the second cause of antagonism between the two. Beyond their disagreement about the expediency of the trial lies Chiàrchiaro's determination to persuade D'Andrea of the actual existence of his supernatural powers. We pass from the social and existential dimension of the situation to an aspect of that vast area of the occult to which Pirandello returned again and again throughout his career.[42] Superstition in this context is no longer a cultural blindness which enlightenment can cure, but a key to a suprarational understanding of reality. Indeed Chiàrchiaro had from the very beginning of his appearance insisted on the authenticity of his magic powers: 'Lei dunque non ci crede?' (So, you don't believe in it?) are his first words in both the story and the play, and later when D'Andrea thinks of humouring him by feigning belief, he cuts him short sharply, 'Nossignore! Lei deve crederci sul serio, e deve anche dimostrarlo istruendo il processo!' (No, sir! You must believe in it seriously, and you must also show that you do by instituting the trial!). But D'Andrea had taken these repeated admonitions no more seriously than Chiàrchiaro's dress or, to be more precise, he had taken them seriously only inasmuch as they were the clue to Chiàrchiaro's deep and intolerable anguish. Now, however, after Chiàrchiaro's emphatic, 'La patente, sissignore!' (The licence, yes sir!) with which in both story and play he counters D'Andrea's benumbed stammer, the window opens unexpectedly and a gust of wind upsets the bird cage on its stand. From this point to the end of the play the only words that D'Andrea speaks refer to the death of the goldfinch. And the very last ones he utters, the disconnected 'Il vento ... la vetrata ... il cardellino' (The wind ... the window ... the goldfinch) – his answer to the excited questions of the Three Judges and Marranca – are the rational interpretation of the accident, in which there is absolutely no room for the action of the supernatural even reduced to its most abstract formulation, fate. Chiàrchiaro disputes this interpretation at once and brings his clinching argument to bear on D'Andrea:

CHIÀRCHIARO (con un grido di trionfo).   Ma che vento! Che vetrata! Sono stato io! Non voleva crederci e glien'ho dato la prova! Io! Io! E come è morto quel cardellino,
     subito, gli atti di terrore degli astanti, che si scostano da lui
così, a uno a uno, morirete tutti![43]

---

42 In Cecchi-Sapegno, IX, 453–7, Macchia has some extremely illuminating observations to make on this point.

43 CHIÀRCHIARO (with a cry of triumph).   What wind? What window? It was I! He didn't want to believe in my power and I've given him proof! I! I! And just as that

The three io's (I's) mark the high point of Chiàrchiaro's transformation. The threat, implicit in the grotesque dress with which he underscored his exclusion from the fellowship of men, tapped out by the rhythmic beating of the cane, at various times openly made to D'Andrea, has become a reality. What D'Andrea had interpreted as play-acting on the part of Chiàrchiaro was deadly earnest. But the argument – the bird's death turned by Chiàrchiaro with lightning rapidity to his interest – convinces only those who have been convinced all along. The TUTTI (All) who answer Chiàrchiaro's intimidation with the usual invocations and entreaties, 'Per l'anima vostra! Ti caschi la lingua! Dio, ajutaci! Sono un padre di fami- glia!' (Think of your soul! May you be struck dumb! God, help us all! I have a family to support!), obviously do not include D'Andrea. If D'Andrea has been defeated by Chiàrchiaro, he has been so only in the sense that his superior learning and his training in dialectic have been unsuccessful in impressing upon the latter the absurdity of demanding official recognition for his fearsome status. As far as the results of a life- time of scepticism are concerned – 'la certezza di non poter nulla sapere e nulla credere non sapendo' (the certainty of not being able to know any- thing and of not being able to believe in anything, not knowing), as the story states – these have not been overturned.

What then is the irreparable something that, in contrast to the story, the final action of the play brings about? While with his specious argu- ments and the various demonstrations of the harm that had been done to him Chiàrchiaro has all along rejected the helping hand proferred him by D'Andrea, it is only through the death of the bird and through his assum- ing responsibility for it that he definitely shuts the door in his face. Hate has triumphed over love. The meanness and stupidity of men have been answered by a cunning and an ill-will strong enough to destroy. The sym- pathy felt for Chiàrchiaro earlier is now suddenly turned to frozen horror. For while Chiàrchiaro's self-congratulation might have been understand- able and even justified as a response to anyone else on stage, it is not so in the case of D'Andrea. The effect is disproportionate to the cause. Chiàr- chiaro has killed – or assumed responsibility for killing, the two things being equivalent here – what D'Andrea held dearest. In D'Andrea's life the goldfinch, the gift of his deceased mother, had taken the place of all human affections and stood for his sense of continuity and identity.[44] It is this that at the existential level Chiàrchiaro has taken from him. The ac-

goldfinch died (*at once all those present draw back from him with gestures of fright*) so one by one you too shall die!

44 The meaning of the goldfinch for D'Andrea is in some respect identical with that of the canary for Adriano Meis (*Il fu Mattia Pascal*, end of chap. IX). While D'An- drea's lines in *La patente*, 'Gli parlo ... che noi esistiamo' (I speak to him ... that we

tion, begun when Chiàrchiaro appeared before D'Andrea, dressed not in his own clothing but in a masquerade costume which revealed his inner being, is concluded. Events will now follow their course. The trial will take place, Chiàrchiaro will lose it, and by losing it he will have found his way back into society, a scarecrow from which men will flee but cannot ignore. Unable to earn his living by contributing to the material well-being of men (his job as a bank clerk thus has a symbolic and not merely a naturalistic meaning), Chiàrchiaro will still have a function in catering to the dark, mysterious underside of their nature.[45] In the final reversal it is not Chiàrchiaro, the apparent victim, who is excluded, but D'Andrea, the man who was isolated all along. Through his progressive swelling, first in the short story and then in the play, Chiàrchiaro has robbed him of his *Lebensraum*.

To find out who and what D'Andrea really is one must, of course, turn back from the play to the story which is its indispensable subtext. D'Andrea, I hope I have made clear, is neither one of Pirandello's chorus figures nor is he comparable to a spokesman such as Laudisi. While Chiàrchiaro stands between Ciampa[46] and 'Enrico IV' on the trajectory of the emergence

exist), can in no way be called a direct borrowing from the novel, 'Non potendo con gli altri ... della nostra vana illusione' (Not being able to do so with others ... of our vain illusion), the two passages follow exactly the same line of development. Morpurgo in his edition of the *Novelle*, p.107 n.34, instead of *Il fu Mattia Pascal* refers to the story *Un gatto, il cardellino e le stelle* (first published in *Penombra* in 1917) as embodying the bird theme. In this story a neighbour's cat finds its way into the house of a carefully guarded and deeply cherished goldfinch and devours it. There are some obvious parallels to the situation of *La patente*: the goldfinch in the story belongs to a couple whose grand-daughter had trained it before dying; their loss is thus comparable to D'Andrea's loss. Less obvious is the fact that the ruthlessness of the cat, a being inferior to man, is very similar to the ruthlessness of Chiàrchiaro. In both stories, as in *Cinci* (1932), nature is a spectator without feeling. The crossing of influences, always significant in Pirandello, is especially interesting in *La patente* because it is an additional indication of the bipartite division of the play: in fact, as far as the bird episode is concerned, it is the mood of the passage from *Il fu Mattia Pascal* that is echoed in the first part of the play; the mood of *Un gatto, il cardellino e le stelle* that is recaptured in the second part.

45 What I earlier referred to as the second *dénouement*, Chiàrchiaro's collecting money from the Three Judges and Marranca in scene 8, is a projection of what is expected to happen later on a larger scale. This scene is incomplete in the *Rivista d'Italia* version, which ends with Chiàrchiaro's defiant 'Io! Io!' The difference between the two versions is further proof of the progressive development of the character of Chiàrchiaro.

46 It is instructive to compare the description of Ciampa and that of Chiàrchiaro at their respective entrances. Ciampa is himself, even though his eyes 'flash like a madman's.' However, he wears thick metal-rimmed glasses, comparable to Chiàrchiaro's horn-rimmed ones. All the details of Ciampa's appearance are naturalistic; none of Chiàrchiaro's is. And yet there can be no doubt that Ciampa's tension is in every way comparable to Chiàrchiaro's, and I would say that the eyeglasses are the outward sign of their kinship.

of the character without an author, D'Andrea is rather much like Serafino
Gubbio, the cameraman whose voice has been silenced by the horror of a
scene he involuntarily filmed. In Pirandello's version of the anecdote relating to the conception of *La patente*, he himself has a role or a possible
role in the life of the unfortunate man reputed to bring bad luck. In
Musco's version there are no second roles: there is only the actor, the
'jettatore.' The stage history of the play reflects this latter vision of it. The
internal history of its genesis and growth, instead, reflects – and how could
it not? – Pirandello's vision of it. In this vision, the complete meaning of
the story of Chiàrchiaro is understandable only in terms of what happens
to D'Andrea. For Pirandello never intended the 'triumph' of the former to
be a cause for rejoicing (as it would have been had only the Manin Baraccas
been his adversaries), but only for reflective sadness at the condition of
'questi poveri piccoli uomini feroci' (these poor little cruel men). So that
without aiming at a comparative aesthetic judgment of the respective
merits of play and story – something which in the final analysis would
only reflect subjective preferences – the greatest pleasure to be derived
from letting play light up story, and story play, is that of once again
watching creativity at work in that great poet of the creative act who was
Luigi Pirandello.[47]

47 This essay was already completed when I located a copy of Nino De Bella's *Narrativa e teatro nell'arte di Luigi Pirandello* (Messina-Firenze: D'Anna, 1962). De Bella
discusses *La patente*, play and story, on pp. 57–9, expressing his preference for the
narrative version because he finds that the figure of Chiàrchiaro is justified only
in terms of D'Andrea. Pirandello's 'humorism,' in other words, is for De Bella only
incompletely expressed in the play.

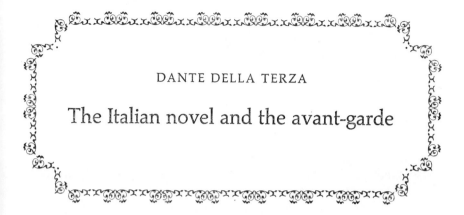

DANTE DELLA TERZA

The Italian novel and the avant-garde

IT MAY BE OPPORTUNE to initiate our discussion of the avant-garde and the novel in Italy by beginning at a moment in history when the word 'avant-garde' was not yet much used,[1] but when two important ingredients of the doctrine it stands for did already exist: the quarrel with tradition-bound culture, and the projection towards the future of ideas and points of view considered to be incontrovertible, new, 'scientific' discoveries, to use the language of the day. The time was the early 1880s, and the discussion focuses on naturalism and in particular on a recently published novel in the new literary style, Giovanni Verga's *I Malavoglia*. If we consider the words of one of the few qualified readers of Verga's book, Luigi Capuana,[2] a critic so interested in the fate of Verga's novel that he turned his review of it into a manifesto of the new literary taste, we see already present traces of what we could call the fervour of anticipation typical of the twentieth century avant-garde. We can find in Capuana's essay for example, diatribes against the romantic–patriotic rhetoric of the Risorgimento dear to the Italian cultural and political establishment, as well as statements of principle which project towards the future, anticipating solutions which seemed scarcely possible in the Italy of the day. However, in Capuana's essay, the relative importance given to the two complementary facets of any authentic avant-garde achievement, polemics and anticipation, seem to be out of balance, since the programmatic aspects of the latter by far outweigh any disruptive discussion of the present state of literary affairs in the peninsula. Capuana limits himself to attacking

1 According to an historian of the avant-garde, Renato Poggioli, the word 'avant-garde' with political, revolutionary overtones already existed around 1878. See R. Poggioli, *The Theory of the Avant-Garde* (Cambridge, Mass., 1968), 9.
2 Luigi Capuana, 'G. Verga' in *Studi sulla letteratura contemporanea* (Catania, 1883).

the Italian public in a vague way, without naming anyone directly.[3] His discourse thus achieves little of objective interest; but when he considers the future, declaring that 'the novel here is a plant that still needs to be acclimatized,'[4] he seems to express concerns and hopes that are less conventional and more in the spirit of what to him appears to be the naturalistic evolution of literary forms. On the one hand, he connects any new, modern, literary effort with the novel, as the only up-to-date instrument for expressing positive, scientific truths; on the other, he hopes to see this new, still fluctuating form, as yet non-existent in Italy, transplanted with vegetal, botanical roots, that is to say solidly and scientifically, as befits the experimental contents it is called upon to reveal.

But can *I Malavoglia* be considered truly an example of this novel of the future according to Capuana? Since Verga's novel is constructed without any concessions to the expediencies of a linear, all-too-predictable plot, and salvages linguistically the sociological fervour for truth preached by the naturalist school, by conserving the flavour, at least, of the Sicilian dialect spoken by the characters in the story, the book would seem, even though not as well organized as Capuana might have wished, to correspond almost perfectly to the characteristics he so anxiously sought.[5] But this is not all there is to Capuana's view of Verga. We should keep in mind his reservations, minor though they were, about the construction of *I Malavoglia*, as well as Verga's equally minor criticism of Capuana's novel, *Giacinta*, which he thought had 'some crudeness in its detail

3 In fact, Capuana seldom mentions any name from the Italian literary establishment. True, a critic not unsympathetic to naturalism, Francesco De Sanctis, is respectfully called to task for having failed to show interest in the *Malavoglia*, but such a polite expression of disapproval cannot in any sense be considered antagonistic, especially if compared to the violent opposition expressed, say, by a Carducci to Manzoni and Manzoni's followers. Capuana's distaste for the artifice and rhetorical tinsel of the Romantics can not have been caused solely by the rather naive practical forms of bad taste in the Italian political oratory of his times. It is our view that Capuana's polemical skirmishes have passively absorbed the spirit of opposition of the French Naturalists to their contemporary fellow writers. As everyone knows, while the brothers Goncourt, in their preface to *Germinie Lacerteux* (1864) condemned the materialistic outlook of the French bourgeois reader of novels, Zola chose as a target the elegant verbiage of Renan's evasive scientific prose and the verbose lyricism of Victor Hugo. They were evidently dealing with more formidable adversaries than the ghosts evoked by Capuana's vague polemical allusions. For this problem see the book by: Roberto Bigazzi, *I colori del vero, Vent' anni di narrativa: 1860–1880* (Pisa, 1969).

4 L. Capuana, 'G. Verga,' 35–6.

5 According to Capuana, the novel does a good job of amalgamating thousands of facts of life, in themselves insignificant, into an organized whole, giving them direction, but it has an excess of minutiae and lacks proportion in its parts.

neither necessary nor appropriate,' and going beyond these external statements examine the structure of the books the two novelists wrote. It is our opinion that the very mild objections which Capuana and Verga exchanged between 1879 and 1881, if projected into the future, crystallize in antagonistic narrative structures, representing two different ways of telling a story, two different roads for the novel to follow. In order to detect them, we shall try to turn our attention to some concrete aspects of the narrative techniques sponsored by naturalism, as they manifest themselves divergently in some episodes in Verga's *Mastro don Gesualdo* and Capuana's *Marchese di Roccaverdina*, both conceived, if not published, during the decade 1880–90.

The scene in *Mastro don Gesualdo*,[6] in which the dying Bianca Trao sends her husband's former mistress, Diodata, from her bedside with a gesture of extreme revulsion, suggests a conflict that is not incorporated into the novel, but whose motives are perfectly discernible to the reader, even though he is unable to trace its genesis or narrative itinerary. If we go back over the story, we find in the four encounters between Gesualdo and Diodata the same glimpses of unexplored possibilities, the same tentative involvement on Verga's part in emotional conflicts that are immediately attenuated by his conviction that the confrontation of one character with another does not in any specific way condition that character's inevitable encounter with his destiny. Thus Diodata's tears and the anger which they provoke in Gesualdo pass without incident, as her emotions give way to her habitual passivity, and his do likewise. The confrontation does not take place, as if the author wished to spare his characters new trials. In a sense, Verga's characters obey a code of action according to which one has the right to choose his own misfortunes one at a time.

But let us imagine that a reader of Verga, at once privileged and impatient, a companion in the naturalist experience, but intolerant of the limits on introspection which Verga imposed on himself in his description of character, decided to rewrite the plot of the novel, in a competitive act of imagination, enveloping Gesualdo's nights in a fog of jealousy, projecting Bianca's hate beyond the instant of delirium in which it is revealed, or conferring on Diodata the aggressive sensuality she lacks. What results would such a narrative expedient yield? The ensuing altered picture of the novel, a working hypothesis reconstructing the Goncourts' path

6 For the text of *Mastro don Gesualdo*, we refer to the Ricciardi edition edited by Luigi Russo in 1955, and for that of *Marchese di Roccaverdina* to the Garzanti edition of 1956.

to realism by an unhurried examination of the characters' deviations from the classical conventions accepted by Verga, while perfectly absurd and abstract in theory, assumes an aura of possibility when considered in the light of the narrative tastes of a Luigi Capuana, for example.

It seems justified to assume that the writer from Mineo might have read these episodes we have mentioned from *Mastro don Gesualdo* as a series of lost opportunities, especially perhaps the one concerning the protagonist's nocturnal visit to the house of Nanni l'Orbo and Diodata, which the latter interprets mistakenly as a return of passion in her former lover. Impatient to conquer new zones of reality for the novel, Capuana, having overcome Verga's still Manzonian modesty in the description of feeling, sees the destiny of Verga's characters in the light of a pathology of remorse, creating in his Marchese di Roccaverdina the aristocratic counterpart of Gesualdo, in Agrippina Solmo a voluptuous Diodata, and in the insidious Rocco Criscione, the counterpart of Verga's acquiescent and opaque Nanni l'Orbo.

From the necessarily mobile point of view of the historian of the avant-garde, called upon by the nature of his task to study intellectual movements and phases in taste in their tension towards the future and hence in their dissolution, the characteristics of Capuana's narrative experience present a curious ambivalence. One is struck on the one hand by the ambition to explore, the defiance of limits, which is a condition of all avant-garde endeavours,[7] the revealing probing of emotions traditionally considered ineffable; and on the other by the all too obvious desire to settle into a convenient schema, into a different but equally classifiable stability. The highly exploratory coefficient implicit in an undertaking that goes beyond the realm of previously established, psychological truths towards the turbid but captivating unknown of instinct, when reduced to reasonable proportions, continues to produce a respectable, popular literature, as long as the narrator limits himself to working with marginal segments of reality – the pathological affliction of characters who are capable in the last analysis of being cured and redeemed, thus leaving uncontested the meaningful structure of reality. Capuana's narrative ideology contains, from this point of view, quite evident tendencies towards compromise and regression: the anthropocentrism which facilitates the descent into the hell of instinct is organized in reassuring dichotomies, allowing one to glimpse the path to salvation alongside the road to perdition the

---

7 For this aspect concerning the sociological behaviour of the avant-garde, see the book by Renato Poggioli, *Teoria dell'arte d'avanguardia* (Il Mulino, 1962), now in English with the title: *The Theory of the Avant-Garde* (Cambridge, Mass., 1968).

protagonists are following. If the Marchese di Roccaverdina by his crime debases the paternalistic function of the nobility to which he belongs, the priest to whom he confesses re-establishes, if not in him certainly for him, that righteous valuation of authority through which principles at least are saved; and though Giacinta and Eugenia seem destined in some other novels by Capuana to a life of dissolution, the prestigious, omniscient doctors Follini and Mola, custodians of the secret wisdom of positivism, are there ready to reassure us as to the exceptional and pathological nature of their disturbances, and thus to save our good conscience as readers.

Paradoxically the two approaches to the naturalistic novel, that of Verga and that of Capuana, do not necessarily lead to their intended respective goals. The re-elaboration of reality in a novel like Verga's, which does not propose to say anything new or go beyond the frontiers of what is already known, is capable of containing a linguistic tension that has a leavening effect on the reality it describes, transforming it; the initial avant-garde premise of a writer like Capuana, however, is doomed to failure in the mediocrity of the results obtained when carried out as it is with stylistic caution by one who is bent on exploring unknown lands without disturbing his readers' peace of mind, and who enters in fact into a complicity with their condition of privilege in respect to the 'degraded' world of novels.

In the general area of Capuana's explorations, that is to say, at the margins of nineteenth-century naturalism, the narrative experiment of Pirandello finds its place. Of what importance is it for the experience of the literary avant-garde in Italy? The answer to this question cannot but be a considered and circumspect one. We must say at once that the partly transformistic nature of the literary avant-garde at work in Italy at the turn of the century facilitated the intemperate proliferation of anecdotes tending to conciliate diverse men and events. Thus the futurists have from time to time presented us with an edifying picture of the period, not unlike a chapter from a schoolgirl's history book of the thirties celebrating the heroes of the Risorgimento, in which we see Gabriele D'Annunzio in full dress uniform presenting a big bouquet of red carnations to F.T. Marinetti, bed-ridden in a hospital in Udine,[8] or Capuana in his last years applauding the initiatives of a futuristic evening in Catania; and Pirandello in an emergency alliance with the futurists against the self-satisfied Roman public during the difficult years of his theatrical reform. But in tracing the history of the relationships existing between the novel and the

8 A. Viviani, *Il poeta Marinetti e il Futurismo* (Milano, 1940), 47.

avant-garde at the beginning of the century, we obviously cannot accept the arbitrary semantic expansion proposed by self-interested contemporary observers. The most healthy methodological attitude consists of placing oneself at a proper distance from events, adopting the selective criterion proposed by the unprejudiced and intelligent neo-avant-garde of the sixties, a criterion which assures us of a minimum of fidelity to the subject under discussion and of sympathy for the task of immediate discrimination which every avant-garde endeavour necessarily demands. It can happen, of course, that when brought ultimately face to face with the actual creative works of the neo-avant-garde, one may be prompted to admit that considerably more intelligence is displayed in their appraisals of the literature of the past than in their own inventions which these judgments were meant to shape. Nevertheless, the criterion for the evaluation of the past which the neo-avant-garde proposes we should adopt is not teleological but historical, to the extent at least that, between the principle of evaluation and the phenomenon to be evaluated, there exists a detachment of a temporal order capable of placing the diverse phenomena under consideration, all on an equal basis. The work of a talented critic who has cast his lot with the neo-avant-garde, Edoardo Sanguineti, can in this case serve as an eloquent example. He is able to advance persuasively a detached judgment of the work of Ardengo Soffici, a writer involved, in the beginning at least, in the adventurous grafting of the expressive force of Rimbaud and Apollinaire onto the cautious Italian tradition, and at the same time attempt a reconsideration of the generally considered thoroughly predictable poetry of Guido Gozzano, which promises to be far-reaching in its effects.[9]

In analysing the literary events from the eccentric point, we have chosen as our principle of evaluation – a working principle which takes the place of an aesthetic criterion, since, like it, it is at once within the work of art being judged and outside of it – all the novels of the early twentieth century stand at an equal distance from this point, waiting to find their place in the dynamics of a still unforeseeable perspective. In the case of Pirandello, what attracts the attention of the selective critic of the avant-garde is the polemic attitude with which he confronts the problem of the novel. The paradox to be gleaned from the second introduction to *Il Fu Mattia Pascal*, when freed of the slightly affected embellishments of Pirandello's mannerisms, delineates with singular clarity the inevitable relationship existing between a mistaken manner of narration and a false ideology of knowledge. In a passage whose similarity in wording reminds

9 E. Sanguineti, *Tra liberty e Crepuscolarismo* (Milano, 1961).

us of a page from Alain Robbe-Grillet criticizing the naturalistic trend in narrative technique, Pirandello in fact rejects, in the words of Mattia, 'the detailed narration full of idle particulars of the type "The Count rose early at eight-thirty exactly ...," "the Countess put on a lilac dress ... ," ' because it seems to him anthropocentric, which is to say Ptolemaic, and hence ideologically backward. However, in Pirandello, the initial intuition that the story should never be an indulgent definition of self, but should dedicate itself to the understanding of existence, is undermined by his summary, still-naturalistic, narrative style. And this occurs because, though seemingly interested in discounting the rhetorical symbolism of appearances, which he calls 'quintilineo,' he remains within the orbit of an interpretation of being as pure content, without adequately meditating on the phenomenology of being as form and style. The ideology which Pirandello evokes with the name Copernican is, in the sense in which he uses it, actually the same as the Ptolemaic – equally anthropocentric, even if in it the ontological realm of being appears related to a background of cosmic improbability. The resulting novels are parables, the events impatient fictions and metaphors of the immutable drama of existence and the human condition.

A neo-avant-garde reading of F.T. Marinetti's narrative work should not exclude a priori the possibility of re-evaluating it as intentional parody. When we read, for example, in the preface to *Mafarka il futurista*, that the great polyphonic novel (*Mafarka*) 'waves in the wind of glory like a banner of immortality on the pinnacle of human thought,' we cannot help asking ourselves if these words are a sacrifice to the D'Annunzian god of vanity, or rather a parody of the narcissistic exaltation which attained unequalled heights in the pages of D'Annunzio's prose. The expansion of the narrative content – the chapters of *Mafarka* describing the rape of the negresses and the attack on the city by the rabid dogs, events typical of D'Annunzio or the Flaubert of *Salammbô*, deformed by the force of a sort of gay, irrepressible madness, seem to suggest deliberate parody. But even so, this could be the case only so far as the extravagant content is concerned, for D'Annunzio's influence on the language is not so much the result of a voluntary mimetic pastiche, as it is the consequence of the pressure exerted by a writer of eloquence and great imagination on one essentially without a language (Marinetti's French bears too much resemblance to the Italian of his translator, Dicio Cinti, and Cinti's Italian is too much like D'Annunzio's 'good' French). Moreover, the derivative nature of Marinetti's work, from a modern reader's point of view at least, is evident even in those works considered to be his literary masterpieces – the futurist manifestos. Those racing cars celebrated for their 'hoods adorned with huge serpent pipes with an explosive breath,'[10] more beautiful perhaps than the Victory of Samothrace, but resembling nonetheless nothing so much as the 1910 automobile parodied for its snaillike pace by Charles Trenet[11] in an amusing song of his, are destined to remain idle fancies of the future, poorly held together by the nominalism of the D'Annunzian vocabulary, unless endowed by an act of our imagination with the visual dynamics of the great Boccioni, who succeeded in capturing with genius the platonic idea of velocity in his paintings.

D'Annunzio's novels, in spite of the obvious attraction they held for all Italian writers of the first part of the twentieth century, remain outside the avant-garde experience. To be sure the scheme of the naturalist novel is modified in them, freed of the appurtenances of provincial life, which represented a cumbersome, folkloric obstacle to the ennobling of the plot D'Annunzio considered the supreme aim of his vocation as an aesthete and a European. And, to be sure, the caste spirit and class morality that constitute the archaic limits of the narrative explorations of a Capuana are sacrificed in the name of a non-restrictive conception of the hero's freedom of action. However, the conflict between the individual and society, life-breath of the naturalist novel, is only nominally abolished, society being absorbed into the individual in a precarious harmony regulated by a diluvial eloquence, which is a kind of fetish that the individual employs in an attempt to placate the external world he is incapable of understanding or modifying.

The legacy of the early avant-garde is to be sought then outside the main roads travelled by the major writers, in the almost imperceptible traces left by Marinetti's parody-jargon, in the limpid crystalline geometry of concentric circles which Massimo Bontempelli inscribes around man's fate, with a detached sense of humour not averse to an occasional pun; or in the ironic reduction of the world of naturalism to its most humble moments, that grotesque–sentimental fragmenting of provincial,

10 The 'Manifesto del Futurismo' we have quoted can now be found reproduced in the beautiful book by Mario De Micheli, *Le Avanguardie artistiche del Novecento* (Milano, 1966).

A try at relaunching Marinetti occurred recently with the republication of some of his writings by Mondadori: F.T. Marinetti, *Teoria e invenzione futurista* (Milano, 1968). In the discussion which followed among the neo-avant-garde (cf. the December 1968 and January 1969 issues of *Quindici*), Edoardo Sanguineti assumed a position antagonistic to the first Italian futurist, while Luciano De Maria expressed himself on the question with a certain, cautious sympathy for Marinetti.

11 This is the song by Trenet which begins with this felicitous refrain: "Aux environs des belles années dix-neuf-cent-dix lorsque le monde découvrait l'automobile ...'

Tuscan life practised, with felicitous narrative verve, by a futurist in rupture with his group – Aldo Palazzeschi.

We must consider separately the Italian equivalent of that far-reaching, middle-European experience that includes Kafka and Freud, the most significant episode the avant-garde can in good conscience claim as its own – the last novel of Italo Svevo. *La Coscienza di Zeno* is, in fact, the most conspicuous example of anti-D'Annunzio narrative method produced in Italy in the first quarter of the twentieth century. And this is because the author dares to concentrate on what is inexplicable and discordant in the world, the stridence in the music of the spheres; and going far beyond his anti-platonic design, on the disparity in man's physiology between muscle tone and the control the will exerts over movement. There is in this connection an extremely interesting page in the third chapter of the book, where Zeno, at the obsessive suggestion of a limping friend, perceives, like an awed observer of a Duchamp or Picabia painting, the peremptory articulation of the whole muscular machine of the leg, with a consequent psychosomatic laceration of the will to move. The success of the *La Coscienza di Zeno* is related in part to the exceptional, if heterodox, use of the psychoanalytic method in the presentation of events. But the true innovation in the novel does not lie, in our opinion, so much in the acquisition of nebulous zones of the unconscious for narrative study, as in the presentation of a vigilant consciousness, recalcitrant to any settlement of its condition, which cannot bring itself to consider definitive any experience other than its own perpetual uneasiness. Zeno refuses to adjust to the condition of healthy men, for sickness endows him with a critical vision of the structure of the world and an ironic contemplation of his own life. The ironic vision of his own contradictory acts and intentions is made possible by his capacity to record within himself the disharmony of the world, without illusion and with the gay indulgence of the wise; the critical vision of reality is inculcated in him by his condition as a sick man, which permits him to observe the world of the healthy from a privileged vantage point as it moves toward total self-destruction in its constant aspiration for ever better health.

At this juncture, after Svevo, we feel swept up with the neo-avant-garde towards more urgent polemics. In fact, the years in which the friction with the past reaches moments of unequalled incandescence are at hand. The premise of fifteen years of wars, in Spain, Ethiopia, and on Italian soil, is followed by the corollaries of a brief five years of palingenetic hopes, and a decade of reassessment, with all its inevitable acquiescence and opportunism. We pass from the complex history of neo-realism to the obsessive and alienated landscape of the so-called industrial novel.

Historical facts and cultural phenomena no longer reach the neo-avant-garde attenuated by distance, but exist on a plane of spatial contiguity, and are therefore confronted with the selective fury that emergency circumstances demand. The moment of truth for the neo-avant-garde, 1960-7, coincides with the most paradoxical and provocatory phases of the polemical dissociation from the immediate past; and the most sarcastic judgments are passed, not only on writers considered to be acquiescent to the established order, such as Bassani and Cassola – 'le Liale 1963' as they were called, but others as well, who had proven themselves ready to risk everything in the name of the most daring experimentation, such as Vittorini, Pasolini, or Calvino.

This is the point where we must part company with the neo-avant-garde, in order to do justice, in the end, to its evident significance. Here too we shall try, out of loyalty to our own tastes and education as a reader, to follow without too much impatience, the useful path of history.

In sketching an outline of the novel related solely to the events of the avant-garde, we would be inclined to exclude the Italian writers of art prose who acquired a certain fame in the years between the two wars. And yet, to take a simile from nature, quiet, even stagnant waters may, unnoticed, be preparing the turbulence of the rapids ahead, representing that imperceptible moment of change. Especially interesting is the declaration of rejection of the novel with which the writer G.B. Angioletti opens an anthology of his work in the thirties, indicating a kind of voluntary isolation of Italian literature from the mainstream of European fiction.[12] It is curious to note that this repudiation of the novel does not follow, as is often the case, a flowering of narrative literature, but is more than

---

12 G. Antonini and G.B. Angioletti, *Narratori d'oggi* (Firenze, 1939).
  I quote from the preface written by Angioletti: 'Scrivere, per certi romanzieri europei (e anche americani) non è più che un lavoro pedantesco di resocontista intento a riassumere fatti sensazionali o monologhi interiori svolgentesi nella mente di personaggi per lo più insulsi e meschini ... Gli scrittori italiani si trovano a formare un gruppo isolato, decisi a considerare ancora molto seriamente il lavoro letterario, perchè essi preferiscono a costo dei più duri sacrifici, puntare proprio sull'arte che non sullo scandalismo documentario o sull'intrigo considerato fine a se stesso ...
  Quando certi stranieri vengono a dirci che gli italiani non sanno raccontare, non possiamo impedirci di sorridere. Gli italiani, se raccontare vuol dire superare la brutalità della materia e la superficialità degli avvenimenti staccati dalle loro cause profonde, sono ancora oggi fra i migliori narratori del mondo.' (Writing, for certain European writers [and American ones too] is no longer anything more than a pedantic work of reportage intent upon giving a summary of sensational events or interior monologues developing in the minds of characters for the most part insipid and petty ... Italian writers form an isolated group, determined to still take literary work very seriously, because they prefer, at the cost of great sacrifice, to rely on

anything else a self-satisfied expression of its absence. We are tempted to repeat the caustic remarks – made several decades later – of two foreign observers:

Les italiens sont supérieurs aux autres par essence. Donc, même ce qu'ils n'écrivent pas est préférable à ce que les autres écrivent. Même ce qu'ils ne peignent pas est préférable à ce que les autres peignent. (J.F. Revel, *Pour l'Italie* [Paris, 1958], 205)

L'intellectuel français méprise la culture étrangère qu'il ignore, l'intellectuel italien envie la culture étrangère qu'il dénigre. (Dominique Fernandez, *L'échec de Pavese* [Paris, 1968], 151)

But to tell the truth, while the statement by Angioletti is not a manifesto avant-la-lettre of the anti-novel, neither is it, in our opinion, solely a manifesto of backward isolationism. The problem is something else. Italian writers, essayists, and critics were opening their arms, perhaps as never before, to foreign culture: the care with which the same Angioletti translated the correspondence of Flaubert is well known. It is less well known, but important to remember, that Emilio Cecchi dedicated a lucid article to Proust's work as far back as the winter of 1922.[13] Let us add that we would perhaps never have had such an intelligent and versatile neo-avant-garde, had we not had the experience of the review *Solaria* as a precedent, or would we have had the ingenious sketches of Arbasino, the globe-trotter, without the scribblings of Cecchi's magic pen in his travel diaries. But what saves these writers from any avant-garde temptations is the Italian tradition of the cult of closed forms, the profound caution with which they approach every possible adventure which might take them outside the safe territory of their insurmountable, intellectual conservatism. Foreign books appear redimensioned by the ever-present, cautious common sense, and never are a mirage, a sorcery of the mind, a witchery, fascination, or vertigo. Romano Bilenchi and Carlo Cassola, two Tuscan

art rather than on documentary sensationalism or on plot, considered as an end in itself.

When certain foreigners tell us that Italians do not know how to narrate, we cannot help smiling. Italians, if narrating means overcoming the rawness of the material and the superficiality of the events detached from their profound causes, are still among the best narrators in the world.), 9.

When we read words like these, written moreover by an essayist of integrity and not even of fascist inclinations, we understand better what a giant Cesare Pavese was in Italy.

13 The article by Cecchi appeared in the daily newspaper *La Tribuna*.

writers who matter, by placing the emphasis on Joyce's *Dubliners* rather than *Ulysses*, are able to assimilate, with very little effort, the most advanced, European, avant-garde tradition, transposed however to a perfectly familiar, homey level. More important than the discoveries themselves are the moderation and profound reservation with which they are irremediably approached.

In a wonderful short story by the versatile Piedmontese writer, Mario Soldati, entitled 'Laurea in lettere,'[14] the young protagonist is carried on the wings of dream to Proust's hotel. Brought face to face with his idol, he is tempted to ask if his friend Giacomino Debenedetti really is the best critic of the *Recherche du temps perdu*. This sudden oneiric degeneration of the encounter, which unexpectedly injects the spirit of a very Turinese *tertulia* into the solemnity of the occasion, seems to me in a way emblematic. Dreams are, of course, only dreams, but we must await the appearance of an illuminating article by Sergio Solmi before it is really understood in Italy to what extent Proust can satisfy the expectations of the contemporary avant-garde. It is for the exploratory exercise of his 'intrepid and desperate rationality' which 'defies the limits of the known,' Solmi tells us, that Proust is relevant to our times. Beyond his extreme but controlled adventure lies the deluge – 'the shipwreck in pure formless matter, in pure object,'[15] in a word, the realm of the avant-garde.

Having indicated the cautious curiosity with which Italian literature viewed the advanced, European experience, it is our duty to point out those cases which depart from the common denominator, exposing themselves to the risks of a more dangerous game. The names which come immediately to mind are those of writers like Moravia, Gadda, Vittorini, and to a certain extent Pavese, who stand aside from the literary experience of the fascist era, supporters of a cause full of import for the future.

The word 'progettazione,'[16] projection, dear to the late work of Vittorini, is perhaps most indicative of the tension towards the future which these writers, for different reasons, share. Moravia, the one who has come closest to realizing the ancient ideal of *nulla dies sine linea*, or of *nullus annus sine libro*, has more than forty years of novelistic craftsmanship behind him. But this long presence in the literary limelight imposes on

14 Mario Soldati, 'Laurea in lettere' in *I Racconti* (Milano, 1957). The volume, whose first edition appeared in 1957, collects stories written between 1927 and 1947.
15 S. Solmi, 'Proust e l'esperienza dei limiti' in *Letteratura*, November–December issue 1947, dedicated to Marcel Proust, 183.
16 Italo Calvino discusses it in the article 'Progettazione e letteratura' included in the commemorative issue of *Il Menabo* (1967) dedicated to Vittorini.

him a continuous effort to keep up to date stylistically, to constantly re-
new his outlook on the more problematic aspects of life in our times. I do
not mean to imply that this is just a result of professional skill; he possesses indeed an uncommon, critical mobility and capacity to place himself in ever-changing literary situations. The other side of the coin is no
doubt a certain impatience in execution, as if, distracted by new subjects
more up to date and more exciting, the mechanism of the novel suddenly
ceases to interest him. The summary disposal of the plot, the entrusting
of the conclusion to the unexpected cathartic devices of the resolving
incident, point to the author's eventual disenchantment with his own
invention. In Moravia, the stylistic tension is proportionate to the fecun-
dity of his thematic inventions. His first novel, Gli Indifferenti[17] as we
know, came into being as the result of a bet among friends; the true sense
of the wager, however, would seem to me to apply more appropriately to
the technical hypothesis on which the novel is based – a sort of challeng-
ing of limits, pure avant-garde geometry. It is a novel built with extremely
rudimentary tools, entirely in close-ups, with no roads, no background
landscapes, and yet it is able to shed light on the misery of a certain
world, a certain society, and the futility of the gestures of the characters
who are unable to rise above their own indifference.

Because Moravia possesses both inventive ability and a critical mind,
he can construct novels and stories as pure working hypotheses, adher-
ing to the substance of the neo-realist commitment, as in La Ciociara, or
accepting the dynamics of the slang 'impasto,' as in the Racconti romani,
or even venturing down the hallucinating road of dissociation travelled by
the industrial novel, as in l'Automa. The latest novel by Moravia, L'Atten-
zione, reveals a writer who accepts the pathos of the neo-avant-garde, at
the same time exposing its limits with lucid rationality. It is a novel within
a novel, since the journalist Merighi, hero of the story, writes the diary
of his attempt at a novel destined to failure, and at the same time tells
the story of his marriage, his wife's infidelity, his frustrated desire for his
stepdaughter, and overwhelming sense of guilt. The anti-plot which pro-
vokes in him a subtle, if belated, attention to the events around him,
destroys the plot of the novel he was writing, in bad faith, since in a
state of inattention. But this is the limit permitted a writer in his regression towards the magmatic point of the convergence of everything into
nothing. In the place of the unwritten novel, we have the sediment of

17 Moravia's first novel, Gli Indifferenti, was published in 1929. All of Moravia's
   works are published by Bompiani, in Milano.

actual experience, which becomes itself an ersatz novel. The pathology of the novel is itself a form of novel and does not signify the end of the novel as a literary genre.

The case of Gadda[18] takes us back in time to the diaries of World War I – the proving ground of so much bad nationalistic prose on both sides of the trenches. And even Gadda's diary is replete with lofty sentiments and the current ideas of *patria* and self-sacrifice, which no matter how noble they may be, do not of themselves constitute good literature. But for better or for worse, the devil of temptation transformed this enlisted soldier into a furious vindicator of his own downtrodden humanity, and behind the mellifluous tones of D'Annunzian patriotism we then catch a glimpse of the grimace of a Céline, and the vocabulary, subjected to the acceleration of a wild, expressive verve, degenerates toward the picturesque impasto of *Voyage au bout de la nuit*. During this long march an eccentric character is born, a most singular writer, who by reason of his own experience outside the mainstream, links up directly with the avantgarde of the sixties, with no need for intermediaries.

The human situation in which the writer finds himself, necessarily represents the naturalistic limit against which his prose struggles. We have before us a man – alone, bitter, cantankerous; an engineer who has been to war, been to South America, who can't stand noise, and can't stand the Milanese who are noisy, talkative, debonair speculators; can't stand Mussolini, but for years cannot say so to anyone, much less say it in writing. These are the seeds of Gadda's prose, transcended by his expressive verve, that linguistic melting pot into which he tosses dialect and professional languages, the language of the bureaucrats and the engineers, and that highly learned language of the pedants. Milan and the Lombard countryside merge with South America in the imaginary country of Pastrufazio; the comic hero Pirrobutirro is at once a small-time, South-American tyrant and Alfieri's self-torturer, he is both himself and the writer, who presents through him a ferocious satire of himself. The police commissioner, Ingravallo is invited to dinner at the Balducci's. A few days later, Mrs Balducci is found murdered, and the inquest is entrusted to the same Commissioner Ingravallo. He does not discover the murderer, but he learns and helps us to learn an infinite number of things about the confusion that reigns in the world, in spite of the watchful eye of Musso-

18 C.E. Gadda, *Giornale di guerra e di prigionia* (Firenze, 1955 and then Einaudi, 1965); *La cognizione del dolore* (Torino, 1963); *Quer pasticciaccio brutto de Via Merulana* (Milano, 1957); *Eros e Priapo* (Milano, 1967). *La cognizione del dolore* appeared in the Florentine review *Letteratura*, during the years 1938–1941. *Il Pasticciaccio* appeared in the same review, beginning in 1946.

lini in the background promising law and order for all. All these things and many more are told to us in *Quer Pasticciaccio brutto de via Merulana*, and the two editions of the book, with the innumerable changes in the text they propose, are eloquent indices of Gadda's stylistic restlessness. Names and dates are purely working hypotheses, and the plot is itself a confused hypothesis. The novel overflows the boundaries of the page, leaving behind long footnotes on Mussolini, which are suppressed in the second edition, but reappear in a new book, *Eros e Priapo*, where they expand into a delirious psychoanalytic discussion of the character of the Duce. Writing has no beginning or end, and to start or to finish is a purely arbitrary act.

The life of Elio Vittorini is perhaps the most coherent testimony to a battle fought for the triumph of the ideals of the avant-garde, a battle for which he sacrificed, with impressive resolution, his own future as a writer. The most inspired moments in Vittorini's art are to be found, in our opinion, at two crucial points: the hymn to the dignity of man in *Conversazione in Sicilia*,[19] and the hymn to the dignity of the worker in *Il Sempione strizza l'occhio al Fréjùs*. But to understand Vittorini one must also consider *Le Donne di Messina*, the book of the crisis that leads to the novelist's long silence which lasted until his death. Novels are for Vittorini, just as they are for the writers of the avant-garde, reifications of eternal emotions, but for him they are also concrete actions of and in themselves, practical acts capable of defining reality and modifying it. While for Pavese the novel counts as an affirmation or negation of the self, an internal clarification that is a science with its own implacable rules of measure and style, but also an adventure, a defiance of the opaque and unknowable world which eluded him until his death, for Vittorini it is an ideology, a way of knowing the world, of understanding others, for which we can substitute political gestures, artistically inferior, but for all practical purposes equivalent to the creative act. As happens with avant-garde writers, the mirage and temptation of keeping up to date weigh on his artistic conscience, and become substitutes for creative drive. The elegy for lost humanity, for the sorrows of the world in *Conversazione* is profound art, because it has its roots in an elemental ideology which originates in an act of love, in thought and total passion that take possession of his whole being. The parable of suffering and of the dignity of the working man is also an elemental movement, which finds an immediate

---

19 Elio Vittorini, *Conversazione in Sicilia* (Milano, 1941); *Il Sempione strizza l'occhio al Fréjùs* (Milano, 1946); *Le Donne di Messina* (Milano, 1949). The second edition of the book, completely revised, appeared in 1964.

echo in the writer's conscience and instinctively identifies with it. But the return to the primordial condition of man, the regression towards the magmatic state of the world, valid in moments of political emergency (life in dictatorial countries followed by elemental demands in an existential, political time) does not survive the appearance of the more complicated world that establishes itself before the writer's eyes after the war. The primitive community of the disinherited who people the pages of the *Donne di Messina* has lost all its charismatic virtue for the writer now and belongs, even as he writes about it, to the past – the echo of an old-fashioned ideology; so it matters little whether the fascist Ventura is punished by the partisans, as happens in the first edition of the novel, or survives, drowning his regrets in alcohol, as he does in the second edition; or whether he does away with the girl Siracusa with whom he lives, or spares her, being content to beat her from time to time. What we are aware of is the writer's ideological detachment from this type of separate, exceptional world which only the experience of the war could have allowed. While Vittorini the writer is left behind, the critic of society and its customs records this new up-to-date edition of the world: the formation in Italy of an advanced capitalism and a consumer society, and the end of the cold war.[20] Vittorini participates in the discussion on the relationship between science and humanism promoted by C.P. Snow, showing us the new frontiers of science and art. Science, he maintains, discovers new worlds and entrusts them to the humanists to be administered; the humanists write and express themselves in archaic terms, they are still Ptolemaic in a Copernican era, but the scientists themselves do not possess the culture of their discoveries, they are backward with respect to their own world, regressing continuously towards the positions of security furnished them by those formulators of reassuring ideologies – the humanists.

It is in this polemical context that we find the latest singular efforts of Calvino (*Le Cosmicomiche, Ti con zero*),[21] who poses himself the problem of the relationship between art and science, finding an artistic solution. The impetus which motivates Calvino is twofold: on the one hand, he sees in the new scientific discoveries, the new vista on the cosmos, a challenge to the condition of the writer in our times, on the other, he interprets the polemics of the *nouveau roman*, of structuralism, scrip-

20 Elio Vittorini, *Diario in pubblico: 1961–65*; 'La Ragione conoscitiva' in *Il Menabò*, n.10, 9–63.
21 Italo Calvino, *Le cosmicomiche* (Torino, 1965); *Ti con zero* (Torino, 1967).

turalism, and all the automatisms of the neo-avant-garde as a desecrating challenge to the author's omniscience.[22] He reacts to the first challenge by adopting the exigencies of the technical language of science, but applying them to a sort of science fiction-narration in reverse, regressing that is toward these magmatic conditions of a universe peopled with primogenous beings in their state of preformation; he reacts to the second by condescending as far as possible, in a sort of paradoxical pretence, to the reductive method of the avant-garde, clear to its point of fusion, to the formation that is of an indifferentiated amalgam of the work of art and the point of view governing it. In this regression toward absolute automatism, Calvino steps out of the zone of influence of Pavese, who had established the priority of myth over the story which explicates it, to adopt the opposite point of view, that the myth crystallizes during the course of the story. A sudden, unexpected encounter between words, recorded and transmitted by the writer, becomes the breaking of a taboo, a discovery. The writer, as he describes the world, with immense astonishment discovers it, reveals its secrets, deconsecrating them. By entrusting his task to the most irrational method of knowing things, he demonstrates for us that the historical conditions of our rationalism are limited and defensive, and that the irrational thrust is nothing more than the refusal to believe there is anything in the world which can be considered foreign to the 'ragione delle cose' (the intrinsic logic of nature).

What can we say about the neo-avant-garde? We admire the lucidity with which it denounces the literary stagnation of Italy in the sixties, the literature industry, and the merchandising of culture in the neo-capitalist era.[23] We can accept its discriminating evaluation of industrial literature

---

22 Italo Calvino, 'Cibernetica e fantasmi,' in *Le conferenze dell'associazione culturale italiana 1967–1968* (Cuneo, 1968).
23 For these problems see especially: R. Barrili, *La Barriera del Naturalismo* (Milano, 1964); A. Guglielmi, *Avanguardia e sperimentalismo* (Milano, 1964); *Gruppo 63*, edited by N. Balestrini and A. Giuliani (Milano, 1964); F. Curi, *Ordine e disordine* (Milano, 1965); Edoardo Sanguineti, *Ideologia e linguaggio* (Milano, 1965); A. Giuliani, *Immagini e maniere* (Milano, 1965); *Avanguardia e Neo-avanguardia*, edited by G. Ferrata (Milano, 1966); G. Scalia, *Critica, letteratura, ideologia 1956–1963* (Padova, 1968).

The essays of Scalia, a critic who has read widely and is well versed in philosophy, contain a theoretical justification for the opening of the neo-avant-garde to the European texts of major importance. The names that are most commonly called upon by the Italian neo-avant-garde critics are those of Hans Magnus Enzenberger, Theodor W. Adorno, Walter Benjamin, M. Horkheimer, Marcuse, and naturally, G. Lukács, although in a sense of absolute aversion. The publishing house of Feltrinelli, and to a lesser extent Einaudi, have put a great deal of their vast re-

and the preference for those novels in which a factual presentation is checked by elements of prodigious inventiveness. The novels of Volponi,[24] where the delirious madness of the protagonists, Albino Saluggia and Anteo Crocioni, serves to shatter the raw material of reality, are certainly positive efforts. But here the problem becomes complicated. When the documentary facts explode to reorganize in hallucinating, unrelated forms where the very relationship to the story is lost, when the initial revolt stagnates in a pure ontology of horror, we seem to behold a return of that committed surrealism the neo-avant-garde considers old-fashioned, but which, to be coherent, they have not the right to disregard. In comparison to such clever but over-rated exhibitions as Goffred Parise's *Il Padrone*,[25] the highly lucid, imposing efforts of the best of Landolfi, if not the technically impeccable but excessively artificial stories of Dino Buzzati, certainly gain in stature in our eyes. And if on the other hand it is true that Robbe-Grillet challenges the industrial society, without confronting the subject matter which polemically concerns it, does not the neo-avant-garde's quarrel with Cassola, who in some ways anticipated the themes of the *nouveau-roman*, seem one-sided? Is there not perhaps some truth to what Dominique Fernandez[26] wrote about Cassola's qualities 'd'agronome et de métreur' connected to an aesthetic of objects and gestures? And does not all this indicate that the narrative effectiveness of Cassola is far superior to the reformistic ideology he has polemically proclaimed, in response to the attacks of the avant-garde?

We share only with reservations the neo-avant-garde polemics directed at the category of mediation, for the idea that ideological instrumentation was the true limit of neo-realism remains to be proven. If that were the case, one would have difficulty understanding the objections raised to the art of Cesare Pavese, who, as Dominique Fernandez[27] has pointed out, was, in spite of appearances, a writer basically recalcitrant to the substance of

sources at the disposal of the neo-avant-garde, in order to make the most prestigious European texts of neo-avant-garde inspiration available in Italian. One of the most singular sociological phenomena of the last few years has been the significance of the neo-avant-garde as a powerful, pressure group within the more advanced and progressive publishing houses.

The most recent interests of the neo-avant-garde run to anthropology and structural linguistics. See the brilliant book by U. Eco, *La struttura assente* (Milano, 1968), especially p. 253–418, where Barthes, Foucault, Lacan, Jakobson, and Levi-Strauss are discussed.

24 P. Volponi, *Memoriale* (Milano, 1962); *La Macchina mondiale* (Milano, 1965).

25 Goffredo Parise, *Il Padrone* (1965).

26 Dominique Fernandez, *Le roman italien et la crise de la conscience moderne* (Paris, 1958), 276.

27 Dominique Fernandez, *L'échec de Pavese* (Paris, 1968).

the ideological commitment. On the other hand, the passionate, poetic composition transcribed in a neo-realist key in Beppo Fenoglio's fine, post-humous novel, *Partigiano Johnny*,[28] has demonstrated that it is possible to begin with a content-oriented chronicle of the war and immerse oneself in the world, in order to discover the mysterious amalgam of harmony and chaos, of coherence and absurdity, which it from time to time becomes for us. Vittorini was probably right in saying that, if ideological conditioning is an obstacle to art in the neo-capitalist era, it does not impose itself in the deterministic way the avant-garde seems to believe. Just as the writer in a non-industrialized society, though bound by its paleo-capitalist structures, expresses himself in the margin of freedom they allow him, so the writer in the neo-capitalist era is not compelled to recognize in the ideological conditioning of the system, any pressure that would destroy his freedom to contest it. Aside from the banal and ungenerous constatation that the presence of the neo-avant-garde is itself tangible proof of the possibility of escaping the system, one is tempted to ask what a literature that adheres to the structures of the world without any mediation really is?

Today in Italy we have several different avant-gardes: a reformistic avant-garde, if one is allowed the contradiction in terms, which bears witness to the modification of the social structure in a given country, and ceases in its task of anticipation once the modifications are accomplished: we think here of Pasolini, the intelligent, compassionate recorder of the jargon of protest in the outlying districts of Rome, who lays down his pen as soon as these districts are incorporated into the city. There is also a conservative avant-garde, so to speak, such as the highly cultivated one of Antonio Pizzuto, who conducts an allusive, intellectual experiment that is purely linguistic in nature. And there is finally a subversive avant-garde, which has known its accords with Marxism, and degrades this initial ideo-logical tension in a descent into the inferno of the undersurface of society, in an exploration of the unknown guts of the universe. But in this case, there is no effort whatsoever at direct knowledge, but rather a prolifera-tion of mediating categories, as in the very learned, if stylistically compo-site novels of Sanguineti, where 'mythological imagination, onirism, Marx-ism, psychoanalysis, obsessive eroticism,'[29] are all mixed together in an interesting, inventive game.

I would not dare to pass judgment on the works of fiction of the neo-avant-garde, for they are not a fact which we can exploit and use, but a

---

28 B. Fenoglio, *Il partigiano Johnny* (Torino, 1968).
29 Discussed with competence by Luciano De Maria in 'Ricognizione sui testi,' an essay included in the volume *Avanguardia e Neo-avanguardia* (Milano, 1966).

becoming, a list of probabilities, a game in the decomposition of the déjà-vue. In Sanguineti's *Giuoco dell'oca*,[30] there is the deep intuition of death as a game, the player immersed in the game of composition and decomposition, weaving the web of his own destiny. I find extremely interesting Germano Lombardi's book, *Barcellona*,[31] inspired by an ethical-political pathos which is drained of its power by the declarative style of the *nouveau-roman*. The novel defuses the epic charge of the Spanish Civil War by studying its effects in a moment of maximum exhaustion and ideological indifference. One is reminded, in contrast, of the polemical gesture with which Vittorini, fascinated by the war in Spain, put the finished story, *Erica*, back in his drawer, or the great emotion the Spanish War aroused in a group of young, middle-class students in France, as told by Jean Francis Rolland in the novel *La Chûte de Barcelone*.[32] In Lombardi, the fragmentation of the story is linked to the isolation of the character, the congealing of passions, the indifference of the world. The story tells of an abortive attempt on the life of a Spanish general, Felipe Acerro, by one Giovanni Zevi, a conspirator without hope, without friends, who acts in the context of a society without genuine faith. The mythic world of the Spain of the 30s is transformed into a world that is impenetrable, petrified by years of self-righteousness, of law and order, of the defence of Christian ethics, in which the prehistoric remains of free humanity flail weakly against an imprisoning net, forlorn and almost forgotten.

The novel *Tristano*[33] by Nanni Balestrini seems to me on the contrary chaotic and derivative. The fact that characters call themselves A, B, or C, is not something that has the power to surprise us these days, not even if C is several people at once, Moreover, the idea that language must deny what it names, or must cancel out reality in the act of creating it, had surely already been said by Maurice Blanchot in *Thomas L'Obscur* and *Le Très-Haut*.

What I find most impressive in these avant-garde writers is their power of divination. To pick one example among many, the pages of Alberto Arbasino dedicated to life in Provincetown, Mass.,[34] present us with an hallucinating and improbable museum of horrors, which becomes a premonition of the carnage at Truro.[35] After that, one must forgive him any-

30 E. Sanguineti, *Capriccio italiano* (Milano, 1963); *Il guoco dell'oca* (Milano, 1967).
31 Germano Lombardi, *Barcellona* (Milano, 1963).
32 Jean Francis Rolland, *La chûte de Barcelone* (Paris, 1952).
33 N. Balestrini, *Tristano* (Milano, 1966).
34 A. Arbasino, 'L'aeroplano per il Cape Cod' in *Gruppo 63* (Milano, 1964).
35 I refer to a recent news item concerning the horrifying murder of an unspecified number of young ladies, committed in the vicinity of Truro on Cape Cod.

thing, even the statement, for me patently absurd, that the waters of the Atlantic are not really cold. The language of the neo-avant-garde anticipates with alarming precision the terminology of the global protest of University students in Italy and the social rupture this terminology reveals. Is it a case of ideological lucidity, or of those magical premonitions primitive societies considered the exclusive prerogative of poets? Only the future can tell.

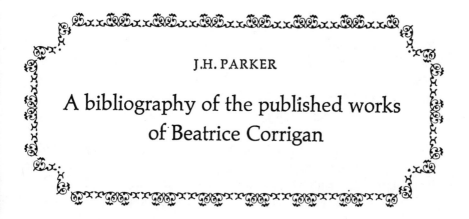

J.H. PARKER

A bibliography of the published works
of Beatrice Corrigan

THE PERUSAL of Beatrice Corrigan's bibliography of published works reveals immediately the catholicity of her interests and the broad range of her literary achievements. Throughout her academic career Dr Corrigan has contributed significant articles to many periodicals in Canada (for example, *Canadian Forum, Queen's Quarterly, University of Toronto Quarterly, Canadian Modern Language Review*) and in the United States and Europe (including *Italica, Publications of the Modern Language Association of America, Renaissance Drama, Romanic Review, Cesare Barbieri Courier, La Bibliofilia*), to mention only a few. Her monographs have ranged from a critical listing of *Canadian Cultural Periodicals* (with Professors Goggio and Parker) and *New Documents Relating to Browning's Roman Murder Story* to a *Catalogue of Italian Plays, 1500–1700*, a translation into English of Alfieri's *Of Tyranny* (with Professor Molinaro) and the recent edition of *Italian Poets and English Critics, 1755–1859*, published by the University Presses of Chicago and Toronto. Dr Corrigan's numerous book reviews have been characterized by depth of understanding, considered evaluation, and sparkling style. Over a period of some years, it is to be noted particularly, she was the bibliographer for the leading journal *Italica*.

The literatures of Italy and Britain have led Professor Corrigan to much successful comparative research and publication in the Renaissance and Modern periods. Few contemporary scholars have taken the time and the trouble devoted by Miss Corrigan to delving deeply into two important cultures and to assessing the interplay and interaction of sources and influences. The Royal Society of Canada, on admitting Beatrice Corrigan to Fellowship in 1964, and the University of Waterloo, on awarding her the degree of Doctor of Letters (*honoris causa*) in 1966, both stressed that she is one of Canada's truly outstanding scholars in the humanities. Added to this is the important fact that she is an inspiring teacher, looked upon with great appreciation and affection by a host of colleagues and students, who do not forget the enriching experience of knowing her. Beatrice Corrigan's PHD was the first doctorate in Italian at the University of Toronto (1932), and since her appointment to the staff of her *alma mater* in 1946, she has encouraged Italian studies at the University of Toronto at both the undergraduate and graduate levels, secure in the knowledge that that institution has library resources, a capable staff, and competent students interested in the discipline. Over the years, Professor Corrigan herself has been a person who has shared her knowledge and discoveries liberally, by means of her published writings, her public addresses, and her class and individual conversations.

As a founder–member of the Renaissance Society of America, as a member of the Modern Humanities Research Association, the Dante Society of America, the Humanities Research Council of Canada, as well as the many scholarly groups such as the Ontario Modern Language Teachers Association, the American Association of Teachers of Italian, and the Modern Language Association of America, Professor Corrigan's inspiration to others has been outstanding in its leadership. As Chairman of the Committee of the Romance Series of the University of Toronto Press, she has been in a position to foster the best in Romance monographs. Beatrice Corrigan's multifaceted talents are indeed reflected in the Bibliography of Published Works which follows. They are also very apparent to the many who know her in national and international cultural circles.

In the Spring of 1971 the University of Toronto Press appointed Beatrice Corrigan Co-ordinating Editor of its *Collected Works of Erasmus*, a fitting acknowledgment of her 'wide range of experience as an author, editor, and translator in Renaissance and modern literary studies' (*Erasmus in English*, 2/1971, 1). Early in 1972 Professor Corrigan was named to the Folger Shakespeare Library (Washington, DC) Editorial Board. At a Spring convocation in the same year her *alma mater* conferred upon her the degree of Doctor of Letters (*honoris causa*) in recognition of her distinguished service to the University and to the world of learning.

ABBREVIATIONS: *BA*, Books Abroad; *CBC*, Cesare Barbieri Courier; *CF*, Canadian Forum; *CL*, Comparative Literature; *CMLR*, Canadian Modern Language Review; *CompD*, Comparative Drama; *DR*, Dalhousie Review; *EM*, English Miscellany; *FI*, Forum Italicum; *IQ*, Italian Quarterly; *ITAL*, Italica; *PMLA*, Publications of the Modern Language Association of America; *QQ*, Queen's Quarterly; *RenD*, Renaissance Drama;

RenN, Renaissance News; *RenQ*, Renaissance Quarterly; *RR*, Romanic Review; *SP*, Studies in Philology; *SQ*, Shakespeare Quarterly; *SRen*, Studies in the Renaissance; *TamR*, Tamarack Review; *UTQ*, University of Toronto Quarterly.

1933
'Harlequin in America,' *CF*, xiv, 62–5

1934
'Sforza Oddi and His Comedies,' *PMLA*, xlix, 718–42

1940
'Canadian Crusaders,' *QQ*, xlvii, 77–88

1941
'The Ill-fated Good Fortune of Francesco Canonici,' *Baylor Bulletin*, xliv, 39–99

1944
'D'Annunzio and the Italian State,' *QQ*, li, 65–71
'Henri-Emile Chevalier and His Novels of North America,' *RR*, xliv, 220–31

1945
'Charles Maurras: Philosopher of Nationalism,' *QQ*, lii, 288–98
'Drieu la Rochelle: Study of a Collaborator,' *UTQ*, xiv, 199–205

1946
'Trieste and the Empires,' *QQ*, liii, 137–46

1947
'Scenario by a Dictator,' *QQ*, liv, 215–22

1949
'An Annotated Commedia Erudita: Giovan Battista Sogliani's *L'Uccellatoio*,' *ITAL*, xxvi, 188–97

1950
Review: Michele De Filippis, *The Literary Riddle in Italy to the End of the Sixteenth Century*. In *ITAL*, xxvii, 188–90

1952
'New Documents on Browning's *Roman Murder* ' *SP*, xlix, 520–33

1954

'Pellico's *Francesca da Rimini*: The First English Translation,' *ITAL*, XXXI, 215–24

REVIEWS: Ernest Hatch Wilkins, *A History of Italian Literature*. In *CF*, XXXIV, 167–8

Niccolo Secchi, *Self-Interest*. In *CMLR*, XI, no. 1, 44

Michele De Filippis, *The Literary Riddle in Italy in the Seventeenth Century*. In *ITAL*, XXXI, 118–20

1955

(With E. Goggio and J.H. Parker) *A Bibliography of Canadian Cultural Periodicals in Canadian Libraries* (Toronto: The Ryerson Press)

1956

Curious Annals: New Documents Relating to Browning's Roman Murder Story. An Edition (University of Toronto Press)

'The Opposing Mirrors,' *ITAL*, XXXIII, 165–79

1957

REVIEWS: Antonio Meluschi, *La fabbrica dei bambini*. In *BA*, XXXI, 76–7

Giovanni Orsini, *Agarista e satelliti*. Ibid., 190

Albert Johannsen, *Phiz Illustrations from the Novels of Charles Dickens*. In *Victorian Studies*, I, 99–100

1958

'Guerrazzi, Boswell, and Corsica,' *ITAL*, XXXV, 25–37

'The Byron–Hobhouse Translation of Pellico's *Francesca*,' *ITAL*, XXXV, 235–41

'*Il Capriccio*: An Unpublished Italian Renaissance Comedy,' *SRen*, V, 74–86

REVIEWS: Pietro Pancrazi, *Italiani e stranieri*. In *BA*, XXXII, 184–5

Giuseppe Antoldi, *Questo disgraziato paese*. Ibid., 317

Mariannina Coffa, *Letters ad Ascenso*. Ibid., 441

Ippolito Nievo, *The Castle of Fratta*, translated by L.F. Edwards. In *TamR*, VI, 85–90

1959

REVIEWS: Gian Gaspare Napolitano, *Il figlio del capitano*. In *BA*, XXXIII, 211

Luis Cernuda, *Pensamiento poético en la lírica inglesa (Siglo XIX)*. Ibid., 335

Giselda Giappi Bertelli, *Più forte dell'amore e dell'odio*. Ibid., 343
P.A. Quarantotti Gambini, *La calda vita*. Ibid., 457

1960
'Browning's Roman Murder Story,' *EM*, xi, 333–400
'Vernon Lee and the Old Yellow Book,' *Colby Library Quarterly*, v, 116–22
REVIEWS: Angela Padellaro, *Dolce nella memoria*. In *BA*, xxxiv, 70
Nelio Ferrando, *Un giornale per Luca*. Ibid., 289–90
Charles S. Singleton, *Dante Studies 2: Journey to Beatrice*. In *DR*,
xl, 401–3
Giuseppe Tomasi di Lampedusa, *The Leopard*. P.M. Pasinetti, *Venetian Red*. In *TamR*, xvii, 71–5

1961
Catalogue of Italian Plays, 1500–1700, in the Library of the University of Toronto (University of Toronto Press)
'Antonio Fogazzaro and Wilkie Collins,' *CL*, xiii, 39–51
'An Unrecorded Manuscript of Machiavelli's *La Clizia*,' *La Bibliofilia*,
lxiii, 73–87
(With J.A. Molinaro) Vittorio Alfieri, *Of Tyranny*. Translated, edited, and with an Introduction (University of Toronto Press)
REVIEWS: Leonardo Vergani, *Eleonora Duse*. In *BA*, xxxv, 84
Giorgio Petrocchi, *La tecnica manzoniana del dialogo*. Ibid., 278
Gino Bacchetti, *Le notti inquiete*. Ibid., 279
Luigi Bartolini, *La pettegola ed altri 19 racconti*. Ibid., 383

1962
'Congreve's *Mourning Bride* and Coltellini's *Almeria*,' *Istituto Universitario Orientale, Annali, Sezione Romanza*, iv, 145–66
'Giovanni Ruffini's Letters to Vernon Lee, 1875–1879,' *EM*, xiii, 179–240
(With J.A. Molinaro) 'Bibliography of Italian Studies in America,' *ITAL*,
xxxix, 289–94; xl(1963), 73–9, 172–81, 271–80, 356–67; xli(1964), 73–9,
181–91, 326–35, 448–56; xlii(1965), 204–10, 285–92, 281–7 (*sic*),
416–23; xliii(1966), 66–75, 190–6, 307–13, 429–37; xliv(1967), 83–9,
233–43, 356–66
REVIEWS: Raffaele La Capria, *Ferito a morte*. In *BA*, xxxvi, 68
Giovanni Pascoli, *Lettere agli amici Lucchesi*. Ibid., 195
Luciano Codignola, *Il gesto*. Ibid., 426
Eric Auerbach, *Dante: Poet of the Secular World*. Ernest Hatch Wilkins, *Life of Petrarch*. Eric W. Cochrane, *Tradition and Enlightenment in the Tuscan Academies 1690–1800*. In *UTQ*, xxxii, 193–8

1963

'Catholic Literature in Contemporary Italy,' *The Basilian Teacher*, VII, 137–44

'The Poetry of Leopardi in Victorian England, 1837–1878,' *EM*, XIV, 171–84

'Erminia and Tancredia: The Happy Ending,' *ITAL*, XL, 325–33

'Italian Renaissance Plays,' *RenN*, XVI, 293–307

1964

'Tasso's *Erminia* in the Italian Theatre of the Seicento,' *RenD*, VII, 127–50

REVIEWS: Luigi Malerba, *La scoperta dell'alfabeto*. In *BA*, XXXVIII, 180

Raffaele Orlando, *L'annaspo*. Ibid., 184

Giancarlo Buzzi, *L'amore mio italiano*. Ibid., 303

Angelo Fiore, *Un caso di coscienza*. Ibid., 304

Italian Studies Presented to E.R. Vincent, edited by C.P. Brand, K. Foster, and U. Limentani. In *ITAL*, XLI, 111–14

Joseph G. Fucilla, *Superbi colli e altri saggi*. Ibid., 350–3

Allardyce Nicoll, *The World of Harlequin: A Critical Study of the Commedia dell'Arte*. In *SQ*, XV, 228–9

1965

'Neapolitan Romanticism and the Social Conscience,' *Studies in Romanticism*, V, 113–20

(A Contributor) *A Concordance to the "Divine Comedy" of Dante Alighieri*, edited by E.H. Wilkins and T.G. Bergin (Harvard University Press)

REVIEWS: Olga Ragusa, *Verga's Milanese Tales*. In *ITAL*, XLII, 299–300

Louise G. Clubb, *Giambattista Della Porta: Dramatist*. In *RenD*, VIII, 219–22

1966

'Pirandello and the Theatre of the Absurd,' *CBC*, VIII, no. 1, 3–6

'Italian Renaissance Plays in the University of Toronto Library,' *RenN*, XIX, 219–28

REVIEWS: Roberto Guiducci, *Dialoghi immorali*. In *BA*, XL, 457

Alessandro Manzoni, *The Column of Infamy*, translated by Fr Kenelm Foster. Cesare Beccaria, *Of Crimes and Punishments*, translated by Jane Grigson. In *IQ*, X, no. 38, 83–6

Vicenzo Paladino, *La revisione del romanzo manzoniano e le postille del Visconti*. In *ITAL*, XLIII, 320–22

1967

'Italian Theatre, 1966,' *BA*, XLI, 398–401

REVIEWS: Mario Tobino, *Sulla spiaggia e di là dal molo*. In *BA*, XLI, 84
Carmelo Bene, *Nostra Signora dei Turchi*. Ibid., 207
Luigi Malerba, *Il serpente*. Ibid., 209
Mario Soldati, *La busta arancione*. Ibid., 336
Pirandello, A Collection of Critical Essays, edited by Glauco Cambon.
In *CBC*, IX, no. 1, 21–2
Marvin T. Herrick, *Italian Plays, 1500–1700, in the University of Illinois
Library*. In *ITAL*, XLIV, 498–9
Philippe Van Tieghem, *Histoire du théâtre italien*. In *RR*, LVIII, 68
*La Commedia dell'Arte vue à travers le 'Zibaldone' de Pérouse. Etude
suivie d'un choix de 'scenari' de Placido Adriani*, edited and translated
by Suzanne Thérault. Ibid., 215–6
Robert M. Durling, *The Figure of the Poet in Renaissance Epic*. C.P.
Brand, *Torquato Tasso: A Study of the Poet and His Contribution to
English Literature*. Louise G. Clubb, *Giambattista Della Porta: Dramatist*.
In *UTQ*, XXXVI, 206–8

1968

Italian Poets and English Critics, 1755–1859. An Edition (University of
Chicago Press–University of Toronto Press) (Patterns of Literary Criti-
cism Series, no. 7)
'Opportunities for Research in Italian Renaissance Drama, 1967,' *Re-
search Opportunities in Renaissance Drama*, XI, 9–20
REVIEWS: Aldo Palazzeschi, *Il Doge*. In *BA*, XLII, 92–3
Massimo Franciosa, *L'arrischiata*. Ibid., 252
Bernardino Zapponi, *Gobal*. Ibid., 254
Antonio Porta, *Partita*. Ibid., 418
Vittorio Alfieri, *Vita*. Ibid., 418–19
Giovanni Gullace, *Gabriele D'Annunzio in France: A Study of Cultural
Relations*. In *RR*, LIX, 232–3

1969

'Commedia dell'Arte Portraits in the McGill Feather Books,' *RenD*, II
(new series), 167–88
REVIEWS. Diego Curtò, *Cronaca di una malattia*. In *BA*, XLIII, 92
Vincenzo Paladino, *L'opera di Corrado Alvaro*. Ibid., 242
Luigi Malerba, *Salto mortale*. Ibid., 244
Michail Bulgakov, *Teatro*. Ibid., 282
Gian-Paolo Biasin, *The Smile of the Gods: A Thematic Study of Cesare
Pavese's Works*. Ibid., 399
Domenica Cara, *Alvaro*. Ibid., 575

Pirandello, Moravia, and Italian Poetry, edited by Michael R. Campo.
In *CMLR*, xxv, no. 2, 123–4

Olga Ragusa, *Luigi Pirandello*. Ibid., xxv, no. 4, 74–5

Giorgio Bassani, *L'Airone*. In *FI*, III, 479–80

Douglas Radcliff-Umstead, *The Birth of Modern Comedy in Renaissance Italy*. In *IQ*, XIII, no. 50, 85–7

Torquato Tasso, *Aminta*, edited by Sarah D'Alberti. In *ITAL*, XLVI, 331–2

Sergio Pacifici, *The Modern Italian Novel from Manzoni to Svevo*.
Ibid., 443–5

Scenarios of the Commedia dell'Arte: Flaminio Scala's 'Il teatro delle favole rappresentative,' translated and edited by Henry F. Salerno. In *RenD*, II (new series), 223–7

Louise G. Clubb, *Italian Plays (1500–1700) in the Folger Library. A Bibliography with Introduction*. In *RenQ*, XXII, 266–9

1970

REVIEWS: Tommaso Landolfi, *Faust 67*. In *BA*, XLIV, 96

Thomas G. Bergin, *A Diversity of Dante*. Ibid., 290–1

Antonio Rufino, *La critica letteraria di G. A. Borgese*. Ibid., 454

Felice Chilanti, *Ex*. Ibid., 458

Giuseppe Paolo Samonà, *G.G. Belli: La commedia romano e la commedia celeste*. Ibid., 641–2

Thomas Goddard Bergin, *The New Science of Giambattista Vico*.
Ibid., 647

Sergio Pacifici, ed. *From Verismo to Experimentalism*. Ibid., 647

Antonio Piromalli, *Grazia Deledda*. In *FI*, IV, 272–4

Attilio Momigliano, *Lettere scelte*, edited by Mario Scotti. Ibid., 621–3

1971

'Foscolo's articles on Dante in the *Edinburgh Review*: a study in collaboration.' In *Collected essays on Italian language & literature presented to Kathleen Speight*, edited by Giovanni Aquilecchia, Stephen N. Cristea, Sheila Ralphs (Manchester University Press), 211–25

'Two Renaissance Views of Carthage: Trissino's *Sofonisba* and Castellini's *Asdrubale*.' *CompD*, v, 193–206

REVIEWS: Giovanni Giudici, *Autobiologia*. In *BA*, XLV, 99–100

Corrado Piancastelli, *Berto*. Ibid., 296

Natale Tedesco, *La condizione crepuscolare. Saggi sulla poesia italiana del '900*. Ibid., 299

Ennio Flaiano, *Il gioco e il massacro*. Ibid., 675

Alessandro Bonsanti, *Teatro domestico*. Ibid., 676

Carlo Castellaneta, *La dolce compagna*. Ibid., 678–9

Galileo Galilei, *Scritti Letterari*, edited by Alberto Chiari. In *FI*, v, 142–3

Luciano Rebay, *Alberto Moravia*. Ibid., 477–8

Piero Guarducci, *Collodi e il melodramma ottocentesco*. In *ITAL*, XLVIII, 102–4

D.G. Singh, *Leopardi e l'Inghilterra*. In *RR*, LXII, 239–40

Leonard Forster, *The Icy Fire: Five Studies in European Petrarchism*. In *UTQ*, XLI, 77–9

1972

'The CWE: A Progress Report,' *Erasmus in English*, no. 4, 1–2

(With J.A. Molinaro) Vittorio Alfieri, *The Prince and Letters*. Translated, with introduction and notes (University of Toronto Press)

REVIEWS: Carlo Sgorlon, *La notte del ragno manaro*. In *BA*, XLVI, 464

R.D.S. Jack, *The Italian Influence on Scottish Literature*. In *CMLR*, XXIX, no. 1, 101

'Humanities.' In *UTQ*, XLI, 362–3

This book
was designed by
WILLIAM RUETER
under the direction of
ALLAN FLEMING
and was printed by
University of
Toronto
Press